Praise for *The Fishing Fleet*

'This book is highly evocative . . . de Courcy takes the reader through an enchanted world' *Guardian*

'This is a fascinating account of the rules, roles and relations of the British Raj' *Daily Telegraph*

'Fascinating and very readable' *TLS*

'Lively and well-researched' *Spectator*

'Anne de Courcy's sparkling book is an unalloyed delight'
The Lady

'De Courcy tells their story with perspicacity and aplomb'
The Field

'A vivid, well-written book, and a delightful read'
Who Do You Think You Are? magazine

'Anne de Courcy's entertaining book . . . may prove perhaps to be the last of a kind, a nostalgic, non-judgmental look back' *History Today*

Anne de Courcy has written eleven books, including *The English in Love*; *1939: The Last Season; Society's Queen; The Viceroy's Daughters; Diana Mosley; Debs at War*; and *Snowdon: The Biography*. She lives in London and Gloucestershire.

BY ANNE DE COURCY

The English in Love
A Guide to Modern Manners
1939: The Last Season
Society's Queen
The Viceroy's Daughters
Diana Mosley
Debs at War
Snowdon: The Biography
The Fishing Fleet

THE
FISHING
FLEET

HUSBAND-HUNTING IN THE RAJ

———◆———

Anne de Courcy

PHOENIX

A PHOENIX PAPERBACK

First published in Great Britain in 2012
by Weidenfeld & Nicolson
This paperback edition published in 2013
by Phoenix,
an imprint of Orion Books Ltd,
Orion House, 5 Upper St Martin's Lane,
London WC2H 9EA

An Hachette UK company

9 10 8

A CIP catalogue record for this book
is available from the British Library.

ISBN 978-0-7538-2896-0

Typeset by Input Data Services Ltd, Bridgwater, Somerset

Printed and bound by CPI Group (UK) Ltd, Croydon CRO 4YY

The Orion Publishing Group's policy is to use papers
that are natural, renewable and recyclable products and
made from wood grown in sustainable forests. The logging
and manufacturing processes are expected to conform to
the environmental regulations of the country of origin.

www.orionbooks.co.uk

CONTENTS

ILLUSTRATIONS

Section Three

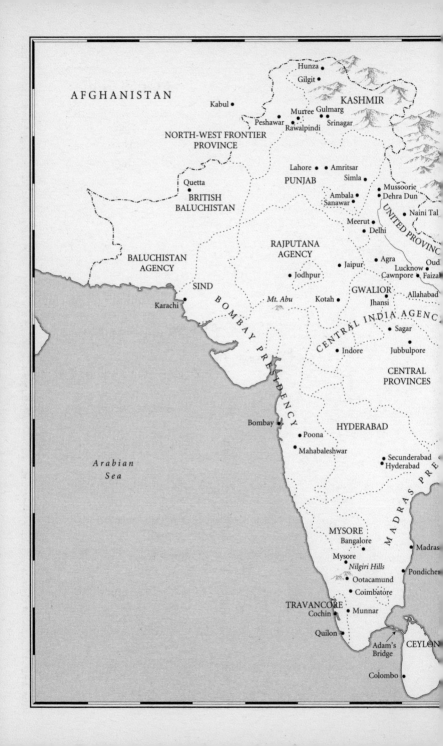

Map of India

THE VICEROYS OF INDIA

—•—

1856–62	Lord Canning (The last Governor General and the first Viceroy)
1862–63	Lord Elgin
1864–69	Lord Lawrence
1869–72	Lord Mayo (The only Viceroy to be murdered in office)
1872–76	Lord Northbrook
1876–80	Lord Lytton
1880–84	Lord Ripon
1884–88	Lord Dufferin
1888–94	Lord Lansdowne
1894–99	Lord Elgin II
1899–1905	Lord Curzon
1905–10	Lord Minto
1910–16	Lord Hardinge
1916–21	Lord Chelmsford
1921–26	Lord Reading
1926–31	Lord Irwin
1931–36	Lord Willington
1936–44	Lord Linlithgow
1944–47	Lord Wavell
Mar 1947–Aug 1947	Lord Mountbatten (The last Viceroy of British India and the first Governor General of free India)

PROLOGUE

'I know you will think me mad'

After describing the weather and how he had overcome his aversion to the smell of durian fruits and now thought them delicious, Lieutenant Stuart Corbett's letter to his father in England continued:

'You must not be surprised when I tell you that I am going to be married on the thirteenth of next month to Miss Charlotte Britten who has got a Brother in the 20th and is of a very respectable family, who reside at Forest Hill in Kent. I shall be able by this step to lead a regular and steady life which I have not been able to do for the last 4 months, the Officers of the 2nd Battn being all single and fond of sitting up till 3 or 4 in the morning which I do not like and still as a single man am not able to avoid it.'

Surprise might well have been the reaction of the Reverend Stuart Corbett in his vicarage in the West Riding of Yorkshire when he received his son's letter, as the boy was a mere nineteen years old, even though young Stuart continued reassuringly:

'I have been considering on the important step I am about to take and I really think I shall be much more comfortable and be able to lead a life more after the manner in which I have been brought up and be better able to take care of my health which is one of the most important considerations in the world as I have now had 3 attacks of fever the last of which was very severe and obliged me to come round to this place [Penang, then known as Prince of Wales Island] for the recovery of my health.'

The year was 1822 and Corbett, a young officer of the East India Company, had snapped up one of the girls then known as the Fishing Fleet – young women who travelled out to India in search of a husband. Trade with India, the jewel in Britain's burgeoning commercial Empire, was vast and the promise of wealth and success – if they survived disease and peril – beckoned the young men of the Company. Once, they had formed marriages or liaisons with Indian beauties but by Corbett's time these days were past – and most British girls stayed at home. So, for both parties, marriage was not so much about passion and romance as a matter-of-fact life choice, sealed by a contract, that had to be arrived at briskly or the prize would be lost to someone who was quicker off the mark.

The story of Charlotte Britten and Stuart Corbett is typical both of how the Fishing Fleet became an established phenomenon and of the magnetic pull exercised by India. It also shows the courage and adventurous readiness to take risks then inherent in the British character. How many parents these days would send a sixteen-year-old daughter on a six-month voyage that might easily end in death by disease or drowning* to a country from which she might never return, even though the golden apple at the end of the journey was that essential commodity, a husband? And how many daughters would consent to go? As did Charlotte and Mary Britten, respectively twenty and sixteen.

In the days of sail, the men who worked for the Company seldom got leave as the only possible route to the subcontinent was via the Cape of Good Hope, a voyage that took several months, sometimes a year. With these travel difficulties, Company employees could expect to return home perhaps only once before retirement, so that finding a British bride was difficult.

To make this quest easier for their employees, from time to time the Company paid the passage out to India of a number of willing women; the first record is of twenty women sent out to Bombay in 1671. Such husbands were desirable as the Company provided an allowance of £300 a year – wealth indeed in those days – for girls who made a Company-approved match and this payment continued for life even if the woman was widowed.

Each shipload of prospective brides was divided into 'gentlewomen' and 'others'; the Company gave them one set of clothing

---

* Four Indiamen were lost in a gale off Mauritius in 1809; in 1840 the *Lord W Bentinck* sank in a storm just off Bombay with the loss of eighty troops and all the women and children passengers, crowds watching from the shore as boats struggled unavailingly to reach her; six hours later another ship was lost in the same way.

each and maintained them in India for a year, during which time they were expected to have found a mate. They were warned that if they misbehaved they would be put on a diet of bread and water, and shipped back to England. Women who were rejected by even the most desperate Company men also had to return home, and were known as 'Returned Empties'.

In those early Fishing Fleet days, marriage was often undertaken with the sort of rapidity usually confined to spotting a business opportunity and pouncing on it, a kind of matrimonial bran tub where it was in the interests of both parties to make up their minds quickly – the girls because they did not wish to go home to probable spinsterhood and the men in case someone else seized the prize.

Charlotte Britten and her sister Mary were part of the 1821 Fishing Fleet; among the civilian passengers on the ship they sailed on were several other single young women, all off in search of husbands. The Britten girls were coming to India at the instigation of their brother George, the eldest of the thirteen children of Thomas Britten, a wealthy merchant, and his wife Anna, who lived in Forest Hill, Kent.

George, who had been educated at the Reverend Dr Samuel's school in Tooting, had successfully petitioned the Honourable Court of Directors of the East India Company to become a cadet in the Bengal Infantry and had left England in 1817. Fortunes could be made by those serving the Company in either a civilian or military capacity – if they survived India's difficult climate and the diseases that could strike from nowhere, rendering a man who was healthy at breakfast dead by midnight. Those who did survive frequently became very rich; and most of these young men were in need of a wife.

By the nineteenth century, India was seen as a marriage market for girls neither pretty nor rich enough to make at home what was known as 'a good match', the aim of all respectable young women – indeed, perhaps not to make one at all. In India, where European men greatly outnumbered European women, they would be besieged by suitors, many of whom would be richer or have more prospects than anyone they could meet in England.

As the century progressed and with it India's economic importance to Britain, so did the country's desirability as a marital hunting ground. No longer did the East India Company send out and maintain young women; instead, they charged a premium to those wishing to go out. This 'bond' of £200* allowed passage (would-be travellers also had to pay their fare) on an Indiaman, as the Company's ships were called, and ensured that the young woman would not be a charge on the Company once she arrived. In a sense, the bond became an affidavit of the girl's social standing and, by extension, behaviour: if her parents could afford its cost, they were likely to be of a class that made their daughter a suitable bride for a high-up Company official.

George's eight sisters fell into this category. They were well-born and would have been schooled in literature, art and the manners of polite society but certainly not in anything that might have helped them fend for themselves. Their father must have wondered how he was going to marry off so many of them, especially in a brief few years – girls were expected to marry young and, if possible, the elder ones first.

With his son George now firmly established with the Company, Thomas did not have to look far. George had himself married a Fishing Fleet girl, Margaret Goullet, in Calcutta in March 1820. No doubt he had told his parents that if some of his sisters came out they too would easily find husbands. It was decided to send two of them, Charlotte and Mary, respectively the fifth and seventh daughters in the family.

The Britten girls took passage on one of the largest and finest East Indiamen, the 1,506-ton *Lowther Castle*, a ship that would carry coal, European stores and manufactured goods and mail on the outward journey, returning with silk, cotton, jute, indigo, hardwoods, ivory, spices, jewels and even apes and peacocks.

For Thomas and Anna Britten the parting must have been sad: if the girls were successful in finding a mate, their parents might never see them again; with journeys taking a minimum of four months it would be up to a year before they could even learn whether their daughters had arrived safely – from time to time, ships were lost in storms or fell to pirates. To defend herself against these or other enemies, the *Lowther Castle* was heavily armed with twenty-six guns.

---

* About £13,000 today.

The Britten girls joined the *Lowther Castle* as she waited for a favourable wind off the coast of Kent. They set sail on 23 January 1821. Before they left the Channel the pilot, as was customary, brought them the latest newspapers. There was plenty in them to read and gossip over, including the topic *du jour*, of intense interest to everyone: Queen Caroline's attempts to reassert her position as Queen in the teeth of the King's resistance.* In *The Times* alone, amid the advertisements for domestic posts, Atkinson's curling fluid and Balm of Gilead ('for ladies who wish to remove wrinkles') were polemical letters and loyal addresses on the subject.

The ship, just under 144 feet in length, was crammed. There were thirty-eight civilian passengers in all, and large drafts for three King's regiments under only two officers, a colonel and a cornet. With them were their 'authorised dependants' – the wives and children that some of them were allowed to take with them – plus twenty Chinese sailors from other ships whom the Company was obliged to repatriate from England (after India, the *Lowther Castle* was going on to China).

The military draft would, as usual, have made the ship pretty crowded forward (the paying passengers would have shared the much more spacious accommodation aft). Mercifully the soldiers seem to have been mostly English – it had been feared they were to be Irish, known as 'wild lads', and unwelcome for both the savagery and the disease they brought aboard. One hundred and fifty-four officers and men crewed the ship and, in addition to its human cargo, there was plenty of livestock, the sound of moos, baas, clucks and snorts gradually decreasing as the animals were eaten during the long weeks of the journey.

---

* Caroline of Brunswick had married the future George IV in 1795. Nine months later their daughter Princess Charlotte was born and shortly afterwards they separated. In 1814 Caroline left England and moved to Italy, where she employed Bartolomeo Pergami as a servant. Soon he was her closest companion, and it was widely assumed that they were lovers. In 1820 George became King and Caroline returned to Britain to assert her position as Queen. She became the figurehead of a popular reform movement that opposed the unpopular George. George attempted to divorce her by introducing the Pains and Penalties Bill to Parliament, but George and the bill were so unpopular, and Caroline so popular, with the masses that it was withdrawn. In July 1821 Caroline fell ill after she was barred from the coronation on the orders of her husband. She died three weeks later.

Two months into the voyage, at a time when there was little wind and the ship crawled over a flat sea, there could have been trouble when a seaman was disobedient and compounded his misconduct by using 'disrespectful language' to his captain. This was smartly dealt with by giving the miscreant four dozen lashes with the cat o' nine tails, after which the cat was not further required. Eight weeks later, in May, there was a happier event: one of the 'authorised dependants' gave birth to a baby. Finally, on 25 August 1821, the ship reached Calcutta.

Here, Charlotte and Mary would have been surrounded. The arrival of a cargo of marriageable females was of intense interest to the numerous bachelors on the lookout for a wife and ready to snap one up at the first opportunity. There was, however, an established ritual for this instant selection. The captain of the ship and well-known ladies whose social credentials were beyond reproach would organise large parties at which the girls who hoped for a husband 'sat up', as it was called, for three or four nights in succession while the eligible bachelors, young and old, rushed there to look the cargo over and make an approach to the one who took their fancy. The church on Sundays was also a recognised venue for young men to try their luck.

What was left of the Fishing Fleet moved on to the *mofussil* (outlying districts) to scoop up husbands from the bunch of unmarried officials, soldiers, planters and businessmen who lived far from the great centres and, with less opportunity to find brides, were likely to be less choosy. With such a multitude of wife-seekers, a young woman had to be very plain or over-particular not to acquire a mate.

The demand for wives was so great that a woman who lost her husband had no difficulty in replacing him. There are accounts of widows being proposed to on the steps of the church after the burial of husbands. Marriage was undertaken at such speed, and illnesses were so often fatal that, according to one authority, there were even cases where a wife would affiance herself to a suitor as her husband lay desperately sick.

Stuart Corbett, who secured Charlotte Britten – at twenty-one, two years his senior – was the eldest of thirteen children born to the only son of Lady Augusta and the Reverend Corbett. He had entered the Honourable East India Company's service at the age of sixteen and although his prospects were good he was naturally a little nervous as to how his family would take the news that he was tying himself for life to a girl older than himself whom he had only known for a few months. 'My dear Louisa,' he wrote to his sister at home in the Rectory near Sheffield a month before his wedding:

'I have now a great piece of news to tell you I don't [know] wether you will think it good or bad but I am going to be married in the middle of next month. I know you will think me mad but these things will happen, my wedding day is to be on the 13th March 1822 when I shall be married to Miss Charlotte Britten who I am sure you will like as she has a very excellent Temper, and is much superior in every respect to the generallity of the young ladies you meet in this country, and has a great stock of good sence.

'One of her sisters who came out at the same time she did, is going home again in the same ship with this letter as the Country does not agree with her and she does not like it near as much as being at home.' Mary, who had celebrated her seventeenth birthday on board the *Lowther Castle,* decided that she did not like either India or its climate and came back to England as a 'returned empty' as quickly as she could (a few years later she too married).

A letter from Stuart to his brother, an officer in the 10th Royal Hussars, stationed at Brighton, spent less time on his proposed nuptials than on the birds his brother wanted him to send. 'I ... have to inform you that I intend to be married on the 13th of this month to Miss Charlotte Britten, you may perhaps some day or other fall in with her father who lives at Forest Hill in Kent. I am sorry I cannot send you any parrots or monkeys by this ship, as the Captain says they drink water and will not take charge of them. I can get you five or six different sorts of Parrots some not larger than a Bullfinch quite green except a small red spek on the breast but I am affraid I shall be never able to find any one who will take sufficent care of them on the voyage home.'

Stuart, like many young men of his generation, was to serve forty years without a break, during which period, unusually, he never once had a day's sick leave. Charlotte, whom he married in 1822, and who never returned to England, predeceased him, dying in India eighteen years later. Stuart finally came home on leave in 1859, returned to India three years later, and was appointed to the Divisional Command of Benares. Two years later he died, in the country where he and so many others had spent most of their lives.

INTRODUCTION

———✦———

The origins of the 'Fishing Fleet' go back to the days when the Honourable East India Company was establishing its trading domain. Sometimes these girls were adventuresses, sometimes they were sent out by the East India Company, sometimes they were gently born but without family or financial support; an example is the sixteen-year-old Margaret Maskelyne, born in October 1735, one of the orphaned children of Edmund and Elizabeth Maskelyne. One of her brothers,* Edmund, in the East India Company, was stationed at Madras, and when he showed his close friend Robert Clive a miniature of Margaret, Clive became so enamoured of her beauty that Edmund urged her to come out to Madras. She did so, sailing with several other young women on the tiny *Godolphin*, a ship of less than 500 tons. By the time she arrived, Clive (later Lord Clive of Plassey or, as he was more popularly known, Clive of India) had become a military hero and amassed a fortune. After a six-month courtship, the couple were married at Madras on 18 February 1753.

As the reputation of India as a place where even the plainest could find a mate grew, so did the number of young women travelling out there. By the middle of the nineteenth century the Fishing Fleet no longer consisted only of girls sent out by the East India Company but of others as well, sent by their families (sometimes against their will) in the hope of making a good match. In England, a land where women outnumbered marriageable men, a girl without beauty, money or grand relations had little hope of this; in India, she was showered with immediate proposals.

Even so, few can have acted quite as speedily as Lieutenant Michael Edward Smith, of the Sutherland (78th) Highlanders. He

---

* Another brother, Nevil, became the Astronomer Royal.

went on leave to Ootacamund in the Nilgiri Hills in August 1847 and on the first Sunday after his arrival saw a young woman in church whom he greatly admired. There and then he decided to marry her if he could. In just over a fortnight he had managed to meet the pretty stranger at a ball – she was staying with her sister, the wife of an officer in a regiment stationed there – proposed, been accepted and married (on 8 September), so that by the time his three weeks' leave was up he was able to take his bride back to his regiment.

After the Indian Mutiny in 1857 the running of India was taken over by the British Government and on 1 November 1858 the Raj was born, at a durbar in Allahbad presided over by the first Viceroy, as the Sovereign's representative in India would be henceforth known. 'We have resolved to take upon ourselves the Government of India, heretofore administered in trust for us by the Honourable East India Company,' declared the Queen's Proclamation, read in all the chief towns.

An Indian Civil Service was installed, for which entrants had initially to pass the same examinations as the Home Civil Service, followed by further education in the laws and customs of the country they were going to govern. Regiments of the British Army were sent out on tours of duty; the Indian regiments originally raised by the East India Company now swore their loyalty to the Crown – as did the planters and businessmen who had settled in India, Ceylon (today's Sri Lanka) and Burma.

With the founding of the Raj, the number of single young women making their way out to India began to increase steadily. When the Suez Canal was opened in November 1869 by the Empress Eugenie (it had been built by the French), the journey time from London to Bombay was cut from months to weeks. The gateway to India was open – and women flooded through, usually at the beginning of the cold weather.

Although the practice of despatching young women to India for the benefit of men working there had ceased, the name Fishing Fleet stuck, attaching itself to the young girls and women who continued to go out to India in sizeable numbers – as a glance at the passenger list of the *Kaiser I Hind*, sailing from London to Calcutta on 12 October 1893, confirms. Reading down the list of names, past Mrs Wright, Mrs Simpson, the infant and ayah (Indian nanny), you come to Miss Max, Miss Cowell, Miss Blyth, Miss Graham ... a long sequence of unmarried women, down to Miss Sandys and Miss Good.

There were compelling demographic and social reasons for a girl to try her luck in this huge, exotic country.

It was an era when for a woman marriage was the desired and only goal, giving her status, financial security, children, a household and a pleasant life among her peers. Without marriage, pointed out the academic Rita Kranidis, a woman's life and her future prospects were as nothing.

If she did not marry, she became (unless very rich) that sad figure: the Victorian spinster, living on the charity of some relation or earning a pittance and despised both by those she worked for and their servants. For middle-class women, the only occupations that were socially acceptable were acting as a companion to some rich, lonely and usually difficult elderly woman, or teaching, usually as a governess (in the 1850s there were over 25,000 governesses in employment). For such women, on an annual salary of only £10–£40, there was no possibility of saving for old age, and of course no pension. And by the late 1860s, even this unrewarding profession was under threat: the new secondary schools for women were turning out young women much better qualified for teaching than those with the superficial education that was all the average young 'gentlewoman' received.

Yet though social life, indeed the whole fabric of society, was based on the assumption that all women would marry, many did not. From 1851 to 1911 approximately one in three of all women aged twenty-five to thirty-five was unmarried; and between fifteen and 19 per cent of women aged thirty-five to forty-five were unmarried. The 1851 census made clear that in a population of around eighteen million roughly 750,000 women would remain single, a number that by the time of the 1861 census had roughly doubled.

Suddenly, it seemed, there were spinsters everywhere. Adding to their difficulties was the then general belief that a girl had to marry or at least become engaged by the time she was twenty or so. The dread words 'old maid' could be applied as early as twenty-five.

These women came to be referred to as 'superfluous women' or 'redundant women' and concern for them was widespread. Society after society was formed for the purpose of assisting them to emigrate to the newly founded colonies, where there was a corresponding shortage of women – but of women prepared to buckle down to the hardships and exigencies of pioneer life, which few with any pretensions to gentility were willing or able to do.

Some tried to help themselves through the increasing number of lonely-hearts columns. 'A young lady, aged 22, the orphan daughter of a country gentleman, of old family, would like to marry. She is a capital housekeeper; can ride and drive a pair; is musical and dresses exquisitely; and wants someone awfully jolly. No clergymen, doctors or learned men need apply, but an easy-going kind of fellow, with a fairish amount of brains, would suit admirably.'* Advertisements like these appeared in the rash of 'marriage' journals that were launched in the 1880s,† but they did not address the central problem of too few men to go round.

The plight of the gently born, softly brought up middle-class woman, in particular, exercised both the Government and the popular imagination: because of her class, most forms of labour were 'banned'; because of her lack of education she was ill-equipped to support herself; because of her lack of independence she could not, like her brothers, seek her fortune overseas – and because so many of these brothers did, her pool of potential husbands was correspondingly smaller.

In 1890 one study by Clara Collett compared the numbers of unmarried women between thirty-five and forty-six (i.e., those considered to be irredeemably single) in Kensington with those in Hackney. Among the Kensingtonian 'servant-keeping classes' (those with an income of £150 or more) there were thirty-six unmarried women to thirty married ones in this age group, but only nine to seventy-six among the working class of Hackney. Small wonder that the enterprising decided to chance it in India, where men outnumbered women by roughly four to one.

One reason for these unmarried women was the attitude of Victorian society. Women had few rights: they could not vote, sue, own

---

* Quoted by Francesca Beauman in *Shapely Ankle Preferr'd*.
† The *Matrimonial Record*, launched in 1882, the *Matrimonial Herald* and *Aristocratic Matrimonial and Marriage Envoy* in 1884, *Marriage Advertiser* 1886 and *Cupid's Cosmopolitan Carrier* 1888. Ibid.

property, take charge of their own money or have a job. Indeed, should this have been possible, they would not have been equipped for it. The Victorian young lady learned only the accomplishments considered suitable for her position – dancing, singing, sketching and how to sit up straight, with needlework to fill in the endless evening hours. Education,* as such, was the province of the male – as, indeed, was virtually everything of importance.

The man who married this sheltered, cosseted creature was expected to provide her with a household – house, furniture, clothing, servants, carriage and, of course, the food and drink necessary to maintain her, the other adults in the house and the numerous children she was expected to bear.

For the men these young women would hope to marry, this burden was often impossible. Younger sons with no prospects, or the sons of parents in straitened circumstances, simply could not afford the expense of a wife. Some of them sailed to Britain's expanding Empire (thus further depleting the pool of available men at home) because here, with luck, they would make their fortunes or at the least be able to live at a standard they could not possibly afford in England. The case of the seven sons (out of thirteen children born between 1860 and 1883) of the Reverend James Du Boulay and his wife Alice is typical. 'The eldest boy became a surgeon,' wrote the Reverend James's grandson, Professor Robin Du Boulay, 'but, at a time of poor prospects at home and widening opportunities in the empire, the others looked overseas.'

Other young men with an income too low for marriage stayed at home, living as bachelors. Filling the gap left by their lack of access to one of the obvious benefits of matrimony were numerous prostitutes. There were so many that it was considered inadvisable for a respectable woman to walk alone even by day in Piccadilly, Regent Street, the Strand or Leicester Square: if she did, she risked not only being scandalised by streetwalkers but also mistaken for one herself and accosted. One leading authority claims that there were about 55,000 prostitutes (in a population of around two million) working London's streets, bars and theatres in 1841 – or to put it another way, there was one prostitute for every twelve adult males.

---

* As late as 1876, the examiners of the Royal College of Surgeons resigned en masse rather than examine three women for diplomas in midwifery.

This high ratio was largely due to the fact that women would often go into prostitution simply because it was very profitable, the hours were good and the other options available for any kind of gainful toil were limited. There was factory work, but conditions were so bad that it killed many. To be a governess a woman had to be 'respectable' and educated. Domestic work was low-paid and, unless in a large house, a dull, relentless grind. Among the very poor, prostitution was regarded as just another, and better-paid, way of earning a living; often, it was something that a woman would dip in and out of according to need. Those living in near-starvation could not afford the luxury of morality.

Another, unspoken reason was that of (male) sexual satisfaction. The image of Victorian married women was that of pure, virtuous mothers and wives, the sweet, untouchable guardians of morality whose distaste for sex led to this explosive increase in the number of prostitutes. The famous Dr Acton, author of a seminal work on male sexuality,* published in 1857, that influenced medical thinking for decades, believed that 'there are many females who never feel any sexual excitement whatever … as a general rule, a modest woman seldom desires any sexual gratification for herself. She submits to her husband, but only to please him; and, but for the desire of maternity, would far rather be relieved from his attentions.' And even that great early feminist, Mary Wollstonecraft, urged† that 'chastity must more universally prevail' – even in marriage, declaring that: 'A master and mistress of a family ought not to continue to love each other with passion.'

Husbands were urged to show restraint towards these innocent, ethereal beings, whereas no such considerations obtained with paid sex. It was the difference between an approach to the Virgin Mary and a romp with Mary Magdalen (indeed, Victorian prostitutes were often known as magdalens).

Although diaries and letters of the period have shown, in contradiction to the general view of the era, that many Victorian women had similar attitudes to sexual enjoyment as women today, these

---

* *The Functions and Disorders of the Reproductive Organs in Childhood, Youth, Adult Age and Advanced Life, Considered in the Physiological, Social and Moral Relations* discussed women only twice, dismissively.

† In Chapter Seven of *A Vindication of the Rights of Women*, published in 1792.

documents were necessarily private. Then, such matters were never discussed. Thus most women, it was thought, were not troubled by sexual feeling of any kind, suffering sex only as a prelude to the sizeable family that they were expected to bear, an example set by the Queen herself. What no one would have known was the gusto with which the Queen approached her own marriage bed, disclosed only years later in her own diaries. It was not until the dawn of the twentieth century that sexual pleasure became 'acceptable' for women as for men, and then only within the context of conjugal love – Marie Stopes's explosive book that tackled the subject, published in 1918, was entitled *Married Love*; indeed, until the Second World War many young women went to their marriage beds in complete ignorance.

As the nineteenth century progressed, more and more men turned their faces outward and soon the words 'Empire builder' passed into the language. Originating with the trading posts and overseas colonies established in the late sixteenth and early seventeenth centuries, these possessions expanded to become, at its height, the largest empire in history. By the time of the Raj, Britain controlled colonies, was unchallenged and unchallengeable at sea and held a dominant position in world trade. To run this empire of around 10,000,000 square miles, more and more settlers, merchants, lawgivers, soldiers and administrators were needed.

India in particular was a goal: schools like the United Services College, Westward Ho! (on which Kipling based *Stalky & Co.*), sprang up, their alumni as a matter of course joining some branch of Government service – the Indian Civil Service, the Forestry Service, the Police – or, with Kipling's Great Game at its height in the 1880s and 1890s, the Army. By the time the Raj ended, on 15 August 1947, many English families had lived in India for generations, with brothers, sons and grandsons conceiving of no other life.

Out to meet and marry them sailed the Fishing Fleet. Some of these girls were returning to join their families after being educated in England, others were going to stay with sisters, cousins, aunts or friends whose husbands worked or were stationed in India, to enjoy its lively social life and extraordinary and magical atmosphere – or to find a husband. Because of the lengthy journey there and back, and the distances to traverse in India itself, such visits usually lasted several months and often a year or more. Although their stories cover the whole span of the Raj, most of the ones in this book focus on the twentieth century – the last flowering of British India before the country gained its independence in 1947.

'Champagne has been known to allay sea sickness when all else failed'

The Voyage Out

'The smell of the earth soaking up the first rain of the monsoon, of watered Lucerne [alfafa], of roasting gram [chickpea from the servants' godowns], of tobacco smoked on the roadside in a communal pipe and the tremendous, heady bitter smell of something in the Simla bazaar – you never forgot and you longed to smell it again …'. Veronica Bamfield, child of a family that had spent three generations in India, was returning as one of the Fishing Fleet.

Some of these young women had been born in India, sent home anywhere between five and ten years of age to be educated, and were now sailing out to rejoin their families. 'Got up very early and went to St Pancras for boat train. Met Lady Steele. Arrived at Tilbury. Got on to boat for India, SS *Mongolia*, cabin 244,' wrote the sixteen-year-old Claudine Gratton on 4 September 1936. 'Said goodbye to Lady Steele.'

Claudine was one of many single girls for whom travelling out to India was a rite of passage as important as the debutante curtsey many of them had already made. In any autumn during the years of the Raj these groups of young women and girls could be found undertaking the voyage, its route marked by distant and exotic ports. 'Port Sudan, the Fuzzy Wuzzies – handsome men with amazing hair – and an ability to stand on one leg at a time for hours. Gully gully men at Port Said, naked brown boys diving for pennies thrown over the side of a ship, islands gold, turquoise and amethyst in the misty early sunlight of the harbour of Bombay,' reminisced Veronica Bamfield in the 1930s.

Claudine, like other young girls of her age and class, was chaperoned every inch of the way, first by her mother's friend Lady Steele to Tilbury (it was unthinkable that she should travel alone on the boat train from St Pancras for Tilbury) until she boarded the SS *Mongolia* for Bombay, on which her mother was also sailing.

'Three awful old hags in my cabin,' she noted – her mother was in smarter accommodation – but within twenty-four hours was otherwise preoccupied. 'The boat rolled. Felt very seasick. Slept on deck all day, very cold. Went to bed. Was sick once. Mummy fainted in the bathroom. Had fever, went back to bed. Had to look after her.' Mercifully, her mother improved the next day.

Departures were always an event, heightened in many cases by the knowledge that this was the last time one might see a beloved face. 'Steamed down Southampton Water under the guidance of a pilot. After three hours the pilot and several others left us,' wrote William Adamson in the 1850s. 'We gave them a parting cheer which they lustily returned – the last of which many then on board would ever give to England.'

Until the beginning of the eighteenth century the leisurely sea route round Africa had been quite sufficient for the needs of the expanding Empire – one of the reasons Britain established colonies along the coast of Africa was to protect the shipping that carried her trade.* But now her mills needed India's raw materials, and fast transport was urgent. The eighteen months or even two years that might elapse before communications from the Company's executive board in London could reach their employees in India and an answer be returned were no longer acceptable. An alternative to the Cape route had to be found.

None of this deterred the eager and determined young women bound for Bombay, as a poem written by Thomas Hood in 1842 makes plain:

* For example, the British were keen to take control of the Cape Colony from the Dutch during the Napoleonic Wars to secure the main sea route to India; for the same reason the islands of St Helena and Mauritius and the coastline of Aden were added. Likewise, soon after the opening of the Suez Canal the British bought a controlling interest in it, to be followed by control of Egypt; with Egypt, Sudan and Cyprus became part of the Empire.

By Pa and Ma I'm daily told
To marry now's my time,
For though I'm very far from old,
I'm rather in my prime.
They say while we have any sun
We ought to make our hay—
And India has so hot an one,
I'm going to Bombay!

. . . .

My heart is full—my trunks as well;
My mind and caps made up,
My corsets, shap'd by Mrs Bell,
Are promised ere I sup;
With boots and shoes, Rivarta's best,
And dresses by Ducé,
And a special licence in my chest—
I'm going to Bombay!

By the time of the Raj, sail had given way almost entirely to steam, although troops were still sometimes carried in sailing ships, which took the Cape route. To judge by the letters sent home by Minnie Blane, the bride of Archie Wood, a handsome captain in the army of the soon-to-be-disbanded East India Company, it could be a nightmare journey.

Minnie travelled on the newly built sailing ship *Southampton* in one of its eighteen passenger cabins. In these early journeys round the Cape all the cabins had to be furnished by the passengers themselves – what they bought was simply an empty space, to be filled at their expense and according to their means. This involved, at the least, a bed or sofa on which to sleep; sheets, looking glass, washstand, chair, candles and a chest for clothes.

The *Southampton* was cramped: there was a dining room but nowhere else to sit except parts of the deck. The ship also carried hens, pigs, a cow, several horses and a pack of foxhounds (which gave tongue just as everyone was falling asleep) that the captain intended to sell when they reached India. The shortage of water meant cleanliness was a problem and during the four months the voyage took much of the food went bad – perhaps the reason Minnie's husband got dysentery.

Sometimes the ship bounced along under a brisk wind with half the passengers prostrate with seasickness; when there was no breeze she inched her way forward under a hot sun. With the insanitary conditions, the endless bouts of seasickness, the effluvia from animals and passengers, one can only imagine the stench, let alone the discomfort. 'Tell Cissy [her sister] never to undertake such a thing,' wrote Minnie. *'It is horrible!'*

Three months into the voyage she reported that 'all the lump sugar is gone and the eggs all went bad and had to be thrown overboard weeks ago, and though there is dessert on the table every day I cannot touch a thing, as biscuits, figs and ratafia are *alive*. I cannot tell you how sick it made me on cutting open a fig to see three or four large white maggots lying comfortably inside!' After intense heat ('I am *melting'*) they rounded the Cape through a terrible storm, waves like mountains and snow falling.

It was so cold when she wrote this that Minnie, normally a bright, cheerful, lively girl, never left the cabin, while her husband wore three or four overcoats at once. A few days later she had retched and vomited so much that one of her eyes was entirely red from burst blood vessels and the doctor had kindly popped in to warn them against the mutton. 'It has all gone bad.' When they finally arrived, the voyage had lasted sixteen weeks and three days. Nor did Minnie know if they would ever return to England.

In those early, smaller ships, seasickness was almost unavoidable, and of a virulence and duration unknown in the passenger liners of today. William Adamson, travelling out in the 1850s on the newly launched *Himalaya,* at 3,438 tons* the largest ship of the infant P&O line, succumbed the moment they left Southampton Water. 'I did not sleep much the first night, my berth being a top one I felt the motion of the ship very much, added to which the night was very boisterous and the noise overhead as well as that of the engines was anything but pleasant. We dined at five o'clock but few were able to sit until the dessert came as they had already begun to feel squeamish.'

---

* Compare this with the 80,000-plus tonnage of the *Queen Mary*, Britain's premier liner between the wars.

When the little *Himalaya* entered the notorious Bay of Biscay she was tossed about like a cork.

'Sometimes a large hill [of water] seemed to bar her progress, at other times we saw one behind looking as if it would engulf us – the pitching and rolling of the vessel did not allow of us walking about so we sat or stood and held on,' wrote Adamson, adding feelingly, 'The Bay of Biscay certainly comes up to my expectation and I can convey no idea of the emotion with which I looked upon it.'

One night the storm and turbulence was so bad that many passengers sat up all night in the saloon, afraid to go to bed in case they drowned in their cabins. Others remained there because they were immobilised with nausea.

In contrast to the cabin furnishings, meals were lavish.

'The bugle sounds at half past eight o'clock, when most of us rise and dress,' wrote Adamson to his father. 'At 9 we breakfast, on hot tea or coffee, hot rolls and hot and cold meat, fowls or anything we may fancy, at 12 we have luncheon of bread and cheese and butter washed down with wine, spirits or ale, at 4 we dine, when we have soup, various kinds of roasts, fowls, pastry, puddings, cheese and celery, dessert of apples, oranges dried fruits etc. During dinner we are allowed an unlimited supply of wine, beer and porter with champagne twice a week. Tea at 8 and Toddy at 9.'

For entertainment Adamson and his fellow passengers had a brass band for an hour in the morning and a string ensemble for an hour in the evening. Otherwise they wrote letters, or played chess or draughts.

In 1830 the East India Company pioneered the Red Sea route with a small steamer, built in India, called the *Hugh Lindsay*. As sail gave way to steam – though the early steamships were often sail-assisted in suitable conditions – and with it the end of the perilous journey round the Cape of Good Hope, the journey time shortened dramatically.

Small steamers began to run across the Indian Ocean between Suez and Bombay. Passengers would leave their ship at Alexandria and, after changing to a Nile boat – even smaller – travel to Cairo via a canal forty-eight miles long that had been built a few years earlier by the Pasha of Egypt, using 200,000 slaves. From Cairo those hardy early travellers were sent off in parties of six in wagons, each with two wooden wheels of the immense strength needed to survive the lumps of stone and small boulders on some parts of the road. Each wagon was pulled by four or six horses (drawn from a stud of 400) that were changed every ten miles or so, when there would be a meal for the passengers; halfway, there was a hotel with bedrooms where the passengers could catch up on sleep for a few hours, for the start of the eighty-four-mile land journey to Port Suez.

'The canal boats are small and dirty,' wrote Adamson to his father, of one of the long, narrow covered boats from Alexandria to Atfe. 'You sleep where you can – sofa, floor or chair. My bed was under the table with my bag as a pillow and my coat as mattress and blanket.' The ladies were allowed to sleep on deck, presumably with wraps and shawls to act as pillows and covering.

At Suez they would catch the steamer that would take them on the last leg of their journey, to Bombay. The coal for this had to come out from England; and was humped across the desert by a herd of 3,000 camels kept for the purpose. By now ships' cabins were furnished, although the minimum wardrobe recommended seems enormous. 'Take with you only six dozen shirts... two dozen pairs of white pantaloons, three dozen pairs of long drawers, a forage cap, a straw hat ...'. Women were advised to take no less than six dozen chemises, four dozen night chemises, four dozen each of drawers, thin cotton stockings, towels and three pairs of stays.

These ships also transported the mail, letters and newspapers packed in boxes about 18 inches by 12, colour-coded in red, blue and black according to destination – enough, said one observer, to fill two large luggage vans. (The mail itself started its journey by going over the Channel and France to Marseilles, from Marseilles to Port Said, then over the desert to Suez and thence by paddle steamer to India.)

When the Suez Canal opened in 1869 passengers were able to remain on the same vessel they had boarded in England, doing away with the dirt and discomfort of the desert route and heralding the luxury of the later ocean-going liners.

By the early 1900s travel was more comfortable, but for some severely regimented. Florence Evans, travelling out to India a few years before the 1914 war, described arriving at Southampton dock and boarding the SS *Nubia*, 'a splendid-looking steamer of great capacity'. In fact, the 5,914-ton *Nubia*,* built in 1894, was a mere 430 feet long – yet, according to Florence, carried 'well over a thousand troops beside women and children, crew, officers etc. [She was] like a small town – one easily lost one's way in her.'

As Florence was not one of the ninety first- or sixty-two second-class passengers the *Nubia* was entitled to carry, routine started early. So rapidly could disease sweep round a crowded ship that she and her companions had to be medically examined and passed as fit before being allowed on board, where they were allotted their beds in the Women's Quarters.

'These Quarters,' she recorded, 'are like a large dormitory with rows of comfortable beds and under each bed is room for the deck box containing clothing for the journey. At the end are the bath rooms (hot and cold water always on) wash house and lavatories also two small hospitals for the sick.

'We steamed out of dock on the Friday morning with our band playing *Auld Lang Syne* and *Where is now the merry party?* These rather saddened us and many both men and women wiped away a few tears as they wished Goodbye to their native land for a few years: then we were cheered by *Soldiers of the Queen* a most lively and inspiring tune which put us all in good humour again.'

She forbore from describing the seasickness that raged after the first day ('I will draw a veil over our sufferings any one who has gone through it understands the horrors of sea sickness'), concentrating instead on the daily timetable: 'We rise at 5.30, breakfast 7.30, doctor's inspection 9, dinner at 12, tea at 4, bed at 8.0' – and sleepy or not, to their dormitory they had to go at eight sharp.

Despite the daily medical inspection, a few days before they arrived at Port Said a rumour swept round that scarlatina had broken out among the children. 'Certainly one child was taken seriously ill, an infant a few months old,' wrote Florence, adding sadly that the child had died before the day was out. 'Poor woman,' she wrote of the mother, 'she had buried three before and this was the last. The little one was buried in the evening, all engines were stopped and the service was read the parents standing by when the corpse was lowered into the deep, it is a most solemn ceremony done that I hope never to see again. Poor mother she was insensible for hours

---

* The *Nubia* was lost outside Colombo Harbour while waiting for a pilot in 1915.

after. She attempted to follow the child at the burial and was held back by force.'

The Bay of Biscay was still so dreaded in the twentieth century that those who could afford it often travelled overland to join their ship at Marseilles in order to avoid it.

One such traveller was the Hon. Lilah Wingfield, daughter of Lord Powerscourt, invited out to India to see the 1911 'Coronation' Durbar, held to recognise King George V and Queen Mary as Emperor and Empress of India. Lilah's fellow passengers were an exceptionally smart crowd, travelling out on the *Maloja* for the durbar as special guests, the married couples all accompanied by their respective lady's maids and valets (travelling second class, naturally). 'As well as the boy Maharaja of Jodhpur with his English army officer companion, Lord and Lady Bute sit at the next table to ours and the Duke and Duchess of Hamilton, he is quite lame,' noted Lilah. 'Lord Leigh and his sister, both elderly, are our next neighbours.'

At first all was excitement and pleasure. Even during the lengthy process of coaling, Lilah could enjoy the warmth and beauty of the night, with its black-velvet sky studded with brilliant stars, listening to Scottish tunes floating upwards. 'Lord Bute's piper played the pipes on the second class passenger deck after dinner and all the maids and valets danced Scotch reels!'

Although Lilah was travelling on the newly launched *Maloja*, one of P&O's larger ships* at nearly 12,500 tons, all too soon the disadvantages of a late-autumn sailing became apparent; and on 17 November 1911 she too was writing: 'A horrid rough night succeeded by a horrid rough choppy sea today and it is no longer warm and sunny either and it rains half the time. I lay in my chair on deck all day feeling very miserable and wretched and too giddy to go downstairs to meals or to do anything … we had dinner on deck and afterwards there was a dance – a queer night to choose for this entertainment as the ship was rolling and pitching like anything.'

But Lilah's natural high spirits and readiness to enjoy herself soon surfaced. 'Lord Bute's piper played reels, Lord and Lady Bute, Lord Mar and Kellie, Lord and Lady Cassilis and the Duchess of Hamilton all took part, and it was a very funny sight as they were all

---

* Sunk by a mine two miles off Dover in February 1916.

lurching against the side of the ship and slipping about in the most comic way.'

Small in size and without stabilisers, ships had little protection from a rough sea – there were even arguments over which was worse: pitching and tossing or rolling from side to side. Sometimes, bags dripping oil were slung over the side in an effort to smooth out the crests of waves so that they did not slap too thunderously on the ship's sides, but the effect was negligible. One ship's bulletin referred to this in its 'Overheard' column. 'Hallo, old man, going to Port Said?' 'Whichever side's nearest. Quick, out of the way!'

'At Marseilles the posh people came aboard,' wrote Maisie Wright. 'There were five maharajas with their wives, children and retinues, and British Provincial Governors returning from home leave, and a bishop.'

By the beginning of the twentieth century nothing halted the relentless gaiety on these voyages. Corseted ladies in flowing Edwardian skirts, holding long-handled spoons in front of them, ran as fast as they were able along heaving decks in the egg and spoon race and, as the *Marmora Gazette* reported (in February 1912): 'in the tie and cigarette race [seeing which lady could tie a tie or light a cigarette fastest, both things which no 'lady' would normally do] the mere men were much impressed by the countless opportunities of displaying genius, even in tying bows, while several ladies were clearly practised hands in lighting cigarettes. After the tea interval with its lively auction most of the time was devoted to spar fighting. How graceful one looks balanced on a thin pole! That amusing event cock-fighting brought the proceedings to a close.'

Invariably, there was a fancy dress ball; Lilah went as an Irish peasant, with a skirt of crimson muslin instead of red flannel because of the heat, her red hair in two long plaits and a scarlet handkerchief round her head. Another girl, rather than be overwhelmed by the elaborate fancy dresses some of the passengers had brought out from England, borrowed one of the young stewards' uniforms and accompanied him serving drinks to guests. She acted the part so well that no one spotted her – and she won a prize.

'After Aden, we had the fancy dress dance, which I enjoyed very much,' wrote Maisie Wright. 'My table companions came in kilts made from bath towels with sporrans of sponge bags and two dangling shaving brushes. But they were drunk by dinner time so I kept out of their way. There was a full programme of social events, with competitions for deck games, camp-fire concerts round an electric fire on deck at night, and a gymkhana.'

Nor did injury deter: on Lilah's voyage a man had four teeth knocked out by a bat during a cricket match on board, although the occasional ladies' cricket match was gentler, if only because the men all had to play left-handed. By the late 1920s and 1930s romping games like sack and potato races had all but disappeared, their places taken by deck tennis (quoits), housey-housey (bingo), sun-bathing and swimming, in canvas pools that slopped about in rough weather; not until 1929 did a P&O liner – *The Viceroy of India* – have a built-in swimming pool surrounded by Pompeian reliefs (it also had a smoking room designed like the great hall of a castle, complete with hammer beams, baronial arms, a large fireplace and crossed swords on the walls).

Lilah shared her cabin with a friend: in the early 1900s there were very few single-berth cabins. By today's standards it was Spartan: there was no heating or ventilation (if a cabin had a porthole and this was left open, water might sluice in dangerously on sleeping passengers). There were no bedside lights and the switch for the cabin light was by the door. The only furniture was a coffin-like upright stand that concealed a primitive basin and tap.

As there were no private bathrooms on P&O liners, passengers would scurry along corridors to 'bath cubicles' in their dressing gowns and, for women – as it was the age of long hair – boudoir caps to conceal their undressed coiffures. These caps were trimmed with lace or frills and the more frivolous ones had bunches of curls or ringlets – often made of real hair – at either side to frame the face. In the cubicles, Indian bath attendants filled the tub with hot sea water, for which a special soap was needed. Across each bath was a tray on which the attendant placed a large wooden container of fresh water with which the bather rinsed off the salt.

Passengers kept the clothes they needed in their flat-topped wooden cabin trunks, marked 'Cabin' and stowed beneath berths. Fresh water for washing clothes was in such short supply that many women who knew they were going to travel saved their most worn underwear and then discarded it overboard on the voyage leaving, one imagines, a trail of dirty, threadbare nightdresses and knickers across the Indian Ocean.

Ruby Madden, daughter of Sir John Madden, Chief Justice and Lieutenant Governor of Victoria, was one who took advantage of this custom, dropping her soiled nightdresses out of the porthole. Ruby, who had been invited to stay with her friend Jeanie, married to Lieutenant-Colonel Claude Hamilton, for the Coronation Durbar of 1902/3, wrote cheerfully that she had very little laundry to do when she arrived as she had 'worn most of the rags and thrown them overboard'.

As evening dress was obligatory at dinner, for a long voyage women had to pack quite an assortment of gowns, some for gala evenings. One little girl, put to bed earlier, watched her seventeen-year-old stepsister dressing in one of these, a confection of white pure silk satin, its skirt caught up with bunches of artificial violets, kept uncrushed in her cabin trunk by layers of tissue paper.

Among garments not needed on the voyage were the special lightweight tropical stays women were advised to take, with shorter ones for riding – much of life could be spent on a horse in India – as in those pre-1914 war years no respectable woman could go without corsets, whatever the weather. Two other essentials in the trunk were a pile of knitted woollen 'cholera belts' and a supply of the long white kid gloves with tiny pearl buttons that were worn on all formal occasions.

It was a time when most women drank little. For men returning to India, there was the custom of the 'chota peg' – the 'sundowner' of whisky and soda or whisky and water, said to be medicinal in that climate, especially against malaria. (Until 1874 all drinks on board a P&O ship had been free – wine, beer, spirits, mineral water and champagne on celebration days like Sundays or landfalls – and the line was still famous for its claret. Many seasoned passengers took advantage of this from breakfast on.)

When a liner reached Port Said it was all change. 'At about 7 pm we got into Port Said,' wrote Lilah in her journal on 18 November. 'The most extraordinary thing seemed to me how marked a difference there suddenly was between west and east.' Here the ship's officers changed into white and double awnings were erected over the decks. Everyone went ashore, chiefly to the famous store Simon Artz (which prided itself on opening for the stay of every passenger liner, at whatever time of day or night) to buy topis* – never white ones, which were considered bad form, but the oblong khaki-brown ones, sometimes known as Bombay bowlers – and any other tropical clothing needed. Here, too, was 'Baggage Day', when all the luggage marked 'Wanted on Voyage' and containing hot-weather clothes was brought up from the hold and exchanged for that marked 'Cabin'.

In later years, Port Said was often seen as a behavioural Mason-Dixon line, with husbands or wives temporarily on the loose casting off the inhibitions that had shackled them on the earlier, cooler part of the trip. As one demure young woman remarked: 'The fun started when they hit Port Said. And then the Red Sea became very hot in more ways than one.'

After Marseilles, Aden was the next port for coaling, a long process during which passengers were sent ashore, to amuse themselves in various ways. Some drove the few miles to the botanical gardens; Fishing Fleet girl Marian Atkins and her mother went to see a well, known for one extraordinary property. Those who looked into the water in its depths, even at midday, could see the stars reflected, even though they were invisible in the clear blue sky overhead.

On board, all doors and portholes were sealed and the coal carried up the ship's gangways by porters bent under the weight of sacks or baskets. Twenty-one-year-old Violet Hanson, travelling to India with her Aunt Mabs in 1920, recalled the scene – when they got back to the ship it was dark and the ship was lit by flares.

'Up the various gangways came almost naked black figures, walking in a constant progression intoning a long loud and monotonous chant, carrying on their heads baskets of coal which they then threw into the hold, only to return for more, chanting unceasingly. They looked like creatures from hell, covered with coal dust, illuminated by the orange glow of flares.'

The mid-Victorian habit of keeping a small farmyard on board and slaughtering pigs, cows, sheep and hens as needed (then, there was no refrigeration) to serve the copious meals demanded had long passed but seven-course meals were still the norm, with beef tea or ice cream at 11 a.m. Service, too, had become more stylish and

---

* Lightweight pith helmets, considered essential to avoid sunstroke.

elaborate: after the soup had been served the head waiter would walk round and, when he thought everyone had finished, beat a gong. In would rush the stewards, pounce on the empty plates and then, as one man, serve the fish.* The same procedure would persist through the rest of the courses. In rough weather, 'fiddles' were placed on the tables. These were mahogany frames with walls about two inches high, divided into little squares in each of which was room for a plate, tumbler and wine glass. Dishes and bottles were placed in the gap between two rows of fiddles.

Precedence reigned supreme, with the most distinguished people – generals, aristocrats, Indian Civil Service† commissioners – sitting at the captain's table, and the rest grouped as nearly as possible with their social equals (meals for the passengers' children, accompanied by their nannies or ayahs, were served in a separate dining room). Most ships were full of British officers returning to India after eight months' leave, businessmen in tussore silk suits and, invariably travelling first class on the top deck, the 'heaven-borns'‡ – governors, commissioners, Residents, judges, often with their wives and chaperoned daughters.

Even with the shorter travelling times after the opening of the Suez Canal, partings could still be for a matter of years rather than months. Maisie Wright left England in November 1928 on the RMS *Rawalpindi*. 'When we arrived, rather late, we found the *Rawalpindi* towering above the P&O dock, with black smoke already billowing from its funnels. After a tearful farewell with my family, knowing that we should not meet again for four and a half years, I found my Second Class cabin. My cabin-mates were a middle-aged Scotswoman, returning from leave to her husband, and a Bright Young Thing travelling to visit relatives.'

In the 1930s, though, partings became more like parties, with cocktails in friends' cabins until the last minute, families lining the quayside and waving, a band playing and long coloured streamers floating from ship to land as the liner edged away in stately fashion.

* Remembered by Assistant Purser Ashley Randall, who joined the *Caledonia* in 1907.
† Known as the ICS, this was the body of civil servants who administered British rule in India.
‡ The ICS, the most desirable men in the marriage stakes, were often compared to Brahmins who, at the top of India's caste system, were known as the 'heaven-born'.

By now, deck quoits, sunbathing and swimming had become favourite deck pursuits – barred to those who had left the necessary smallpox vaccinations until the last minute.

'My vaccination, red and swollen and at its worst, prevents me from swimming in the pool and from taking any exercise apart from the daily promenades round the deck,' wrote Margaret Martyn. 'I soothe my arm with boracic powder several times a day and wear a protective wire frame.' These vaccinations were quite painful: instead of the usual needle and syringe, the smallpox vaccine was given with a two-pronged needle, dipped into the vaccine solution, then the skin was pricked with this several times. It usually left a scar, so thoughtful doctors would do it on the legs of women rather the upper arm, where it would be seen in evening dress.

Even as late as 1934, sailing across the Bay of Biscay could still be terrifying. Bethea Field, aboard SS *Mantua* (a P&O ship of just under 11,000 tons) and fortunately immune to seasickness, ran into a storm so bad that she was one out of only twelve – the ship's full complement of passengers was 600 – who made it to the dining saloon; but when she returned to her cabin she found it impossible to climb into her bunk, the top one. 'I changed into nightclothes and dressing gown and rested for a time on the floor. The ship was being battered from every side and there was a wild shrieking from the rigging and crashes.

'Next morning it was wilder than ever. Sofas and armchairs were sliding about the saloon in every direction. Even the grand piano joined in the dance. The dining saloon was deserted and I heard that an order had come down from the bridge that all elderly passengers were advised to stay in their cabins – in their bunks. We found refuge in the divan room, a narrow saloon that ran from port to starboard of the ship. There were wall seats on three sides on which some people were lying – others were sitting on the deck holding onto anything that seemed stable.

'The deck steward came in and enquired for breakfast orders. As so few passengers were about, the dining saloon was closed. I think I said "buttered toast and an apple". A few other orders were taken but most kept their eyes shut and shook their heads.' The ship was rolling so alarmingly that the returning steward crashed with his loaded tray, watched by passengers clinging to upright supports. Those who wanted a drink had to haul themselves to it hand over hand along 'storm ropes' lashed in place by the crew. 'I ordered a "horse's neck" [brandy and ginger ale]* and that, with apples and sandwiches, became my main sustenance for the next three days as the cooking galley was closed,' wrote Bethea.

Until stabilisers finally came,† finding one's sea legs was always a problem. One early authority, pointing out that 'chloroform taken in water is one remedy', added 'I think no one should ever embark without a few bottles of the very best wine that can be procured; champagne has been known to allay seasickness when all else failed, and in the weakness and depression which invariably follow, good port wine is quite invaluable.'

---

* A drink supposed to settle the stomach.
† The first stabilisers were introduced during the early part of the twentieth century, but it was not until the 1930s that a much more effective type was invented.

2

'Happy hunting-ground of the single girl'

The Women Who Went Out

'The Fishing Fleet would come out for August week, and the chaps would go along to the Galle Face Hotel to look them over as they sat on the veranda,' said former tea planter Mike Waring, describing the arrival of some of the girls in Ceylon; others sailed on to the ports of India.

'There would be around fifteen or twenty of them, and they came in stages. They would be asked for a dance at the Galle Face, which might be holding a rugger night. The girls always wore long dresses and the men mostly dinner jackets or white sharkskin. There were also tea dances. There were quite a lot of romances and marriages.'

August Week, which began in 1890, was the great social week of the year for the tea and coffee planters with estates in Ceylon; at the beginning of August, it fitted neatly between the end of the south-west and the start of the north-east monsoons. The girls who came to try their luck with the eligible bachelors who had come down to Colombo for the annual festivities were the more adventurous contingent of the Fishing Fleet, if only because marriage to one of these men generally meant a life spent on an isolated plantation.

Others were more like nineteen-year-old Katherine Welford, who viewed her invitation to stay with an aunt in India simply as a chance to see the country and have fun. 'I felt I was too young to marry and I don't think I wanted to live in India.' Katherine, born in Toorak, Melbourne, was an only child; her father owned a sheep property in New South Wales, where he spent much time, with another in

Western Australia. Her aunt, who thought Katherine would enjoy an Indian 'Season', had met her own husband in Colombo.

The voyage from Australia, in 1932, took a fortnight and the fare on Katherine's one-class ship, the *Mongolia,* was £30; she had a cabin to herself but no bathroom. At the start of the journey she was plagued with seasickness ('the Great Australian Bight is as bad as the Bay of Biscay'), after which there was the usual fun, games and dancing. 'There was a canvas swimming pool on board and we used to play deck quoits. You changed into a long evening dress for dinner. I had about a dozen evening dresses. My favourite was a gorgeous gold colour one with a cowl neck that was backless – you couldn't wear a bra but one was very firm in those days. Backless was very fashionable then. I don't think I drank at all until I got on the ship and then I would have one before dinner. Every night there was dancing after dinner, to which one was escorted by some chap.'

At Colombo, where the palm trees and spicy food made an immediate impression, she was met by friends of her aunt, with whom she stayed for a few days. 'I was taken out to the Galle Face for dinner, and to the races, then up to Madras, which took two days, where my aunt and uncle met me.'

Others of the Fishing Fleet were simply returning to their families after an English education. In the eyes of those who served the Raj, there were compelling reasons for sending their offspring home to England.

To begin with, medical advice was uncompromising on this point. In 1873 Sir Joseph Fayrer, whose decades of service in the Bengal Medical Service had rendered him an expert, had declared: 'It has long been known to the English in India that children may be kept in that country up to five, six or seven years of age without any deterioration, physical or moral ... But after that age, unless a few hot seasons spent in the hills should enable parents to keep their children in India until a somewhat later age, to do so is always a doubtful proceeding. The child must be sent to England, or it will deteriorate physically and morally ...'. As with many pronouncements from renowned doctors, it was a view that echoed through the years (in this case, until well into the 1930s), despite the fact that child mortality was actually greatest in the *under*-fives – British cemeteries in India are scattered with little cholera graves.

There were also pressing social reasons. By the twentieth century, there were excellent boarding schools in India – but in English eyes, they had one fatal flaw: the accent of their alumni. Many of the pupils at these establishments were Eurasian, the children of Eurasian planters or of the railway community, who spoke with the sing-song Eurasian accent, commonly and derogatorily known as 'chi-chi'. The fear that a British child might pick up the accent of – or become too friendly with – Eurasians was very real in the India of the Raj. (When Iris James attended All Saints College in India for a few months to complete her education, her mother was so anxious lest she 'pick up the accent, like some unpleasant disease' that she was not allowed to join her schoolmates for curry lunches but had to sit on the hillside by herself eating hotel sandwiches.)

Such apartheid had not always existed. In this hot climate where life expectancy was low and to which few white women travelled, what Robert Clive's great rival Joseph Dupleix* called '*la rage de la culotte*' meant that marrying or cohabiting with Indian women was accepted as perfectly natural for men who were likely to spend their entire lives in India. Many of their offspring were sent back to Britain to be educated, often marrying there.†

Then came the Regulating Act of 1773, which created the post of Governor-General of Bengal with administrative powers over all of British India. When Lord Cornwallis – the man who surrendered to George Washington at Yorktown in 1781 – was chosen for the post in 1786, these powers were enlarged and he immediately began a programme of edicts that would eventually result in the impassable barrier between British and Indians during the Raj.

The first of these diktats, issued almost at once, banned the children of British men and Indian wives from jobs with the East India Company. At the same time, it was forbidden to send such mixed-race children home to be educated. Five years later, an order was issued that no one with an Indian parent could be employed in the civil, military or marine branches of the Company (though at this point, as 'Indian' rested largely in the eye of the beholder, the light-skinned still slipped through) Finally, all jobs paying more

---

* Joseph Dupleix was appointed Governor-General of all French establishments in India in 1742.

† Lord Liverpool, British Prime Minister 1812–27, had an Indian grandmother.

than £500 a year were reserved for British men born and hired in Britain.*

The thinking behind these earlier laws was rammed home with a vengeance when, in 1800, Lord Wellesley (the successor to Cornwallis), banned Indians, and Britons born in India, from all Government social functions in Calcutta, a practice that spread steadily to the other parts of India under British domination. The machinery for separation, and the creation of an Anglo-Indian society that could fill only the lower and less lucrative posts in India, was now in place.

As these laws hit home, Indian wives and mistresses began to disappear. No man wanted to see his children penalised because their mother was the wrong colour or to see his wife viewed as a social outcast. At the same time, despite the difficulties, more British women began to travel to India.

To the general public, as to Queen Victoria herself, India had always been a land of compelling fascination. Its silks and muslins, its spices, jewels, ivory and tiger skins breathed an exotic glamour with overtones of romance and danger that must have been irresistible to an adventurous young woman. These early members of the Fishing Fleet were put off by neither the discomforts and dangers of the journey nor the high mortality rate among Britons working in India. What lay ahead was the Holy Grail of the Victorian miss: a pool of eligible, financially secure bachelors.

By the time the Raj was installed in 1858 the 'us and them' attitude was part of the British mindset, as was an unquestioning acceptance of the need to maintain purity of blood and links with the motherland.

So home – as England was always called, even by fifth-generation Anglo-Indian families – went the small boys and girls born to the servants of the Raj, sometimes as young as five, sometimes to see parents only once or twice during those years. Some were lucky enough to stay with loving aunts, cousins or grandparents, others could find themselves lodged somewhere that lacked all love, warmth and laughter; yet others had to remain at school during the holidays while everyone else left to join their

---

* The Act of 1793 that renewed the Company's charter expressly stated this.

families, enduring years of separation and misery.

Iris James, born in 1922 and brought to England as a small child by her parents, only saw her father twice during her childhood after he had returned to India. He was 'a stranger for whom my feelings were neutral'. During the holidays she stayed at the vicarage at Potten End, then run as a home for children of the Raj, where she was half-starved. When her mother returned home two years later she removed Iris at once; thenceforth holidays – Iris became a boarder at eight – were spent with aunts or her grandmother. The experience of the six-year-old Iris was all too common.

Nor, as she grew up, did the idea of going back to India appeal. She had a withered right leg, due to early polio, undiagnosed, untreated and never spoken of. 'My nickname in the family was Jane, short for Plain Jane,' she wrote. 'So by the time I was educated and ready to be taken to India to find a husband, my chances were considered to be poor, especially by me.

'Another, crippling disadvantage was a good brain. Men hated clever women, my mother never ceased to point out, adding that even quite old very clever men in the Indian Civil Service would prefer not to have the silence in their remote outposts disturbed by intelligent conversation.'

Negating as far as possible the effects of intelligence was something Iris's mother could, and did, do something about. In undeviating pursuit of the goal of marriage, she practised a cruel deception on her hapless daughter, concealing from Iris, who longed for an education, that her school had been confident she would get a scholarship to Oxford. Instead, she was whisked away from school at the end of summer 1938 and brought out to India and the marriage market.

Unsurprisingly, Iris dreaded the idea of tea dances and tennis playing and although her withered leg was never mentioned in the family, her teenage life became dedicated to trying to disguise it. 'To cross a room became an exercise in camouflage. Even in the hottest summers, and the summers of the thirties were very hot, I carried a coat over my right arm, to drape itself down my side and conceal my leg. Neither my mother nor my aunts thought of giving me slacks to wear. I dreamed and schemed of buying myself a pair, but in the days before dress allowances this was impossible. Why did I never ask? I don't know, the young were so tongue-tied then, the adults so crushingly in control.'

Marjorie ('Billy') Gladys Fremlin was another of the returning young women who had been sent home to be educated. Marjorie, who returned to India aged seventeen in the Fishing Fleet of 1924, had been born in Bangalore; she was the second of the three daughters of a coffee planter, Ralph Fremlin, whose wife, Maud, came from the next-door plantation, about four miles away. The Fremlins' early married life had been full of the tragedies that so often happened to Anglo-Indian families: four sons had died, two at birth, two at a year old. Marjorie, always known as Billy, was treated as a boy by her father.

The three little girls were sent home when Billy was five, to stay with their aunt and uncle, a Norfolk parson, during the holidays. Like many of the children sent back like this, the shock and narrowness of English life after the warmth, sights, smells and teeming human and animal life of India was profoundly depressing. Billy's first impression was of the chill of England after India. 'We struggled through those years, they were cold and unexciting,' she says in her spoken memoir. 'Most of my memories were not very happy.'

When war was declared in August 1914 her parents came home, her father to fight, her mother to take them to a rented house in Lowestoft, where sometimes they saw drowned sailors washed up on the beach. One night a zeppelin came over, later a sea bombardment destroyed the railway, and their mother removed the small family, along with their Indian ayah, in a horse-drawn cab. Finally, in 1924, Billy, a skinny, beautiful, blue-eyed blonde, returned to India like a prisoner released to rejoin her father, now back on his coffee plantation. Even a Bay of Biscay storm during the voyage out on P&O's *Khyber* did not depress her. 'I was so happy and it was so exciting I could hardly believe it.'

Ten years later Beatrice Baker was openly calling herself 'a member of the fishing fleet', which she described as 'the daughters of British families stationed in India, who went out to join their parents, uncles, aunts and friends with the idea of finding a husband. In my case finding a husband was not a specific idea as my family were a long-established family in India. My great-grandfather, Henry Baker, had gone out to India in 1819 as a Church Missionary Society missionary, one of the first in South India. It was always presumed that on leaving school, Malvern Girls' College, I would return to India, where I was born, to enjoy the wonderful life on our family estate Kumakarom.'*

In January 1934 she sailed from Tilbury in the SS *Orsova* for Colombo. As the only unattached girl on board – there were two other young women, sailing to meet and marry their fiancés in Colombo – Beatrice came in for a lot of attention from the ship's officers. Her father was waiting for them on the quayside in Colombo, magnificent in a tussore silk suit, highly polished brogues and rakishly angled topi. Then came a journey by ferry and train to mainland India and down canals to their estate.

Another who expected to return to India was Iris Butler,† the daughter of Montagu Butler, later Governor of the Central Provinces of India.

For Iris, her childhood in Rajasthan meant that 'pictures and talk about England were fairy stories. India was real.' The Butler children would listen to stories of Indian gods and heroes and, as a family, would attend festivals like Diwali, passing shrines built into mud-banks between the fields, 'each with its tiny offering of marigolds, a handful of cardamoms, a saucer of ghi'.‡

In 1911, when Iris was six, she, her mother and her siblings sailed for England from Bombay and settled in a furnished house in Hove to be near the preparatory school of her brother Austen (thenceforward to be known as Rab, the nickname he was given at this school). 'The house was on a steep street going down to the sea front, windswept, cold and seemingly always grey,' she wrote. Another terror for this small child, used only to the 'thunderboxes'§ of India, was the pulling of the lavatory plug, followed by 'an overwhelming rush of water. Where, oh where, was the kind, efficient sweeper?' The contrast with India could not have been more acute.

While many of the Fishing Fleet had been schoolgirls only months previously ('In the afternoon unpacked, wrote to Mummy. Have moved up a form,' wrote Claudine Gratton, adding gloomily, 'Exams. Fail.' a few weeks later), others were going to India with a definite purpose. For Ruby Madden this was, quite simply, to enjoy

---

* Now known as the Taj Garden Retreat.
† She was the younger sister of the politician 'Rab' Butler.
‡ A type of clarified butter, used like cooking oil..
§ The equivalent of a commode, emptied by sweepers.

herself, to see – and be seen. Ruby's letters and diary focus to a large extent on what she was wearing, or what someone she admired was wearing, and the effect on spectators. Even her trousseau for the ship was huge. 'I get unmercifully chaffed about my clothes because I have a new thing on every day and a handkerchief to match,' she wrote on 27 November 1902. 'They all watch with interest to see what I have on when I go upstairs.' For the shipboard Sunday service she wore 'my white muslin dress with blue sash and ribbons and hat with blue veil,' noting that she 'got quite a cheer when I came on deck and old de Passeb reeled off compliments about looking like Dresden china etc till I had to escape from him …'.

A number of the Fishing Fleet were travelling to India to stay with married relations or friends, sometimes just for fun but often because the wife was having a baby. In 1900, one such girl was Lucy Elinor Hardy. 'My brother Willie, serving in a British Mountain Battery at Umballa, asked me to stay for the winter – his wife Jessie was expecting a baby and he had to be out in camp a great deal of the time.'

It was a chance not to be missed. She came of an Army family – her father, Major-General Frederick Hardy, of the York and Lancaster Regiment, had fought in the uprising of 1857, at the second relief of Lucknow – and her parents must have known what an enjoyable time their daughter would have, as they bought her a return ticket that would only expire after a year. She sailed on 9 October on the P&O *Arabia** with two other girls, also going to brothers, the three considered responsible enough to chaperone each other – 'one, Mary, being a daughter of Austen Dobson the poet,' wrote Lucy.

Occasionally girls were shipped out because their parents or guardians wanted them out of the way – perhaps relations at home were strained, perhaps some bad behaviour had to be lived down and a change of scene might give them a fresh start or provide a breathing space or perhaps because the last hope of finding a husband was more likely in the Raj.

Dulcie Hughes was the daughter of the Mayor of Marylebone, London, and the eldest of three sisters. She was extremely attractive, dark and slim with come-hither eyes. She was also very difficult, with a jealous, vindictive nature that erupted to cause problems

---

* Sunk in the 1914–18 war.

within the family ('probably due to pre-menstrual tension,' said one of her relations. 'But that wasn't a subject discussed then …').

Dulcie despised bluestockings, was bored by academic achievement but, at a time when marriage was everything, knew how to get men interested – in her eyes, the only talent a woman needed. 'The only thing that is worth having in this world is sex appeal,' she would say. 'If you don't have sex appeal you might as well give up. Without it, it's pointless being alive.'

But the years passed and there was no sign of a marriage. By the time she was twenty-eight her parents had become disenchanted and frustrated, so when in 1934 the chance came to send her off to stay with friends in India they leapt at it. 'You can go off to India and try and find a husband,' said her mother. 'It's the only thing to do. And I think it would be nice if you took Dorothy [her younger sister] as a chaperone and companion.' Off went Dulcie and Dorothy, aged twenty, for a year's visit, during which they had a wonderful time and Dulcie received thirteen proposals. But alas, she became, in the dreaded phrase, 'a returned empty', as she turned all her suitors down; back in England, she gave as the reason that 'they were either after my money or my body'.*

Another despatched for behavioural reasons was Marguerite Lucie Chouillet de Jassey, always known as Bébé. She was one of six children of a Huguenot family, brought up in France. Her father, a pastor, spent a lot of his time in Paris and the Hague, where at one point he was personal priest to the Queen of Holland. With their mother, the family spent every summer in Brittany, renting the same house each year. Here Bébé and her sisters and brothers ran wild.

Bébé's two elder brothers were killed at the end of the 1914–18 war, but the four girls and their mother continued their long summer visits to the Brittany coast – in Bébé's case for another seven years until she was twenty-five, an enchantingly pretty young woman with red-gold hair and brown, flirtatious eyes that attracted a string of admirers.

She had also imbibed the new freedoms that had come with the war. With whichever sister was around, she would swim naked. 'This was much to the fascination of the local male population, who would pursue them into the sand dunes behind the beach,' said

* Dulcie later married in England, but not very happily.

Bébé's son. 'Eventually, my grandmother got a bit fed up with this and said: "Look here, enough is enough – I'm not having all these men chasing you over the beach." My mother – Bébé – was about twenty-five when Granny shot her off to India. I think she got fed up with the chasing over the sand dunes. So she sent her off to stay with her eldest, married sister, who lived in Delhi and Simla. Basically, she wanted my mother out of the way.'

That most of these girls did marry was unsurprising. Until the Second World War, the whole emphasis of their upbringing was on becoming wives and mothers;* any thought of a career was usually discouraged, with arguments ranging from 'Don't be silly, your husband will support you,' to 'You will be taking the bread out of the mouth of someone who really needs it.' Thus whether or not they actively planned to look for a husband, the subliminal quest for a mate was necessarily there from an early age.

As far as the Army was concerned, girls from Army families often regarded a spell in India as the equivalent of a debutante Season. They 'sailed joyfully away by P&O liner to join the "Fishing Fleet", see the Rock, the Grand Harbour, the Taj by moonlight and find a husband,' wrote Veronica Bamfield, herself the daughter and grand-daughter of soldiers who had served in India. 'This practice was well established long before it became part of army ritual and had been a fruitful source of supply of wives for the Honourable East India Company.'

Not all of the Fishing Fleet were successful, as this sad little verse written in 1936† shows:

Now sail the chagrined fishing fleet
Yo ho, my girls yo ho! Back to Putney and Byfleet
Poor girls, you were too slow!
Your Bond Street beauty sadly worn
Through drinking cocktails night and morn
With moonlight picnics until dawn
What ho! My girls, what ho!

---

* Until the Second World War there were only 600 places a year for women in Oxford and Cambridge and about 300 in London; most of the few provincial universities did not take women.
† From *The Illustrated Weekly of India.*

Violet Hanson, aged twenty-one and with an unfortunate marriage behind her, was one of those sent out to India by her mother to
find a husband of the 'right' social and financial standing. She was
the daughter of Sir Francis Hanson and his wife Pearl and brought
up like most children of her age – the Edwardian era – and class
largely by her nanny, seeing her parents for an hour after tea dressed
in her best frock and on her best behaviour. Occasionally, perhaps
for her birthday, they would come and say goodnight to her.

Towards the end of the 1914–18 war, when she was seventeen,
she fell in love with her brother's tutor, an attractive young man of
good family, with a private income, who for medical reasons had
not been conscripted. Her mother, keen that her daughter should
marry well and pleased to have such a presentable, eligible young
man to hand when so many others were losing their lives in battle,
decided that he would be a suitable husband for Violet, and went
into action. 'Somehow or other,' Violet wrote in her memoir, 'Billy
was persuaded to propose to me'; they became engaged and, when
she was eighteen, they married.

Like almost every girl of her time and age, in similar families,
Violet was sexually ignorant: it was an era when sex was never spoken of and certainly not to a young and innocent girl. Numerous
mothers could not even bring themselves to enlighten daughters on
the eve of their marriage. This was the case with Violet.

'After the wedding Billy and I went off for our honeymoon to a
suite in the Savoy Hotel, London,' she recalled. 'I don't know what I
really expected would take place between us, but I suppose subconsciously I must have realised that this relationship of ours was not
usual – after dinner the first night I retired to my room, Billy to his,
and no more was seen of him until the next day.'

She had, in fact, married a man who was homosexual – another
unknown area in the dark and dangerous field of sex. For the teenage Violet, homosexuality was not merely a closed book – it was a
word she would not even have recognised. Later she was to write:
'I shall never understand how my mother, and indeed everyone else,
allowed me to marry Billy. Even in those days it must have been
apparent to intelligent adults that he was a homosexual. Naturally I
had no idea, for I didn't know what homosexuality meant.'

She was fond of Billy and he had an interesting circle of friends
– writers, painters and actors; and at eighteen she enjoyed being

surrounded by these personable, amusing young men who were always ready to take her to theatres and parties. Life was pleasant, full of affection and, as she had no real knowledge of what marriage should be, any misgivings were pushed away. It was only when she got to know the local doctor that enlightenment came. Experienced with human nature, and able to question her gently, he quickly realised what was wrong. 'I don't know that I was really surprised,' wrote Violet, 'as I subconsciously knew that there was something very odd about our marriage.' Her doctor friend explained that, as she was still a virgin, she could get the marriage annulled and this she did.

In her mother's eyes, remarriage would be the quickest way out of the delicate and faintly scandalous situation of a daughter returned home because her marriage had gone wrong. At twenty-one, the veteran of a *marriage blanc,* Violet was persuaded by her family to accompany her Aunt Mabs to India – Aunt Mabs's son Geoffrey Byron was an officer in the very smart 4th/5th Dragoon Guards, then stationed at Secunderabad, in the Deccan. It must have seemed highly likely that in the exotic surroundings and social whirl of regimental India, and surrounded by fit and attractive young men, a romance leading to marriage would develop and the unfortunate early marriage could be quietly airbrushed away. Violet herself certainly believed that her aunt had been given instructions to get her suitably married off. She would be successful – but not in the way her mother had hoped.

3

'Kisses on the boat deck'

Love at Sea

'This evening Judy told me that the Comte de Madre had informed Lady Strefford that he had come simply and solely on this voyage for the purpose of finding an English wife!' wrote Lilah Wingfield, travelling to India on the P&O vessel *Maloja* for the Coronation Durbar of December 1911.

'She said that he was very anxious to marry and that he considered there were more opportunities on board ship for getting to know a girl well than in any other place, and he particularly wished for an English wife and did not want a very young girl – no Miss of eighteen – so he had set his selection on me! But I would ten times rather marry the black boy who prepares my bath!'

For Lilah and her friends, 'spooning' couples or those engaged in a purely shipboard romance were a common sight – and a bit of a joke. 'We all stalked around the deck to watch a ship flirtation which was going on at the far end of the bows, a very affectionate couple who held hands and gazed into each other's eyes, oblivious of all of us who walked by.' Sometimes their little group did more than stalk. 'We all nag Colonel Mitford over his infatuation for a pretty little Miss Gauntlett, it is a regular ship-flirtation. We composed a letter and had it given him by the deck steward, supposedly to be from "Mamma" Gauntlett, asking him his intentions! But he found out we had done it, so the joke fell flat.'

Lilah travelled out at a time when a strict and rather ridiculous apartheid existed between the P&O's officers and its passengers. 'There is a rather fascinating ship's doctor aboard but unluckily none of the ship's company is allowed to dance, which seems an absurd rule,' she wrote sadly. 'They looked longingly on at the rest of us.' As one Commodore of the line, Captain D.G.H.O. Baillie, recalled: 'We were never allowed to appear on passenger decks in the day time before half past four in the afternoon, and we had to be off them by half-past nine. Drinking with passengers, either in one of the public rooms or a cabin, was rigidly forbidden and officially we were not permitted to dance.'

The reason was that earlier the P&O ship *China* had run aground on the island of Socotra at the southern entrance of the Red Sea – no one was hurt but it was considered a disgrace to the line. When it was found that some of the officers had been dancing with passengers during a party on board, the Company concluded that this was a contributory cause of the error in navigation and decided to ban all officers from on-board gaieties.* This, said Commodore Baillie, fomented a real grievance, especially in the Australian mail ships, 'where rows of pretty and partnerless young girls would be sitting or standing round the edge of the dance space'.

Even more *verboten* was any hint of romance. But determination often found a way. As Captain Gordon Steele pointed out, although Company regulations forbade him from speaking to passengers, happily there was no rule against passengers addressing him – when, of course, politeness demanded an answer.

Apart from the attraction of a uniform, the officers of a liner in the P&O fleet had an aura of importance and dignity. When Steele – then younger and more junior – performed the simple operation of marking the ship's noon position on the track chart by means of a small circle, it was quite a ceremony. He had a quartermaster to assist him. 'He opened the frame and held the dividers for me, and walked discreetly behind me as we wended our way to the First and Second Saloons.'

One day, said Steele, he found a pretty woman waiting by the First Saloon track chart. The following day she was there again. The third day she murmured to herself, sufficiently loud for Steele

---

* This was so resented by the P&O officers as a body that in late 1913 they chose to hold up one ship, the *Arcadia*, for three days as a sign of their discontent. Very wisely, the Company withdrew their prohibition.

to hear: 'How beautifully he does it!' The embarrassed Steele not only dropped the dividers but also wrote down the latitude a whole degree out. The next day she asked if he would correct her wrist watch for longitude. He lingered so long over this operation that two elderly ladies thought they were holding hands, one whispering to the other, 'A boy and girl attachment – how sweet!' Every day Steele corrected the young woman's watch. By now he had altered the routine so that the quartermaster went straight to the Second Saloon while he, alone, attended to the First – and to Jean, as the girl was called.

But they could not hope to escape notice for ever and Steele, while longing to see more of Jean, could not afford to jeopardise his chances with a reprimand – or worse. He happened to be the officer supervising the lifeboats on the ship's port side, so had Jean transferred from the starboard lifeboat list to the number 2 port lifeboat, of which he was directly in charge – while leaving her mother on the starboard list. He then ordered extra lifeboat drill for his port passengers ... which meant helping Jean to put her life-belt on, tying it round her, and assisting her to climb into the boat. But he was too steeped in the Company's traditions to make any further move.

Finally came the moment when the passenger tender arrived alongside the ship in Bombay and the passengers prepared to disembark. The queue was filing past the hatch where Steele was making up accounts; Jean, noticing this, left her mother at the head of the queue and herself rejoined at the very end. With everyone else ahead of them, Steele managed to give Jean a long and tender farewell kiss – their first.

For the next week, he recalled, 'I was miserable.'

For others, these late-autumn sailings held a storehouse of possibilities.

As most men took their leave during the English summer, largely to avoid the heat of the plains and also often to take advantage of the London Season, ships going out in the autumn usually carried not only Fishing Fleet girls but also returning soldiers and administrators, most of whom would be single.

Some might have taken their furlough with the specific aim of finding a wife, but failed ('If she doesn't respond within a week, I move on,' said one ICS man) and were happy to meet a willing girl on the ship. Others made a mental note of a 'possible' girl, keeping her in mind for future encounters in India – or found that a meeting on board ship led to love in the future.

One of the latter was Jim Acheson, going out in 1913 to join the ICS. Curiously, it was also an ocean liner that nearly destroyed his chance of happiness – by sinking with his proposal of marriage on board. Jim was a young Ulsterman from County Armagh, who had done outstandingly well as both scholar and sportsman at Trinity College, Dublin, before passing into the ICS as a 'griffin' (as newly joined members of the Service were called).

In the tender taking passengers from the Tilbury quayside to their ship, the P&O *Arcadia*, Jim had noticed a Mrs Field, 'whom I mentally described as a typical memsahib,'* and her daughter Violet, then aged almost twenty, who at the time made little impression on him. He also saw a number of girls going out to join their parents in India – called, as he knew, the Fishing Fleet. 'It was perhaps ill-natured of the old hands in the services to refer to the P&O and other liners sailing east [in the late autumn] as the "Fishing Fleet". We had our full quota of these maidens on the *Arcadia*.' For them, as he also knew, he would be considered a desirable target. But at twenty-four and only at the start of his career Jim was well aware that any thoughts of marriage were out of the question.

By the end of the voyage Jim had had enough conversations with Mrs Field and Violet – 'whom I admired at a distance' – for Mrs Field to give him their Indian address and for him to promise to send them his when he knew where he would be posted. The Fields were bound for Meerut, a big cantonment in the United Provinces where Violet's father, Colonel Charles Field, was stationed as Cantonment Magistrate.

That first Christmas Jim exchanged Christmas cards with some of his shipboard friends, including Violet. The following summer, on 4 August 1914, war was declared between Great Britain and Germany. Jim, like most young men, wanted to fight for his country and applied for permission to join the Indian Army Reserve of

---

* 'Sahib' was a form of respectful address for a European man in India. With the addition of 'mem' – a corruption of 'ma'am' – it was applied to their wives.

Officers (IARO). He was flatly turned down by the Lieutenant-Governor of the United Provinces (to which he had been assigned) on the grounds that he could not be spared, although he did receive a promise that, should circumstances change, the position would be reconsidered.

The next time he sent a Christmas card to the Fields, Jim, now stationed at Lucknow, happened to mention he was recovering from a cold. He was immediately invited to stay with them for Christmas and recuperate (in Indian terms Lucknow, less than 300 miles away, was quite close to Meerut). Feeling very run down and delighted at the idea, he accepted gladly.

He was met at the station by Violet, a memory he always cherished. 'I was greeted by a pretty, strange young woman, with what I can only describe as a gallant bearing, neatly gloved and neatly shod and with the brightest eyes I had ever seen and one of the sweetest voices I have ever heard.' Later he noticed that she had thick, glossy hair, with a reddish-gold glint. 'I have a crow to pluck with you, Mr Acheson,' she began, going on to point out that he had got the day of his arrival wrong. She led him out of the station to a smart English trap, with her mare Bunty between the shafts (there were only one or two cars to be seen), handling the reins efficiently through the crowds outside the station and in the bazaar.

It was a happy week. Jim rode, played tennis at the famous Wheler Club, met an old friend from on board ship, took part in his first large-scale snipe shoot and attended a New Year's Eve ball. The time slipped past all too quickly in those crisp sunny days of perfect weather – but not too quickly for Jim to become increasingly close to Violet.

They remained in touch and, by the time Violet was sent home early in 1915, along with other wives and daughters of Army officers ordered to the UK or elsewhere on active service, they were exchanging weekly letters, albeit on a firmly comradely basis. Jim, however, who had now been promoted to the two important positions of City Magistrate of Agra and Superintendent of the two Agra prisons (Agra Central Prison and the District Jail), had already decided that he was going to ask Violet to marry him.

What caused him to hesitate about proposing to her was not only the fact that Violet was doing war work but – much more of

a consideration – ships were being sunk daily by German U-boats*
in the Mediterranean, which was inevitably traversed by any passenger to India. And if Violet agreed to marry him, she would in
all likelihood feel bound to come out to join him in India – with
the possibility of terrible danger en route, for which he would feel
himself responsible.

The impasse was resolved when Violet wrote to him to say that
she had decided to accept an invitation from a friend, the wife of a
Hussar officer stationed in Meerut, to come out and stay with her.
Jim resolved to act: if she was coming out anyway, why should she
not come out as his fiancée – that is, if she accepted his proposal …

He wrote a letter asking her to marry him and it was duly despatched. Showing the forethought and intelligence that would later
enable him to become one of the most distinguished members of
the ICS, he then set himself to discover on which P&O mail boat
the precious missive, so laboriously worked over, would travel. This
turned out to be the SS *Arabia,* a single-screw liner built in 1898.

The bad news he had been fearing came about. Three hundred
miles off the coast of Malta the *Arabia,* a passenger liner, was torpe-
doed without warning on 6 November 1916 by the German submarine UB-43. Jim read the news in the *Civil and Military Gazette,* the
Lahore newspaper that included the daily list of sinkings. Providen-
tially, few lives were lost but all the home-bound mail went down
including, of course, Jim's proposal of marriage.

Swift action was needed. Jim rushed to the Agra Central Telegraph
Office, where he composed a cablegram that was in effect a short-
ened version of his letter. He sent it off and waited anxiously for
Violet's answer, hardly able to concentrate on the cases appearing

---

* After the sinking on 7 May 1915 of the *Lusitania*, with its large complement of
(neutral) American passengers, there was such outrage that in June the Kaiser
forbade all attacks on large passenger liners; but on 19 August 1915 the White
Star's *Arabic* (with three Americans among the losses) was sunk off the coast of
Ireland by the German submarine U-24, without any form of warning whatsoever.
After this, the Kaiser decreed that crews and passengers of merchant ships should
be given the chance to abandon ship; but in the Mediterranean a sinking without
warning policy was adopted, since large merchant ships were attacked 'on suspicion
of being transports or auxiliary cruisers'. Finally, Germany declared unrestricted
submarine warfare on 1 February 1917; by 21 March seven American merchantmen
had been sunk. President Wilson summoned Congress and on 6 April 1917
America entered the war.

before him in the stuffy, crowded Lucknow court room.

When her cable came the answer was 'Yes' followed by a letter saying she would be sailing a fortnight later in P&O's *Khyber*. This time, his anxiety during the three or four days the *Khyber* was in the Mediterranean was of a different order of intensity – with consequent relief when Violet's ship reached the safety of Port Said.

Then, just before Violet was due to arrive in Bombay, Jim received a telegram from the Lieutenant-Governor's secretariat. 'Be prepared to leave at shortest notice for Mesopotamia, Persian Gulf or NWF [North West Frontier],' it read. The telegram was followed by a letter saying that although the Lieutenant-Governor still adamantly forbade Jim from joining the IARO – which meant, effectively, from any kind of the active service he had wanted – all Indian provinces had been asked to send in the names of those officers who could be spared on loan to fill a single temporary gap in the Foreign and Political Department cadre. Jim's was one of the names put forward. 'At least,' ended the letter drily, 'You will be closer to the firing line.'

With his bride-to-be nearer every minute, Jim was at a loss. The only thing to do was to appeal to a higher authority. He went to see the Viceroy's Private Secretary – the Viceroy was on tour at Agra at the time – laid his dilemma before him and was advised to put it to the Deputy Foreign Secretary in Simla. It was back to the Telegraph Office again, this time to send a cable including the words: 'Am just about to get married stop please allow decent interval and post to Quetta* stop Acheson.'

Jim's request was granted and he and Violet were married on 1 March 1917 at Meerut. Shortly afterwards, they were posted to Quetta.†

For those in love the sea in peacetime – when calm – was a perfect setting. 'There was the excitement of sleeping on deck which we did if the nights were excessively hot as the tiny cabins were like ovens after the day's heat,' wrote Violet Hanson in 1920. 'It was a lovely

---

* The reason for Quetta was that men stationed there were allowed to have wives.
† Jim was appointed early to the political department of the ICS. Most of his postings were in the sensitive tribal areas of the North-West Frontier and Baluchistan; as a brilliant linguist, he could negotiate well with the local population, who were often extraordinarily difficult. He was also Deputy to the Viceroy's Foreign Secretary. His final post was a Resident in Kashmir from 1943 to 1945. He was knighted in 1945.

experience to lie under those brilliant stars and watch the tall mast gently swaying against the marvellously clear dark sky. The pleasure of the little wafts of air after the heat was wonderful.'

Romances that had been tentative bloomed in the perfect temperature and tranquillity of the Indian Ocean. 'Here, the water looked like brilliant sapphire blue jelly,' wrote Violet, 'and the flying fish skimmed in flocks over the scarcely moving sea. At night phosphorescence glowed over the ocean, it was cool again and there was the excitement of nearing the end of the voyage. Shipboard romances were coming to an end with a great exchange of names and addresses and promises to meet.' These, she wrote with a touch of cynicism, were seldom to be fulfilled.

But for the sophisticated Edwina Ashley, one of the Fishing Fleet of late 1921, the dances and fancy dress balls were just so many humdrum episodes in a boring three weeks. In love with Lord Louis Mountbatten, who was accompanying his cousin David, the Prince of Wales, on a royal tour of India and Japan in 1921, she had decided to cut short their separation by securing an invitation to visit the Viceroy.

As a young unmarried girl, socially prominent, Edwina could not travel alone without giving rise to scandal: a chaperone was essential. She found one by the simple method of going to Thomas Cook's office and asking to look at the passenger list. The name she landed on was Olwen Carey Evans, Lloyd George's daughter, eight years older than Edwina and, as was essential, married. Edwina scarcely knew Olwen but Olwen's husband, Thomas Carey Evans, of the Indian Medical Service, was personal physician to the Viceroy, Lord Reading, with whom Edwina was going to stay.

Whatever her feelings, Mrs Carey Evans was not likely to refuse a girl who was going out to stay with the Viceroy during the visit of the Prince of Wales; in practice, she found Edwina difficult and self-willed, and was constantly worried that there would be some troubling episode on board the ship that would cause scandal. For most, though – in the words of Joan Henry, an eighteen-year-old Fishing Fleet girl returning to India after years of boarding school – 'kisses on the boat deck with the moon making a silver path over a smooth sea was as far as it went or was even expected [to go]'.

When Kathleen Wilkes travelled out in 1922 to take up a post as a governess, warm weather and romance arrived together. 'In a few days under a full moon on the Red Sea we became engaged, much to the delight and interest of many people on board ship.' Her fiancé was a returning ICS man; as the older, rather snobbish woman with whom Kathleen was sharing a cabin remarked: 'You've done well for yourself, haven't you? He's one of the heaven-born.'

One girl who found romance on the voyage not once but twice was Enid Shillingford, the daughter of a planter in Purnea (near Darjeeling). When she was seven her parents divorced and Enid returned with her mother to England, where she was educated, spending the years of the 1914–18 war at home. Her father came from an old family of indigo planters, but because of the decline in the indigo market when aniline dyes were invented in the early part of the twentieth century, he turned to tea planting, at which he became extremely successful.

Purnea was an area where there were a lot of Eurasian families, who tended to group together as – among the British in India at that time – those with Eurasian blood were stigmatised. Enid was a quarter Indian, very good-looking, pale-skinned with medium brown hair, a agile dancer and keen tennis player with a lithe, athletic figure. She had no idea that her heritage could ever cause her problems, especially as her cousins, with the same proportion of Indian blood, had been happily accepted into the Life Guards, where they were contentedly serving.

When the war, with its terrible slaughter, ended she was twenty-one. Her father, who shared the prevailing belief that a woman's life would be nothing if she did not marry, and knowing that many of the men she could have married had been killed, became increasingly worried as the years ticked by that his beautiful daughter would not find a husband in England. So in 1921, when Enid was twenty-four, he paid for her passage to come out to India and stay with him. 'She told me several times that that was the specific reason she was sent out,' said her son Charles Greig.

Enid found romance almost the moment she boarded the ship. She and an attractive young man fell in love with each other, he proposed, was accepted and they agreed to marry when the ship reached Colombo. Two days before the wedding she was informed – correctly – that he already had a wife, in Calcutta. Enid was devastated. She returned immediately to England, catching the next ship home from Colombo; she refused even to go on to Calcutta, where her father would have met her.

Five years later, in 1927, when Enid was twenty-nine, her father, still determined that she should find a husband, again paid for her passage out to India. Again she fell in love on the voyage – this time with a happy ending. Thomas Stock, born in 1891, was in the Forestry and Agriculture Department of the ICS. He had just been appointed to a post up-country in Mogok,* Burma, and was returning from leave in England. This time there was no impediment and they were married within three weeks of landing in Rangoon.

The 'shipboard effect' was well summed up by the youthful Cecile Stanley Clarke, travelling with her mother in 1928 to stay with her sister and brother-in-law Hubert Gough, tutor to the son of the Nizam of Hyderabad. 'One old man, who must have been quite forty, had kissed me on the boat deck, but I had dismissed this lightly, having been told that the boat deck and the phosphorus on the water had funny effects on the most sober of men, especially as the aforesaid man had gone to great lengths to tell me how much he loved his wife. This was my first insight into the curious make up of the masculine sex; they can love one Woman with their Whole heart and at the same time get quite a lot of enjoyment from kissing another, and it is no good getting on one's high horse about it, it is just something to do with masculine hormones.'

For Ruth Barton, writing in the spring of 1931, a voyage was a magic time. 'The Mediterranean was calm and balmy and from the Red Sea onwards the nights were very hot, the stars brilliant and there was a waxing moon. At night we danced on deck and then went down to the Promenade Deck – invariably deserted at that hour – and leant on the rails, looking over the stern of the ship. The ceaseless silken swish of the double wave below us, creaming away across the moonlit sea and leaving an endless green track in the wake of the speeding ship, soothed and fascinated us. It needed an effort to break away and go down to a scruffy cabin – no air conditioning then.'

So dazzling was the romantic potential of sea travel that it could spill over into ordinary life – in one case, it even acted as a subliminal advertising medium. In the 1939 film *Love Affair* – the story of

* Famous for its rubies.

two strangers who meet aboard an ocean liner and fall deeply in love despite the fact that they are engaged to marry other people – there is a scene where Charles Boyer and Irene Dunne gaze into each other's eyes while sipping pink champagne. Immediately, sales of the then little-known drink rocketed.

Unsurprisingly, many of the Fishing Fleet found husbands even before arriving at Bombay, Calcutta, Colombo or Rangoon. There was a pretty good chance on the ship itself, filled as it was with a number of bachelors, some of whom had tried unsuccessfully to find a bride during their months of leave and were delighted to be offered another chance. Thus many romances started on the voyage out, as warm starlit nights succeeded the fogs of a British November, waltzes from the ship's band echoing faintly in the air as the couple gazed dreamily at the glimmering phosphorescence in the ship's wake.

Sometimes the engagement lasted only a matter of days, with a wedding the moment they arrived. Bombay, Calcutta and Rangoon were full of churches to facilitate this: the authorities very much disliked the idea of unattached European women in India; they had to be there as someone's wife, mother, daughter, sister, aunt or niece and the man to whom they were related or who was their host was responsible for them (women teachers, governesses, missionaries or doctors were the responsibility of their employers). But for a member of the Fishing Fleet and the bachelor who had struck lucky on his return voyage this plethora of churches was often an answer to prayer – if only because both sides were anxious that the other should not change his or her mind.

4

'£300-a year man – dead or alive'

The Men They Met

In the days of the East India Company, a favourite after-dinner toast was a pun on the mournful phrase 'alas and alack-a-day'; aspiring Company men would drink to 'a lass and a lakh a day' – the acquisition of 100,000 rupees and an Indian mistress.

The ethos behind the Raj could not have been more different. The bribes that piled up East India Company fortunes were a thing of the past and miscegenation was discouraged. Give or take a few bad apples, the men who governed India throughout the latter half of the nineteenth century up to independence in 1947 came from another mould altogether. They were not motivated by pure self-interest, rather by a sense of mission. Trade, of course, was still a main concern but they believed equally that the world would be a better place if ruled by Britain – as much of it was. They also believed in their responsibilities to those they ruled.

It was a time when horizons seemed to be expanding in all directions. New inventions were proliferating, new peoples, in barely mapped parts of the globe, were being added to the Empire almost daily. For two and a half centuries India – so far away, so mythic in the tales, the exotic silks and spices brought back by travellers – had been a fabled land. With the Raj, the 1876 incorporation into the Empire and the greatly shortened journey time, the great subcontinent exercised a gravitational pull on the popular imagination. More than any other tribe, province or country, India embodied the idea of Empire. To rule it required almost a new breed of men: tough, hardy, able to withstand frequent loneliness, adaptable yet capable of maintaining standards, just, impartial and not afraid of responsibility.

Their nurseries were the public schools, with certain of these almost wholly dedicated to producing the desired result, a custom started by the East India Company with its East India College. With the disbandment of the Company in 1857 the College was closed down and in 1862 a new school, Haileybury, took over its former grounds and buildings – and its eastward-looking attitude, with the result that many of the old boys of the former College sent their own sons there. 'To the student at Haileybury the abiding subject of interest was the expansion and maintenance of British rule in India ... Many a Haileyburian had been dandled as a child in arms which had help to bind a province together or bring savage tribes into subjection.'*

India demanded so much of its servants that some families lived there for several generations, sending offspring home for the obligatory English education. Although over half of India's viceroys had been educated at Eton, not many of the families involved in the day-to-day running of the country earned enough to send their sons to the 'great' English public schools, so that several schools were founded to provide an education acceptable, in those class-conscious days, for the children of gentlefolk but at a lower fee. Thus the United Services College at Westward Ho! in Devon was founded in 1874; it, too, looked outward towards the Empire, indeed recruiting its first headmaster and initial group of pupils from Haileybury (with which it later amalgamated). Bedford School was another; endowed by the Harpur Trust, which kept fees low, so was the choice of many of the poorer Anglo-Indian families.

Cheltenham College, founded in 1841, also attracted the sons of Anglo-Indians – Cheltenham was a place to which many of them retired – gradually becoming one of the two leading schools for boys who wanted to join the Army (virtually all regiments served a tour of duty in India). The other was Wellington College, founded in 1859 to commemorate the great military Duke. It, too, kept its fees low: in 1912 it charged between £84 and £103 for boarders (Eton and Harrow charged £166 and £153 respectively).

All these schools based their curricula on the needs of a future

* Haileybury Archives 10/2 (1893) 357–832.

career in the Empire. For the future ICS man this meant the classical education necessary to achieve the essential good degree at university as well as equipping him for a society that became steadily more sophisticated and steeped in the nuances of protocol and etiquette as he climbed the ladder. On the 'Army' side, boys were tutored for the entrance examination to military academies.

Permeating everything these institutions taught was an ethos that came to be known as the public school spirit. As the influence of the great Dr Arnold (headmaster of Rugby 1828–41) trickled out through boys, masters and parents, so did his belief that the primary aim of education was not purely to instil learning but to form 'character' – the character of a Victorian gentleman. So from the schools that produced the soldiers and administrators who ran India emerged young men with a belief in team spirit, the prefectorial system, the importance of both moral responsibility and games (read 'sport' in later life), the health-giving virtue of cold baths and the need to maintain a stiff upper lip at all times. Today the latter is often mocked; then, it was essential – for a young man sent out at twenty-five to run a district the size of an English county any display of emotion would instantly weaken both his authority and his dignity in the eyes of those he was governing.

The Indian Civil Service – the 1,000-odd* Government officials, administrators, judges, collectors and commissioners who ran that vast country – were the cream of Oxbridge graduates. In an average year about 200 candidates competed for around forty places in the ICS; by 1900 the ratio was about four to one. They took the same entrance examination as that for the Home Civil Service; if they were successful they then had to spend a year on probation, during which they had to pass a riding test – much of their time as juniors would be spent on a horse – learn about Indian history and law, and receive a grounding in the language of the province to which they had been assigned. Much was expected of them and standards were high, hence their nickname 'the Incorruptibles'. As there was no home leave for eight years, young men often left in the knowledge that they would never see someone dear to them again.

---

* By 1922 the number had risen to 1,200; by the end of the Raj there were only 500 British ICS men.

There were three presidencies: Madras, Bengal and Bombay, and seven provinces;* and while governors of presidencies were sent out from England, the provinces were governed by senior members of the ICS. Many were classical scholars, the mark for decades of an educated man. Their knowledge of these ancient worlds often spilt into the routine work of their departments, from the days when Major-General Charles Napier despatched his one-word report 'Peccavi'† to denote his capture of the province of Sindh to junior ICS man Edward Wakefield's agricultural notes written in flowing Virgilian hexameters.

Wakefield, who had been sent on a three-week course of instruction at an agricultural college, found that the lectures on wheat cultivation reminded him of the advice given to farmers by Virgil and, feeling bored, decided he would write up his notes in the same way. His *jeu d'espirit* had a sequel: the instructor, sensing something was wrong, reported him to the Punjab Government. When sent for by the Chief Secretary he was told that his notes had been found unsatisfactory. He sat there apprehensively only to hear the Secretary remark: 'I am sorry to say that they contain at least one false quantity. Nevertheless, they are in other respects admirable.' They were placed on record in the archives.

ICS members served in three main departments: judicial, executive or political. The political service was an elite corps, drawn from both the Army and the ICS, which represented the British Raj in the more important native states such as Kashmir. Members of the judicial department served as judges in the districts with some in the High Courts, while most Executive officers remained in the districts.

The key man in all this was the District Officer whose job, described by one of them, L.S.S. O'Malley, was all-embracing in his district, where he was responsible for the maintenance of law and order, for the prevention of disorder as well as its suppression and, for the collection of taxes over hundreds of square miles. He also, as O'Malley put it: 'has to be able to deal with anything from

---

* Punjab, United Provinces of Agra and Oudh (now Uttar Pradesh), the North-West Frontier Province, the Central Provinces (now Madhya Bharat and Maharashtra), Bihar and Orissa, Assam and Burma.

† Latin for 'I have sinned'. A possibly legendary story, but one which certainly appeared as a cartoon in *Punch* in 1844.

riots to flood, famine and cyclones.' Of Rupert Barkeley-Smith his Fishing Fleet bride, Honor Penrose, wrote: 'Most of my husband's days were spent keeping a balance between the Hindus and the Mahommedans and preventing them from scratching each other's eyes out.'

Edward Wakefield spent much of 1931 trying to eradicate locusts from Ajmer, in the heart of Rajputana. His success illustrates the kind of lateral thinking expected of these men. Against what might be thought heavy odds he succeeded through an ingenious campaign based on knowledge of locust habits. When the insects settle to lay their eggs the females deposit 300–400 eggs each a few inches below the surface of the ground and die within a week of doing so. A fortnight later the eggs hatch out into tiny ant-like hoppers. These hoppers move slowly across the countryside, devouring wholesale everything in their path. After a month they are as large and active as grasshoppers; six or seven weeks from the date of hatching they fly in a cloud, bringing ruin to every farmer on whose crops they may choose to settle.

Edward Wakefield began by flooding the fields where eggs were known to have been laid. When the hoppers emerged, he organised the digging of deep trenches in front of the direction in which they were moving while setting up canvas screens alongside the hurrying army to funnel them towards these trenches. Then, when each trench was full of hoppers, his men instantly buried them under mounds of earth, stamping it down hard. It was work that went on for several weeks but in the end all were destroyed.

At the top of the ICS were nine posts of Resident, First Class, all of whom had started in the lowest rank, that of Assistant Magistrate, during which they learned their trade from a senior or seniors. The experience of William Saumarez Smith is typical. After successfully passing both the entrance exam and that at the end of a year's probation, on riding, Indian law and the history and language of the province to which he had been assigned, he was sent out to his first job.

This was as Subdivisional Officer, or Assistant Magistrate, of Madaripur, a district roughly the size of Herefordshire in the Ganges delta, East Bengal. The population of the subdivision was more than a million – he was under twenty-five. The annual rainfall was seventy-three inches and the rivers changed course constantly, flooding some fields and leaving other riverbeds suddenly dry, so that many disputes were about who had the right to harvest the crops of rice and jute. There were no real roads, a horse was no use, the nearest railway station was over fifty miles away and all communication was by water. Several ICS men had been murdered during the terrorist campaign that raged in Bengal during the 1930s.

The young Subdivisional Officer's work varied from a report on an unsatisfactory headmaster, making a speech in Bengali or cross-examining witnesses in an abduction case to inquiring into a petition by villagers who claimed their land had been washed away by floods but that they were still being forced to pay rent on it. There were no real office hours, months were spent under canvas and the only leave was local.

Marriage was not on the cards. It was an iron rule of the Service that no one married before the age of thirty: the young ICS man had to be mobile and undergo any necessary hardship. In 1859 one of them, John Beames, described the ideal of a District Officer as laid down by John Lawrence, the man who subdued and reformed the Punjab,* as 'a hard, active man in boots and breeches, who almost lived in the saddle, worked all day and nearly all night, ate and drank when and where he could, had no family ties, no wife or children to hamper him and whose whole establishment consisted of a camp bed, an odd table and chair or so; and a small box of clothes such as could be slung on a camel.'

The cross most of them had to bear was extreme loneliness coupled with sexual deprivation, as evinced in the case of Charles Maurice Ormerod, born in 1904 in Brighouse, Yorkshire. Charles Ormerod, born to a wealthy father who owned silk mills and retired to a large place in Westmorland, was one of four clever children – his eldest sister became a doctor (then extremely unusual for a woman), his brother a barrister. Charles, the brightest of the lot, got a Double First at King's College, Cambridge, after which he was attracted by the idea of the ICS. With his classical education and excellent degree, he was just the type they wanted and when he passed their exam was appointed

---

* John Lawrence later became Viceroy of India 1864–9 and was created 1st Baron Lawrence.

to the Punjab (where he eventually spent twenty years).

During his first ten years he was on his own, moving from village to village, occasionally returning to the office of his immediate superior. Eventually the isolation and lack of congenial company became an overwhelming burden. One day, as he later told his daughter, he was sitting in an up-country village not too far from a railroad, when he said to himself: 'I could get on that train – that's all it would take and I could go back home. What is it that keeps me here in India? I don't know. I'm here with just this one man and we're on our own and I'm spending all this time in the real wilderness in India, and I'm getting older. The people here who have a better life are the ones who are married. So when my next leave comes up I'm going to go back to England with the idea of getting a wife.' As we will see later, this is exactly what he did.

Another who wrote home unhappily about this emotional and sexual black hole was William Saumarez Smith. 'As long as I am in the junior ranks of the ICS I shall not marry. It is absolutely unfair to ask any Englishwoman to live in a station in Bengal. The alternative is celibacy, in the monastic sense of never seeing a female face from week's end to week's end. A bachelor in England will at least have female relatives and friends, but my work is exclusively with men, so that practically speaking I live in a world populated by one sex. This is unnatural and abnormal.'

What effect did it have? 'My life was as sexless as any monk's at this time; and in a sense I was only half alive, lacking the companionship of women. But what is good for the Roman priest is good (I suppose) for the Indian Cavalry subaltern, who has work to do (like the priest) which he could scarcely perform if hampered by family ties,' wrote Francis Yeats-Brown, a subaltern in the Bengal Lancers, in 1905. 'I do not know how far discipline of the sex life is a good thing. But I know that a normal sex life is more necessary in a hot than a cold country. The hysteria which seems to hang in the air of India is aggravated by severe continence of any kind …'.

Pay and conditions, however, were good. All ICS men had to contribute to a fund that, after a certain number of years, paid the widow of an ICS man who died on duty £300 a year – roughly the same salary as a junior received – hence the phrase 'a £300-a-year man, dead or alive'. ICS men also stood at the top of the social tree together with Army officers, in the Raj their only social equals.

For the Fishing Fleet, an ICS man was considered the crème de la crème – once he was eligible. 'Mamas angled for us for their daughters,' wrote John Beames. 'The Civil Service was in those days [1858] an aristocracy in India, and we were the *jeunesse dorée* thereof.' Or, as Jim Acheson put it in 1913, 'The young ICS men were generally supposed to be the chief quarry – the turbot and halibut of the matrimonial nets.'

Army officers were also a catch; again, the under-thirty rule applied. This meant that most had to be captains before they could start looking for a wife, though some managed it a year or two earlier. On 17 February 1896 twenty-seven-year-old Lieutenant Leslie John Germain Lavie, newly engaged to Miss Florence Ross, told her in his daily letter: 'I wrote to Major Wood yesterday and he wrote back ... he said the reason he had not congratulated me was because he thought I was too young to marry and so this would not have been sincere. But he wished us the best of luck and said he hoped I would not leave the Regiment [Lavie was in the 20th Regiment Madras Native Infantry].'

The highest social strata of the Army were the 'good' regiments, in particular the (British) cavalry who were, on the whole, richer than most of their contemporaries – often young men from wealthy families who had joined because they were attracted by the hunting and polo that were then considered a part of cavalry life.

It was the same in the Indian Army; there, the cavalry, too, considered themselves the cream. To a young and impressionable girl, their colourful, romantic uniforms of long jackets, cummerbunds, turbans and breeches with English boots had an irresistible dash and glamour, from the yellow coats of Skinner's Horse to the dark blue jacket, scarlet and gold cummerbund and striped gold and turquoise turban of Probyn's Horse.

Possibly the most desirable *partis* in India were the ADCs and Private Secretaries to the Viceroy (and, in descending order, to governors and generals). Most were from backgrounds that were impeccable financially and socially (many were or would be peers), wore clothes well, knew how to put people at their ease and were entertaining enough for the Viceroy and his family to enjoy having them as part of their household. If soldiers, they usually came from a 'good' regiment; if from the ICS they were likely to be future stars – just the sort of man, in fact, that a Viceroy might hand-pick as a son-in- law. Owing to constant, daily proximity, marriages between viceregal daughters and their fathers' ADCs were common; and to the outside world these gilded young men were regarded, in some subliminal sense, as viceregal property. So if one of them looked elsewhere it caused a mild frisson – as when Mary Tribe, the daughter of a clergyman (then, as now, paid little) secured as a husband a young man destined to become one of the richest dukes in England.

Mary du Caurroy Tribe, born in 1865, was the younger daughter of the Reverend Walter Tribe, a parson who had come out to India with his wife Sophie in 1867, largely for financial reasons – he felt that in India he could earn more, live at a higher standard and also save. Their two daughters, Mary aged two and her older sister Zoe, four, were left behind with a beloved aunt. They were educated at Cheltenham Ladies' College (then becoming so famous for its emphasis on proper education that it elicited complaints from many parents who believed that too much education in a girl was a serious handicap to her matrimonial chances). Mary loved school but was longing to leave and go to India, not so much to see her parents – whom she hardly knew – but for the thrill and excitement of what awaited her there. She loved an outdoor life: there would be tennis, riding, parties, friends of her own age and, for the first time, of the opposite sex.

She was sixteen when she arrived in India. She was not yet 'out', she did not know how to dance or make small talk but she was beautiful, bright and had, as her sister Zoe commented, 'such a lovely *figure*!' By nineteen she was a magnet to young men. She became engaged to one faithful swain but then broke it off ('I have nothing left in life now to hope for, nothing to work for,' he wrote to her mother in an attempt to make Mary change her mind).

Early in 1886 her father was appointed Archdeacon of Lahore. From then on there were summers at Simla with regular invitations to dance at Viceregal Lodge. On 15 September that year she was recording in her diary of one of these: 'Very jolly dance. Danced 4 with Lord H.' Soon Mary's dance cards were filled with 'Lord H', her diary with appointments to ride with him; and he was deeply in love with her.

Lord Herbrand Russell, a Grenadier Guards officer, was then

twenty-seven to Mary's twenty-one, and the second son of the 9th Duke of Bedford; he had been personally selected as one of his ADCs by the Viceroy, Lord Dufferin – who had two unmarried daughters, aged twenty-two and eighteen.

Herbrand was under no illusions as to why the Viceroy had chosen him as an ADC. After he and Mary were engaged, he wrote to her to explain the need for dealing delicately and tactfully with the Dufferins. 'Because … Lord and Lady Dufferin always meant me to marry someone else and not your own dear little self at all. This parental plan you have entirely upset. It was this idea that kept me on the staff, otherwise, being the worst of ADCs, I should have been sent away with several fleas in my ear long ago.' As it was, the Duke's permission was eventually extracted, Mary and her Herbrand were married on 30 January 1888 and – on the death of Herbrand's elder brother George in 1893 – she found herself a duchess.*

In the 1930s, the army officer in India was allowed two months' privileged leave, to give him a break from working in the hot weather, when the plains were an inferno until the monsoon broke. The heat took a toll on almost everyone. 'I'm in an awfully bad temper and feel very liverish. Everything has been going wrong this morning,' wrote Lieutenant Lavie to his fiancée Florence (always known as Flossie), on 18 February 1896. 'I'll tell you what I do every day … so you may give me the benefit if I don't write so fully. Getting up at 5.30 a.m. it's parade we go to at 6.30 a.m. get off at 8.00 a.m. Sometimes orderly room and always duty till 9.00 a.m. when breakfast, 10–12 office, 12–1 or 1.30 my letter to you. 1.30–2.30 office, 2.30 tiffin, 3–3.30 learning new Sword Exercise, parade 4.00. Racquets or something 5.15. Mess for Billiards or Whist 6.15–7.30. Dinner 8.00, bed 10.30.' There were few diversions. A month later Lavie was writing to Flossie: 'Last night we had quite a gathering at the "At Home" – you must not get bored at my perpetually talking about this weekly excitement – as we mustered four ladies!'

All this was in the sweltering, draining heat. Partly to offset it, there were also three 'casual' leaves a year of up to ten days, spent

---

* Later she became known as the Flying Duchess when she took up flying in her early sixties. She disappeared on her last flight, aged seventy-one, and no trace of her has ever been found.

by many on shooting or fishing expeditions. Once every three years there was home leave for eight months, to include the journey (flying, which began just before the war, took three days). 'Not always enough time,' remarked one, 'to find a wife.' Many of them married Fishing Fleet girls who had come out to stay with sisters or aunts married to brother officers, but for most, especially those serving where action was to be found, the lack of female company, and sex, could be torture.

'It is useless to pretend that our life was a normal one,' wrote John Masters of his life as a subaltern in the 4th Gurkhas in the mid-1930s. 'Ours was a one-sexed society, with women hanging on to the edges. Married or unmarried, their status was really that of camp followers. But it is normal for men to live in the company of women, for if they do they do not become rough or boorish and the sex instinct does not torment them. In India there was always an unnatural tension and every man who pursued the physical aim of sexual relief was in danger of developing a cynical hardness and a lack of sympathy which he had no business to learn until many more years had maltreated him. Of those who tried sublimation, some chased polo balls, and some chased partridge, some buried themselves in their work and all became unmitigated nuisances through the narrowness of their conversation.'

After soldiers in the social pecking order came railway engineers, businessmen, other civil servants, missionaries, police superintendents and tea, jute or indigo planters. Tea planters, too, were usually single throughout their twenties. 'Before The Second World War, a tea plantation manager would probably have to do ten years without leave, except for local leave,' said former planter Mike Waring. 'Before you owned your own estate you couldn't go away. Most of the tea planters who married would be thirty or over. They often met someone on the ship.'

It was the same for indigo planters. In Bihar in the north-east, on the borders of Nepal, a centre for the industry, at its height in the late 1890s, the highlight of the year was the Meet – a week given over to enjoyment with others of one's kind. Every District had its Meet, to which planters, their assistants, ICS men, police officers and businessmen and their wives flocked by train, horse, pony and trap, with their luggage arriving by bullock cart. The most popular were the couples who could produce a Fishing Fleet girl –

single women were notoriously scarce while lonely bachelors were plentiful.

Some found it hard to wait until custom and their financial state allowed marriage and set up irregular ménages with local women, known as 'polls'. Said Waring: 'It wasn't exactly done but it was accepted – as long as you didn't produce children. You didn't mess around with your own staff or labour force – you got your poll from somewhere completely different. The girls knew the men wouldn't marry them but they also knew they would be looked after. The man would give the girl or her family a nice little house somewhere – and if she did produce a child that would be looked after too. A lot of the cleverer half-castes, who became lawyers, doctors and teachers, went to Australia, because they could produce proof of white ancestry.'

For most of the young Raj bachelors, sport had to take the place of sex. Brought up in the athletic games-playing tradition of the public schools, they flung themselves into everything India had to offer – and this varied from adaptations of what they knew from home to the exotic. Key to most of it was the horse – from pig-sticking, polo, gymkhanas and horse shows to jackal hunting with packs of foxhounds brought out from England and masters and hunt servants in pink coats. All could be risky but, as Desirée Hart (who arrived in 1939 to take up a post as social secretary to the Resident of Kashmir) in Sialkot noted, 'the hardest and most dangerous time was playing polo on the dry hard ground where bones got broken, heads bashed, limbs bruised and that winter "one death"; all bumps and accidents, even fatalities, accepted as part of the game ... Play starts off with a spurt of dust and rattle of hoofs on the iron ground, and in no time at all all that could be seen was the arc of a swinging stick through billows of white dust. As the tournament progressed the games got tougher, the finals becoming a deadly battle.'

There was also fishing and shooting, from duck flighting to – if you were lucky – a tiger shoot on elephants with a maharaja. Indeed, sport, including games like tennis and cricket and early morning rides when the air was fresh and cool, played a large part in the lives of all the British in India, where most people were young or youngish: it was both exercise, fun and the sublimation of one of humankind's most pressing instincts – an instinct to be heavily discouraged until the servants of the Raj could fall thankfully into the arms of suitable brides.

In part this reasoning was to maintain the social distance between the rulers and the ruled; in part because if a man had an Indian mistress he would not be perceived as impartial – Indians, whose loyalty was to caste or clan, would believe that such a man would always favour the family of his wife or mistress in any dispute. There was also the question of prestige: if a man was seen to frequent the same courtesans or prostitutes as, say, his Indian colleagues, the respect owed to the Raj would be subtly diminished. Nor could such behaviour be kept secret; India was a land where privacy was impossible ('everything in a man's private life is public property in India,' said Kipling), and gossip of this type would spread like wildfire round bazaar, cantonment or village. As one ICS man remarked, the District Officer, 'living as he did, under constant public inspection, particularly when he was in tour or on camp, had of necessity to be something of an anchorite, or possibly even a stylite.' Said another: 'This was one of the sacrifices I thought I was making for the Raj.'

At the same time, it was realised that such considerations would weigh not a jot with the average private soldier – young, healthy and deprived of female companionship – a fact recognised by his commanding officers. Almost from the start, the solution had been licensed brothels, with Indian girls under the jurisdiction of a madam who were regularly examined by the regimental doctor. The rigour of this system owed much to the Contagious Diseases Act of 1864 which allowed police to arrest known or suspected prostitutes, who were then medically examined; if found to be suffering from venereal disease they were forcibly incarcerated in locked hospitals ('Lock Hospitals') until cured.

The repeal of the Act in 1886 (in India this occurred in 1888) coincided with the growing power of the social purity movement which sought, among other aims, to abolish prostitution. The expected (by senior Army officers) happened: with the repeal of the Act and the consequent discontinuation of compulsory medical examinations, the incidence of venereal disease shot up among the troops: between 1889 and 1892 roughly half the British soldiers in Bengal were treated for venereal disease. The Army response was pragmatic: Lock Hospitals now became 'voluntary' and a blind eye was turned to the discreet return of brothels for the troops. But there were no such facilities for their officers.

Both campaigners and the Government were fiercely against the idea of European prostitutes – the campaigners from a moral point of view, the Government because if Indians could use them, they might stop viewing the British as the ruling elite. It was, therefore, easier for purity campaigners to try and tackle 'vice' in large towns where, if European girls were found – there were several hundred in the largest ports – they would hope for Government backing. In Calcutta and Bombay these girls worked in the well-established red light districts – respectively in Free School Street and Cursetji Sukhlaji Street (described by one missionary as 'the seething hell of European vice') – so that the target area was easy to find. This led to what were called the Bombay Midnight Missions, when these streets were patrolled at night by missionaries and purity campaigners trying to dissuade potential customers from the wares on offer, making the prostitutes so furious at their loss of custom that they would pour water and 'other fluids' out of upstairs windows onto the heads of passing missionaries. For the police, this meant endless trouble: the missionaries complained and so, too, did the respectable women whom the missionaries mistook for ladies of easy virtue. Finally, after the women had been told that the courts of justice were open to them as to everyone else for redress and the missionaries had been reproved for interfering with the liberty of citizens to enjoy themselves, things settled down again.

Businessmen, often known as boxwallahs, usually lived in or around the larger cities. European trading firms were doing well; nor had Indian mills become serious competitors in the making of cotton cloth. Particularly popular were the strong grey, unbleached shirtings beloved by the Pathans, and muslins, known as 'mulls'. For most young businessmen, too, marriage was not on the cards if only because they did not earn enough. Thus young men usually lived in 'chummeries'; with several bachelors together sharing the expenses of a household, all of them could manage a fairly pleasant life. Only when they reached managerial status could they afford a bungalow to themselves – essential if they wished to marry. Meanwhile, even if they could not afford a horse of their own, plenty of people had a full stable, and were keen to get their horses exercised.

One of these young businessmen was Sam Raschen, who went to India in January 1913, to a chummery in Karachi. 'When I arrived there were fewer than a dozen cars in Sind. There was no tarmac on the roads and the dust was all-pervasive and often almost blinding.' But money went a long way. As an impecunious bachelor Sam managed to belong to three clubs (Sind, Gymkhana and Boat). Every bungalow had a fair-sized compound and large servants' quarters and, while there was no electric light or electric fans, there were paraffin lamps and punkah coolies pulled a rug or blanket suspended overhead in a steady rhythm.

Standards were high. 'In India, even as the newest joined "chota sahib" one automatically assumed the responsibilities of a man ten years one's senior,' found Sam. Export was the backbone of the business then, with wheat in particular; this came down in train after train from the Punjab, to be unloaded, sampled and generally passed through the cleaning machine to remove dust, barley and other seeds, then rebagged ready for shipment.

Two years later, Sam Raschen left to fight in the 1914–18 war. He was badly wounded, and returned home to convalesce. Then, in January 1918, he met Maj, a girl he had encountered some time earlier; two months later they were married and, in December 1918, the young couple sailed to India, where Sam returned to his old job. With the birth of their daughter Adelaide in October 1920 their happiness seemed complete – especially when Sam, a keen rowing man, won the Sculls, spending the prize money on a christening mug for their daughter.

A week later, Maj contracted puerperal fever and ten days later she was dead. To Sam, it seemed 'as if the world had stopped and I had been flung off into space with nothing to which to cling'. He packed up their personal treasures, sold their furniture, left his job and sailed home on the *City of Baroda* for England. It was the roughest trip he had ever made and he had to look after a two-week-old baby – the kind woman who had offered to help him was incapacitated by seasickness.

He took the baby to his parents in Maidstone, Kent and, believing that he would easily find one, began to look for a job. With the press of those seeking work after the war, none seemed available so when after a few months his former firm, Ellerman, City and Hall, offered him his old position back, he took it, although it meant leaving behind his child, the living memento of his wife. But his story had a doubly happy ending.

Katherine (known as Kitty) Irwin, born in November 1888, was the seventh of eight children, and the fourth daughter. Her family, well known in Cumberland, lived in a large house, Justicetown, six miles from Carlisle. Although the family had fourteen indoor servants and a coachman in the gate lodge, and her father was a former High Sheriff of Cumberland, Kitty led a restricted life. Her eldest sister married young and the next two were sent to London to 'do the Season' but Kitty – with no independent means to support herself otherwise – perforce had to follow the Victorian custom whereby the youngest daughter was expected to stay at home and keep her mother company, helping her where necessary.

When her mother died and her eldest brother and his wife inherited the house, she had to leave. She had come into a little money and bought herself a flat in London's Stanhope Gardens. She spent the war years in London, doing voluntary work making minor munitions such as gas masks. As a pretty woman, with lovely blue-green eyes, she had several boyfriends, but all were killed (two of her elder sisters were also widowed).

So she was delighted when she received an invitation from a married friend, Zinnia Patterson, to come and stay with her in Karachi. Kitty was such a bad sailor she chose to go overland to Venice, then on 4 November 1920 she sailed on the SS *Innsbruck* to Karachi, arriving in India on her thirty-second birthday. She spent six enjoyable months there with the Pattersons, then went to Kashmir on a round of visits, returning to Karachi on 6 November 1921.

Next day, at a dinner party, she met a young widower recently returned from England. It was, of course, Sam Raschen; and her impact on him was immediate. Later he wrote: 'We had been at the same dinner party and were at the dance afterwards but were never formally introduced.* Her dance card was fully booked up but somehow I managed to arrange a dance with her. She told me she was returning home after spending some months in India and I discovered that she intended to call at our office to arrange her passage home.

---

* Such was protocol that this was often an insuperable barrier.

'In the office I gave strict instructions that Miss Irwin was to be brought in to me when she arrived at our Passenger Department.'

Kitty duly arrived. And in Sam's words: 'Then, instead of choosing her a cabin, I managed to persuade her to marry me.'*

---

* Their wedding took place in Karachi on 22 February 1922.

5

'Welcome to India'

Arrivals

For the Fishing Fleet, arriving in Bombay was extraordinarily exciting. There before them lay the vast landlocked harbour, the towers and flat roofs of the city, the tugs ready to tow, push and nudge their liner into her berth. Beyond was the country that to some of them was home – a home they had missed almost more than they had realised, its sights, sounds, and above all smells, bringing back the India they knew and loved. Where a girl arrived depended on where her family or friends lived or were stationed – Bombay for Rajputana and much of Central India, Calcutta for Bengal and the United Provinces, Madras for much of southern India.

'Arriving in India then, and always, was dazzling and familiar,' wrote Iris James (later Macfarlane), who had travelled out with her mother. 'The smell of burnt gram and open drains, of sweat and spices, was carried in a warm breeze. The noise was deafening, the crowds jostled and shrieked but in the days of Empire we white women had paths cleared for us and my mother's Dalmations.'

To newcomers it was a land so strange that the only way forward was acceptance. On the quay, towards which passengers looked anxiously for those who had come to meet them, humanity swirled, shouted, begged, pushed and swore in different incomprehensible languages and dialects. The brilliant colours of saris in shrill pinks, emerald green, orange or red gleamed against dark skins, men in white uniforms mingled with sellers of fruit, curry, sweetmeats and rolled-up leaves with red betel nuts inside – when the juice was spat out it looked like blood.

The first glimpse of the other great seaport, Calcutta, where Minnie Wood arrived in 1857, was very different. Her little sailing ship passed through the mangrove swamps of the Ganges delta, with jungle running down to the edge of the various tributaries; next came the large, well-kept riverside villas of rich European merchants and officials; then, round the final bend, Calcutta itself, with its packed, busy harbour, scarlet-coated soldiers on the ramparts and, amid the crowd of coolies, bullock carts, camels and traders, crinolined Englishwomen and men in top hats awaiting the arrival of friends.

The colour, the light, the heat and above all the teeming mass of people could be almost too much to bear. 'I honestly confess that the overwhelming crowds of people frightened me,' wrote Anne Wilson in 1895 of her arrival in India. 'What were we in the land, I thought, but a handful of Europeans at the best, and what was there to prevent those myriads from falling upon and obliterating us, as if we had never existed?' As there were never more than 300,000 Britons in India, amid an indigenous population of 250 million, her apprehension was understandable.

Sometimes those whose destination was Calcutta, by the time of the Raj the capital of India and its main port, travelled overland from Bombay; sometimes they approached through the Hooghly River and green jungle. Wherever they arrived, Fishing Fleet girls were met, by parents, friends or, for some, the bearer (personal servant) of their hosts. For Desirée Hart this was the servant of the Resident of Kashmir's wife. 'At last I was cleared by the doctors and immigration officials and descended the gangway clutching my small luggage to find myself surrounded by hordes of beggars showing stumps where hands and feet should have been,' she wrote. 'Many were children with fly-encrusted eyes, others were so lacking in limbs that they propelled their truncated bodies on roughly made trollies ... I began to despair of ever getting to the station until my salvation appeared.

'"Shut up, be off with you," I heard an authoritative voice declaim and saw the crowd part by the exit to allow through a tall fierce-looking Indian. How he picked me out from the crowd I never knew.

'"Miss-Sahib?" he enquired haughtily.

'I nodded suspiciously and he handed me a large buff envelope embossed with a gold coat-of-arms, then raised his right hand, palm inwards towards his pugri, bowing his head at the same time in one graceful movement.

'"Welcome to India," I read in the letter from Lady Fraser. "My personal bearer, Dost Mahommed, will escort you on the journey. He speaks adequate English and you can trust him with your life." … in no time my status was transformed from buffeted nonentity to veritable princess.'

After the port of entry – Bombay, Karachi, Calcutta, Madras, Rangoon – came the rail journey, often of several days, to station or cantonment. So long were these train journeys that when Lord Ripon travelled from Bombay to Simla to be installed as Viceroy in the summer of 1880 his chaplain was depressed to learn that there were coffins in readiness at every station along the line in case a passenger succumbed to one of India's fatal illnesses *en route*.

The first sight of the station could be unnerving, with its jostling, thronging crowds and loud cries. Sweetmeat sellers, their sticky sweets swarming with flies, thrust their wares at you, fruit sellers offered plates of 'jolly decent fruit!'; there were sellers of flower garlands, curries, water from sheepskin bags. Long lines of sleeping men, shrouded in white, waited for their train, their wives squatting patiently beside them. And when the train came, few Europeans could have survived the general scramble to climb aboard, friends pushing each other through windows, families colonising every spare inch, with makeshift bedding and cooking arrangements in corridors.

For those who had been born in India, even if they had left it as a small child, residual memory held back the shock of the new. 'The Gateway of India was as familiar as the bustling crowds, the poverty and wealth, the squalor and the splendour of Bombay, even the smells,' wrote Richard Slater, who had left India as a baby, to return to it to take up his first posting in the ICS. 'The green upholstered compartment of the Frontier Mail in which I headed for the Punjab, so unlike anything in the experience of the traveller back home, was not unexpected, any more than the white incandescence of midday over the endless plain as we rattled north, the wallowing buffaloes, the toy villages barely distinguishable from the mud from which they were made, the Persian wheels, the temples and the mosques …'.

Like so much in India, train travel for the servants of the Raj managed to combine luxury with hardship. Trains were extremely comfortable owing to the broad gauge of the rolling stock (most were around 5 feet 6 inches), and the absence of corridors meant first-class carriages (routine for Europeans) were more like sitting rooms, with fans, leather sofas and private bathrooms attached. The attention of your personal servant (who travelled in the scrum of an adjacent third-class carriage), who brought you tea, soda water or hot water for washing, meant that you did not have to deal with luggage, food or any other arrangements.

Everyone travelled with a bedding roll, with which your servant made up your bunk at night. Another piece of travel equipment was a leather-covered enamel basin that doubled as a sponge bag. The cupboard-like bathroom at the side of the carriage had room for a thunderbox and an overhead pipe from which dripped a thin flow of water, a form of primitive shower.

'We took a train up India for two days and nights,' wrote Iris James. 'Of course, we had a carriage to ourselves, and in the evenings unrolled our "bisters" – canvas sausages that held our bedding, with pockets at each end for towels and a chamber pot. The dust rolled in clouds through the open windows and the studded leather seats grew slimy under our sweating thighs. At stations men handed in trays with teapots, and plates of bread covered with rancid butter, and little green bananas.' Their destination was Naini Tal, a hill station 6,560 feet above sea level in the Kumaon Hills.

There were no restaurant cars but stops of about an hour were made at suitable times at wayside stations. Here British travellers would proceed to the station restaurant, where a meal was provided. Usually this consisted of stringy curried chicken and a caramel custard as dessert. If it were evening, when you returned to your carriage you would find your bedding laid out and everything ready for the night.

Fishing Fleet girl Bethea Field crossed India from west to east when she journeyed the 1,500 miles from Quetta to Calcutta to meet her fiancé, leaving Quetta one late afternoon in December 1919.

'Sleep was often disturbed from a stop at some big station. The clamour was unbelievable and nobody could have slept through it or the garish lights. The Indian would-be passengers ran in all directions and shouted to each other as they ran. The sweet sellers, the water sellers, the tea sellers, all announcing their wares at the tops of their voices. Here and there a khaki-clad policeman with his lathi* prepared to restore order should the crowd become too turbulent. The guard would walk up and down the platform near the train, shouting out the name of the stations. Indians have the most powerful larynxes and no amount of shouting seems to exhaust them.'

Apart from the stations, Bethea would also often wake up when the train was about to cross one of the many long bridges, as its rhythm would change from the steady double jolt of the train going over the sleepers laid on ballast to a hollow, booming sound. The pace slowed and she felt a frisson of tension. 'The bridges were magnificently built but there was always the chance that some pier had been undermined. In December, the dry season, the great rivers were trickles between sand banks but I remember once crossing the Jumna in the rains when the brown floodwaters, crested with creamy waves, almost reached the sleepers of the bridge.

'In the dawn one saw small boys with little sticks driving the cattle, who had been herded during the night in the small village enclosures surrounded by thorn barricades, out into the fields to graze the day away. They shouted and whacked as the still-sleepy cattle and goats stumbled along. Dim figures emerged from the thatched huts. Women drew water from the village well and took it to the men who gargled and spat and rinsed their faces before girding themselves in their loin clothes and tying their big turbans in preparation for the day's toil in the fields. The dogs came out and barked at the crows – the innumerable carrion crows of India.

'Through the United Provinces it was all fertile, the fields green with the young crops, mango plantations in between and on the hillocks the animals grazed. Villages were frequent, the huts hung with pumpkin vines growing over the thatch. Sometimes, more distant, there was a small town with whitewashed houses and a Hindu temple or a mosque with minaret. The grand trunk road mostly ran alongside the railway, carrying its traffic of horse-drawn vehicles and the occasional motorcar or lorry. We arrived at Howrah station, Calcutta at 6.30 in the morning.'

---

* The equivalent of a bludgeon or truncheon: a stick, often made from the male bamboo and bound at intervals with iron rings.

Some carried travel comforts to extremes. Sixty servants were thought necessary to look after Lord Reading, Viceroy from 1921 to 1926, when he, Lady Reading, their assistants and their guest Edwina Ashley paid a three-day visit to the Maharaja of Alwar, a state known as one of the hottest parts of India (here India's highest-ever temperature, 50.6°C, was recorded on 10 May 1956). They travelled in the Viceroy's personal narrow gauge train; on arrival they were met by a fleet of Rolls-Royces; four lorries for the luggage and an omnibus for the servants.

But even in the luxurious, white and gold viceregal train on the way to the hills from Delhi the door handles were too hot to touch and, as Lilah Wingfield had noted ten years earlier: 'It is a bore not to be able to drink any water from now on and the boiled or condensed milk one has in one's tea or coffee is very nasty.' The dust and the smutty debris of the coal-fired locomotives penetrated everywhere, in spite of the three layers of glass, wire gauze and slatted Venetian blinds against extreme sunlight on the windows of the carriages. 'We had clean clothes twice a day and our pillowcases and sheets were just black,' wrote one woman after three nights and several changes; and often it was difficult to take enough (safe) water to satisfy.

Most people, like Lilah, travelled in the cooler weather. In the heat it was not so much travel as an endurance test. 'The drill was to set out with a wet towel round the head,' wrote Humphrey Trevelyan in May 1936, about to leave the baking heat of Gwalior for a few weeks in Poona. 'Keep the windows of the car tight shut against the scorching wind, get in the burning hot train with a large block of ice, eighty pounds of it, in a container between the seats, dip a towel in the ice water and tie it under the fan, shut the windows and shutters, dip your own towel in the ice water and tie it round your head again, lie down and hope that you would still be alive the other end.'

Desirée Hart was lucky enough to enjoy an air-conditioned carriage until Delhi, after which she was settled into a small ladies-only compartment in a train that had been waiting in a siding all day under the blazing sun. To render it tolerable a slab of ice was placed in a flat tin on the floor under a whirring fan. At first, the air was deliciously fresh but inevitably the ice began to melt and Desirée spent much of the time trying to keep her feet out of the growing pool of water, as a film of red dust that had percolated through the closed windows gradually covered both her and the carriage.

When Jean Hilary left Calcutta to travel to Sialkot the journey came as a shock. Her father Henry Hilary had first come to Calcutta in 1903, and ten years later had become Chief Executive of the Calcutta Port Trust. When the 1914 war broke out he had returned to England to fight for his country and was killed in action near Arras in June 1917, aged forty-one. He had been involved in plans to build a new dock for the port, finally opened in 1929. His widow had been invited to the opening but, with two boys still at school in England, she sent her twenty-two-year-old daughter Jean to represent her. Jean, Fishing Fleet material *par excellence*, had constantly to reassure her mother that she was not going to marry one of the many men who proposed to her. 'Don't imagine anything will happen as I definitely don't care enough, and find other men much too amusing,' she wrote home of one luckless suitor.

Because by the first week of April she was beginning to find the heat of Calcutta oppressive she accepted the invitation of another admirer to stay (suitably chaperoned) in Sialkot. The friends with whom she had been staying in Calcutta sent their bearer with her as escort. 'This journey is being pretty good hell and my only consolation is that I am travelling alone,' she wrote in one of her weekly letters to her mother. 'Most of the day I have been just lying on the bed, with only a petticoat on (no stockings) and a dressing gown to throw over me at the stations. All the windows and jalousies are up and it's fearful – one simply can't bear to be touching anything for long as it's red hot. It's quite impossible to touch any part of one's own body with any other part. I have lemonade and soda water brought to me at every stop as one has to drink it at once or it's hot. I am now having tea consisting of *petit beurre* biscuits and fizzy lemonade. I am just full of *eau gaseuse*.

'Simon the bearer is good and kind, comes along at each station and stays with my things while I eat. I paid thirteen rupees eleven annas for his ticket and twelve rupees ten annas for mine, and I have to pay him a return second class, as he goes back alone. Reggie got all the tickets for me and sent his bearer down with my baggage. I have a bottle of Evian for my teeth and have not forgotten soap or Bromo [toilet] paper! I have some good books to read which are saving my life as it's too hot to sleep.' But arrival at Sialkot did not bring the longed-for relief from the heat; soon afterwards, Jean was writing: 'I can't imagine why I left Calcutta because it was getting hot – it's hotter here and none of the facilities for coping with it. Each bungalow has [only] one fan and some have none, and it's turned off periodically during the day to save the current.'

Fishing Fleet girls who had come out to rejoin their families might easily find themselves somewhere remote – one planter's daughter scrawled 'It is very *boring* here!' across a photograph of her father's bungalow many miles from their nearest (planter) neighbour.

When Charles Ormerod was still a junior member of the ICS his parents decided to send his younger sister, Hrefna, out to stay with him to see if she could find a husband. For Hrefna, used to a smart social life in England, arrival in India to find primitive sanitation, newspaper pasted up on the windows of her bedroom in default of curtains and the lack of other amenities such as electricity and long-distance telephone calls came as a jolt.

The culminating shock was Charles's brisk way with rats. 'They were having dinner when all of a sudden my father saw a rat scuttling along the wall of the dining room,' recounted Charles's daughter Penelope Mayfield. 'Without a moment's thought he pulled out his revolver and shot it dead. Hrefna was astounded but to my father that was normal. He had always been a good shot – at Cambridge he was in the Shooting Eight – so to him this was part of life.' (Hrefna, happily, overcame her shock sufficiently to find a husband later in the visit.)

Girls who had been invited out by relations or friends usually arrived at a reasonably sizeable destination. They could expect to find themselves in a station or cantonment, with a club or Gymkhana as its social heart. The club could be anything from a few rooms where you could read old newspapers, buy drinks and meet the (often lamentably few) other Europeans in the station, to much grander affairs with tennis courts and golf links, a library and Saturday dances. Its rules were much the same as English clubs, with the addition that almost all excluded Indians, even as guests. Women were kept in their place, often a special annexe, and generally not allowed near the bar.* Sometimes segregation was such that if a

---

* In the Madras Club, Humphrey Trevelyan records that women were not even allowed to watch the men playing tennis.

husband was in the club and his wife was in the hen house, as the ladies' annexe was familiarly known, the couple had to send each other notes by a servant if they wanted to leave together.

Often stations were near or had sprung up round a local Indian town or village – but never too near. The huddled dwellings, rudimentary sanitation and often filthy alleys made for a noisome atmosphere. Sam Raschen, driving with a friend in the Mohmand region on the North-West Frontier, was some distance away when he heard a sound like a factory at work, 'as of high-powered engines and driving belts'. When he asked his companion what it was, he received the laconic reply: 'Flies.' And it was – 'houseflies by the million crawling and swarming over everything'.

Thus when the British built stations and cantonments they were separate and upwind from any nearby Indian village, both for fear of infection and to avoid smells. Cantonments were laid out with wide roads and, usually, sizeable gardens round each bungalow; these had spacious, airy rooms with high ceilings and whitewashed walls. Each bedroom had a bathroom leading off it, with (before running water was installed) a hole in the wall through which water drained when tipped out of the bath, large 'ali baba' water jars and the familiar thunderbox.

Pre-Mutiny bungalows generally had thick walls to withstand the heat, and deep verandas. As, in the early days, disease was supposedly often spread by a 'poisonous miasma', densest in ravines, gullies and clefts, bungalows were frequently raised on a platform above ground level. This served to counter the danger of the dreaded white ants (termites) that could eat their way through anything from a wall to a library full of books, and also meant that bungalows tended to be more airy.

The main drawback to the average bungalow was lack of privacy, as rooms led into one another and a servant might appear at any moment; against this, as the novelist Maud Diver pointed out in the early 1900s, there were no gas-pipes to leak, no water-pipes to freeze, no boilers to burst, no windows to clean, no grates to polish – and many more servants to do the minimal housework.

The new arrival would quickly learn that certain precautions were a routine part of daily life. Milk and water were boiled, fruit peeled or washed in permanganate of potash, care was taken to ensure food was kept fly-free, topis were invariably worn out of doors, mosquito nets hung over beds and an eye kept out for rabid dogs. Bathrooms were routinely checked for snakes that had crawled in through the drainage hole and wrapped themselves round the cool water jars and no one walked through the beds of lucerne, often grown in large gardens to feed horses and polo ponies, in case a cobra might be nesting there. In the early days, antique furniture legs had to stand in saucers of water to minimise the chance of destruction by white ants and silks and satins mildewed in the rainy season.

The new girl would have been struck at once by the formality of much of life and the protocols that governed it. In the Raj, as with royalty, attitudes and behaviour were well behind contemporary custom and usage, with everything from etiquette to medical theories preserved in a kind of social formaldehyde. This sprang from the hierarchical nature of the governing institutions: the ICS and the Army. When junior members of either arrived in India, they naturally took their lead from the top; by the time they in turn had reached this exalted position, they carried with them the customs and habits imprinted on them in their youth.

Thus the iron rule of precedence regulated social intercourse, from whom you called on to whom you sat next to at dinner. As the position of every official and military officer was detailed in a graded list known as the 'Warrant of Precedence', published by the Government of India, it was possible not only to seat people according to seniority but for a new arrival to deduce everyone's place in the pecking order. There were sixty-six categories in the Warrant; at the top, of course, was the Viceroy, at the bottom, sub-deputy opium agents.

Businessmen did not figure on the Warrant of Precedence but were nonetheless graded according to equally arcane rules. The broadest division among them was that between 'commerce' and 'trade' – the management of plantations was the former, and higher; selling something directly to the public was the latter. Other markers were education – a good public school and university elevated, as did long familiarity with horse, gun or rod – a decent address and a car. Even clothes came into the equation, with the wrong ones an immediate one-down mark: Owain Jenkins, a young man working in the Calcutta office of Balmer Lawrie, was quickly told by a colleague to buy a 'better hat'. His topi had been bought in Port Said and was covered in cheap cotton cloth, with a chinstrap resembling cardboard. 'Acceptable hats ... were covered in gabardine and had chinstraps of suede,' he was told.

Women were ranked according to the status and seniority of their husband or father, the senior ladies having 'their' seat on a favoured club sofa reserved for them, first shuttlecock in a game of badminton served to them and getting first use of the loos after dinner; nor could anyone leave a dinner party before the most senior lady there. (When the Hon. Margaret Ashton married Hugh Whistler of the Indian Police in 1924 there was much scratching of heads: did Margaret's status as the daughter of a lord raise that of Whistler – or did his lower hers?)

Most people still changed for dinner, if only because of the pleasure of washing away the heat, dust and sweat of the day and of putting on clean clothes – laid out by one's bearer – and for women, long skirts were a protection against mosquitoes. Another, more subliminal reason was that the consciousness of being the ruling elite permeated virtually every aspect of daily life.

Where the old East India Company had based its intercourse with India on trade, with intermarriage not only accepted but often welcomed, the British of the Raj were there to govern, and govern they did. As with anyone in a dominant position maintained by acceptance and good will rather than purely by force, and in a nation accustomed to the magnificence and dignity of its princes,* behaviour and outward show counted for much.

The British preoccupation with hierarchy, and the ceremonial that went with it, was not, therefore, a subject of mockery to the Indians themselves, but the reverse, something they understood since ceremonial and ritual had long been part of their own lives: their rulers were accustomed to unquestioning obedience and palaces full of servants and panoply as impressive as they could muster on occasions of importance.

Similarly, for the British, standards not only had to be maintained, they had to be shown to be maintained – and dinner dresses, white gloves and hats were simply one way of expressing this. 'Yesterday night I dined with the Hoddings; neither he nor the Major dress for dinner apparently when they dine on the quiet,' wrote Leslie Lavie

* In 1900 there were roughly 680 princely states.

disapprovingly (on 21 July 1896) to his fiancée Flossie 'I don't like the idea of not dressing at all, but I remember the Major used to say the same thing, and he seems to have dropped into the way of it. I hope I shan't and, darling, I hope you won't.' Edward Wakefield, writing in the 1930s, described changing for dinner 'even in camp'.

Even mourning emphasised the importance of the regime and by extension that of the Viceroy; following the death of a Sovereign, officers wore black armbands and their wives wore black for three months. In Government House, even the death of a lesser member of the royal family received the same treatment. 'Rushed off to shops and bought some white material with wee black spots on it as we've all got to wear black or white or black and white for weeks at GH on account of Queen Maud of Norway,'* wrote Claudine Gratton, then eighteen, on 1 December 1938.

The Raj was shot through with protocol of different sorts. First, there was the complicated caste system of India. A gardener – a fairly lowly job – could be a poor man but of a high caste; if he was a Brahmin and your shadow fell on the food he was eating, this had to be thrown away because your impurity had defiled it. Most table servants were, in fact, Muslim. Only those of the lowest caste could be sweepers, who brought in and emptied water for baths and emptied the thunderboxes.†

What would probably not strike the newcomer for several days was the homogeneity of the society into which she had arrived. Except in the ranks of British regiments, the British 'working class' was poorly represented – Indian labour, cheaper and local, took its place – as were children over eight and teenagers (only a few remained with their parents and were educated by the PEN system); and almost no old people.

The formality of much of English life often contrasted unhappily with the elegance, colour and fluidity of the inhabitants of their adopted country. As Lilah Wingfield noted appreciatively: 'The way these Eastern women of the bazaars, the very poorest of the poor, walk with lithe grace, carrying a pot of burnished brass on their

---

* The fifth child of Edward VII and Queen Alexandra, who had died on 20 November 1938.
† Government House in Calcutta was not fitted with a bathroom with running water until 1905 – the last year of Curzon's viceroyalty – and flush lavatories did not reach Simla until just before the 1914 war, arriving in Delhi even later.

heads, apparently so easily, supported by one shapely raised arm, and the stealthy, noiseless tread as they pace along with bare feet in the dust, more gliding than walking, with that inimitable gracefulness of movement and poise that marks the east from the west will always remain a wonder and a delight to me. I love watching them.'

Katherine Welford leaving for India in 1932 on the P&O liner SS *Mongolia*.

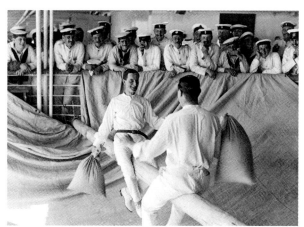

Male sports, such as this 'spar-fighting' competition, required great athletic ability.

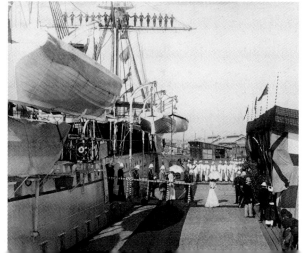

The arrival of someone important was always marked by ceremonial – note the lascars on the mast of the ship.

A group of bachelors living together to share household expenses, such as in this one in the Mahalaxmi district of Bombay, was known as a 'chummery'.

The five ADCs of the Viceroy, Lord Elgin, in full dress for a levée. As the only one of the close personal staff not a soldier, Henry Babington Smith (*centre*) wears Court uniform.

The Hon. Lilah Wingfield, just arrived in India for the Coronation Durbar of 1903, wears a dust veil over her topi to use if necessary.

The Viceroy, Lord Curzon, processing through the streets of Delhi on his way to the Coronation Durbar of 1903.

The Viceroy's Private Secretary, Henry Babington Smith (*centre, front row*), with his staff.

Lady Elgin seated in a silver tonjon (portable chair), carried like a palaquin on single poles resting on the shoulders of four bearers.

When the Viceroy went on tour, an army of tents would spring up, such as this one in Jodhpur.

Picnics were popular with everyone from the Viceroy down, who is seen here (*centre, next to his daughter Bessie*) in the Hills in the 1890s.

Bessie Bruce and Henry Babington Smith before their engagement.

A hunt breakfast for the Bangalore hounds in 1935. Horses were a central feature of life in the Raj, whether for hunting, riding, racing or playing polo.

Marian Atkins, seen here at the seventh and final day of the Calcutta paperchase in 1934 on her horse 'Kitty', was an assured rider.

(*below and right*) Hounds were transported to the meet by camel cart in this part of north India in 1905.

A day at the races in Ootacamund. Jerry and Sheila Reade, with the Maharaja of Mysore standing between them.

Annette Bowen, in 1932, aged seventeen (*left*), in *Daphne* at the Royal Madras Yacht Club Regatta (*centre*) and with three friends at the Madras Hunt Gymkhana Races in 1935 (*bottom*).

6

'A *hell* of a heat'

The Climate

What struck new arrivals first was the heat, sometimes like a scorching blast from a hot oven, sometimes sticky and damp.

To Europeans, the sun was the enemy; to protect against its assault, one garment was essential: the topi. 'We were all convinced that to abandon it even for a moment meant sickness and death,' wrote Owain Jenkins, in 1929. Most of the Fishing Fleet would have bought theirs at the invaluable Simon Artz on the way out. This lightweight helmet, made from the pith of the Indian plant sola and covered in khaki cloth, was worn almost to the last days of the Raj. Earlier, the spine pad was also deemed essential for soldiers and sportsmen: this object, about seven inches long by three inches wide, filled with cork shavings, hung down from the collar of jacket or coat (it disappeared in the early 1900s).

One of the stranger habits of the Raj was the insistence on wearing flannel next to the skin, advocated by virtually all doctors until well into the twentieth century. 'There are few of the ordinary diseases in India, which may not in the majority of cases be traced to the action of cold on the surface of the body, relaxed by the antecedent heat,' ran one piece of medical advice.

As flannel was thought to absorb perspiration more successfully than cotton or linen, this fabric was recommended as underwear – in one of the world's hottest climates. In the 1880s it was a 'must' for outdoor exercise, usually in the shape of a long-sleeved flannel tunic and flannel drawers. In the 1890s, as the heat in Simla increased, poor Lady Elgin, the Viceroy's wife, spoke anxiously to their doctor about wearing winter clothing in such heat. He answered firmly, 'No underclothing was to be changed.'

The stomach in particular was considered to be most at risk through over-rapid cooling, so a special flannel belt was designed, known as a cholera belt, supposed to protect against the disease. This quickly became a standard item; it continued to be worn long after the discovery of the cholera bacillus and the way that this was transmitted. In 1902 Ruby Madden was writing: 'I wear my belt every night and find it a comfort.' Unsurprisingly, perhaps, when she wanted to take a cold bath to counter the heat, Ruby was told that she couldn't, as it laid one open to 'all sorts of illnesses'.

As well as stifling in flannel underwear, women invariably wore corsets – it was a girl's ambition to have, at marriage, a waist measurement no more than the number of years of her age – together with several petticoats, trimmed with frills or lace, beneath long-sleeved dresses. (In the nineteenth century, the fashion for crinolines and bustles had led some Indians to believe that European women had tails.) As the Raj was several years behind England in customs and fashions it was not until the 1920s that cotton dresses and light underwear made their appearance. Yet even as late as 1929 Jean Hilary was writing home, with a touch of excitement: 'I found I could keep my stockings up rolled round garters, so wore no stays on the journey, which was much cooler!'

What sometimes caused even more problems was the question of dealing with the monthly menstrual cycle. Before tampons, women relied on sanitary towels or, sometimes, washable towelling squares. Adding to this inconvenience was the silence and embarrassment surrounding the subject; the thought of buying these necessaries from a male assistant in a chemist's shop would have sent most girls away scarlet-faced. In the Raj, a girl caught unawares could only rely on female friends; although most had washable towels tucked away in case of emergencies, this was not always foolproof. Jean Hilary discovered, to her slight indignation, that the dhobi (washerman) in one house was too high-caste to undertake this task 'so shall have to have mine burnt. Such a bore, as I seem to have very few left. They were always done in Calcutta.' To a girl brought up with servants, now in a land where women did even less, the idea of doing such an unpleasant job herself simply did not occur.

The seasons – cold, hot or wet – dictated the pattern of British life in India. The start of the cold weather, lasting from November to April, was marked by the flowering of social life, the arrival of the Fishing Fleet and the return of the British officers and ICS men who had been on leave in England – most of them took leave to coincide with the English summer, though some in cavalry regiments preferred the winter, with its chance of a season's hunting with a crack pack.

In Calcutta, the capital of British India until 1911, the seasons were predictable and easily dated. During the four winter months it was, in the opinion of Marian Atkins, 'perfect summer weather, 70°F and no rain except for a few days either before or just after Christmas and therefore known as the Christmas rains.' November was a popular month for weddings; it was also the month for a number of Indian festivals, such as Diwali. Christmas was celebrated as at home – from which presents had been ordered as early as October – but with local variations such as peafowl instead of turkey and perhaps a swim later in the day instead of an energetic frosty walk.

Delhi Week, with the Viceroy's Ball as its climax, signalled the end of the cold-weather season. On 12 March the men changed into white and the hot weather officially began, with the temperature gradually increasing up to a maximum of around 45°C (or 130°F in the shade).

Even in the cold weather, though, the dust in Delhi was a byword. 'Quite a foot deep on the road and powdery white stuff – you can't see a yard in front of you,' wrote Ruby Madden, who went out riding with a veil to protect the pink and white complexion she was so proud of. 'When I got home my veil was perfectly white one side and green the other, so it showed what I had been saved.'

'We are beginning to feel the real heat,' wrote Lady Canning, wife of the Governor-General* in March 1856. The shutters were shut and the punkahs kept going but the Calcutta heat took its toll. 'Any attempt to go out, even in a carriage, makes one gasp, and dissolve

* Two year later he became the first Viceroy.

immediately, and an open window or door lets in a flood of hot air, as though one were passing the mouth of a foundry,' wrote Lord Canning. Other seasonal hazards were snakes and monkeys. Lady Canning wrote that in her bedroom were lizards, running about the floor, and bats. 'One evening I had five in the room flying about and squeaking and worse in the night; I was glad of my mosquito net for protection.'

'The Punjab [then in the north-west of India, now in Pakistan] has a bad climate,' wrote Bethea Field. 'For the four months of the so-called "winter" it is pleasant – sunny, though chilly at night. Through February and early March, it is enjoyable. Then suddenly the great "heat" starts. In April and May there is relief from time to time from a sandstorm, bringing in its wake a cooler wind. Late May, June and July is a hell of heat, with daytime temperatures up to 120°F in the shade. In August the monsoon arrives, bringing relief from the high temperatures – but also so much humidity that the human body has to exist in a state of sweat.'

In the time of the Raj, long before air conditioning had been invented, the hot weather was an appalling strain for Europeans unused to its intensity – the heat, the flies, the dampness, the general discomfort, the glare. It was dreaded by everyone; some felt the northern part of India (except the north-west, which did not get the monsoon rains), where the temperature rose to great heights, was the worst, others that the damp heat of Bengal or Karachi, where the humidity was often 90 per cent or more and clothes had to be changed several times a day, was intolerable.

'This is the way the hot season begins,' wrote Lady Dufferin. 'Day by day the wind gets hotter and hotter till it scorches as though it came out of an oven. The sound of a strong wind on a warm day is very depressing – there is something unnatural about it.'

Those who could stayed indoors all day, venturing out only just before sundown. Windows were shut by 7.30 a.m., and large screens made from reeds were kept wetted and hung over windows to cool any breeze that came in. At night, sleeping on verandas under mosquito nets was common. Sometimes it was possible to eat outside. 'We used to have dinner on the lawn – dining tables and chairs, drawing-room furniture and standard lamp were carted out there every evening,' wrote Rosemary Redpath, then living in Indore State.

When the hot weather really took hold it was no good relying on the proverbial 'good night's sleep' to repair the ravages of the day: the heat, the noises of the night and the discomfort saw to that. It was the season when frogs croaked, cicadas sawed away relentlessly and jackals howled, an ululating, almost human shriek that rose and fell around the horizons or nearer – the drains in cantonments or stations were favourites for dens – setting off the barking of the numerous pi-dogs (mangy, feral skulking beasts with no owner) that scavenged round every village.

The summer was the time of year when rabies was most prevalent and if your dog had been bitten by a rabid dog it was often put down at once. For humans too the hot weather was intensely debilitating: boils, eczema, infections and fevers were common. Prickly heat* was almost impossible to avoid and although not health-destroying, could be appallingly unpleasant. Lord Minto, who was Viceroy from 1905 to 1910, described one of the Madras judges, Sir Henry Gillin, discovered by a visitor 'rolling on his own floor, roaring like a baited bull,' so tormenting was it.

'Sitting on thorns would be agreeable by comparison,' wrote one young lieutenant, 'the infliction in that case being local; now, not a square inch of your body but is tingling and smarting with shooting pains, till you begin to imagine that in your youth you must have swallowed a packet of needles, which now oppressed by heat are endeavouring to make their escape from your interior.'

As the temperature rose, so insect life increased. Lady Canning remarked that her dinner table in Calcutta 'was covered in creatures as thickly as a drawer of them in a museum'. Sometimes floors seemed alive with beetles; Lady Canning described huge cockroaches ('as big as mice') in her bedroom, 'some moving away, side by side, like pairs of coach horses'. Before the days of electric light, flying ants and bluebottles incinerated themselves in candles and lizards grew fat. Green flies piled up round the base of the kerosene lamps and there were moths everywhere.

Some of these creatures were not simply a nuisance but the cause

---

* If excessive sweating causes the sweat glands to become blocked, the sweat is trapped under the skin in swollen pockets, seeping into nearby tissue and causing a rash and irritation. In the days before antibiotics, if a bacterial infection developed, these could turn into boils.

of lesser or greater physical unpleasantness. Stinkbugs, the tiny black shield bugs with a horrible, penetrating odour, arrived in their thousands. One earwig-like insect, the blister-fly, which could settle on people without their being aware of it, left immediate large and painful blisters on the skin if crushed while removing it. 'Some crept up gentlemen's sleeves, others concealed themselves in a jungle of whisker,' wrote one guest at a ball that had suffered an invasion of these insects. 'One heard little else all evening but "Allow me, Sir, to take off this blister-fly that is disappearing into your neck-cloth" or "Permit me, Ma'am, to remove this one from your arm".

'This, however, did not stop the dancers and they polka'd and waltzed over countless myriads of insects that had been attracted by the white cloth on the floor, which was completely discoloured by their mangled bodies at the end of the evening.'

Slippers and shoes had to be shaken before being put on in case a scorpion had climbed inside. There were hornets that could give a powerful and painful sting, and would fly into rooms to build tiny clay nests on the legs of furniture, in which they laid a grub, fed by pushing caterpillars through the hole they had left. 'We had to watch out when playing tennis as poisonous black bees hung in great clusters from the porch,' wrote Betsy Anderson, a Fishing Fleet girl of 1923. 'Directly they were seen moving we had to take refuge inside while the special bee men were fetched. They cleverly swept and shook them into sacks and carried them off to an unknown destination.'

Up to and including Lord Curzon's time (1899–1905), jackals would howl in the shrubberies after emerging from their dens in the drains and stinking civet cats would climb to the roof of the house, occasionally entering the bedrooms – Mary Curzon once woke to find a civet cat drinking her bedside glass of milk.

In the hot, damp weather, with its extreme humidity, mould destroyed books and shoes or rotted dresses so that they hung in strips, white ants gnawed at the foundations of houses. These, properly called termites, could eat through a whole trunkful of clothes in a single night; the only wood that can withstand their ravages is teak, one reason for the prevalence of teak furniture in the Raj. (If spotted, through the grey powder deposits they left, paraffin poured over them was a sure killer.)

'You seem to be going in for enormous temperatures up there

judging from the *Madras Mail* reports,' wrote Leslie Lavie to his fiancée in Secunderabad on 9 April 1896. 'We have nothing like that degree of temperature here (96°F being our highest up to date) but the heat here has certainly been much greater than anything I ever felt in Secunderabad, I suppose from the fact that this is more or less a damp heat here.

'The worst of these damp heat places is that one's skin gets covered in prickly heat and all sorts of unpleasant-looking things, while a dry heat does not seem to have that effect at all. I thought I was too much of a veteran for prickly heat as I never got it in Secunderabad but I've got it everywhere now and in addition I've got that most irksome of all the minor ills that flesh is heir to – a stye in my eye. We've all had them in succession – Hudson, Searle, Storr and myself.' Next day he told her that the four of them had been obliged to shut their house up to avoid the scorching wind that blew in. 'The nights are as hot as the days and sleeping inside is unbearable. Storr and I sleep in the garden always, and are the cynosure of many a passer's-by eye, in the morning.'

'In hot weather sleep was a real problem,' wrote Monica Campbell-Martin. 'Punkah coolies would fall asleep and have to be woken, brilliant moonlight by which you could read a book roused dogs to bark, echoed in villages for miles around, jackals howled, night birds screeched and chattered, led by the brain-fever bird.' Sleeping outside, under a mosquito net, was the only alleviation. People tried everything, from dining with a block of ice (harvested in the cold weather and buried in pits until needed) under the table to damping pillows, sheets and the screens across windows.

Those who could left for hill stations like Simla, Mussoorie, Darjeeling; Srinagar, Gulmarg and Sonmarg in Jammu and Kashmir; Manali, Naini Tal, Gangtok and Kalimpong in the east of India, and Munnar, Ootacamund (Ooty) and Mahabaleshwar. In practice, this meant the women and children, with the men escaping from the scalding heat of the plains for a brief week or two when they could. The exception was the bureaucratic heart of government, which rolled up to Simla, files and all, to make it the summer capital of the Raj.

Then came the monsoon – India's climate is dominated by monsoons, strong, often violent winds that change direction with the season, blowing from cold to warm regions (because cold air takes up more space than warm air). They blow from the land towards the sea in winter, and from the sea towards land in the summer. As a result, winters in the north, though hot, were dry (the Himalayas acted as a barrier to the north-east winds), with perhaps a little rain around Christmas, while the summer monsoons, roaring into the subcontinent from the south-west, loaded with moisture from the Indian Ocean, brought heavy rains from June to September. These torrential rainstorms can cause landslides, sweep away villages and flood thousands of square miles.

Lady Canning wrote of a hurricane during her first May in Calcutta. 'The house shook, windows crashed and smashed, shutters were blown here and there. In my bedroom the windows had been left open and though the shutters were shut, the rain came in horizontally and drenched everything, even on the far side of the room, and left it ankle-deep in water, which rushed down the stairs in a cataract.' Her shoes turned 'furry with mildew' in a day, her husband's dispatch boxes looked 'white and fungus'y'. Crickets, grasshoppers, huge black beetles and cockroaches appeared everywhere, so much so that the wine glasses on the dinner table had to have lids to cover them.

'The chota bursat (little rains) may arrive ahead of the real monsoon,' wrote Monica Campbell-Martin in Bihar. 'You think the monsoon has arrived, because rain has fallen for a few hours. Your burning skin is relieved, your prickly heat is eased, but only for a short time. All over again, the days grow hotter, and back you go to where you started, steadily dripping. Once again the clouds pile up in thunderous beauty. You breathe air that is a dank and heavy substance, almost tangible. Around you everything is still. Every living thing seems waiting. Each night after each burning day seems waiting, too, in deathly quiet.

'Suddenly, with a crash, the sky disintegrates in a vast avalanche of water. It rains for about three and a half months with intervals of hours, or of a few days, until the cold weather. There is no gentle season of the falling leaf. There is no spring. There is the cold weather, the hot weather, and the rains. On the Northwest Frontier there is not even a monsoon. When the rains fall everywhere else, on the Frontier it grows hotter and hotter.'

That year the monsoon, which had swept up the Bay of Bengal, broke on 14 June, and the streets were flooded on and off until the cold weather, which began at the end of October. By Christmas Monica needed a blanket on her bed.

In the Punjab there were often dust storms, 'upheaving, whirling and carrying everything before them,' said Anne Wilson, on a camping tour of duty with her husband, a Deputy Commissioner. The Wilsons were on horseback for that day's march, when suddenly they saw a dust storm on the horizon. 'The air had become warningly cold. We cantered as hard as we could but in spite of our pace we were overtaken by the storm; darkness that could be felt enveloped us; straw, dust and leaves whizzed past us, thunder rolled, hail beat on our faces.'

As her frightened horse began to plunge, her husband dismounted to hold it still and quiet it, whereupon his own horse tore itself free and galloped away into the darkness. After the dust storm had passed they made their way in heavy rain to the camp, which their servants had taken the precaution of pitching on high ground, with mounds of earth heaped up protectively against the outer wall of the tents. Even so, in the morning they were surrounded by a lake and had to organise the digging of channels to carry the water away.

In Calcutta, the monsoon eased off from September on. 'By the end of that month a collection of coolies could be seen replanting the tennis courts everywhere, with a grass that "ran" like strawberry runners,' commented twenty-one-year-old Marian Atkins in 1931. 'So by November 1st we were playing on a perfectly level, entirely covered, good hard grass court! The sight screens were of hessian dyed with indigo so were almost navy blue – they were first class courts. The Saturday club had hard courts *lighted* – I emphasise this as it was a new concept and enabled the "box wallahs" to get exercise after office hours. The Club also had a few squash courts and a new swimming bath – all in the middle of built-up Calcutta.'

In Simla, Lady Dufferin was writing joyfully on 3 September 1885: 'It is true the monsoon is really over. Oh! It is a comfort; you can't think now tired one gets of the gloom and the everlasting drip, and the impossibility of settling beforehand to do anything out of doors.'

7

'Parties, parties, parties'

The Social Whirl

Apart from her sola topi and an open mind, the Fishing Fleet Girl's most important accessory was her calling card. Without it, she was a non-person, socially invisible.

'The first thing my aunt did when I arrived was to have some cards printed for me and then take me round to all her friends and to Government House to leave cards,' Katherine Welford told me. 'This ensured an invitation to dinner. And all the young men would call on my aunt and leave their cards and then she would invite them to dinner parties. And then they would ask me out dancing. I met hundreds of them. It was lovely.'

Violet Hanson, who had come to India to stay with her aunt in Malabar Hill – one of the best quarters of Bombay – was familiar with the practice of calling from staying with her grandmother, who would summon her carriage and drive round to various ladies' houses.

The etiquette of calling had been firmly established in English nineteenth-century life, as a means of keeping in touch with a wide circle of social equals, of establishing oneself in society, or of rising in it (if one's call was accepted), for these small rectangles of pasteboard could keep social aspirants at a distance until they could be assessed as suitable – or not. In the Raj, this complicated ritual had been refined down into the simple matter of dropping a card in a box. When Olive Douglas paid calls in 1913 she went out with a list in her hand and asked the servant who answered at the first house for the 'bokkus' (the wooden box into which calling cards were dropped). As she wrote: 'If the lady is not receiving he brings out a wooden box with the inscription "Mrs X not at home", you drop in your cards and drive on to the next bungalow ... If she is receiving, he comes out with her salaams and you go in for a few minutes but that doesn't often happen. The funny thing is one may have hundreds of people on one's visiting list and not know half of them by sight, because of the convenient system of the not-at-home box.'

It was exactly the same for men, especially for the numerous bachelors if they wanted any kind of life away from the confines of club or chummery. Sam Raschen recorded, also in 1913: 'Armed with a carefully prepared geographical list of names and with a box of cards, one set off in one's best suit and a gharry [horse-drawn cab], driving from bungalow to bungalow dropping cards into the box hung outside every door. In due course the calls were returned by the husbands of the ladies called on; cards with your name written on were placed in the racks provided for the purpose at the Sind Club or the Gymkhana. It may sound very formal, but it served its purpose of drawing attention to a newcomer's arrival, and an invitation to a dinner party, picnic or tennis soon followed.'

If a family was temporarily leaving the area, perhaps to go to the hills, they wrote 'P.P.C.' (*pour prendre congé*) on their cards when they called, as a reminder that they would soon be back.

By the late 1920s calling was just as necessary but even more of a hollow ritual, with not even a pretence that the caller might be asked in. 'One of my first duties after arriving at Lyallpur* had been to pay a round of social calls,' wrote Edward Wakefield. 'I was given a list of thirty or forty names and told to leave my visiting card in the little black tin box that I would find attached to a board at the entrance to each bungalow. Each box had painted on it in white letters the words "Not at Home". Conscientiously, on a bicycle, I did the tedious round, gradually working through the list.'

When he left out one because he could not find the bungalow, its indignant owner wrote to Wakefield's superior, the Deputy Commissioner, declining an invitation to dinner at which Wakefield would be present: 'as he has not had the courtesy to call on us we would

---

* A town eighty miles from Lahore and over 700 from Karachi, now known as Faisalabad.

prefer not to meet him.' The matter was rectified by the speedy dropping in of a card. To avoid this kind of gaffe, people would keep little leather booklets, like diaries, entitled 'Register of Calls', headed 'Date and Calls Received' on one page and on the opposite, facing page, 'Date and Calls Made'.

Equally imperative was the ceremony of signing the Book, kept either in the house of the Divisional Commander or near the gate of a Governor's residence, if you wished to be included in any of the top-level invitations. So vital was this considered that Katherine Welford, invited with her aunt and uncle to dinner at Government House, found herself tracked down during the day of the dinner by a flustered ADC, who told her reprovingly: 'You're supposed to be dining with us tonight but you haven't signed the Book!' She had to be driven immediately to Government House in her uncle's car to sign the Book and then dash back home to change for the dinner, returning to Government House an hour or so later.

'It's surprising how touchy people are about this whole business of calling,' reflected Margaret Martyn. 'They compare notes to see if so-and-so has called on you and not yet on them, and vice versa, and Mrs A won't invite young Mr X for dinner or drinks – he's so uncouth, has been here a week and hasn't called yet.'

Nor was distance considered an obstacle. In 1920 Fishing Fleet girl Bethea Field was a new bride and the wife of the most senior Government official in the district, which meant that cards were left on her first 'and then I had to return them. Some of the nearer ones I could do on foot but those further away I had to post. My callers left their cards on the way to the Club but I had no means of going the fifteen miles or so to return them. Even so, there were whisperings that I was "slack".'

By contrast, going out to dinner was often by the most informal kind of transport. 'In the army stations, very few people had or could afford cars,' explained Valerie Welchman (née Pridmore Riley). 'So you went out to dinner on your bicycle. You picked up the corner of your skirt and both of you pedalled off to dinner, or a dance, and pedalled back afterwards. In cantonments, the roads were built up high with deep gutters each side so that the water could drain down in the heavy rainfall of the monsoons. If someone emerged from a dance having done rather too well it was quite easy to fall down the side into one of these gutters.'

*

Cards were not the only form of protocol of which the Fishing Fleet had to be aware. Girls whose fathers had risen to high-ranking posts while their daughters were at school in England had to learn the rules when their formal education ended. They were taught how to behave at dinner parties ('talk first to the man on your right; then to the man on your left; start a conversation but never close it; never shut up either man'), told always to wear long white gloves at vice-regal dinners, and to carry frilly parasols to race meetings; to invite to parties only young men who had officially 'called'.

The 'right' clothes were needed: '... it is so funny having to think so much about clothes as one has to out here,' wrote Lady Elisabeth Bruce, daughter of the Viceroy Lord Elgin, when she arrived for the Calcutta Season of 1897. 'Dress at 7 to go out. Dress at 9 for the morning. Dress at two for luncheon. Dress at 4.30 if you walk or play tennis. Dress for dinner. And though one seems to have cupboards full of clothes, one never knows what to wear and has to think a long time so as to have something different on different days.'

Many of these clothes had to be formal, sometimes to emphasise your own status, sometimes to recognise that of others. To meet the Maharani of Travancore Beatrice Baker and her mother dressed rather as for Ascot, in flowered silk dresses, large sweeping hats, gloves, silk stockings and high-heeled court shoes. The Maharani and her daughter wore filmy saris, gold sandals and bare feet, with their long, thick, glossy dark hair decorated with flowers.

When Jon and Rumer Godden went out to India in 1914, all Englishwomen wore corsets, stockings, petticoats, dresses with high necks and long sleeves. The real benefit for women came when, in the 1920s and 1930s, linen or cotton dresses replaced the Victorian and Edwardian assemblage of voluminous underclothes, corsets, whalebone collars and ankle-length skirts.

Seniority was the touchstone when it came to seating and uniforms were not only a part of (Army) life but often a reflection of an individual's status – a status clearly marked wherever that individual might be. As Edward Wakefield put it: 'Never, I am sure, has there existed in England such an elaborate structure of class distinction as British exiles erected for themselves in up-country clubs in India.' At the heart of government, pomp and circumstance ruled even more so – papers for the Viceroy's attention were carried in by orderlies in long scarlet gowns trimmed with gold lace. (Of one huge pile Curzon remarked: 'I have perused these papers for two hours and twenty minutes. On the whole, I agree with the gentleman whose signature resembles a trombone.')

Sometimes the insistence on formality became stifling. When Monica Campbell-Martin, newly married and aged twenty-one, walked to the gate of her bungalow with the elderly official who had called on her with a message about tennis, and chatted to him for a few minutes before he got into his car, she was reprimanded the next day 'for having been seen talking, for so long, on the public road, to a gentleman, alone.'

The higher up the social scale, the more repressive life could be When Nancy and Daisy Leiter came to stay with their sister Mary Curzon, the Vicereine, in April 1899 these two free-spirited young American girls found the stiffness of Viceregal Lodge hilarious. Curzon, well aware that as the King's representative he ruled over almost ten times as many subjects as the King himself, was treated with more reverence than was royalty at home. The Leiter girls, rich, pretty and not disposed to bow the knee to someone whom they could now call 'family', had to be taken aside by Mary and spoken to sternly: they must not call the Viceroy 'George' except when they were alone, and they must always give him precedence. The girls' reaction was mockery by overblown obsequiousness: at one public ceremony they prostrated themselves before Curzon in exaggerated fashion. This so shocked everyone and horrified the viceregal staff that they were sent to their rooms in disgrace. 'Socially the advent of the Leiters has done great harm,' wrote Walter Lawrence, Curzon's Private Secretary, in his diary.

There were other misdemeanours and to add to it all, both put on a great deal of weight in a mere two months – like most of the British in India, the Curzons' cuisine was largely English (achieved brilliantly by cooks working in primitive conditions and with no knowledge of what a dish should taste like). Daisy gained fifteen pounds; 'her sit-upon is perfectly enormous and she is bursting out of her clothes,' wrote Mary, who added that there is 'no one on our staff who will be a matrimonial danger and I won't allow any flirtation.' Whenever the girls went to dances they were heavily chaperoned by sophisticated older women. Nevertheless, neither the sisters' behaviour, the attentive chaperoning nor their increased girth stopped both of them meeting their future husbands when staying with the Curzons – and both of these men were Curzon's ADCs.

Chaperoning, as in England, was a constant for young girls, with the added ramification that a single woman who might in England be considered old and sensible enough to read a railway timetable and get herself from station A to station B was in the Raj regarded as more of a parcel to be handed on from host to host. 'Even ... in 1933 I found a girl could not easily travel about independently,' wrote Helen Rutledge. 'Or rather geographically she could, but was discouraged from being too independent and doors would not have opened for her ... Even very distinguished travellers, who "knew the ropes" [and were] hardened to every discomfort, like Gertrude Bell, relied on their letters of introduction and being "passed on".'

With such letters, or invitations to stay, visitors could rely on hospitality of the most generous kind. Friends of friends would be happily pressed into service to meet an arriving Fishing Fleet girl if her parents were unable to get away. 'I was met by a friend of my uncle's, Archie Ricketts, who took me to stay with other friends,' said Katherine Welford of her arrival in Colombo en route to Madras. 'Archie must have been kept busy entertaining people passing through Colombo, expensive and time consuming for him but I was given a wonderful time during the four days that I was there. We went to the races and dined at the famous Galle Face Hotel and to Mount Lavinia.' In the same way, someone who wanted to stay on after the cold weather and see what a hill station was like could rely on being asked up to one.

When the cold weather began in mid-October, it was the signal for four months of non-stop gaiety – race weeks, polo weeks, ICS weeks, horse shows, race meetings, gymkhanas, paperchases, moonlight picnics, garden parties and constant dinner and cocktail parties. For anyone still at a loose end, most twentieth-century cantonments, towns and hill stations had a cinema. With books in short supply, no television or – for the most part – no radio, films were often the focus of evening entertainment. At Bangalore, Claudine Gratton managed to see several most weeks; during the week of 19 November 1937, for instance, there was Harold Lloyd in *The Cat's Paw* and Jack Hulbert in *Jack Ahoy*.

'From now on for the following year life became a glamorous fairy-tale,' wrote Betsy Anderson, who had been brought out to India, aged seventeen, in the Fishing Fleet of 1923 by her mother after years at an English boarding school, followed by presentation at Court and a London Season. They stayed for a few days with friends in Bombay, in a house that reminded Betsy of Rome, with its black and white marble floors, high ceilings and windows with long venetian blinds.

'I had been to some big dances at home, and to the May Week balls at Cambridge, by which time we would be looking somewhat dishevelled. They had been tremendous fun – sometimes arriving in a punt, dancing the Charleston with great vigour, and ending with a breakfast picnic on the river at Grantchester.

'But here at the Yacht Club everything was perfection – gorgeous evening dress, the men in uniform, and we danced on a superbly sprung floor. The gardens, which were discreetly lit, had well-watered smooth green lawns looking across the harbour to the ships twinkling with lights – all very romantic and unreal.'

Betsy's father held the important position of Resident, at Neemuch, Central India, and so the Andersons had the largest bungalow in the place, its best feature its shiny stone floors. Betsy and her mother set about making it looking attractive with yards of pretty coloured silks from the bazaar and huge vases of bougain-villea, canna lilies and other plants. 'There were dances at the Club, and this was fun for me, as the Gunners had just arrived from the Frontier and a young girl – the only one in the place – was a nov-elty. I was thoroughly spoilt, sought after for the dances, taken for picnics and out riding. At which I was not at all experienced.

'I fell blissfully in love with the handsome young subaltern who tried to teach me to ride, also because he was a divine dancer – this did not last long as, during the cold weather, my father's work had to be carried out while camping and moving from village to village.'

Betsy was one of the lucky ones taken to see India's most famous sight: the Taj Mahal. Her parents had met in Agra and her mother insisted that Betsy's first view of this extraordinary building must be by moonlight. 'We waited together silently around midnight in the stillness of the soft, warm, starlit Indian night,' she recalled later. '[My mother] slipped through a door in the large arched gateway, beckoning me to follow. We stood, hardly daring to breathe, watching the amazing sight before us.

'As the first light of the full moon rose glowing behind the immense and incredible dome and minarets, it appeared as a translucent, ethereal vision about to float into the sky ... its shimmering reflection was mirrored in the long stretch of water in the garden, making a pathway almost reaching to our feet.' An old priest took them down into the vaults, 'demonstrating that if one sang the notes of an octave the complete chord would be repeated high up in the vast dome ... we stood singing different chords for a long time'.

In Calcutta, Marian Atkins's day began with riding a pony lent by friends – her parents thought it not worth buying a horse for her as her father was due for home leave in four or five months. Sometimes on Sunday mornings she rode with friends from the Jodhpur Club.

'These were red letter days as we went at least ten to fifteen miles into the "jungle" round about. "Jungle" was a misnomer as it consisted of paddy fields, dried up for harvest in the cold weather after the monsoon, and guava orchards. These were always on made-up ground as Calcutta was built on the Ganges delta, its particular branch being the Hooghli. Guava trees are prettier than apple trees, having bark which peeled off regularly, like London plane trees, and wiggly branches. The fruit is apple-sized and green ripening to yellow.'

On Friday mornings the great excitement was a paper chase, in India always played on horseback. 'The Paper Chase Club met early at 7.00 a.m. at one of the milestones on the Diamond Harbour Route out beyond Jodhpur Club and the Dakuria Lakes (Father's handiwork),' wrote Marian in late 1930.

'They were great occasions; all my friends from the Calcutta Light Horse rode if their horses were sufficiently trained by then. The jumps were mud walls and coconut leaves, making a similar course to a point-to-point at home. Two of the officials rode round first, laying the paper trail. The rest of us, who for one reason or another preferred not to chase, watched the start and finish. The points gained were added up for the final result at the end of the season. After the chase we lazy or incapable ones went round through the holes or over the tops, as we fancied.

'On one occasion I nearly fell off and found myself suspended from the saddle by my bent knee. There was always a large crowd of Indians watching – they are mad keen on sports – after all, we got polo and gymkhanas from them, to say nothing of tent-pegging.* They all roared with delight at my predicament but I managed to climb back into the saddle, raised my bamboo riding stick in salute – and got an even louder roar as I rode on.'

The largest pool of eligible bachelors in India was in Madras, often known as the catchment area for the Fishing Fleet because of the number of single men working both for the Government and for businesses – Madras had been a centre of trade and industry since the early days of the East India Company and had continued to flourish. A British regiment was always stationed in the Fort; an Indian regiment out at St Thomas's Mount. There were other resident young men in banks, import and export firms, connected with cotton mills and railways, the Forestry Department, the Public Works Department and of course the ICS. Life was social to an almost frenzied degree, with any Fishing Fleet girl sure of an endless supply of admirers.

Annette Bowen found herself at the heart of it. She had been brought back to India by her parents in the autumn of 1933, aged almost eighteen, after being educated in England, finishing with a term at Queen's College, Harley Street. Her engineer father, Charles Henry Croasdaile Bowen, had worked most of his life for the Madras & Southern Mahratta Railway; his special line was bridges, and over the years he designed many over the rivers emptying into the Bay of Bengal. In 1933 he was Bridge Engineer and Chief Engineer, based in Madras.

'Here I spent nearly three years of sheer pleasure and interest,' Annette reminisced. 'There was the Indian scene to explore plus the social pattern of dancing, riding, swimming and picnics, Mah Jongg and amateur theatricals, choir singing, a course with the Governor's Mounted Body Guard, trips up country in my father's inspection cars, visits, social work (almshouse visiting and library duty on vernacular books), snipe-shooting, paper-chasing, rowing on the Adyar

---

* Contestants would ride at full gallop, attempting to spear a narrow wooden peg stuck in the ground with a long lance, then raising the lance and carrying the peg away. It is supposed to have originated from the idea that cavalry could charge through the camp of the enemy, carrying away the pegs of the tents so that these would collapse on the sleeping occupants, causing complete chaos.

river and plenty of friends of both sexes for the first time in my life.'

She dined out several times a week, sometimes invited to dinner parties, sometimes in parties she and her friends organised in clubs or chummeries, usually going on to a cinema, or to dance all night, often followed by a day in the saddle. 'Early mornings were spent riding or hunting, when horses were sent out to a planned milestone, miles out from Madras and we, changing from dance clothes to riding clothes, drove straight out in the dark and moved off in the dawn mist through flooded paddy fields and coconut plantations, through pale dusky-laned hamlets smelling of dung fires and coffee. Meets [of the hunt] were usually on Sundays, so we got back for gargantuan late breakfasts, then slept, and reassembled for evensong in the huge cool cathedral.'

Fancy dress and 'theme' parties were taken seriously. Annette once designed a 'circus' dance, with herself in the costume of the ringmaster – 'black silk stockings stitched to my briefs, a borrowed scarlet tailcoat, black topper and whip'. Sporting events also meant parties, parties, parties – Race Week, Rugger Week, Cricket Week, Rowing Week, 'when hordes of delightful young men would arrive from all over India and require accommodation and entertainment. A complete rugger team of planters from Ceylon once slept on our upstairs veranda, and we also hosted some of the MCC on tour.' It was girlie heaven.

In the grand villas left by eighteenth-century merchants, set in spacious grounds, the entertaining was more formal but just as easy and frequent. Katherine Welford's diary describes her days in Madras.

'My uncle was manager of the Burmah-Shell Oil Company in South India. Labour was cheap and they had many servants. First thing in the morning the butler brought me a cup of tea. Then we went out for a swim at Elliot's Beach, about a quarter of an hour's drive from their house. Lovely warm water. We swam about eight or half past then came back and had a bath and breakfast. My aunt and I would go with my uncle in the car to the office, leave him there and then go shopping. Lovely shops – gorgeous silk underclothes, all hand-embroidered. Sometimes we would play mah jongg at another bungalow.

'After lunch (always a different curry), we had a siesta. Even in what was called the cold weather, Madras was hot during the day.

Lying under the mosquito net I could watch the little lizards running up the walls. After a cup of tea, my aunt and I would go for a drive or a walk round Nungumbaukaum, the part of Madras where they lived, and when my uncle came back we'd have drinks on the balcony upstairs and more often than not a young man would call for me and I'd go out.'

Often Katherine, her aunt and uncle went to watch a polo match and there was a regular twice-weekly visit to the races; her uncle was senior steward of the Madras Race Course, where the jockeys came from Britain and Australia. The gardens there were beautiful, with seats beneath shady trees and brilliant tropical flowers to gaze on. As he was a senior steward, her uncle had his own box. They would drive out in time for a delicious lunch at the course, for which some of the food had been sent out from Fortnum & Mason, London's most expensive and prestigious grocer. Launching the proceedings, the Governor and his wife, Sir George and Lady Beatrix Stanley,* would drive down the Straight, in an open carriage, behind mounted bodyguards magnificent in their colourful uniforms.

'Sometimes we would go to the Adyar Club for drinks on the terrace that overlooked the Adyar River. It was a large white colonial building with lovely grounds, a lawn that sloped down to the river and lights in the trees – a very romantic place. There was a big veranda where people sat and had dinner – if you were having drinks there and a young man asked you to dine, you went back and changed into a long dress. There was a ballroom inside where dances were held twice a week. We often stayed for a late supper, or if we'd been dancing all night, for a breakfast of kippers, sent from the UK, at three or four in the morning. Then we'd go home about six.'

Another diversion was a weekend at the seaside. From Calcutta this meant Puri, staying either at an hotel or at one of the guest houses or hostels built by various of the companies and businesses based in Calcutta. Here beach 'boys' (some were in their sixties) in conical straw hats patrolled the shore to escort bathers into the sea – entering was difficult because of the surf. Others came round with 'tiffin boxes' slung from their shoulders, offering food for lunch.

* Youngest daughter of the 3rd Marquess of Headfort.

Jean Hilary, taken there by friends, wrote of the relaxed freedom of that weekend in 1929. 'We wore no stockings! only kicks, petticoat and dress.'

As most young women would notice pretty quickly, there was little mixing with Indians, apart from the servants in every bunga- low. Indeed, it was possible for many Englishwomen – in particular for regimental wives, where the social life of the community took place almost entirely within that community – never to meet any- one Indian except their own servants and those of their friends. (Even here, potential difficulties could emerge. 'Before dinner my ayah brushed my hair. It had got very dirty but it had somehow not occurred to me that I could let those skinny little black hands actu- ally touch me but after a bit I got used to the idea and acquiesced and felt no repugnance as I thought I should have done,' wrote Lilah Wingfield on 29 November 1911).

Today, it seems extraordinary that an impassable gulf existed between the two races; and that sophisticated, intelligent, well-edu- cated Indians, descended from a civilisation far older than that of their overlords, should have been so snubbed. At the same time, advantage was taken of their innate good manners: if some grand personage – a governor, a viceroy – wanted a tiger shoot, it was expected that the chosen maharaja would lay one on.

Long gone was the time when it was accepted that many East India Company men and soldiers took Indian wives; with the Raj came the barrier most forcibly expressed by Kipling in *Plain Tales from the Hills*: 'A man should, whatever happens, keep to his own caste, race and breed.' It was an elitism fostered by what was seen as the need to emphasise the difference between the rulers and the ruled, underlining what was then the sincerely held belief that belonging to the British Empire – which then held sway over three-fifths of the earth's surface – was the best possible fate for any nation, race or creed.

Men in the ICS did, of course, work with Indians to a certain extent and were well aware that posts filled by Indians would increase. But, as Edward Wakefield wrote ironically: 'It was unthink- able that European women should have to receive medical attention from an Indian doctor.' It was the same socially, no matter how grand the Indian. When Beatrice Baker became a friend of a good- looking, charming Indian prince her mother quickly saw him off.

*

Some of the girls who went out to join their parents were called Raj debutantes. For others the outlook was less hopeful. The fashion-conscious Ruby Madden, youthful, blooming and determined that she would not remain in India (its effect on her complexion was already being noted), described an encounter with two of them. After tea in their dressing gowns she and her aunt dressed for a drive. 'I wore my crash [coarse linen] skirt green silk blouse and hat with blue silk and white ruffle and we started off in the victoria at 5.00 o'clock. We went shopping, then I was introduced to two girls, quite nice but rather worn and old-looking. They are husband-hunting, I believe, and it looks as if it didn't agree with them.'

The most beautiful girls were known as Week Queens: girls asked to all the 'Weeks' of the cold-weather season – Calcutta Week, Lahore Week, Meerut Week, Rawalpindi Week, Delhi Week, each with horse shows, polo, gymkhanas, tent-pegging contests, tennis tournaments, dances, dinners, fancy dress balls and cocktail parties every night. These Weeks were the highlight of the cold-weather season, with Delhi Week – once Delhi had replaced Calcutta as the capital in 1911* – the culmination and peak. Here, civet cats rustled in the thatch of bungalows and hyenas howled at night and Urdu – the 'language of the camp' invented by the Moghuls for their multi-racial armies – was still the speech. There was always a New Year's Day parade with cavalry and infantry marching and galloping across dusty parade grounds.

To entertain as many as possible during the Week there was a huge viceregal garden party – 'sweet peas and roses, delphiniums and carnations, hibiscus and jasmine, grew in every garden,' wrote M.M. Kaye, the daughter of the Deputy Chief Censor, Sir Cecil Kaye, in 1927. There was also a ball at Viceroy House and a fancy dress ball at the Imperial Delhi Gymkhana Club, with a band playing tunes like *You just You, You're the Cream in my Coffee, You were Meant for Me, Wonderful You*, with supper after eight dances, mostly assorted foxtrots and waltzes (spelt valses).

On New Year's Day every station had its parade, with uniforms at their smartest, buttons gleaming in the sun, the band playing

* The Government felt that administration would be easier from Delhi, a northern city, rather than from the coastal city of Calcutta.

and complicated manoeuvres performed, all in honour of the King-Emperor. Everyone turned out to watch this spectacle. 'Went to the New Year's Parade,' ran the youthful Claudine Gratton's diary for 1937. 'Michael came in to drinks and we all acted the goat, and he lay down on the sofa with his head on my bosom, the angel. In the afternoon slept in the garden.' In the evening was the inevitable film. 'Went to see Joan Crawford, Franchot Tone and Robert Taylor in *The Gorgeous Hussy*. Very good and rather sad.'

For Katherine Welford, New Year's Day held more than the parade. It was the day the Burmah-Shell agents came from all over South India to pay their respects to her uncle. 'We were up very early (after seeing the New Year in) to receive them. We stood on the wide veranda and one by one the agents salaamed and placed beautiful garlands round our necks. I still have one of these, made with fine gold thread.

'They brought presents, cases of champagne, tropical fruits and Elizabeth Arden cosmetics for my aunt. It was a company rule that only presents that could be consumed were to be accepted. Uncle Maurice told me that one year he was given a silver salver with his crest engraved on it, not one but several, making a design all over it. Of course, it had to be returned.'

Not all the Fishing Fleet girls, however young and pretty, met a future husband. Katherine herself, who arrived with about twenty others, commented that only three of them became engaged during that cold-weather season. 'I met stacks of young men,' she said. 'It was marvellous. After a visit to the Hills I returned to Madras for eight days – and went out with eight different men. I almost lost my heart – but I felt I was too young to settle down.'

8

The Viceroy's Daughter

Elisabeth Bruce

As a daughter of the Viceroy, Lady Elisabeth Bruce, known in the family as Bessie, was in the highest echelon of the Fishing Fleet. She was pretty, modest, self-contained, helpful to her mother in her public duties and a companion to her father on his walks What made her unusual was a great power of observation, put to good use in the comprehensive diaries she kept from the moment she came out to India. The husband who eventually captured her heart was, in the best tradition of viceregal circles, one of His Ex's household.

Bessie arrived in Bombay in January 1894, aged sixteen and a half. As her father, the 9th earl of Elgin, was the incoming Viceroy, they were received with much pomp and ceremony. Brought up in Scotland, Bessie was amazed by the contrast. 'It *is* a new wonderful undreamt of land ... a few minutes ago, along a scarlet carpet spread from the bungalow to the chief entrance [of Government House] passed a little procession. H[is] E[xcellency], supported on each side by two attendants dressed in scarlet, holding brass clubs; followed by Her E. in a low dress, with a man carrying a parasol over her head. She wore the tiara, the diamond necklace, two diamond bracelets, her diamond ring and the Fleur de Lys, on a plain black gown, which suited her very well.'

It was an effective introduction to the formality and grandeur that would henceforth surround the Elgins and the impressionable Bessie realised this at once – even in her private diary she refers to her father and mother as 'His Ex.' and 'Her Ex.', so much so that it is sometimes difficult to remember that she is talking of much-loved parents.

Before they set off for Calcutta, then the seat of government, there were visits, and a state banquet and reception. Bessie, still in the schoolroom at sixteen, did not attend but kept a watchful and admiring eye on the clothes. It was an era when in the evening silks and satins predominated, 'jewels' usually meant diamonds, and feathers, lace and flowers were the accepted accessories. Her mother 'looked beautiful' in a white silk dress with bunches of purple anemones, pearls and diamonds and Bessie's young cousin, Elsie Bruce, wore 'a bride's white satin dress'.

Elsie was an unabashed member of the Fishing Fleet: before leaving England she had announced her intention of marrying within the year. She had come out as lady-in-waiting to the Vicereine. The Viceroy's staff was of course much larger – a Military Secretary, a Medical Adviser and various ADCs, about four at a time, officers seconded from their regiments, with the honorary rank of captain, and a Private Secretary, a twenty-nine-year-old civil servant called Henry Babington Smith. He was a rising star; he was also extremely good-looking and, as Bessie was to learn later, a wonderful dancer.

The viceregal party arrived in Calcutta on 27 January 1894 to a huge reception, 'troops, colours, a dazzling and *most* orderly crowd, from which came a kind of low buzzing that rolled on with the procession (the people here never shout, they only salaam and smile), shops were closed, every balcony crowded, the body guard and volunteers following H.E.s carriage rattling their swords ...'. They were met by the outgoing Viceroy, Lord Lansdowne, who led them through the marble halls with their chandeliers and busts of Roman emperors (captured from the French) but, regretting the absence of the electric light she was used to, Bessie noted that 'there does not seem to be much likelihood of our having other light than parafine [*sic*] lamps and candles'.

A ceremony that deeply impressed this young Scots girl was the reviewing of the Bodyguard, the Viceroy's personal corps, 'at the beginning by daylight, at the end the lances were glittering in the moonbeams. It looked such a perfect little regiment, as divided into six columns, with the sergeants in front; they moved round their reviewing field, then passed in single file before His E.'s carriage, the first five officers with swords, which they lowered as a salute;

the two British captains have a leopard skin over the saddle and have horse clothes beautifully embroidered in thick gold thread; they themselves have white helmets, & in every thing else resemble other soldiers; all officers' horses have a red tassel underneath the chin. It was quite wonderful to see them keep in line so beautifully & manage their horses so well, when they had become impatient from waiting such a long time.' Unfortunately, her father was very tired after long hours in Council and 'his carriage being stationed under a tree, the mosquitoes fell upon him in droves'.

One of the Viceroy's chief recreations was to go for long walks, often accompanied by Bessie and only marred by the standing regulation that a policeman had to accompany the Viceroy whenever he went for a walk. Fortunately, the officer concerned was thoughtful and empathetic: 'such a nice man, who so entirely understands what a disagreeable thing it must be to be constantly dogged in this way that when we stand still, he hides behind a tree, or pretends to be near us by accident, in such a way that H.E. has said several times that he does not care how many policemen are *behind* him'.

An important feature of the household was the viceregal band, which played at dinner and at dances, and followed the Viceroy up to Simla when he moved there for the summer. Mercifully, rehearsals were conducted some way away; after the arrival of the Elgins the band began to practise playing reels.

Soon the hot weather began. By 2 March, with the heat increasing daily yet the routine remaining as rigid as ever, 'when the gong rang, panting forms in muslin, flannelette or silk gathered in the Throne Room for luncheon, which is still supplied with roast beef and boiled puddings, like on a day of 0° at home …'. It was a relief to Bessie when, on the evening of 9 March, she set out on the thousand-mile train journey to Simla in the company of her two younger sisters, Christian and Veronica, two ADCs, their governess, a ladies' maid, countless Indian servants and two dogs, arriving there three days later.

Bessie's days in Simla were strictly organised. She worked with her governess and sisters in the schoolroom from eight until nine in the morning, followed by breakfast, then an outing, usually in rickshaws, from ten until half past eleven. After this there was more schoolroom work until 1.45; then came luncheon, more work from three until five, the end of the schoolroom day. In the evening the young ladies were taught tennis by the ADCs, with the rickshaw men as ball boys 'who will on *no* account lend each other a ball and sometimes nearly fight'.

Sometimes the girls 'had dinner with the gentlemen' (the four young ADCs and Henry Babington Smith) and afterwards danced – reels, polkas, valses – ending up with the full curtsey they would have to make to their father on formal occasions. There were visits to The Retreat, the Viceroy's weekend cottage in Mashobra, six miles from Simla and a thousand feet higher, in spring surrounded by banks of violets in the pine woods, wild roses and pale pink and white begonias. Here there were walks, scrambling over the rocks, more tennis and in the evenings teaching the ADCs the Scottish dances the Elgin family loved and in which the young men had to be proficient for the Simla Season about to begin.

After Simla, with its greater freedom, the viceregal household with the Government of India in its train returned to Calcutta, arriving on 15 December 1894. There were reviews, investitures, parades and a formal visit from the Maharaja of Mysore. 'His Excellency looked very well in white silk stockings and white knickerbockers instead of trousers. Her Excellency stood beside him in dark blue velvet with her diamonds ... all the dresses were like long dinner gowns; only one or two had court trains; very many had a veil and feathers.'

The relentless round continued, with entertaining, church parades, a garden party on 27 December and an evening party where H.E. and his hostess sat on a sofa on a dais 'quite commanding everything, with their feet on a large tiger skin'. There was a fancy dress ball, a state ball, grand dinners at Government House every Thursday, as the heat gradually grew worse: on 19 March the garden party at Government House 'fortunately did not last long as the rain began and there was a great deal of lightning all evening I hope a storm will come; it might clear away the smallpox which is so bad'.

Bessie was lucky enough to leave again for Simla on 22 March, staying en route at Lucknow, where 'the mosquitoes were quite dreadful, they sing and buzz round one's head all evening', reaching Simla after sunset on 29 March, where it was very cold, followed by rain and thunder for the next few days. As the weather warmed, there were expeditions, the usual round of formal entertaining, dancing after dinner with the ADCs and Henry Babington Smith and, sometimes, games. 'Mr B.S. played backgammon with me & I lost three times & went to bed. It is such a very nice game – he plays very well indeed.' The summer was notable for the arrival of a primitive telephone service, beset with unlikely teething troubles – a bell that would not stop ringing at the other end, 'ear tubes' that did nothing but crackle and the need sometimes to shout at the top of one's voice.

The days passed with their storms, mists, rain, brilliant sunshine, visits to Mashobra, walks, the household's discovery that their servants were much better at using the telephone than they were themselves and, for Bessie, the planning, rehearsing and performing of an eighteenth-century gavotte with her sister, two friends and the male members of the household. There was also the incipient idea of a flower collection, that typical pastime of Victorian young ladies, which would have an unexpected outcome for Bessie.

They left Simla in late October 1895, returning to Calcutta via several states, travelling in the Viceroy's special train. In the first coach, the Royal Saloon, sat H.E., in the second Royal Saloon were Bessie, her mother and an English maid, then came coaches devoted to dining and cooking, followed by those for the staff; in the final five carriages the first two were for the sixty-odd servants, the last three for luggage and horses. They wound up at Poona – more ceremony, parades, reviews and a grand ball – followed by another train journey to visit the Nizam of Hyderabad, supposed to have 800 wives, who gave a dinner for 360 in their honour.

Back in Calcutta, Bessie's father finally succumbed to one of the illnesses that then abounded in India (classified by the viceregal doctor as a chill on the liver). Combined with the poor health of her mother, who had suffered from chronic fatigue, headaches and general malaise since arriving in India, this made for a depressing Christmas. Towards the end of January 1896, with both Excellencies still ill, they were ordered that universal Victorian panacea, 'sea air', in the form of a cruise on the SS *Warren Hastings*, leaving Bessie as the nominal hostess in Government House – a challenge indeed to an eighteen-year-old girl.

Fortunately (for Bessie) the death of Prince Henry of Battenburg, husband of Queen Victoria's daughter Princess Beatrice, meant that

Court mourning was announced soon after her first dinner party and this put an end to all formal entertaining – but did not prevent a visit to a museum with two friends and Henry Babington Smith. 'Then we had tea in Mr B.S.'s room and he showed us his microscope which is a Christmas present. It is most interesting, & I do not at all like hearing it called a toy; it is a real instrument …'. A few days later she joined her parents on the *Warren Hastings* cruise; by the time of the final return to Calcutta in early February, her father had completely recovered; and on 27 March they left for Simla again. Here, for the first time, she danced at the state ball, though retiring from it early.

But the past two years had been so punctuated by illness of one sort or another, afflicting everyone from the Viceroy down, that sporadic sickness had come to be taken for granted. The ADCs suffered everything from sunburn, inflamed mosquito bites and injuries from polo and the newly fashionable sport of bicycle riding, to fevers of different sorts; the Vicereine was never really well and even the robust Bessie herself was sometimes under the weather. Finally, after another exhausting tour of the princely states, with its accompanying succession of formal dinners, hours watching parades and reviews and the entertainment of various worthy dignitaries, with the Vicereine newly pregnant and the Viceroy in poor health and with a broken finger, the viceregal party arrived back at Calcutta on 10 December 1896.

It heralded the most important year of Bessie's life – a true Victorian courtship that concluded in a happy marriage.

The Calcutta Season began well for her, with a new ADC, Lord Burford ('very shy'), at Government House to greet them. At first, Lord Burford seemed to hold the inside track. When he was in waiting for the first time Bessie found him 'very pleasant to speak to'. He told her he had to look out for orchids and carpets to take home, quests that undoubtedly appealed to her. The first major ceremony was a levée on 17 December, with H.E. in his uniform with blue Star of India ribbon and his stars, the men in full dress processing into the Throne Room.

Then, on Saturday 19 December, came a Drawing Room, the equivalent of the Queen's Court at home, where presentations took place, dreaded by Bessie as her first Court. She had a new dress for it, blue satin, with spangled net on the bodice and she was instructed by the dressmaker that to suit the new fashions she should wear her hair in a little bundle high on her head, with a rose or a small comb as ornament – only married women could wear whole coronets of flowers. Her sister Christian wore white satin trimmed with white violets and Her Ex. a long skirt of shot mauve and maize-coloured brocade with a crystal fringe round the bodice, a broad band of purple velvet across the shoulder and sleeves of diamond-spangled net. With it, she wore a diamond necklace; and collar and three diamond stars on the velvet band.

Nervous though she was, Bessie was able to train her observant eye on the presentations. 'They say the fashionable curtsey is an athletic-looking bob but when some people attempt this their knees give way and they either sway a good deal or seem to be sitting on the ground for a second. It also adds greatly to the graceful curtsey if the head is well held; some keep their eyes fixed on the ground as before a shrine and others fix them on Their Exes.'

Christmas Eve was spent peacefully at Barrackpore, and the family lunched by themselves under the banyan tree. But there was one drawback to alfresco meals: 'The hawks and kites are growing much tamer. One of them carried off HE's beef just as it was being put on the table; after which he ordered men with sticks to stand near to guard the table and the stove.'

By now their social circle was much enlarged. Both older sisters, very well liked, were quite different in looks and personality, Christian much shorter and, as described by her cousin, 'soft and fluffy & always laughing & talking a great deal', whereas 'Bessie is tall and quiet and has a dignified way of doing things, especially evening things'. Unsurprisingly, perhaps, 'Bessie's chief friends are among the ladies, the men out here do not like her style as much as C's on the whole'. But in the race to the altar, Bessie would be an easy victor.

In the middle of the social season, then in full swing – a Christmas party for eighty-four children, boys' presents in one bran tub, girls' in another, nine stockings for the gentlemen of the household hung on a line, photographs, parades, reviews and a state ball – while H.E. coped with famine and restlessness, there was news that shook them all. The *Warren Hastings,* on which Bessie and her parents had cruised and which had taken home the outgoing Viceroy, Lord Lansdowne, had gone down. Most of them knew the ship and no one could talk of anything else. Fortunately, there had been minimal loss of life.

That January, 1897, the *Warren Hastings* had left Cape Town bound for Mauritius with 993 passengers, including the headquarters and four companies of the 1st Battalion, The King's Royal Rifle Corps. At 2.20 a.m. on 14 January, eight miles off-course and steaming at full speed, in pitch darkness and pouring rain, she ran straight into the rocks on the coastline of the French island of Réunion.

There she stuck fast, allowing time for the troops to fall in below decks without noise and in perfect order and at 4 a.m. the captain ordered the troops to begin leaving the ship down rope ladders slung from the bows; as the *Warren Hastings* appeared so firmly stuck, his intention was to leave the disembarkation of the women and children until daybreak, when it would be easier and safer for them.

However, twenty minutes later the ship suddenly began to list badly so the captain hastily ordered the men to stand fast while the women, children and sick were helped off the ship. As the position on board became ever more dangerous, the men were told to scramble ashore as best they could. By 5.30 a.m. all the troops were on land – later, even some of the baggage was recovered. Miraculously, only two lives were lost: two Indian members of the crew (no lascar could swim). The French on the island rallied round and soon the passengers boarded another ship for the final 125 miles to Mauritius. But the *Warren Hastings* was gone for good; for many, it was almost like losing a friend. 'I always felt that ship was alive,' said one of her captains.

With her mother's health never good and her confinement nearing, Bessie found herself thrust into the role of hostess. She carried it off with grace and dignity but hardly had time to think of anything else. Once more in Simla, she enjoyed its familiarity and charm – and a new and enjoyable prospect opened up before her. As she wrote to her Aunt Louisa on 21 April: 'Now I will tell you something very serious; I am learning Latin with Mr B.S.'

Henry Babington Smith had offered to help Bessie with her flower collection and, as she told her Aunt Louisa: 'It was so impossible to remember the names of the flowers we collected that I asked him if he did not think the best plan would be to learn Latin. He said it would help me and I said – half in fun – that he would have to correct my exercises. He said he would – quite seriously – and then bought the books. So I began at the end of the Calcutta time. Then, coming up while we marched, he used to give me Latin sentences out of his head ... it is so much more interesting to have a subject like that to talk about with people to whom one cannot make the usual society conversation because it has been all said years ago. And he is most clever when he teaches ...'.

Babington Smith was indeed a clever young man. His father was a lawyer and mathematician, one of his brothers became an MP and the other Keeper of Greek and Roman Antiquities at the British Museum. He had been educated at Eton College and Trinity College, Cambridge, where he read Classics, as did so many of the upper echelons of the Home and Indian Civil Service. Before joining the Elgin household, he had been Principal Private Secretary to the Chancellor of the Exchequer, George Goschen. Born on 19 January 1863, he was now thirty-four to Bessie's nineteen – an age difference that would have seemed perfectly unexceptionable at the time.

Bessie, who as deputy hostess for her mother often found conversation difficult in the limited society of Simla, where everyone knew each other and the constraints of her position prevented too much freedom of opinion, frequently found the postbag contained more original and interesting news. On the same day that her father received a letter from the Queen and a cheque from New York for the Famine Fund, she heard from a friend at Jhabrapathan. 'The people there are so unsettled that 300 troops have just been sent to keep them quiet. The other day a panther was caught which had eaten three children; Major Jennings wanted it to be shot or sent to the Zoological Gardens, but the people would not listen and said that as it was a man-eater it must be trampled to death by the state elephants. All the parents of the eaten children looked on ...'.

Her flower collection was now of paramount interest. On May Day 'Mr B.S. told me that we ought to make a list of all the flowers we have collected and print it. That means a good deal of work, for they must all be arranged in families, and I have been trying to begin it today ... Next morning Mr B.S. came up to the sitting room and told me how to write out the list; each family must be on a different sheet, & only one side of the sheet may be written upon. At present I know of 38 families but there must be a great many more.'

Nothing must be allowed to stand in the way of this absorbing project. On 10 May she was explaining to Aunt Louisa that she was giving up her music lessons, because of the heavy demands on her time made by her flower collection (which she drew and painted). 'We have only one more spring here and the collection must be as good as possible.' Often they thought they had found a new specimen but with most bushes with white flowers looking the same in the distance, she and Mr Babington Smith necessarily had to walk to them all to inspect them at close quarters. However, two new ones were discovered.

Henry Babington Smith was clearly determined to capitalise on Bessie's enthusiasm and, he hoped, growing interest in him. As she told her aunt: 'Mr B.S. means to add an account of our walks round Simla (100 he thinks will do). It ought to be rather interesting but it means a *great* deal of work for him and I cannot think how he is able to do it beside all his real business. But he is ... altogether growing so friendly that I almost think he *is* a friend; shall I tell you why? Because the other day, at dinner, he told me something about other people – and in Simla, from a man like that, this means a good deal ...'.

She also spoke of how her Latin was progressing – or rather, of her Latin teacher. 'He takes so much trouble and is *very* clever in the way he teaches; he never grows angry, he only sometimes smiles when a thing is wrong and that makes one sorry; and he is not frightening ...'.

The Season continued with the state garden party, races at the end of May, the state ball and state dinner party the following week (moved from Thursday to Tuesday to allow the Eton dinner to take place correctly on the Fourth of June for the twenty-three Old Etonians then in Simla).

On Tuesday 22 June, the day of the Queen's Diamond Jubilee, celebrated in Simla as everywhere else under British rule, the weather was appalling. Rain poured into the rickshaws, thunder roared in the hills round about and, as there was no awning leading to the town hall entrance, most people got soaked. It did not stop Bessie recording the highlights of the ceremony, such as the presentation of gifts. 'Some of the caskets were very handsome, some were in embroidered bags, one only in a large envelope. Many of the deputations came from Bombay, two or three from Calcutta, one from

Lahore, others from Benares, Allahabad etc. There was a good deal of draught and wind and poor Lady Cohen arrived saying that she had her feet soaked and she had only just got out of bed, where she had been for four days with a sore throat; and Lady White was wet and many others.'

Jubilee honours and knighthoods were bestowed. 'Mr B.S. is made CSI [Order of the Star of India, ranked above the Order of St Michael and St George in the British honours system]. He *certainly* deserves it,' wrote Bessie warmly, 'for he works so very hard.'

Next day there was a reception at Viceregal Lodge, where the newly honoured were congratulated, sometimes with a touch of envious spite. Sir William Bisset was the only 'honoured' person Bessie had been able to congratulate but he did not escape scot-free. 'There are so many "ladies" and so many Sir Williams you can call anyone "Sir William", somebody said disdainfully; but I think it was from envy; for people seemed as pleased as they might have done 200 years ago before all the democrats and presidents were talked of. However much people may speak, they will always like to be distinguished; and what more so than "Her Ladyship" ...'.

Wet weather and disturbing events that required the attention of H.E. and his Private Secretary put a temporary stop to the collection of flowers.

At the beginning of June there was an earthquake in Calcutta, which damaged the spire of the cathedral and cracked many houses. Fighting broke out at Malakund, which saw a number of the soldiers depart. Later came news of another outbreak on the frontier, near Peshawar. As the month progressed, half the soldier ADCs left for active service with their regiments.

Although fighting was endemic on the frontier with Afghanistan, when the Pathan tribes revolted in 1897, as Bessie's diary recorded, British officials and soldiers blamed the Afghan Amir, Abdur Rahman, for causing the trouble. They thought that, as the self-professed champion of Islam, he had commanded the tribes to undertake holy war against the British and that these calls for jihad might be heard and answered within India and even beyond. Because they ruled more Muslims than any other empire, the British were always very sensitive to any idea of Islamic hostility. At the same time, they wanted to preserve friendship with the Amir, not solely to keep peace in this volatile area but also because of fears of Russian expansion (Kipling's Great Game).

Even during the work entailed by the fighting on the frontier, the routine and exigencies of life at Viceregal Lodge were maintained – and the flower collection continued. When Henry Babington Smith went off for a few days' shooting he sent Bessie a collection of flowers from the camp; on his return there was another flower gathering expedition and in October, at Mashobra, 'Mr B.S. arrived just in time to join the walk after luncheon ... it was a very delightful evening; the stars were so bright, the Pleiades were rising as we came in.' And towards the end of November her diary ('written with a new quill pen!') records that 'Mr B.S. sent up the "dedication" he had written for my flower catalogue', generously allotting all the credit to Bessie.

Back in Calcutta after a tour through Darjeeling, the Season began in earnest with a long levée, and a Drawing Room at which Bessie's youngest sister Veronica 'came out'. For her presentation she wore white satin. 'H.E. wore a white brocade gown with a small Star of India blue silk band round the waist, a panel of the same silk down one side. She had her tiara & her diamond necklaces were hung like chains among the beautiful lace on the bodice.' Poor Veronica, in a state of quivering nerves, confided that the thing she dreaded most was talking to the ladies after dinner parties. 'I can hardly think of it, it will be so much more than dreadful from all B. and C. tell me.' But all passed off satisfactorily and Bessie was able to tell Veronica afterwards that she had looked 'very stately'.

As the winter rolled on, the words 'for the last time' began to be heard: in 1899 Lord Elgin's term as Viceroy would end and he and his family sail for home.

First, there was an investiture on the evening of 13 January, attended by 1,700 people, a red velvet canopy above the raised throne on which her father sat in front of gold and scarlet embroidered hangings. 'H.E. wore his blue robe and collar of the Star of India; his two little pages, Jimjack Evans and a son of the Maharaja of Cooch Behar, walked behind him. They wore white satin suits, white shoes with blue bows and garters, and black wigs.' It was a glittering scene, with women in evening dress, sparkling aigrettes and opera cloaks, festooned with diamonds, and uniforms everywhere, the civil dark blue embroidered with gold, the military scarlet. Next day Bessie's two aunts who had been staying with them left for Darjeeling; their places were taken by other guests. One was a Mr Churchill. 'He is short, with reddish hair and face, blue eyes – and some of his father's characteristics.'

Winston Churchill, then in the 4th Hussars, was less kind, writing of his visit to Government House to his mother in dismissive fashion. In his letter of 2 January 1897 he poured scorn on the Liberal-appointed Viceroy and his family. 'The Elgins are very unpopular out here and make a very poor show after the Lansdownes. The evil that a Radical Government does lives after it. All the great offices of state have to be filled out of the scrappy remnant of the Liberal peers. And so you get Elgin Viceroy. They tell me that they are too stiff and pompous for words – and "Calcutta Society" cannot find an epithet to describe them by.' (Nevertheless, eight years later, when Churchill was a junior minister in the Liberal Campbell-Bannerman Government, Lord Elgin was his Secretary of State at the Colonial Office.) For Bessie, other things were more interesting than the arrival of a young red-haired subaltern rather too full of himself.

It was clear that Bessie preferred the quieter Henry Babington Smith, and was flattered by his showing her an article in *The Times* about the new Rowton Houses.* After the great excitement of a total eclipse of the sun on 22 January – the temperature fell by ten degrees and as many Indian spectators who could bathed in the Ganges during the ninety seconds of totality – the next important date, recorded for the first time, was 29 of January: 'Mr B.S.'s birthday'. To celebrate it, they went to Barrackpore in the afternoon. 'The mango trees and lilies and violets are so fresh after the rain. H.E. sang some songs after dinner and Mr B.S. gave me two reed pens to draw with.'

By now some of his most trivial remarks were finding their way into the diary. 'Mr B.S. told me at the dance that his horse shied at the flashes [of lightning] as he came back from dinner at the Fort.' 'I showed Mr B.S. a sketch of the blue convolvulus I think of working [embroidering] for the Maharani of Gwalior. He thinks each flower

---

* Rowton Houses were a chain of hostels built in London by the Victorian philanthropist Lord Rowton to provide decent accommodation for working men in place of the squalid lodging houses of the time. George Orwell later wrote of them enthusiastically, in *Down and Out in Paris and London*.

ought to be distinct, and he is right.' 'Mr B.S. told me he had been to the place where Tennyson wrote "Flower in the Crannied Wall".'

On Tuesday 29 March they set off on a final tour that would take them eventually to their last Season in Simla. It began with a journey of two days and three nights in the train to Pathancot on the border of Kashmir, where the railway ended; after this there was a march – in carriages, dandies* and on foot – of over 150 miles through mountainous country to Simla. It was to be completed in about three weeks.

They reached Pathancot early on the morning of Friday 1 April and set off at once to avoid the heat of the day. They stayed in bungalows and small villages or towns on the way; as they gradually climbed from Pathancot's 1,090 feet, views of the mountains were revealed.

By now 'Mr B.S.' was clearly occupying a great many of Bessie's thoughts; and to judge by his behaviour towards her, the same was true of him. Then came the intimacy of the camp in romantic scenery, with its scarlet-flowered pomegranate trees, ferns, indigo bushes, lime bushes with sweet-smelling leaves and gentians and primulas beside mountain streams – a catalyst for both Bessie and Henry Babington Smith. On Easter morning, after tea at the top of a hill, the two went to look at a nearby small temple, surrounded by fir trees and palms. Here Henry proposed to Bessie and was accepted – although even in her diary he remains 'Mr Babington Smith' until the day of the public announcement when, at last, she can allow herself to call him 'Henry'.

For Bessie, everything now had a rosy glow, from dinner en route with a retired general and his Afghan wife – 'such a feast! Asparagus, ices, entrees, everything quite as grand as in Simla' – to a fruitless search for flowers along a hillside path, 'so we sat down & then the time passed so quickly that we were nearly late for luncheon'.

Once at Simla, the concerns of the world reasserted themselves. Tongues were wagging and though Bessie agreed with her fiancé and her father that the engagement should not be announced until the replies from home had been received, 'so that it should be clear

---

* A travelling conveyance used mainly in the Himalayas, a dandy consists of a large hammock-like piece of strong cloth fixed to a pole borne on the shoulders of two or more men.

to all that H.E. is fond of him,' she found it 'horrid to be talked about'. She was also worried about deserting her father, to whom she was devoted and, with her mother so constantly ailing, who had come to rely on her companionship.

But eventually the day dawned, when the gossip and speculation surrounding her ceased. The engagement was announced in the papers on Wednesday 18 May, to be followed by a blizzard of letters of congratulation, all of which had to be answered, although she did manage to escape from time to time for some walks with Henry and a search for more flowers. Finally, after much discussion, it was decided that the wedding should take place in Simla in September rather than wait until they arrived home. For both Bessie and Henry it was a great relief that the engagement would not be prolonged. Her sisters were to be bridesmaids, together with four young friends.

'Henry looks happy, always, now,' she wrote to her Aunt Louisa, 'and has arranged what he is to wear and what to buy. He thinks a frock coat and grey-blue silk tie for the wedding, and a grey or light brown suit for going away. Mother thinks for my going away dress a fawn stuff with a white velvet toque trimmed with fowl's feathers. Then Mother thinks I should have a tailored gown of dark bluish grey lovat mixture for London and ordinary use here; a little gown of tussore silk trimmed with blue ribbons and insertions ... Henry wants to give each of the bridesmaids a turquoise brooch.' (These were made of three interlocking rings, shaped like a trefoil.)

A month before her wedding she was telling Aunt Louisa how fond her parents were of Henry. 'They love Henry and they are always so pleased to see him ... I cannot help looking back sometimes and being sorry that for so many years I have often imagined him proud or despising when he was all the time far too good for either. He naturally thinks "the kind thing" which again and again reminds me of father ... he has decided with Father and Mother that I am not to take his name Babington which is only a Christian name.'

At the opening of the annual Simla Picture Exhibition she and Henry made their first public appearance as a couple. 'H.E. drove with Her E. and I came after with Henry. He wore grey clothes and I had a white dress with small tan hat trimmed with feathers & a white ribbon to match.'

The next day, at 10.30 in the evening, as her father was playing patience, an office box was brought to him in the drawing room by one of the scarlet-coated orderlies – to disturb H.E. at such a time meant news of great importance. Lord Elgin opened the box and saw therein one telegram. Folding it and clasping it tight he left the room, saying in a low voice as he passed his wife the one word: 'Curzon!' Next day the news that Curzon was to succeed him as Viceroy was officially announced.

On Friday 16 September the staff of the Private Secretary's Office and Printing Press laid on an elaborate entertainment in honour of Bessie and Henry. There were addresses, a concert, snake charmers, a flower boy who sang and presented flowers, songs by the brides-maids and an appearance by the god and goddess of love. Henry was given a handsome salver, made a graceful reply and then *God Save the Queen* was sung.

At last the great day dawned. Thursday 22 September was a blue and cloudless day, the church was decorated with bamboos, pampas grass and big white and pink lilies. Bessie wore a white bro-cade dress draped with old Brussels lace, a Brussels lace veil held in place by a myrtle wreath, a bouquet of lilies and myrtle and the pearl necklace Henry had given her. Bride and groom left the church under the raised swords of a guard of honour from the Punjab Light Horse. The bridal party went to the reception by carriage; everyone else followed by rickshaw or on horseback.* The 700-lb wedding cake, for which 4,000 eggs had been used, was carried round on large silver plates. The presents were admired – the jewellery was not put out but there were three tables of silver things – business was suspended at the Government office and the employees given a half holiday, and the happy couple left at 5.15 in a carriage, to spend their honeymoon half at The Retreat and half at Naldera.

Henry Babington Smith turned out to be a prize Fishing Fleet catch: he went on to become one of the most successful civil serv-ants of his generation, known for his sense of unselfish service. On their return from India he and Bessie were sent immediately to Natal (he went as Treasury Representative in the South African War). There followed a variety of posts, from President of the National

---

* Only the Viceroy, and by extension his family, and the Commander-in-Chief were allowed carriages.

Bank of Turkey to Minister Plenipotentiary on Lord Reading's 1918 visit to the United States. He died at only sixty, loaded with public honours* but declined a peerage because he did not feel rich enough to support it and he wanted his nine children to make their own way in the world. Bessie survived him by more than twenty years but never remarried, dying at sixty-six.

---

* He became Sir Henry Babington Smith, GBE, CH, KCB, CSI.

9

'There are so many "Ladies"'

Viceregal Entertainments

Viceregal entertaining was of a glamour unknown to the courts of Edward VII, George V and George VI, let alone that of Queen Victoria, thanks to the size and vistas of the viceregal palaces, the plethora of servants in their scarlet and gold uniforms moving noiseless and impassive among the guests, the scents of the flowers, the brilliance of the light and, above all, the presence of the princes.* Their dark skins gleaming in satin coats with jewelled buttons, diamond and emerald aigrettes that flashed in the light of the candelabra adorning their silk puggris, and swathed in ropes of pearls and diamonds worn with a regal insouciance, they were figures of dazzling exotica. 'Pearls as big as thrushes' eggs, uncut emeralds of enormous size lay on their chests like green lakes,' wrote Gertrude Bell, one of the guests at the 1903 Durbar. Less flatteringly, of the dust she said: 'You eat it, you drink it, you live in it.'

The greatest 'party' during the time of the Raj was undoubtedly the Coronation Durbar of 1903, held to celebrate the coronation of King Edward VII and Queen Alexandra as Emperor and Empress of India. It was devised in meticulous detail – as he did everything – by the then Viceroy, Lord Curzon. It lasted two weeks and was a dazzling, dramatic display of pomp and power, made possible by the precision of superb organisation and split-second timing.

---

* The princely states had remained loyal to Britain throughout the Mutiny and, in return for this steadfastness, the various maharajas, rajahs, ranas, nizams, gaekwars and nawabs continued as rulers under the paramountcy of the British Crown.

In a few short months at the end of 1902, a deserted plain was transformed into an elaborate tented city, threaded with a temporary light railway stopping at sixteen 'stations' to bring the crowds of spectators out from Delhi, containing a post office with its own stamp, telephone and telegraphic facilities, a variety of stores, a police force with specially designed uniform, a hospital, magistrates' court and complex sanitation, drainage and electric light installations. Tents, many with fireplaces, were laid out in streets that were outlined by plants in pots and lit by electric light. There were three tent cities, the Viceroy's, the Commander-in-Chief's, and that of the Bombay Presidency.

The ceremonies began on 29 December 1902, with a parade of elephants (the actual Durbar Day was New Year's Day 1903). Then came rehearsals, reviews and parades, foot soldiers marching, drilling and presenting arms, mule batteries and teams of big white bullocks pulling guns, softly plodding camels, the cavalry galloping and wheeling, the glint of weapons, the gold and silver cannons of Baroda dragged by white bullocks caparisoned in gold and silver, rearing elephants, horses that walked on their hind legs and the flash of brilliant uniforms glimpsed through clouds of dust.

Ruby Madden, then aged twenty-six, was a fascinated but dispassionate observer. She had already been to an evening reception at Government House ('I wore a black and white dress with cerise roses on the corsage'), where she was introduced to the Maharaja of Mysore. 'Quite young, with the most exquisite emeralds and diamonds you ever saw. He had a collar round his neck and then chains to his waist of huge pear-shaped stones, an aigrette in his turban and armbands to match and he was dressed in yellow satin. He speaks English beautifully and is so good looking.'

She had also had a ride on an elephant, climbing up a silver ladder on to a gold-clad one that belonged to the Maharaja of Kashmir, and she admired the bearing and splendid uniforms – white frock coats, glistening with gold embroidery, blue cummerbunds and turbans with diamond aigrettes – of the Imperial Cadet Corps, the sons of the Indian aristocracy, on their black chargers bedecked with the skins of snow leopards.

Yet despite their looks, wealth, power, breeding and exquisite courtesy, neither the Maharaja of Mysore nor any other prince could hope to pass through the portals of an English club – although they were welcome guests in viceregal palaces and Government houses. The feeling that the British were the superior race was so strong that it even marred Curzon's Durbar.

Some time before, three British troopers of the 9th Lancers had beaten an Indian cook to death. When Curzon heard of this he was furious and when the men were shielded by their officers he became even angrier and insisted that they were punished. The 9th Lancers were a smart and popular regiment, and public sympathy for them, even in England, was such that there was a general outcry. In a Minute on this, Curzon wrote: 'If it be said "Don't wash your dirty linen in public". I reply "Don't have dirty linen to wash!"'

Curzon was undeterred by the general sentiments against him and the criticism that he was 'on the black man's side'; and he and the Commander-in-Chief, Lord Kitchener, decided to withdraw leave privileges for all the 9th Lancers for six months – a smarting public humiliation for such a proud and honoured regiment. There was also talk by the military authorities of not allowing them to take part in the durbar but, magnanimously, Curzon overruled this ban.

It resulted in a shaming display of disregard for natural justice and poor manners on the part of the British spectators. In the words of Dorothy Menpes:* 'Just before the 9th Lancers passed, the atmosphere was electric. As the regiment came into view the whole stand rose and cheered itself hoarse; women waved their handkerchiefs … men flourished their sticks and shouted bravados … There is no doubt about it, the fact of the Viceroy's guests standing up and cheering showed exceedingly little tact … this was hardly a fitting moment to give vent to their feelings. It was a distinct stab at the Viceroy … He did what from his standpoint he knew to be absolutely right. For his own guests to choose that moment to insult him seemed hard and ungenerous. Let me add that Curzon had spent £3,000 of his personal money to host these low people at the Durbar.' (Curzon had the gift of facing embarrassment with equanimity: when he heard that on the last night of the durbar seven soldiers from a Welsh regiment had beaten a native policeman to death outside Delhi, he merely remarked to his wife Mary: 'It is

* Author of *The Durbar*, published by A. and C. Black in 1903.

a pity that we cannot have another Review for them to receive a popular ovation.'*

Although most people arrived well beforehand, the durbar festivities – for that is how they were generally seen – began after the opening ceremony on 29 December 1902, with the state entry by elephant into Delhi, the Curzons themselves sitting in a gold how-dah underneath a gold umbrella. There were cavalry and gymnastic displays, bands, parades and polo matches, with dinners and dances given by notables encamped in 'tent city' in the evening (it must be remembered that Eastern tents were so luxurious and sophisticated that Napoleon had one of his rooms at Malmaison decorated like the inside of one, with drums for occasional tables). There were fire-work displays, special medals were struck, and dinners and dances galore.

Ruby Madden was invited to one of the grandest dinners. It was given by Lord Kitchener, then at the height of his reputation. The victorious General of the South African War, he had been heaped with honours and he remained – in the eyes of the public – the pre-eminent military figure until his death by drowning in 1916. 'I robed myself in my best black with velvet in my hair which went up rather nicely and white roses,' she wrote on 23 December. 'I looked quite nice and Claude [her brother-in-law] and I drove off in our Victoria, he looking a love in uniform.

'I was opposite [Lord Kitchener] so had a good look at him. He is just like his pictures but with a dreadful squint in his left eye. It turns right out when he is talking at you. It fascinated me so I could hardly listen to what he was saying. The dinner was excel-lent and we ate off lovely silver plates, used for the first time … The candle sticks were all gold and huge urns and salt cellars were all gold, presentations from the different cities. He has all the late Queen's Indian servants. They came to him and said they thought she would like them to serve him. They are all dressed in white and gold with a huge coronet and "K" on their chests.' Later in the even-ing Lord Kitchener asked her to sing – there was even a grand piano in the tent – and came to stand beside her at the piano, listening. 'He thanked me so nicely. It was a most successful evening and I enjoyed myself hugely.'

* Quoted by David Gilmour in *Curzon*.

After the durbar came the state ball. Here, according to Ruby Madden, the rajahs looked like walking jewellers' shops – one, in the Imperial Cadet Corps, could not wear his jewels himself so brought with him an attendant dressed in yellow satin to display them instead.

Although British India was ruled from Calcutta up to 1911, all of the three important durbars were held in Delhi. With its 3,000-year-old history and ancient buildings and its past as capital of the Moghul empire, it was the obvious choice for these later imperialists.

The first durbar, held over a fortnight during December 1876, marked the proclamation of Queen Victoria as Empress of India (on New Year's Day 1877), and was largely an official occasion, although attended by about 100,000 people, all eager for spectacle. Again, it was a tent city, with the encampment of the Viceroy (Lord Lytton) illuminated by gas. Sixty-three princes were present as well as several hundred nobles. After the proclamation, which took place on an open plain, there was a *feu de joie* that caused the elephants to bolt, scattering the crowd in all directions.

Twenty years later, the Queen's Diamond Jubilee was celebrated in Simla, where the Viceroy, now Lord Elgin and his family, had moved during the hot weather (the actual Jubilee Day was Tuesday 22 June 1897).

Gifts were presented by deputations from Bombay, Lahore, Calcutta, Benares, Allahabad. Next day attention was directed to Viceregal Lodge. 'A dais was arranged in the big drawing room, which was covered with a gold carpet, and two chairs of state were behind,' wrote Lady Elisabeth Bruce. 'Everyone who comes to the reception tonight is to pass by and shake hands with their Exes [the Viceroy and his wife]. Then they can go into the ballroom and look at the caskets presented by the deputations. The English people shake hands and pass by; the natives are all to be announced ... Her E wore her blue velvet gown with the tiara, diamond necklaces and order and looked very lovely indeed. She stood beside H.E. who was in uniform.'

The third grand durbar was the Coronation Durbar of 1911, attended by the newly crowned King George V and his Queen, Mary – the only one at which a ruling Sovereign was present. For this, a twenty-five-square-mile 'coronation city' of tents, many of the greatest luxury, housed potentates, participants and their visitors. There were dining tents, drawing room tents lined with pink brocades, smoking room, billiards room and banqueting room tents. By now motor cars were popular; along the forty miles of dirt road – covered with a thick layer of black oil to damp down the inevitable dust – drove the fleets of cars belonging to the grander princes.

Here Lilah Wingfield, accustomed to the conventions and etiquette of the British social Season, was a guest, with an ayah instead of a lady's maid. 'We each had a large tent to ourselves, which was luxuriously furnished. We had luncheon in the mess tent. Roads and railways built, post offices and shops erected and all for ten days' festivities this huge amount of money has been spent.' Everyone brought their finery: one visitor noted that for the finals of numerous polo matches the onlookers wore 'Ascot frocks', as they watched and listened to the massed bands of 2,000-odd performers.

'There are a good many women in camp, nearly all visitors, as few of the officers are married,' wrote Lilah. 'I heard jackals howling at night …' The Delhi weather varied daily from hot to cold. 'We take thick overcoats and furs with us when we go out in the afternoon with a boiling sun overhead and wearing a linen frock. It got bitterly cold when the sun went down at five o'clock. Basil [the brother of her friend Sylvia] and I call each other by our Christian names now, he treats me like another sister and it is delightful being able to treat him with no formality.'

One night they were asked to a dance by Lady Bute. '[It] was only from 9.30 until 12 as everyone had to get up early to be in their places for the King's State Entry into Delhi. I found an old friend, Ronnie Fellowes, and I danced the first dance with him and he brought up two other men whom he said wanted to be introduced. Lady Bute introduced me to the Maharaja, a slim boy of about twenty-one, gorgeously dressed in pale blue satin brocade, pale blue satin trousers turban and wonderful jewels.'

Once again, Lilah found herself enjoying the experience – common to so many Fishing Fleet girls – of being mobbed by eager young men. So much so that, after the State Reception she and her friend Judy went on to a dance at the club ('with a Mrs Starkie, who promised to chaperone us'), she received a declaration from one of them. But the level-headed Lilah was not swayed.

'Jorrocks *thought* he was in love with me and said so but I told him it was only moonlight and romance and the spell of the East, which offended him rather I'm afraid!'

For the State Procession she and Sylvia had good seats outside the Fort, with overhead shelter. 'It started at 11.30 and took two and a half hours to pass. The King, looking rather small and insignificant, rode between Field Marshals, just in front of the Queen's carriage, and behind for miles and miles stretched native troops and English Lancers and Dragoons, in all their varied brilliance of uniforms, with the sun glinting on swords and gold trappings.' Two days before Durbar Day, there was a State Church Parade – 'miles and miles of troops in white helmets and scarlet tunics and many coloured uniforms and a long line of red carpet to the dais where the King and Queen sat throughout the service'.

Then came Durbar Day itself. The huge arena was lined with thousands upon thousands of people in brilliant uniforms. The procession was headed by trumpeters, glittering with gold thread and blowing silver trumpets, on grey horses, and heralds – 'like walking kings of cards'. The King and Queen, in robes of purple velvet and diamond crowns, drove in open carriages escorted by the Imperial Cadet Corps, the sons of maharajas, rajahs and the highest nobles. 'Their uniform is quite lovely – white tunics with lots of gold lace, pale blue and gold scarves round their waists with a pale blue turban with lots of gold, gold aigrettes,' wrote Maude Bingham, another guest at the durbar. 'They all rode fine horses so it was one of the finest sights of the entry ... retainers carrying flags, musical instruments, arms of all sorts – old guns, blunderbusses, muskets, bayonet guns. The Begum of Bhopal, the only woman who reigned over a princely state, got an ovation. Her retainers were in brown with white and gold sashes and brown, white and gold turbans. She was strictly veiled, only little eyeholes.'

Arriving at the Durbar Pavilion to a 101-gun salute and a *feu de joie*, the King and Queen proceeded along a red carpet, gold and crimson umbrellas held over their heads and eight little pages holding their purple velvet trains, with Lords Durham and Shaftesbury walking backwards in front of them the whole way. Inside the pavilion was a raised dais; here the King and Queen sat on solid gold thrones beneath a crimson canopy held up by ropes of gold, with the Viceroy and Lady Hardinge and other important people on their right and left. Several small pages, the sons of rajahs, stood on the steps of the dais, as the native princes came up one by one to pay homage; the elderly Maharaja of Kashmir, in black silk and gold, kissed his sword three times, then laid it at the King's feet.

It was at this durbar that it was announced that the seat of government would now be Delhi rather than Calcutta. 'The transfer of the capital from Calcutta to Delhi ... was an absolute surprise and one heard whispers of approval and disapproval going on all round,' recorded Maude Bingham, noting that 'Everything was so well arranged we got our motor in half an hour and were back at our hotel by 3.30!! That was far better than getting away from the Opera at home! The crowd, we were told, trooped on to the ground afterwards in thousands to kiss the red carpet and ground on which they [the King and Queen] had trod.'

The hierarchy of the Raj was so well established that even Lord Dufferin, who loved parties – at one fancy dress ball he dressed up so successfully as an Arab that even his wife failed to recognise him – found himself writing to a friend: 'It is an odd thing to say but dullness is certainly the characteristic of an Indian Viceroy's existence. All the people who surround him are younger than himself; he has no companions or playfellows; even the pretty women who might condescend to cheer him it is better for him to keep at a distance.'

For a viceregal couple, the pomp and circumstance with which they were surrounded could at times be overwhelming; when the little Curzon daughters went out with their flock of attendants, a special policeman was deputed to carry their dolls. All the principal viceregal servants wore scarlet and gold; the men who waited at table had long red cloth tunics, white trousers, bare feet, white or red and gold sashes wound round their waists and white turbans, with gold-embroidered waistcoats for the higher-ranked ones and a 'D' and a coronet embroidered on the chests of the lower ones. 'All the "housemaids" are men with long red tunics, turbans and gold braid – oh! so smart – while every now and then a creature very lightly clad in a white cotton rag makes his appearance and seems to feel as much at home here as his smarter brethren do,' noted Lady Dufferin in 1884. 'He is probably a gardener and he most likely presents you with a bouquet of violets.'

When the Viceroy was guest rather than host, there was even more of a scramble to get things right and maintain the rigid security then enforced. When Lord Minto paid a visit to the Governor of Bombay in 1909, Jim Du Boulay, Chief Executive of the Bombay Presidency, wrote: 'I have to spend weary and useless hours in examining and correcting programmes for his official arrival and for the arrival and reception of various Chiefs [Princes] who count their guns and watch their ceremonies with lynx eyes.'

Jim's wife Freda described the measures taken for the Viceroy's safety. 'This place is arranged as though we were going to be besieged: sixty-two policemen in the grounds, two companies of soldiers on guard. Quantities of native and English detectives and some of the bodyguard, while there are boats rowing round the whole place on the three sides of the grounds which overlook the sea. My room and the verandas round Lady Eileen Elliot's [the eldest Minto daughter] and Lady Antrim's, who are in the same block with me, have sentries all day and all night, and as the heat is intense and I am obliged to open all the windows and doors, there is nothing the sentries can't tell you about the details of my toilette.'

What struck her even more forcibly were the intricacies of the caste system. 'One "caste" arranges the flowers, another cleans the plate, a third puts the candles in the candlesticks but a fourth lights them; one fills a jug of water while it requires either a higher or a lower man to pour it out. The man who cleans your boots would not condescend to hand you a cup of tea, and the person who makes your bed would be dishonoured were he to take any other part in doing your room. The consequence is that, instead of one neat housemaid at work, when you go up to "my lady's chamber" you find seven or eight men in various stages of dress each putting a hand to some little thing which needs to be done.'

Others had no difficulty enjoying the lavish hospitality of the Sovereign's representative. Ruby Madden, for whom who wore what – in particular herself – was central to any evening's entertainment, adored these evenings. 'Wore my white crepe de chine, with white roses and fern leaves in my hair. Captain Cameron looked a dear in the mess kit of the Imperial Cadet Corps, dark blue shell jacket with pale blue facings and overalls with white cloth stripe and narrow blue one. The same on the cap, with a wide top.'

After the Byculla Ball on 18 February 1903, she described gardens 'lit up like fairyland and flowers and palms banked everywhere. About 400 people were there but dancing was quite easy in the huge dining room. There were some lovely frocks, Lady Jenkins's the most wonderful from Paris! White chiffon embroidered with green and purple grapes and jewelled to represent dewdrops … I had the whole twenty-three dances booked almost at once and had some good turns with Mr Scott.' As Mr Scott was ostensibly the cavalier servente of a predatory married woman this must have been particularly satisfactory, especially when, at a reception at Government House, 'Mr Basil Scott and I sat on a sofa and talked until it was time to go home. Mrs Chitty was there too but he must have given her the slip!'

Little changed through the years, least of all the ceremonial surrounding viceroys and governors, and the preoccupation with how to dress for one of these important dinners or receptions. In 1931 Meriel McKnight, visiting family friends Lady Noyes and her husband Sir Frank, a member of the Viceroy's Council in Delhi, was writing of a viceregal garden party on 15 November 1931:

'Enid [Lady Noyes] wore a Wedgwood blue georgette with silvery embroideries, a large and becoming black hat and light stockings and shoes. F had the grey morning suit and a fascinating grey topper, a white slip in his waistband and spats. I put on the cream lace, with my black hat and shoes and Enid lent me a black georgette sunshade so I was quite happy and never thought about myself the whole time. The dresses were mostly of the patterned georgette or lace with coatees … We processed up a marble staircase having been directed that way by a friendly aide-de-camp in navy blue and gold braid (coats to the knee).'

Lutyens's great palace, the largest residence of any head of state in the world, was a truly imperial building, with its grilles, dome, fountains, statues of elephants, loggias and courtyards. On the stairs, as Merial entered, were 'men in scarlet-coated uniform and turbans with pikes standing at intervals like blocks of wood, they are not supposed to move their eyes, all Indians.'

'We reached the Library with books, chairs done in tomatoey-coloured leather of the loveliest shade, marble inlaid yellow floor, a huge globe at which we whiled away the time until we were called into procession', she wrote. 'Their Excellencies stood in the Durbar Hall, a really magnificent marble circular hall with a dome that can be opened to the sky. It is open by arches to the surrounding corridors in which stood scarlet soldiers etc. You walked down two steps on to the floor.

'[Their Excellencies] were standing in front of gilded chairs with servants and aides behind, he was in morning dress and she in a gay flowered chiffon and hat to match. Our names were read out. E and F had a most warm welcome and quite a stoppage of the procession to hear of their time at home. Then my name rang out and I had to step forward, shake hands with him first and curtsey and about three steps further and the same with her. They were most cordial ... the band in scarlet coats and white topis were playing pretty well all the time in the garden but as we went in they were on the balcony behind the Durbar Hall so that our procession was done to soft music. Their Exes came down into the garden and talked to the people.'

Punctually at 5.45 Their Excellencies walked up the centre of the garden path, preceded by two aides-de-camp and followed by another, through their lined-up guests, bowing to them all and saying goodbye. The male guests bowed, the women bobbed a half-curtsey. When they reached the door of the house the viceregal couple stood there while *God Save the King* was played, then turned and walked indoors – the signal for their guests to leave. This took time, as although it was only a comparatively small party, there were many cars.

Protocol was just as evident at a dinner party on 28 November. 'We were received at the door by ADCs who showed us the way to remove our coats. Then we sailed up the marble staircase with the gorgeous bodyguard on either side and along corridors to show the way – black top boots, white trousers, scarlet coats to the knee and huge black, blue and gold turbans on top. We went into the drawing room and by degrees were all ranged on one side ...'.

When the Viceroy gave a state banquet, formality was even greater. Behind each chair the length of the huge table a servant stood motionless, his hands raised to his forehead in salute until the Viceroy took his seat. With their evening dresses, women wore long white kid gloves almost to the shoulder, with a row of pearl buttons at the wrist; during dinner itself, these buttons were undone, the hand slipped through the opening and, if possible, the flapping empty 'hand' of the glove tucked back into the glove arm. It was the same at balls at which the Viceroy was present, with the difference that once the viceregal couple had left or retired, ladies were permitted to pull off their long gloves, usually with a sigh of relief. When the Vicereine swept up the ladies at the end of dinner, each as she left had to make a full curtsey in the doorway to the Viceroy,* who had risen to his feet and made her a 'Court bow' (from the neck only) in response.

It could be said that the Viceroy's House in Delhi, Lutyens's grandly impressive creation, demanded the splendour and state that attended the Viceroy: it was larger than Versailles, with a porch capable of receiving a ruler on his biggest elephant, howdah on top, thirty-seven splashing fountains and wonderful gardens that required a staff of more than 450 (some of them simply to keep birds away). Inside was a hundred-foot dining room where, in Lord Irwin's day, dessert was served on the priceless gold plate he had brought with him. Even the door handles, shaped like resting lions with crowns on their heads, exuded imperial opulence, while behind the scenes it resembled a small self-contained city, with its own bakery, tailor's shop, dispensary, operating theatre and hospital ward; outside was a swimming pool, a nine-hole golf course, cricket pitch, eight tennis courts and stables and kennels for the horses and hounds of the Royal Delhi Hunt.

'One would mount the long flight of red stone steps,' wrote Bethea Field when asked to dinner there. 'Steps flanked by the troops of the Viceroy's bodyguard – Sikhs in their glorious uniform with silver spurs on their high boots, beards perfectly trimmed into a band under the chin for no Sikh may cut his hair. Such handsome dark faces and above, a turban of pale blue muslin so perfectly wound that each fold was *exactly* half an inch above the other. They stood, with their lances at rest, as still as statues. They may have cast an eye at the British women and their low bosom dresses beneath them but it was not obvious.

'At the top of the long stairway we were greeted by the aides-de-camp. Charming, handsome young men in their various mess dress.

---

* In a custom started in 1905. It was not until the viceroyalty of Lord Irwin (1926–31) that, after gaining the necessary consent from George V, this was changed to the practice of the British Court, where only the ladies on either side of the King made a full curtsey.

They ushered us in to the reception hall where we stood with our backs against the walls to await the arrival of "Their Excellencies". This was heralded by a fanfare of trumpets from a gallery. We all held our invitation cards and as the aide preceded the Viceroy and his wife round the hall, he took them and announced us – each one. The men bowed and the women curtsied. Then we followed into the Banqueting Hall, each to his or her allotted place.

'The food was handed round by scarlet-clothed Viceregal servants wearing white cotton gloves so as not to offend the Indian guests. At the end of the meal, the Vicereine got up and led out the ladies. She curtsied first to H. E. and then we, in pairs, curtsied as we followed her to the drawing room. It was a time to chat together or pay a visit to the cloakroom. H. E. and the men joined us for coffee and after a decent interval when the sexes interchanged, Their Exes retired. We were given whisky and sodas and relaxed in the care of the aides. Not for too long however. As their glances grew cool, we scampered back down the long red stairway – now no longer guarded by the handsome soldiers, to our cars and our homes.'

The highlight of the week was the Viceroy's Ball, with its gorgeous setting – black crystal panels lined the walls of the ballroom, with light brackets of Kashmir crystal carved into tulip shapes – and the presence of the princes, festooned with waist-length ropes of pearls, rubies and emeralds, diamond aigrettes in their jewel-hung turbans, wrists and fingers sparkling with more gems. They were popular with Lady Willingdon (her husband was Viceroy 1931–6), who clapped them on the back and called them by their Christian names.

One step down from viceregal entertaining was an invitation from one of the governors of the three presidencies (Madras, Bengal and Bombay). Government House in Madras was a huge white colonial building, to which Katherine Welford was often asked, girls being scarce. 'Dinner there was a very formal occasion. On arrival the car would draw up under a portico and drop us at the foot of shallow red-carpeted stairs leading up to the entrance hall. We would be handed our dance programmes, also a diagram of where we were to be seated, by a servant dressed in white with a scarlet and gold turban and cummerbund. It was always a matter of great interest to see who was going to take you in to dinner, as he would be sitting on your right.

'Then we would be greeted by an ADC and passed on to a reception room to stand in line to shake hands with the Governor [Sir George Stanley, brother of Lord Derby] and his wife, after which they would come round and talk to everyone. I was always impressed how the ADCs – there were three of them – remembered everybody's name. You always wore long white gloves, with sixteen buttons, for dinner at GH – but then, you always wore stockings when you went out, no matter how hot, and a hat or, quite often, a topi. Bands played *Tea for Two, Always, Mountain Greenery* on palace lawns.'

No story of viceregal entertaining would be complete without mention of the most famous faux pas of the inter-war years. The Viceroy had his own orchestra, which used to play throughout dinner, and once when he recognised a tune but could not put a name to it and nor could anyone else, an ADC was sent to ask the bandmaster for the song's title. When the ADC came back everyone was talking so he patiently waited his turn. Finally the babble of conversation ceased and the young man seized his chance. Leaning forward and gazing at the Viceroy, he announced into the sudden silence: 'I Will Remember your Kisses, your Excellency, when you Have Forgotten Mine.'

'I told him it was only the moonlight'

Courtship

'Broadly speaking, European women in India may be divided into two classes: those who are or have been married, and those who most assuredly will marry,' wrote Claude Brown in 1927.

Courtship in the Raj took various forms. From the point of view of the husband-hunting Fishing Fleet girl, single men also fell into two categories: those who had passed the age barrier after which marriage was permitted, and financially possible, and – a much larger category – those who had not.

As few Raj bachelors were allowed to marry until they were around thirty, husbands were nearly always quite a few years older than their wives, an age difference so usual that at one time its desirability was firmly embedded in the national psyche. 'You ask my age,' wrote Lieutenant Leslie Lavie to his fiancée Flossie Ross on 10 February 1896. 'I was 27 on January 3rd last, so that I've got exactly four months the better of you. I suppose this is alright; some people have a fad that the man should be older than the lady, but provided they like one another, I don't see much what age has to do with it, do you, darling? My mother used to say there should be six or eight years difference, and I've had lots of discussions with her about it, without either of us convincing the other ...'.

The converse of this was that girls were supposed to marry young, with only a few years of bloom before falling victim to the dread phrase 'on the shelf'. When Minnie Wood's sister turned down a suitor in 1859 Minnie's comment was more of a warning: 'She had better take care as she is twenty-two in a few days and could be an old maid!' A few years later another young woman was noting that 'if a girl did not marry or at any rate become engaged by twenty she was not likely to marry at all'.*

The male age barrier meant that, however attractive the dashing young cavalry subaltern who escorted a marriage-minded young woman on a (suitably chaperoned) moonlight picnic, he had to be regarded as nothing more than a glamorous playmate. Marriage, for him, was well in the future – unless he wished to send in his papers and give up his Army career.

Although many of these parties undoubtedly seethed with unrequited lust – for young, extremely fit, women-less young men the influx of these girls must at times have been overwhelming – behaviour was seldom 'bad'. Although so distant from home – a factor that often loosens the moral straitjacket – there was none of the sexual free-for-all that characterised the Happy Valley set in the Kenya of the 1930s. For one thing, in Kenya hedonistic individuals were just that – individuals – responsible only to themselves and, perhaps, husband, wife or lover, whereas in the Raj almost everyone was responsible to a direct superior.

The moral climate of Victorian England held sway among those who governed, as did the belief that sexual misbehaviour would tarnish the impeccable image of probity they struggled to maintain. Another, equally powerful, factor was that during the years of enforced celibacy young men were either up country and working all hours or in a closed community where transgressions would be spotted and suppressed by (safely married) senior officers. But the main reason for the unblemished moral behaviour of the vast majority of the Fishing Fleet was that from the inception of the Raj in 1858 and up to the outbreak of the Second World War gently born young women were brought up in an ambiance where sex was never even discussed, let alone condoned.

As one of them told me: 'At seventeen I was so ignorant I thought you could start a baby if someone kissed you. The thought of becoming pregnant was held over our heads like a flaming sword.' The stigma of giving birth to an illegitimate baby was so great that most such children were given away for adoption, and the girl herself thrust out of sight where possible. With premarital

* Quoted by Francesca Beauman in *Shapely Ankle Preferr'd*.

chastity thus the required social norm, few men with pretensions to honour or decency would attempt to seduce one of these sheltered creatures – and so destroy her chances in the all-important marriage stakes.

Plenty of men flocked round Ruby Madden but she was a forthright, independent creature who knew her own mind and would not be swayed by the romance of her surroundings in a distant land. 'I rode in the morning at 6.30 and enjoyed it except that Major Pollard, poor little man, would propose to me and I have seen it coming for some time and tried to avoid it by talking hard about mundane subjects such as "should you take cold baths in India?" but all to no good. Poor little man, he seemed very much in earnest …'.

Poor Major Pollard did not give up easily. At a fancy dress ball soon afterwards he stalked up to Ruby looking, as she wrote to her mother, 'a speaking likeness of the lunatic in Dotty Ville who thought himself a poached egg or a rooster … he is rather short and fat and had a furious red beard and moustache glued on very insecurely. Mustard-coloured tights … a doublet of sorts slashed in every direction with maroon satin and to crown all a huge felt hat with rather a coal scuttle tendency, presuming to be covered with flowing ostrich plumes, instead of which there were three miserable bones, two standing out at the back and one in front like the feeler of a cockroach. I never recognised him till nearly the end of the evening when he came up to me as I was talking to Lady Clarke and asked in a sepulchral voice, for fear of blowing off his beard if I had remembered to keep his dance.' She hadn't – 'and the feathers wore a hurt expression as he stalked away'. It was the end of Major Pollard.

Ruby had been determined from the start not to marry and settle down in India, one probable reason for her 'hands-off' attitude. For everyone else to be surrounded by eager young men was a heady experience. Lilah Wingfield, in India for the Coronation Durbar of 1912, wrote of a dance to which Lady Bute had asked her and her friend Sylvia Brooke: 'It is a pleasant sensation to be so much in demand as one is at dances out here! India being a country full of men, the few women find themselves very popular.' It is a sentiment that recurs again and again in the journal of her visit to India.

At the same time, so rigid was the hierarchy of the Raj that even flirting with a girl that a senior officer had his eye on was thought to be risky. 'The first part of the time the boys in the regiment rather avoided me if anything and I wondered why,' wrote Lilah Wingfield in December 1911. 'It appears that because I was the only girl in camp who was the Colonel's guest and *no* relation or friend of any of the other officers they had got it into their heads that the Colonel must be in love with me and that we were shortly to become engaged! ... they all looked on me for a certainty as their Colonel's future wife and as such treated me with due respect and did not talk to me much when he was present, as I suppose they thought he would not like it!' When Lilah heard this rumour she asked a friend, married to a brother officer, to tell the young officers that there was no truth in this supposition 'and from that time on they ceased to look at me as another man's property and no longer kept up the avoiding me and the deep respect'.

In virtually all Fishing Fleet flirtations, a kiss was about the summit of fantasy for most girls (if only because many of them had no clear vision of what could happen next). Betsy Anderson was typical. In Neemuch she had soon met a young man in the Royal Artillery for whom she had fallen, but who had been sent to a station elsewhere.

It was from him, when she was eighteen, that she received her first kiss. It was a matter of huge moment. 'The Gunners we had met at Neemuch were now stationed not far off. There was to be a big dance and I lived in anticipation of seeing my first love again,' she recalled later. 'To my joy he was amongst the subalterns who had been invited and arrived looking resplendent in full-dress uniform. I was in a transport of delight as he danced with me most of the evening.'

Fortunately for Betsy her mother, usually a vigilant chaperone, was also a beauty, and so much in demand that Betsy and her sub-altern managed to evade her and slip into the cool garden. 'It was bathed in blue moonlight and filled with the intoxicating scents of jasmine and frangipani and I felt as if I was going to swoon when he gave me my first kiss as I think I imagined myself as an Ethel M. Dell heroine – the only love stories I had, surreptitiously, read. It seems ludicrous these days,' she wrote later, 'that the stirring of first passion which this evoked made me feel guilty and unable to tell my mother in whom I usually confided.' But there was no Ethel M. Dell ending: when Betsy later met her Gunner he told her he had become engaged to the girl he had left behind.*

The repression engendered by years of celibacy and, often, loneliness, coupled with the shortage of nubile young women and the lack of opportunity for meeting them, meant that frequently a man of marriageable age would seize the first chance he got to acquire one of these desirable creatures. Even in the 1930s, this was sometimes a matter of mere weeks. Patience Winifred Horne, born on 24 September 1910, became engaged to her future husband within six weeks of landing in Calcutta. He had spotted her immediately but she could not remember him. 'It was the day after I had arrived, a Sunday, and I went to the cinema with Tommy,' she wrote to him. 'I remember a party sitting in the corner but not you I'm afraid.'

Patience was the daughter of the Reverend Francis Horne, a hunting parson (though he would never hunt during Lent), brought up in the large Georgian rectory of Drinkstone, near Bury St Edmunds. Although the family hunted, and lived in a large house, money was tight – country parsons have never been well paid – and all there was went on her brothers' education, first at prep school and then at Charterhouse and Stowe. Patience, who longed for an education, taught herself to read, and used to pray each night that she would be sent to school.

She grew up pretty, clever, an excellent rider and county-level tennis player. Although she was presented in July 1930, she did not 'do the Season' and the chance to meet suitable young men in the heart of rural Suffolk was limited. The result was that at the age of twenty-three she was considered to be 'on the shelf' and sent off to India in October 1933 on what her family called 'the marriage boat'. There she stayed with family friends, Aline and Hugh ('Bodie') Aldous and their daughter Louise in Poona – Hugh was the son of Bury St Edmunds hunting neighbours.

She scored an immediate success, with young men flocking round. 'I'm coming back from the wars on Saturday temporarily until Sunday. Will you have a party with me on Saturday night and do something with me on every occasion on which you are not doing something with someone else? Darling I love you. A toi Johnny' wrote a young soldier in the XIX Hyderabad Regiment.

* Betsy herself went on to make a happy marriage, described later.

And again: 'Loveliest Patience, are you doing anything after dinner on Saturday? If not will you dance at Murator's and Louise? They have a reasonable band there on Saturday night and some amusingly frightful people. I want to dance with you, in fact I think if I don't dance with you I shall pass quietly away. Desperately, Johnny.'

Another proposal came from 'Ian' on 30 November, only a few weeks after she had arrived. 'Have your feelings changed at all regarding me? Please answer this question soon ... Patience darling, is there any chance for me. Do you still love someone, or have your feelings changed?'

By Christmas 1933, a mere five weeks after she had arrived, she was engaged, but neither to Johnny, Ian, nor Tommy. Her fiancé was Captain Harold Edwin Collett-White, born on 28 September 1902. His father worked for the Indian railways but he was a soldier; he had been to Woolwich, become a Gunner officer and then transferred to the Royal Horse Artillery. When Patience met him he was stationed at Bangalore, as ADC to General Jeffreys, the GOC.

There is no record of how the others felt but Tommy took it on the chin. 'I saw Tommy last night at the Club, he was just back from camp for one day and congratulated me very nicely and hoped we should be very happy,' Patience told her fiancé. 'We left him sitting there saying he was going to get so drunk he would forget me and as he had had five brandy and sodas in about ten minutes it looked as if he was going to succeed. A ridiculous fuss about me.'

Collett, as Patience always called him ('I can't do Harold') was tall, dark, good-looking and much sought after. 'Mrs Ainley was very amusing,' runs one of Patience's letters to her fiancé. 'She said the girls of Poona were jealous of me for being engaged to you as you were supposed to be the nicest and most difficult man to catch in Poona!' Mrs Ainley appears to have been right, as on 7 December the newly engaged Patience was writing: 'My darling Collett, I wonder whether you are sitting in the train now or if you missed it! I hope you are thinking of me and not feeling worried about my parents' consent or regretting your hasty action. I was hauled out by the noble Louise the minute you had gone to play badminton to keep me from crying too much.

'We met Yola Jenkyn on the way down and told her the great news ... she was so horrid about it I came to the conclusion she was jealous, and her saying she didn't like you didn't make much impression on me except one of extreme rage ... I really was so angry I couldn't speak because you see when I said: "I'm engaged", she said: "Who to?" and when I said you she said: "Good heavens, you can't marry that man." I said: "Why not?" She said: "He's the most awful little pipsqueak."

'So Louise said in a determined voice: "One more word and I push you into the ditch" and she said: "Oh well, I'm engaged you know only I can't announce it yet," so we realised she was overcome with jealousy, which I don't wonder at. I should be very jealous of anyone who was going to marry you.'

Patience and Collett decided to get married in England so that her family could meet him. She sailed for home on 9 March, on the *City of Simla* ('only a month and we shall be together again. I am longing for it. Lots of love and all my kisses'), straightaway running into an old friend. 'The first person I saw was my dear friend Stewart Brown and he started teasing me about you and the successful fishing fleet!'

Money, as so often in the Raj, was a worry. Even more than in the English countryside, in India horses were both a focus and a preoccupation – and they were expensive animals both to buy and keep. Another letter from *City of Simla* shows that Patience, like a good Raj wife-to-be, had got her priorities right. 'We will do without anything for the sake of the horses, won't we? I don't mind doing anything as long as you are nice to me always. If I have you and a horse nothing much else matters, does it?'

Hunting was also a priority with Valerie Pridmore Riley, born on 1 April 1913, a Fishing Fleet girl who lived in Somerset and, unlike most of the Fleet, only reluctantly went out to India. After leaving finishing school in Paris she had returned home, where her life became centred round hunting and skiing. When her close friend Rosemary Sandys-Lumsden, whom she had known since she was eleven, and Rosemary's Aunt Katie asked Valerie to come out to India for the winter she refused unhesitatingly. 'I was having far too good a time at home to want to go,' she told me. When offered a second chance for a visit, she refused again.

A year or so later, in 1936, Aunt Katie and Rosemary invited Valerie out for the third time. On an earlier visit, Rosemary had got engaged to the best man at the wedding of her brother, who worked in the family tea firm in Calcutta, but as they were so young they had to wait a year or two. Now, they told Valerie, they were going out for Rosemary's wedding; would Valerie come this time, to be bridesmaid to her old friend?

Valerie was still hesitant to leave the life she was enjoying so much at home. But, urged on by her mother, and the telling fact that her hunter was getting old and she had not yet found another horse, she agreed. And, of course, there was the compelling reason of being bridesmaid to one of her greatest friends.

'So in the autumn of 1936 I became a member of the Fishing Fleet,' said Valerie. Once she was safely on the ship – *The Viceroy of India,* the most modern and luxurious in the P&O fleet – with her bridesmaid's dress safely packed in a trunk in the hold, the other two disclosed to Valerie that the wedding was off and that they were not going to the brother in Calcutta but to a cousin of Aunt Katie's in Delhi. 'We didn't tell you before,' they said, 'because we were afraid if we did you wouldn't come.' But Valerie enjoyed the voyage, acquiring both a boyfriend and the reputation of being the only girl never seen in either shorts or trousers and managing to have a good time while never drinking anything stronger than orange juice.

In Delhi they stayed at the Cecil Hotel, where a lot of English people lived. 'I'd met a Royal Fusilier on the boat, who became a bit of a boyfriend, and his regiment was stationed near Delhi.' Life became even gayer at Christmas, when they went to stay in Calcutta, where Rosemary's brother and cousin were and where the two girls were asked constantly to dances and parties. 'Then we went back to Delhi, stopping off en route at Lucknow for Army Cup Week – Rosemary had friends in the Devon Regiment, who were stationed there and they wanted us to come – girls were at such a premium in India.

'Aunt Katie allowed us to go together, and stay at an hotel, without her to chaperone us on condition we stuck together – she made us promise. We had a wonderful time. It was a very gay week, with lots of polo. All the regiments had their teams. The first afternoon I went to watch the polo a chap in the 14th/20th who had known me in England recognised me and we then had about four days of drink parties followed by dances. Every night one of the regiments would give a big cocktail party, followed by a dance. Non-stop.

'It was great fun being surrounded by all those young men, and being so in demand, especially after England where in our part of the world there were no young men around because there weren't the jobs for them.'

After returning to Delhi, Aunt Katie took them to Agra, to visit the Taj Mahal. Back in Delhi, she sent them off one day in the car she had hired for six months with an Indian chauffeur to see the Red Fort. As they came out Valerie recognised on the sentry on guard the red, white and green ribbon of the Welch Regiment. 'I'd had a boyfriend since I was about fifteen, in the Welch Regiment, who used to send me Christmas cards, so I knew those colours.

'I said to Rosemary: "The Welch Regiment must be here" and she said: "I wonder if that chap Roger Welchman, whom I met two years ago, at a dance in the Berkeley, is with them?" Apparently they'd got on rather well, though as he was going back to India the following day they hadn't seen each other since. My friend John from the boat was motoring up to Delhi from Bombay and he came to dinner with us in Lorries Hotel and Rosemary kept on about this chap Roger Welchman she had met, but John could not help either. She looked at the various young men having drinks on the veranda speculating if one of them could be Roger – after all, it was two years since she'd seen him.

'Then in the middle of dinner a young man came up to the table and said: "You're Rosemary Sandys-Lumsden and we met at the Berkeley!" Of course it was Roger. He asked what we were doing that night and we told him we were going to see the Taj by moonlight and he said he'd like to come too. So he escorted Rosemary and I went with John.'

Back in Delhi, the girls soon saw Roger again, when he came to their hotel with his sister Joan, who was staying at Umballa, 121 miles away, for the winter. 'I saw him quite often,' said Valerie, 'but I reckoned he was Rosemary's boyfriend and we didn't believe in poaching. I got on very well with Joan, and several times went to stay with her in Umballa, which was great fun because it was a smaller station – just the Brigadier and his staff, some Gunners, one or two Indian regiments and at least one British regiment.'

One day Valerie told Joan that she had originally come out to India to be a bridesmaid but that on the ship it had been disclosed to her that it had been all called off. 'I'm getting married,' said Joan. 'Come and be bridesmaid to me.' Her wedding was to be a few days before Valerie's date for sailing home, so she agreed. 'At that time I looked on Roger as a very nice chap but I certainly wasn't sighing secretly over him,' recalled Valerie. 'We'd only met on three weekends when I'd been staying with Joan for a dance or something and he'd come to Umballa. Joan asked me to stay for the week before the wedding and Roger came up to Umballa to give Joan away. The night of the wedding we all went to see Joan and her new husband off on honeymoon on the Frontier Mail, which went through Umballa somewhere around midnight. Then we went back – and Roger asked me to marry him! I was dumbfounded. You see I liked him very much but I hadn't thought of marrying him – I hadn't thought of marrying anyone then actually.'

In any case there seemed little chance of getting married. Roger was Adjutant in his regiment and he had agreed not to get married while he was Adjutant, because part of the job was looking after the young officers in the mess, which a married officer could not do. Nor did Valerie feel that she could leave her mother for another winter so didn't see any prospect of coming back to India again. 'So I told him I didn't believe in long engagements. I said: "We can write to each other and then when you next come home on leave we can take another look at each other." I made it quite clear that we weren't tied in any way so if either of us met someone else, well, fine.'

Valerie sailed for home in the spring of 1937 – again, on *The Viceroy of India* – expecting a long exchange of letters. But she had reckoned without Roger, who was determined not to let her slip through his grasp. A few days after arriving home she got a letter telling her that he had tackled his Colonel about getting married – he was, after all, twenty-nine, so at the age when marriage was permissible, and coming to the end of his adjutancy. The Colonel had said: 'Well, I can't spare you now [it was summer] but I'll give you two months' leave in the winter to go home and get married.'

Hastily Valerie got friends she had known in India to write to her mother, who had never met Roger and knew nothing about him, to vouch for him in case her mother objected violently. She arranged the wedding and she met his parents, eliciting a splendid letter from her eighty-year-old future father-in-law to his eldest son in the Navy. 'Last week Mrs Riley and Valerie visited us for two nights and contact seemed to lead to mutual approval. Valerie is a delightful girl, a good looker without being exactly beautiful, well set up and natural, without any cosmetics, which pleases me, and I judge enormously practical, both in her attainments and her outlook on life. I do not think Roger could have made a better choice …'.

They married in November 1937 but only had a few days' honeymoon because Roger's leave was up and he had to return to his regiment. They travelled back to India on the same P&O ship, *The Viceroy of India*. As Valerie went up the gangway at Tilbury, with Roger behind her, the ship's doctor was standing at the top.

'Oh, how nice to see you again!' he greeted her. 'What are you doing?'

'You took me out as part of the Fishing Fleet last year,' she replied. 'This year I've got my catch and I'm going back!'

Up to the outbreak of the Second World War – and the virtual end of the Fishing Fleet – the sharply drawn borderline beyond which sexual intimacies were not permitted was maintained. Planter's daughter Joan Henry, who had met Geoffrey Allen, the young man who would be her future husband, was even more restrained when it came to physical liberties. Her hospitable father often asked him to stay weekends for early morning duck flighting; and on one of these weekends Geoffrey tried to kiss his host's pretty twenty-one-year-old daughter – but she turned away. 'I knew that he meant more to me than a casual kiss,' she wrote later, 'and I wanted no part in what could become a frivolous affair.'

In the late 1930s, seventeen-year-old Claudine Gratton's private diary breathes a similar sexual innocence, as depicted in entries from May and June 1937. All that year, her diary is filled largely with a dizzying number of names of different young men – many of whom she thought she was in love with – and films or dancing.

'M[ummy] asked me why I always asked R[ichard] to everything and we had a bit of a discussion. He is so adorable I can't help asking him to everything!!!' Two days later: 'He drove me to his house, showed me his horses, and kissed and squeezed me goodnight. The darling. We had a long talk trying to arrange parties for Bangalore.

I want to see him lots more before I go,' followed mournfully by 'My last dance with R. He was simply wonderful. We lay out in the garden. He went to sleep. He's not feeling well. He won't eat (because of me). We kissed each other goodbye. I cried. He is going to Simla. I don't suppose I shall see him again for a long time.' Three weeks later, another man was 'adorable'. On 4 March it was Eddie, in April Richard again, then a new admirer called Pooky. 'At about 2 a.m. started home. Eddie and I in back of Humber. He held my hand and kissed me etc. Poor Eddie!! Dropped them all home, got into bed at about 4.15.'

Back in Poona the brisk switch around of affections continued. 'Met Richard, the darling. He hasn't changed a bit, thank God. Swimming, dinner, then swimming again. He kissed me several times in the [swimming] bath. Oh, the angel. We had dinner, danced, then went home, and sat and talked.' Next day she saw Richard again. 'He was so simply adorable I wish he was never going to leave me. Kissed him goodbye, took him to the station, and rushed home, miserable.' But by December: 'Thought a lot of darling Pooky, wish he'd marry me.' The next day reads: 'Up late, cried for P. I do love him so. Can't last long without him.'

During the Raj, marriage between Englishmen and Indian girls, however beautiful or well-born the latter, was frowned upon. Long gone were the days when Edward Sellon, who arrived in India in 1834 as a sixteen-year-old cadet, could write enthusiastically: 'I now commenced a regular course of fucking with native women.'* In those days, no one – either English or Indian – frowned on the eager young white man for keeping an Indian mistress or visiting Indian prostitutes, many of whom were more akin to the cultivated, sophisticated Greek *hetaira* than to the drabs who then thronged London streets.

But as more and more European women arrived in India, to become the wives of the men who governed it, so the old *laissez-faire* attitude disappeared. Husbands might work alongside or with Indians, but for most of these women, whose lives revolved around their homes, Indians were servants. Miscegenation was proscribed and the almost obsessional attitude to 'keeping up standards' extended

* Quoted by Lawrence James in *Raj*.

to preserving the purity of a European bloodline.

With Indian women and young English girls out of bounds, any affairs had become the prerogative of the married. In the Raj there were often massive barriers to extra-marital love, from the contemporary attitude to marriage – lifelong and unbreakable – and the difficulties of keeping any affair secret in a town or cantonment where everyone knew everyone, to the effects, possibly fatal, on career or profession. In a lonely or isolated setting, illicit love could cause anything from scandal to mayhem; in a closed society such as a regiment, often stationed in distant cantonment for several years, an affair with a brother officer's wife and the consequent disruption to close working relationships was the cardinal sin.

Of course it happened from time to time, but any such affair needed more than the usual cloak of secrecy. 'I love you, my dear,' wrote 'Pat', a young man in the 1/5th Gurkha Rifles in April 1937. 'Don't take this as a passionate outcry (though sometimes it is like that towards you) but as a clear statement of fact put out or prompted by every fibre of my being … I am glad that you came up in this room glad that I kissed you in front of this very fireplace. You mean more than life itself to me. For ever and ever, Your own Pat.'

'Pat' went on sending letters to his married lover, and even claimed a photograph from her. But when the affair ended, he informed her of this abruptly and from a distance; when he wrote to her tersely in the spring of 1938, what misery she felt had to be kept strictly to herself if she was not to ruin several lives. 'Just a letter to tell you that I am going to marry a girl called Sibyl Rouse, who is in Peshawar. It all happened very suddenly and both of us just fell completely, so there it is. The Regiment have given their blessing and I am crazily happy.'

Another obstacle to the seduction of the Fishing Fleet girl was the same as that at home: the likelihood that she would seldom be alone. 'Hoped to go out to a hunt with Michael tomorrow but Mummy as usual butted in and she is coming too,' wrote a disappointed Claudine Gratton on 1 January 1937. Next day she got up early so that her admirer could take her to the meet but 'Mummy came too, to chaperone me'.

Dances were another matter. Here there was a certain amount of licensed flirtation, with specially arranged darkened nooks and crannies for young men to take the girls on whom they had their eye for a little longed-for privacy. These *kalajuggahs*, or dark places, were sought after and, sometimes, fought over. 'Before dances the young subalterns used to rush around and borrow things like curtains and heaven knows what else to make something called a *kalajuggah* – a dark place,' wrote Grace Nori. 'They all used to have their own to which they used to take their best partners and to which no one else was allowed to go.' Other 'dark places' could be a sofa for two pushed into a dimly lit corner, an area screened by potted palms on secluded verandas, or even one of the club's attics.

Magdalene ('Magda') McDowell, who went out to India in 1906, got engaged in one of these 'dark places' while at the regimental club ball of the Jat Lancers in Bareilly. 'All the officers were in full mess kit,' she wrote later. 'The whole building was picked out by tiny oil lamps and lanterns hung in the trees. It looked like fairyland and there I met Ralph [Hammersley-Smith] again. Between dances one didn't return to a chaperone, but went into one of the cleverly and prettily arranged *kalajuggahs* where you and your partner sat among or under palm branches and chatted. Here we got engaged.'

Ruby Madden had little time for them. At a fancy dress ball in Bombay in early 1912, she talked in a robustly dismissive tone of being 'initiated into the mysteries of *Kala Jugga*, which means little sitting-out places made of trellis work and palm leaves, so you can see out and not be seen. "Nothing but traps for spiders," I said. I was invited into one but said that I preferred the open with great emphasis. I think it is an extraordinary idea.'

But in a hill station, with its floating, changing population, human nature fought back. As on shipboard, lightning romances might spring up between grass widows whose husbands were working in the plains and officers or administrators who had snatched a few weeks' leave in the cool of the hills, with Simla in particular known as a centre of gossip, flirtation and intrigue. Ruby Madden, whose judgements were nothing if not crisp, wrote to her mother of an early morning ride she had taken. 'Mrs Crowe was there with her own young man,' she told Lady Madden.

'Everyone sports an "own young man". And she has such a dull little husband I suppose it's necessary for her to have a change now and then.'

11

'It would be a pleasure to be in his harem, I thought'

Maharajas

For sheer magnificence there was little to touch the splendour of the maharajas. Their palaces, their clothes, their jewels, their retinues, the gold and silver trappings of their state elephants, the largesse they showered on fortunate guests, seemed to sum up everything that was meant by the phrase 'the gorgeous East'. It was not surprising that some Fishing Fleet girls, given the chance, found them irresistible.

There was little to touch the lavishness and generosity of their hospitality. As the daughter of the Resident of Neemuch, Betsey Anderson made several visits to native states with her parents.

'We watched jugglers, musicians, dancers and the private individual armies of the Princes in all manner of unique uniforms. The halls in which banquets were held were stupendous pillared rooms, some with colourful scenes depicting the ancient days and former rulers, others with magnificent embroidered hangings, fine lattice screens, cut-glass chandeliers and mirrors making a dazzling effect. For the diners, long tables were laid with spotless white cloths laden with gold and silver plate, immense bowls of fruit, cleverly festooned with exotic flowers.

'We would be seated before the Maharaja appeared, surrounded by his courtiers. They were all resplendently dressed, their long coats looking like cloths of gold. Each one would wear different headgear according to his caste and these creations would have made any milliner proud, adorned as they were with fabulous jewels and feathers.' Afterwards guests were entertained with dancing girls.

For those lucky enough to be invited to stay in a maharaja's palace, it was an unforgettable experience. Often the first stage was a train journey, to be met by one of their host's cars (the Maharaja of Mysore had fifty-two Rolls-Royces). 'It was dusk when the train pulled into Ratlam,' wrote Evelyn Barrett, who with her husband had been invited to stay for Christmas with the Nawab of Jaora in 1935. 'Followed a drive through the jungle. Great trees hung like lace against the stars. Once twin points of light became a stare of green. "Wolf!" said Ali Khan [the Nawab's son]. Then the jungle broke and before us lay a green river full of stars. On the far side lights twinkled.

'Crossing the river, and bypassing the moonlit palace with its forest of guest-tents, we drove through gates guarded by sentries to a white house standing in a garden. Light poured from the open doorway where servants, in the colours of His Highness the Nawab of Jaora, stood waiting. Five minutes later we were doing justice to a delicious dinner, served with iced champagne in a bucket. Beside each of our places was a printed programme of fixtures for the next ten days, with a list of numbered cars, and the names of the guests allocated to each one.

'Next morning we went hunting. The Meet was at 7.00 a.m. at the palace, His Highness maintained his own pack of hounds, some bred by himself, but most imported from England. The Hunt staff were beautifully turned out and mounted. All wore scarlet, as did H.H. and the Princes. The going was black cotton soil, varied by ridges of rock and sand. A troop of cavalry, armed with spears in the event of flushing out wolf or panther, followed at a distance. We had excellent sport, killing three jack, but the most vivid memory of that morning was great Sarus cranes, crimson crowns glistening above mists, stalking in the cotton fields, and of their melodious, clanking calls.'

The days that followed were a succession of hunts, shoots and polo, with golf and squash thrown in. In the mornings guests were expected to amuse themselves. At noon, followed by a servant bearing aloft, on a long silver handle, a huge, silver-fringed pink umbrella, H.H. would emerge from the palace. Shaded by the umbrella, he would descend the steps between kneeling rows of those who had received audience, to greet his guests assembled by the waiting cars. The evening before a shoot, one of the princes would wander unobtrusively among guests, ascertaining that everyone was equipped with gun or rifle and, if not, inviting selection from some of HH's beautiful weapons.

'On these outings it was my privilege to drive with HH,' wrote Evelyn. 'For shooting he wore a Norfolk jacket, a striped silk shirt, the neckband looped with a string of pearls and fastened with a Woolworth gold safety pin, cotton jodhpurs and brown boots. The ubiquitous diamond stud completed the outfit. In the dashboard of the car was a recess containing cigarettes and sample-size bottles of Coty's scent. Before lighting up, a cigarette would be probed with a scent stopper and the resultant cloud of Chypre and Abdullah luxuriously inhaled.'

Evelyn found herself forgetting that her hosts were of a different race and creed from herself. One day, riding alongside a little wood, Ali Khan remarked, 'We never shoot that wood because of my great-uncle.'

'Your great-uncle?'

'Yes. He's a jinn. He lives there, in the form of a white blackbuck.'

'Have you ever seen him?'

'Oh yes, but it is not good to see him, so we will ride on.'

Once there was an escorted visit to the harem, guarded by enormous eunuchs, where Evelyn was received by the youngest wife, aged fourteen and already a mother. Later in the visit, Evelyn asked the Nawab:

'Do your wives never get envious of these wonderful parties?'

For answer H.H. raised an arm so that the light fell on an embroidered sleeve. 'Beautiful, is it not?' he asked. It was an exquisite design of leaves and flowers, worked in gold and silver thread. 'The work of my youngest wife,' remarked H.H. complacently. 'The only one who gives trouble. Such a garment takes six months to make. When she gets restive I merely ask for another coat.' He grinned. 'She is doing one now!'

Even the route that led to the princely domains could be glamorous. Here is Violet Jacob, writing from Mho at the beginning of December 1896 of the drive to the great ball given by the Maharaja of Indore at his palace, the Lal Bagh. She was accompanied by her husband, Captain Arthur Jacob of the 20th Hussars, resplendent in his full dress uniform of blue with crimson busby-bag and yellow plume.

'In the evening we started for the Lal Bagh, four miles off ... It is difficult to give you an idea of that drive, as you have never seen an Indian city. There were three miles of lights. We drove through a blazing road, so bright that surrounding objects were as distinct as in the day. On right and left, at the height of a man's head, was a double row of lights on parallel wires about eight inches apart. Behind this in many places small trees were hung with paper lanterns with another row of lights under the boughs; this sent up a great glare into the blue-black sky and made the whole skyful of stars look like steel. In the smoke that hung round the houses, many of which were carved about the windows, some buildings stood out dark and some light.

'The entire female population stood, sat and leant out from roofs and verandas in a confused tangle of wood-smoke, glare, teeth and brown arms, and dressed in every colour of the rainbow. This made a seething background on which the gold and silver of bracelets and nose rings shot out like flashes of moonlight on water ... Below, in the light, the male population swarmed in its holiday clothes, kept back from the road by Holkar's cavalry whose lances made dark points in the crowd and whose half-broken horses stamped and squealed.

'There is a square in Indore about the size of the Campo dei Fiori in Rome and here there are two palaces, one on either side, one stone built, the other stucco and painted a raging blue. Both can be seen far out into the country as they are much higher than the other buildings ... When we got to the Lal Bagh gardens elephants were looming like castles in the shadows under the trees ... As one looked at [the palace] ablaze, like everything else, the gardens were on the right, full of high trees and strong-scented jasmine and on the left the river. At the top of the steps the Maharaja Holkar stood, receiving his guests in a white silk coat and rose-coloured puggri ... I had just time to see that his only ornament was three rows of pearls as big as peas.'

The jewels of these princes were beyond price. The most amazing belonged to the last Nizam of Hyderabad, who had enriched his fabulous hoard with boxes of diamonds, rubies and emeralds that had belonged to Tsar Nicholas II. Next in importance were those of Baroda. To meet the Prince of Wales (later Edward VII), the young Gaekwar of Baroda wore a seven-string necklace of pearls the size of marbles. A 128-carat diamond known as the 'Star of the South' was the centrepiece of a necklace made of five rows of diamonds and two of emeralds, with a diamond plume worn in his turban. When the Prince visited he was met by the Gaekwar's own elephant, its face and ears painted and bedecked with gold anklets and caparisoned with a gold howdah, up to which the Prince climbed on a silver ladder. In 1930 Rosita Forbes described the Maharaja of Jodhpur as having writing table sets encrusted with precious stones, children's balls set with rubies, women's shoes sewn with diamonds and an expanding cap made of the finest solitaire diamonds.

The Maharaja of Dholpur had a nine-row necklace of pearls as big as gulls' eggs. The Maharaja of Patiala, six foot tall, on ceremonial occasions wore at least four ropes of pearls to the waist, a belt of diamonds, a gold lamé scarf held by a four-inch emerald, with more necklaces of diamonds and emeralds and a jewelled sword. At a state banquet for the Viceroy, Lord Reading, he wore, on his maroon brocade coat, the Empress Eugenie's diamond necklace, a three-row pearl collar, the ten diamond stars of his order, the pale blue ribbon and diamond jewel of the Star of India with – on his maroon puggri – an enormous diamond tiara from which hung loops of diamonds, pearls and emeralds. 'He looked wonderful,' wrote Yvonne Fitzroy, who had come out to India in 1921 as Private Secretary to the Vicereine.

Curzon might have remarked loftily to Edward VII that 'The native chiefs ... have been deprived of the essential rights and attributes of sovereignty,' but to their people they were absolute rulers, venerated almost as gods, moving in an aura of wealth and power. Violet Jacob, accompanying the Nawab of Jaora on one of his ceremonial trips, saw this first-hand.

'We passed through about twenty villages, mud-walled, most of them, and buried in a world of poppies brilliant in the sun, with high mango groves like clumps of plumes standing in their midst. Great banyans put down their aerial roots making arches and pillars of twisted fibres and wood, many with stone shrines hidden in their sinister darkness. Village people, according to custom, ran to meet the Nawab, presenting him with small coins which he touched and gave to his tonga* man; the women came separately, some beating tom-toms. Peacocks flew about, trees loomed grey and heavy in the hot morning air, poppies blazed and native cavalrymen galloped and pranced and on we went again.'

Annette Bowen, invited with her parents to the Dasera Durbar ceremony of 1933 by the Maharaja of Mysore, had several days of dinner parties, race meetings and garden parties as well as the main reception. At this, wearing a ball gown and long white gloves (men wore tailcoats or full dress uniforms), she was presented to the Maharaja, 'who sat, jewelled to his fingertips and with jewelled thimbles to keep the rings on, and flashing in cloth of gold and silver.

'We had to approach over carpets embroidered with pearls, crunching underfoot, and curtsey. He gave us each a stiff bouquet, drenched in rosewater – in the old days, each bouquet would have contained a piece of jewellery. All the city of Mysore was strung with fairy lights … [there were] daily processions of elephants, faces painted, ears studded with huge emeralds and gorgeously caparisoned, tusks and toenails gilded with real gold leaf, and all the time strange scents of spices and incense and charcoal fires, rosewater and frangipani, and oriental music and singing.'

The maharajas were as keen on protocol and precedence as the British – in some cases even more so. How people were placed at dinner, how many palace steps the Maharaja went down to greet someone, whether an elephant walked half a pace behind or half a pace in front of a neighbouring ruler and, above all, how many guns that particular ruler was entitled to as a formal salute from the British† were matters of intense and heated debate, often filling whole files of correspondence between officials as one prince vied to outdo another.

Sport and hunting – the peacetime substitutes for warfare – united both the British and the princes. For young officers, who had to be ready at any time to be sent to quell a local uprising or repel an

---

* A light, two-wheeled horse-drawn vehicle, seating up to four people.
† According to rank, each prince was entitled to a gun salute that rose by odd numbers from nine to the twenty-one given for the five most senior: Hyderabad, Baroda, Mysore, Gwalior and Kashmir.

incursion by one of the warring tribes of the Frontier, it was often almost a religion, encouraged by their superiors: a young man who was fit, hard, a good rider and a quick, accurate shot was the sort needed on active service.

Yet even here precedence counted. To produce the best tiger shoot was for the princes a matter of honour, often involving the luring of tigers to a particular locality by the staking out night after night of cow or goat; and it was equally important that the most important guest, especially if he were the Viceroy, bagged the biggest tiger. To achieve this, there were even special tape measures, made with only eleven inches to the foot.

At one time, tiger shooting had a certain social justification. When tigers in Bengal were common, they were often seen along the roads in daylight, and killed large numbers of people. The terrified peasants, in particular the forest workers and wood cutters, would naturally refuse to go out to work until the tiger had been despatched, usually by a District Officer or one of his subordinates to whom a message had been sent. In the large blocks of jungle, an eye was kept on the tiger population: there had to be enough to keep the numbers of pig and deer in check or these would eat and destroy the villagers' crops in their search for food.

Often, though, tigers were killed purely for sport, something difficult to comprehend now. It was generally an arduous and uncomfortable business. As tigers lay up in the heat of the day, climbing into a *machan**, and despatching beaters could be done unobtrusively. Then came a long, motionless wait in the midday silence, with heat, somnolence and flies the worst enemies and the gun barrels, too hot to hold, resting on a handy branch. After a distant shot signalled the beginning of the beat, shouts and the rattling of bamboo canes against branches drove an army of creatures towards the machan – peafowl and jungle fowl, jackal, perhaps a mongoose or two, small birds and screeching emerald parakeets. 'Soon the form of the tiger is viewed through the vista of bamboos and tree trunks,' wrote Colonel Burton of his first tiger shoot in 1894. 'He looks huge; small chance has anything borne down by that massive form, gripped by those terrible jaws. His ruff stands out white on either side of his neck. The placing of the first shot is everything.'

---

* Platform hide, usually built in a tree.

So much, indeed, did tiger shooting evolve into a rite of passage for the Englishman in India* that it became almost an industry, with the Madras taxidermy factory of Van Ingen and Van Ingen acquiring a global reputation for the tiger-skin rugs once found on the library floors of so many returned Anglo-Indians. Skinning of a shot animal had to be done on the spot if possible – dragging over rough ground would scrape off large patches of fur – and within a few hours, or the fur would begin to slip and the pelt to decompose, so an important shooting party would include a skinner or two among the beaters. Once removed, the skin had to be dried, which meant stretching on a wooden frame in the shade if the party was of several days' duration, and salted, so that it was in treatable condition when it reached the Van Ingen workshops. Between 1928 and 1937, this firm handled 400–600 tigers a year from all over India and Burma (then part of the Raj).

'Tigers are a necessary part of every Viceroy's experience,' wrote Yvonne Fitzroy. 'You can have a beat, sit over a kill or a drinking pool, or walk up the quarry; you can shoot on your feet, from a *machan*, or from the back of an elephant – but since risk on these occasions has to be reduced to a minimum an elephant or, in some cases, a tower is chosen. Important shoots demand weeks of preparation; the tiger has first to be located and then if possible kept in the district by the lure of an easy meal in the shape of a tame buffalo tied up in the vicinity. To prevent his wandering a fresh buffalo is provided whenever necessary, and once he starts killing it is easy to keep track of him. He will usually lie up after a heavy meal and sleep off the effects, and with the heat of the day as your ally this is the best moment to work his undoing ... on each occasion it is a matter of great moment to the host that the Viceroy should get his tiger and as far as possible the uncertainties of the jungle are defied.'

Dinner parties were equally impressive. Cecile Stanley Clarke declared that the most wonderful dinner party she had ever been to was given by an Indian prince 'whose name I could not pronounce'.

---

* At one time it was almost *de rigueur* to return home from India with a tiger skin or two – and more if you were a Viceroy. Curzon took home five and used one as an opening salvo in his courtship of the beautiful red-haired novelist Elinor Glyn, sending it round to her dressing room when he saw her on the stage in the adaptation of her scandalous novel *Three Weeks*. He was irritated to discover later that Lord Milner had done exactly the same.

'He had an enormous Arabian Nights palace of glittering white, just the kind I should ask for if I ever uncorked a genie. The dinner was held in the garden under gold canopies. The air was heavy with jasmine and the fountains were sending showers of sparkling water into the starlit sky. Somewhere a band was playing soft Eastern music. Soldiers in glorious gold and scarlet uniforms were standing about, two of them leading a cheetah in a gold and jewelled collar, which snarled at us in the moonlight.

'I was taken in to dinner by a very handsome Indian. He was obviously very amused by my excitement. It would be a pleasure to be in his harem, I thought – provided I was Number One wife and could poison the others. The dinner went on for hours and hours. I nobly tried to eat a bit of everything, having been warned not to go all out on first courses. This proved good advice, as after about the tenth, just as one was thinking "Well, that's that", an enormous dish of peacocks, complete with tails, appeared. The chicken pilau was perhaps the most sensational, as it had real gold dust sprinkled over it. It gave one a lovely feeling, eating gold! I was very thankful that the prevailing fashion didn't favour tight waists. Little silver boxes had been put by the side of each plate as a present.'

After dinner came another revelation of princely splendour, albeit in a more basic direction. The female guests were escorted by ayahs to the ladies' powder room. 'We were all looking forward to seeing this, having been told that the plumbing was sensational. It had just been installed, all the way from Paris. And this was, so to speak, opening night. Nor were we disappointed! The room was of cathedral-like proportions and all down one side, stretching as far as the eye could see, were rows and rows of 'pull and let goes' in a variety of glittering colours. On the opposite side were bidets. The floor was made of black and gold mosaic and at the very far end there was a sunken bath.'

Yet despite their wealth, power and hospitality, Indians, from the grandest maharaja down, were excluded from virtually all of the British clubs. The Raj Kumar of Mysore (the maharaja) was often in Madras during the season and, as Katherine Welford told me: 'One would meet him at Government House, the races, or the Gymkhana Club. But he was not allowed in the Adyar Club – no Indian was allowed there, nor would one meet an Indian at a dinner party. He was often a guest of the Governor and I could, and often did, dance with him at Government House – but never at the club.'

When an Indian prince showed a preference for a white woman over his own kind the highest Government circles were drawn in – and many maharajas did, especially those who had been educated in England. Letters would fly back and forth between the Viceroy's aides and the Resident of the state, the telegraph wires would hum and veiled threats be issued to both parties. Even as 1920s' idol, film star Rudolph Valentino, was enrapturing female fans with his portrayal in *The Sheik* of an Arab with whom a titled Englishwoman falls in love, the Agent to the Governor-General of the Punjab States was writing to his superior of the Maharaja's wish to bring his French mistress, Mademoiselle Seret, to India. 'From discussions I have had with the Maharaja, it is apparent that his Highness is utterly miserable unless he has a European lady to associate with. Indian women neither satisfy nor interest him, and the few months he spends in India every year are a penance, unless he is accompanied by his mistress.'

The Maharaja made this clear in a letter of 1 December 1924, while assuring the British Establishment that nothing untoward would happen provided he got his own way. 'I have no intention of marrying a European or Indian lady again, but should unforeseen circumstances unavoidably impel me to a fresh matrimonial alliance I cannot imagine how a domestic occurrence of this nature should in the slightest degree impair the cordiality of my personal relations with the British high officials whose friendship I have invariably sought and shall always seek to cultivate. Apropos of visits of European friends of either sex to me in my state or outside I am sure my mature experience and discretion will be fully relied upon to ensure that no departure from conventional decency shall be allowed to occur.'

A few days later, on 8 December, the Agent passed on this ultimatum:

'His Highness made it clear in conversation that, if he were prevented from bringing Mademoiselle Seret out to India, he would be compelled to marry a European or to stay away from his State for much longer periods. Either of these alternatives is open to strong objection, and it would be far preferable, in my opinion, to let his Highness bring Mademoiselle Seret to Kapurthala when he visits India, as we can rely on his discretion not to create a scandal. The lady would reside in a house well away from the Palace and would not be in evidence when any high official visited the State. His Highness even offered to send her elsewhere on such occasions, if it were thought desirable.'

When the matter reached the Viceroy he sensibly decided to turn a blind eye, as a letter of 30 December to Colonel Minchin makes plain:

'I am now desired to inform you that his Excellency does not desire any inquisitorial enquiries to be made regarding visitors to Kapurthala. There have been no open scandals and as long as there are no scandals of an open and public character, in his Excellency's view it is no concern of ours what visitors come to stay at Kapurthala. Of course if a lady was produced on a public and formal occasion or at a social entertainment when European officers were present at the Maharaja's invitation and the lady in question were known to be the Maharaja's mistress, a different situation would arise; but so far as His Excellency is aware, the lady to whom you refer has always been kept in the background and has not appeared on such occasions. There are therefore at present no grounds for offence.'

The first to actually marry a Fishing Fleet girl was Rajendar Singh, the rich, glamorous, hard-playing, philandering Maharaja of Patiala. He was famous as a sportsman: he was a brilliant shot, his polo teams were the best in India and he was the first maharaja to engage English cricket professionals to coach his teams – he was so keen on cricket that he once had the top of an 8,000-foot mountain levelled off to make the highest cricket pitch in the world – and in 1892, aged twenty, he imported the first motor car to India, a De Dion Bouton, with the number plate Patiala O and a speed of 15–20 km an hour.

Horses and women were his great weaknesses. He owned 700 of the best thoroughbreds in India, bought for him by his great friend Lord William Beresford, VC, the horse-mad third son of the Marquis of Waterford. These studs were managed for him by an Irishman called Charles Bryan, the son of the head clerk of the Central Police Office in Lahore. When Charles Bryan came to Patiala in 1890 he brought his three young sisters with him.

The Maharaja seduced them all – and fell so deeply in love with the eldest, Florrie, a quiet, gentle girl, that he determined to marry her. He confided this to Lord William Beresford and, knowing that

Mary McLeish with her fiancé Nigel Gribbon. They had known each other for only a fortnight before they were parted; six years later he proposed to her by telephone – and was accepted.

Katherine Welford, aged twenty, at the time she went to stay with her aunt and uncle in Madras.

Jean Hilary, during a 1929 weekend with friends at Puri. She wears one of the conical straw hats worn by the bathing 'boys' on Puri beach, who escorted bathers into the water, helping them through the surf.

A view of Simla, showing the enormous crowds gathered to attend the wedding of Lady Elisabeth Bruce to Henry Babington Smith in September 1898.

The view from Observatory Hill, Simla, looking north-east.

Simla was famous for its amateur dramatics, as in this 1930s staging of
The Gondoliers.

Something in the air in the Hills seemed to encourage the British love of
dressing up, as seen here at the Viceregal Lodge in the 1890s.

A picnic in the grounds of the Residency, by the Dal Lake, Srinagar, Kashmir, in the 1920s.

A walk in the hills.

Hut 102A in Gulmarg was rented by the Lloyd family every year and regarded as their second home.

The finals of the Gilgit polo match. These contests were fiercely fought between rival clans. Spectators who could not crowd on to walls perched in the trees.

In isolated areas cricket matches were a popular social fixture. Billy Fremlin's father, Ralph, is on the front row, second from left, in this photograph of the Kadur Club cricket team, 1910.

Miss Florence ('Flossie') Ross (*left*), newly engaged to Lieutenant Leslie Germain Lavie of the 20th Regiment Madras Infantry (*right*). At twenty-seven Lavie was considered young for marriage.

Grace Trotter, the girl who got away from her 'tainted' heritage.

Tiger shooting from an elephant: Grace's sister, Mabel Trotter – hatted, corseted and gloved – with G. P. Sanderson, the Superintendent of Keddahs for the Maharaja of Mysore.

A bullock cart for use on roads, drawn by the white bullocks of Mysore.

Bethea Field and her mother – always known as Madre – in their garden in Poona in 1906.

Violet Field pictured by a river at Bhola, a noted beauty spot near Meerut, in June 1914.

Bethea when she returned to India aged nineteen, just after the Great War.

Jim and Violet in their courting days. Although Jim was a genial person, he could never manage to look cheerful in front of a camera.

The 'wrong' Major Williams, Arthur de Coetlogon Williams, who became Bethea's husband.

it would be frowned on by the British, asked Lord William to be his intermediary with the Viceroy.

Beresford's intervention brought the expected result. 'I have mentioned the matter to H.E. the Viceroy,' he wrote to his friend the Maharaja, 'and I feel bound to tell you that H.E. regards your intention with the strongest disapproval, and that he will not, in any way, countenance this marriage. An alliance of this kind, contracted with a European far below your rank, is bound to lead to the most unfortunate results. It will render your position both with Europeans and Indians most embarrassing. In the Punjab, as you must be well aware, the marriage will be most unpopular.'

The twenty-one-year-old Maharaja, accustomed to being absolute ruler in his own large state, took no notice. On 13 April 1893 the *Civil and Military Gazette* carried the news of his marriage on its front page. 'The Maharaja Rajendar Singh of Patiala has secretly married Miss Florry Bryan, sister of Mr C. Bryan, in charge of H.H.'s stables … the marriage was by the Hindu and Sikh ceremonies united … the bride's name was changed to Harnam Kaur. The Maharaja left for Dholpur the same night with his new bride.'

Florence was already five months pregnant; her son was born on 20 August 1893. But her married life was brief and unhappy. In spite of her adoption of her husband's religion the nobility of Patiala took no notice of her; and she was spurned by European society. Worst of all, her son was poisoned. By 1896 a Foreign Office file refers to her as 'the late' – it is believed she died of pneumonia while accompanying her husband on a campaign in the Himalayas. Rajendar himself died a few years later, on 1 November 1900, following a riding accident.

12

'Us and them'

Brits and Indians

Much of the view of Anglo-Indians, as seen by the eyes of those at home, has been influenced by the differing attitudes of those two literary giants, Rudyard Kipling and E.M. Forster – in the case of Kipling, by a large body of work but with Forster by only one seminal book, *A Passage to India*.

Of the two, Kipling's approach is the more straightforward. He believed in the British Empire, the Pax Britannica, and in the almost mystical right of the British to rule; the Kipling view of Empire also held that there were grave responsibilities for those who ruled. Supremely fitted for this task, he thought, was the British public schoolboy, ably supported by the British soldier. The ideal English hero, in his stories, was brave, strong, imbued with the public school ethos, always fair, chivalrous towards women, and a leader.

At the same time, only someone with admiration and respect for Indians could have written books like *Kim* or the Mowgli stories, let alone the poems 'East is East' and 'Gunga Din' ('You're a better man than I am, Gunga Din'). Yet, however close the relationship – the bonds of loyalty and affection between master and servant, or that linked fellow soldiers or brave men of whatever colour or creed – one line could never be crossed. There must be no mixing of blood. For Kipling, writing in the late nineteenth century, intermarriage was the unpardonable sin.

A hundred-odd years earlier it had been perfectly acceptable; in the early days the East India Company had even offered a christening present of five rupees to the children of their soldiers and their

Indian wives. At that time many Englishmen preferred an Indian wife or mistress. Major-General Charles 'Hindoo' Stuart of the East India Company, who went to India in his teens, in the late 1780s, wrote enthusiastically of the charms of Indian women rather as if describing a Miss Wet-Tee-shirt contest: 'the Hindoo female, modest as the rosebud, bathes completely dressed ... and necessarily rises with wet drapery from the stream. Had I despotic power, our British fair ones should soon follow this example; being fully persuaded that it would eminently contribute to keep the bridal torch for ever in a blaze.'

'Hindoo' Stuart – so called because of his devotion to and knowledge of all things Hindu – was admittedly well known for his passion for women ('He has the *Itch* beyond any man I ever knew,' wrote a contemporary), but the fact that he considered Indian women more beautiful and desirable than their English counterparts would not have been considered particularly strange at the time he was writing. One eighteenth-century senior Resident of Calcutta even had himself circumcised* in order to improve his relations with Muslim women, and the experienced roué Captain Edward Sellon, writing of India in the years 1834–44, said enthusiastically of its women: 'They understand in perfection all the arts and wiles of love, are capable of gratifying any taste, and in face and figure they are unsurpassed by any women in the world ... it is impossible to describe the enjoyment I have had in the arms of these syrens.'

Forster's view, more complex and of a later date than Kipling's, as expressed in *A Passage to India* (published in 1924), was contemporaneous with the rising power of Mahatma Gandhi and the first stirrings of the struggle for independence. He wrote enthusiastically and sympathetically of Indians, but created a searing portrait of those who ruled over them, charting an attitude the polar opposite of that of 'Hindoo' Stuart. Such was the book's blazing success that for many people it has irrevocably coloured their view of the British in India. Forster's tone towards them is notably hostile: they appear as the arrogant, bombastic sahibs of caricature, expecting

---

* Circumcision, though routine among Jews and Muslims, only became an acceptable practice (apart from medical reasons) in Britain in the late nineteenth century, and then only among the better-off. But by the 1930s, exactly one third of the British male population was being circumcised – again, with a preponderance among the upper classes.

all to bow down before them and with wives who do not scruple to treat all Indians like dirt:

'You're superior to them anyway. Don't forget that. You're superior to everyone in India except one or two of the Ranis, and they're on an equality,' says Mrs Turton, the Collector's wife in the novel, who has already refused to shake hands with any of the Indians at the mixed party her husband has made her give, while the various British officials are constantly expressing loathing and disdain of 'the natives'.

Forster, who had fallen in love with an Indian in 1906, a passion that lasted for many years, was predisposed to dislike the sons and daughters of the Raj before even meeting them. To one old friend he made his attitude clear. 'Over the Anglo-Indians I have to stretch and bust myself blue. I loathe them and should have been more honest to say so.'

Among the letters of praise on this brilliant novel's appearance were also letters of complaint, largely from those who had lived and worked in India themselves. One,* who congratulated Forster on his depiction of the Indians in the novel, said that when one turned to the Anglo-Indians one was 'confronted by the strangest sense of unreality. Where have they come from? What planet do they inhabit? One rubs one's eyes. They are not even good caricatures, for an artist must see his original clearly before he can caricature it …'.

The book also caused a serious breach with one of his oldest friends, Rupert Barkeley-Smith, who had gone out to join the ICS in 1908 – they had met on a Greek cruise intended for serious classical students. Forster stayed with Smith in 1913 during his first, two-year visit to India, recording that 'Smith seemed to dislike every class of Indian except the peasant'.

Despite his reservations, on his second visit in 1921 Forster again went to stay with Smith, now a Collector, in Agra, with an Indian friend of Smith's as a fellow house guest. When the book came out Smith was so enraged by what he saw as the unfair depiction of those who lived and worked in India (plus a jibe at Smith's own bungalow as the most uncomfortable in the station) that he wrote

* E.A. Horne, who had served in the Indian education service and was the author of *The Political System of British India*.

a furious letter. The friendship was broken off, not to be resumed again until thirty years had passed.

For some Fishing Fleet girls coloured skin came as a cultural shock. Others, who had been brought up in India as small children, with ayahs instead of nannies, servants to play with and chatter to (all Indian servants loved children), often camping, and always familiar with the sights, sound and smells of India, found acceptance easy.

Iris Butler, daughter of liberal parents, had Indian friends who often came to stay all her life. When a small child she was woken every day by the calling of the sacred peacocks. She and her sister and brother were often taken for picnics by a huge lake full of crocodiles fed on camels' stomachs that would crawl up out of the lake when called by the Rajput keeper. 'This was by invitation of the ruler, whom we all called Andatta (bread-giver) as did his subjects. I owe the Andatta the inestimable gift of Indian friendship, for he and my parents were devoted to each other, and thus from the first it never entered my head that Indians were any different from anyone else.'

Cecile Stanley Clarke spent many a happy hour in the zenana of the Nizam of Hyderabad. She would often go to tea there, sitting cross-legged among the zenana women on the floor to eat delicious sticky cakes. She was fascinated by the paraphernalia for making the delicacy *paan* (chopped areca nuts mixed with lime and various spices and wrapped in a betel leaf, chewed throughout India). 'It corresponds, I suppose, to our smoking habit. Beautiful boxes were brought in by the ayahs containing all the ingredients, which were carefully mixed together and wrapped in a betel leaf secured with a clove. The first time I was given one I chewed and chewed with tears pouring down my face, swallowing the red hot juices instead of spitting them out, and the grand climax came when I could bear it no longer and swallowed the lot, clove and all. I nearly died. What I should have done, of course, was to have delicately spat out the lot.'

After tea they would play shuttlecock (badminton), 'or something like it, though there were never any rules or tiresome things like scoring, and we were five or more a side'. Like exotic butterflies in their brilliant saris, the girls of the zenana would flutter about in the sunshine. When they were all tired they would sit round one of the fountains in the courtyard, sipping refreshing cool drinks. 'Or we might wander in the garden, which was the most beautiful I had ever seen.'

To generalise, the higher the official, the more open the approach. Many viceroys had found the business of 'us and them' distasteful. A long time earlier, the 8th Earl of Elgin, the second Viceroy of India (1862-3) had written: 'it is a terrible business this living among inferior races'. In Government House, he disliked walking about among the salaaming servants 'with perfect indifference, treating them, not as dogs, because in that case one would whistle to them and pat them, but as machines with which one can have no communion or sympathy'. When an English soldier was sentenced to death for killing an Indian while trying to rob him, Elgin refused to grant a reprieve despite public opinion.

Eventually Lord Minto, Curzon's successor as Viceroy, in his efforts to breach the social barriers between the British and the Indians, helped to found the Calcutta Club, which admitted both.

As early as 1885, with the encouragement of the Viceroy and the support of several British officials, a group of Indian lawyers and other professionals, of all religions and from all parts of India, had founded the Indian National Congress as a forum for debate and to express Indian opinion to Britain. This was followed in 1906 by the All-India Muslim League and the Morley-Minto reforms of 1909, which enlarged the Viceroy's Council to include an Indian member and allowed Indians to elect representatives to the provincial legislative councils.

The fledgling Indian independence movement was given wings by the terrible massacre of Amritsar in 1919, when British troops under the command of General Dyer fired on an unarmed crowd of thousands, killing about four hundred. This was followed by more reforms – the Montagu-Chelmsford Reforms of 1919, which increased power at provincial levels – and the rise to power of Mahatma Gandhi, who changed the Indian National Congress from a small group of educated men to a mass party of millions. By the late 1920s and 1930s, most of those who joined the ICS realised that sooner or later Indian independence was inevitable.

Gradually, barriers were breaking down. While all over India the clubs maintained their rigid rule of racial and sexual apartheid, Indian colleagues worked alongside British Government officials and, especially up country, in the smaller, more isolated stations, there was more mingling. Educated Indian colleagues would be asked to dinner or, in some cases, join the club. 'The Club was basically a planter's club,' wrote E.F. Lydall, an ICS man based in a tea-growing district in the late 1930s. 'There was no actual colour bar. An Indian medical officer who took over during my time automatically joined the club.' Indian officers in the Indian Army, though on a level with their British brother officers in the Mess, could not be full members of the Peshawar Club, remembers Lydall, 'though they could be members of the Cavalry Club in London'.

Iris James, in a sign of the times – the late 1930s – was allowed to go out with maharajas. 'There was something about their being very rich that overrode the colour thing.'

Generally, though, for a youthful Fishing Fleet girl who had married a soldier or junior official it was little use trying to counteract loneliness by friendship with Indian families. So strong was the barrier between the ruler and the ruled and hence the unwritten law forbidding even social mixing, that most minds were set against it; and in a society where conformity to received protocols and attitudes was the accepted ethos, it required a young woman of extraordinarily strong character to run counter to this.

There was also – and not least – the attitude of Indians themselves. Muslim women were kept in purdah, driven about in enclosed vehicles, and veiled. Hindu women, encouraged to consider their husbands as gods, were similarly treated; nor would the men of either religion have allowed their wives to attend dinner parties or dances where, as was normal British custom, men were present.

Honor Penrose, who had been sent to India to find a husband and who married the brilliant ICS man Rupert Barkeley-Smith in 1914, was one of a large family accustomed to sociability and often spoke of the difficulty of making friends across the race barrier. 'Purdah was very strictly enforced. English men got on with Indian men but couple entertaining was awkward as the fourth of the quartet was always missing and it was difficult to get going. Also, as a woman, you were conscious that the men were looking at you and thinking you were a bit of a hussy to be publicly about like this and that you ought to be behind purdah.

'Occasionally I would go and see wives but it was very difficult as you could not see them when you talked, and sitting behind purdah, doing nothing, made them very lethargic. On one of our camping tours one man took his wife into camp, where she lived in two bell tents. When we moved the curtained bullock cart was drawn up beside the opening of one and she was decanted into the cart. She never saw the fresh air at all.'

It was the same in palaces. 'We dined with the Maharaja at a large banquet – men only, of course, except for me,' wrote the newly married Violet Hanson; she and her Indian Army husband Podge Gregson had been invited to spend their honeymoon in the state of Dhranghadra (its maharaja was the uncle of one of Podge's brother officers).

'There was a curtained-off part of the banqueting hall behind which gathered the Zenana ladies. One could hear muffled giggles and tinkling of bangles during dinner. We went out on shooting parties and sightseeing tours. One of the young princesses, who spoke a little English, insisted on taking me out into the city in her purdah car. It had dark blue glass windows so that no one could look inside. The young Princess drove at breakneck speed through the bazaar, regardless of what or whom she might knock over. However, everyone got out of the way, salaaming deeply as they scattered.'

Today the barrier between the races has been knocked down and intermarriage is common and accepted. But in the days of the Raj it was, like the Berlin Wall, almost impossible to cross and dangerous to try to do so. 'I was told who was within my marriage range and who wasn't,' said Iris James. 'Anybody, however old and decrepit, bald or dull, was a possible husband, as long as he was white. But anybody with the slightest touch of colour wasn't.'

13

'I thought my heart was going to jump out of my body'

Grace Trotter

'Understand clearly that there was not a breath of a word to be said against Miss Castries – not a shadow of a breath. She was good and very lovely ... But – but – but – Well, she was a very sweet girl and very pious, but for many reasons she was "impossible". Quite so. All good Mamas know what "impossible" means. It was obviously absurd that Peythroppe should marry her. The little opal-tinted onyx at the basis of her finger-nails said this as plainly as print ... It would have been cheaper for Peythroppe to have assaulted a Commissioner with a dog whip,' wrote Rudyard Kipling in *Plain Tales from the Hills*.

By the 1880s 'tainting' the blood of pure-born Britons by mixed marriages had become something to be avoided at all costs, even by force if necessary: in Kipling's story the hero is kidnapped to save him from a fate – marriage to a beautiful and charming girl whom he adores – considered worse than death because the fact that the girl has some Indian blood will ruin his promising career. As for the girl, she is expected to marry someone who, like herself, is Eurasian, and to lead her life in the Eurasian community, regarded as socially inferior by Europeans and as casteless by Indians.

Indoctrination started young. In the 1870s one mother was writing to her thirteen-year-old daughter, at school in Simla, 'I very much hope the other girls are ladies. As for those who are dark, ignore them. It is a sad fact that unions are made in India of the nicest of men of the best families, and women of no breeding who have coloured forebears. The sad result we must simply accept as part of God's plan, but there is no need either to speak or even have physical contact with these poor creatures. I know Mama can trust you not to have such a girl as a close friend or a friend of any kind.'

Only a few of those with Indian blood managed to clamber out of this undesirable no-man's land. One was Grace Trotter, a girl who must have been twenty when Kipling published his story.

Grace Minna Trotter was born on 29 November 1868, in Calcutta, where she was baptised. Her family had lived and worked in India for several generations, beginning with her great-grandfather, Alexander Trotter.

Alexander Trotter's father, John, had been a man of substance, one of Scotland's gentleman merchants. He died young in 1798 when Alexander was fourteen. A financial disaster had forced his executors to sell his charming Ibroxhill estate in 1800 and leave the residual funds to maintain Alexander's mother and sister (who later suffered grievously in the inflation of the Napoleonic Wars). Alexander himself obtained a post with the East India Company as a cadet in the Bengal Army and, after training in England, arrived in India in 1801 and was promoted to Lieutenant of Infantry in 1803.

So far so good. But three generations back, Grace had a secret. She had Indian blood – at least an eighth, and quite possibly more. In the British India of the Raj, this would not only have put paid to any hope of a 'good' marriage but also sent her crashing down to the bottom of the Raj's rigid class structure. As a Eurasian, she would have moved in a parallel world, alongside the English but never of them, alongside but despised by Indians. She would have belonged to a community in which she could expect to marry a husband who would never have risen to the top in the ICS or been an officer in the regular HEIC regiments;* instead, he would have held one of the vital but less eminent 'Anglo-Indian type' jobs – as a pilot on the Hooghly, for instance, as a hospital steward, as non-commissioned personnel in the Army, in middle management, in the railways, telegraphs or other jobs connected with the infrastructure.

In Alexander Trotter's India, although the practice of marriage to – or cohabitation with – an Indian woman was beginning to die

* See Introduction for details

out, it was certainly not frowned on (in any case, there were very few British women in the country). A few years earlier the Governor-General, Sir John Shore, had publicly kept a native woman and the British Resident in Delhi, contemporary with Alexander, used to take the evening air accompanied by his thirteen *bibis*, as these unofficial wives or consorts were called, mounted on elephants.

So Alexander's cohabitation* with a woman described in his will as 'a native woman of Hindoostan' would have raised few eyebrows. She was clearly well born: one of her names, Khanam Jan, means the equivalent of 'noble princess'. Most of Alexander's fellow cadets died of disease or on active service; even so, there were few opportunities in this period for glory and swift promotion.† When he was invalided out of active service in 1825, he commanded a regiment of Native Invalids until his death in 1828.

Their son William, described in his father's will as his 'natural son', was born in 1814. By the time he was grown up native marriages were dying out, from a combination of factors: earlier edicts banning Eurasians from the best jobs, nineteenth-century religious fervour and the growth in the numbers of European women. So although his father was a gentleman, William, as half-Indian, was slithering down the social ladder. He started his career as Assistant to the Military Board of the East India Company in Calcutta and made a very early marriage indeed: at the age of nineteen he married a widow of eighteen in the Cathedral at Calcutta and died aged thirty-two in his father's native Scotland.

His son, William Henry Trotter, born in 1837, was Grace's father. He had a career, working at times as a stockbroker and for different banks, almost always in Calcutta. His personal charm must have counterbalanced his Indian blood, as he married a young woman called Sarah Honoria Boote of a fairly humble background (both her father and maternal grandfather were non-commissioned soldiers). Both William's mother and wife probably also had Indian blood, believes Grace's great-grandson Charles Arthur.

Two of their daughters, Grace, born in 1868, and her elder

---

* Even if both regarded it as a marriage, no British clergyman would have married an unbaptised Indian and no Indian cleric would have married a practising Christian.

† Promotion in the HEIC was solely by seniority. Every officer would eventually become a general if he lived long enough; until the Mutiny generals were often in their seventies.

sister Mabel, were pretty, light-skinned girls who could pass as English – and were determined to do so. Grace's is the story of someone who managed to transcend her origins in the teeth of a highly stratified and critical society in a most remarkable way.

When Grace was only eleven her father died. Now, with a mother who looked English and their own similar appearance, there was nothing to suggest that Grace and Mabel's blood was not as purely English – or Scottish – as any of the young men and women this well-established Calcutta family mixed with. But the knowledge of her heritage must have made her feel that making a 'good' marriage was essential if she were finally to shed something viewed as so discreditable.

'Grace and Mabel teamed up to extricate themselves from the ghastly predicament into which the curse of mixed blood cast them in late-Victorian India,' says Charles Arthur, who to his surprise discovered that William Trotter had had another four daughters. 'They must have been darker-skinned and followed a Eurasian way of life, marrying other Eurasians who pursued Eurasian careers. At any rate, Grace and Mabel cut themselves off and the other girls were never mentioned to their descendants – perhaps my grandmother did not even know of them.'

When Grace was nineteen she met a good-looking 'griffin' in the ICS. William Henry Hoare Vincent, born in 1866, was the third son of the vicar of Carnarvon, who had died in the cholera epidemic of 1869, leaving his wife with seven young children and little money. Fortunately in 1871 a compassionate cousin bequeathed to them a house and small farm at Bangor, but the sons relied on scholarships for their public school education.

After school William went to London to train for the ICS entry examination, in which at the age of just nineteen he was placed seventeenth out of a field of about 200, most of whom had had the advantage of further education at Oxford or Cambridge, a high placing that made him a man to watch. Training periods at Trinity College, Dublin, and in London followed and in December 1887 William arrived in India to start his career in Bengal and Bihar and Orissa. Soon after his arrival he met Grace but was then sent to his first posting in Dacca.

In 1888 Grace and her elder sister Mabel were invited on what must have seemed the trip of a lifetime – exciting, glamorous, romantic and in the company of the most eligible young man in all India; in short, the *ne plus ultra* of any aspiring Fishing Fleet girl. Their friend, George Sanderson (always known as GP), the most famous elephant hunter in India and the Superintendent of Keddahs* for the Maharaja of Mysore, had asked them to join the tiger-shooting trip he had arranged for Lord Clandeboye, the twenty-two-year-old eldest son of the Viceroy, Lord Dufferin. For two weeks they would be constantly in his company in the romantic setting of jungle camps, with the added spice of excitement and possible danger. It was the equivalent of two British debutantes being asked to go on an exclusive safari with the unmarried Prince of Wales. To Grace, it was so important that she wrote a daily journal of it.

The trip began on Tuesday 24 April, at Mirzapore camp. As it was thick jungle the shooting would be from elephants. To make sure that Lord Clandeboye had sufficient opportunity to get a good tiger, GP had sent some cattle to the camp to act as bait if necessary; shooting at least one tiger had become almost obligatory for the Englishman in India and Lord Clandeboye, due to return to Britain later that year when his father's viceroyalty ended, was not going to miss the chance.

The next day they got to the jungle by boat on the river in about half an hour. 'It was very big and dense enough to have been the home of wild elephants,' wrote Grace. 'Mr Sanderson and Lord Clandeboye went a little way into the jungle and took up their positions in a tree towards which the tiger was to be driven – Mab, Bertie [a friend] and I remained outside on a narrow strip of *maidan*† that separated the jungle they were beating from another piece the other side.

'The heat began and after two hours of intense silence only broken by the occasional trumpeting of an elephant we heard a shot fired, which was followed almost immediately by shouts from the line (which was very close now) and savage growls from the tiger as he tried to break through before he finally did ... Lord Clandeboye said that when the tiger came near his tree he fired and wounded it in the shoulder. It rolled over once and then walked away; and

---

* The capture, followed by the taming, of wild elephants.

† Open space.

finally as we heard broke through the line into the heavy jungle beyond. We beat for him until about 3.30 then gave it up as hopeless. It rained hard nearly all the time, and we returned to the boats wet, hungry and disappointed … and slightly seasick. In spite of all our efforts to be cheerful we felt very melancholy and depressed at the loss of the tiger. It is the first time we have ever lost a tiger we've been after and having wounded it made it harder.'

The rain went on bucketing down, the camp ran out of mutton ('I was rather melancholy all day at the thought of the mutton having come to an end, and that henceforth we must live on fowls, duck and pigeons. I don't like any of these. However we had mushrooms for dinner and that cheered me a little.' There was nothing to do except play with the cat that Grace and Mabel had smuggled in, and no sign of any tigers.

'Another idle day in camp,' wrote Grace on 28 April, as the rain continued to pelt. 'Lord Clandeboye is not very fond of Bengalis … Today he told one of our boatmen who was speaking rather loudly that he would tie a rope round his neck and hang him over the side of the boat till he learnt to speak more quietly before ladies! He keeps the men in good order and not one of them dares disobey him.'

Just as Grace was writing 'I think we were all beginning to feel a trifle mouldy after so much rain,' everything suddenly changed. The rain stopped, news came in of a kill across the river and immediately after breakfast the party set out to find the elephants waiting for them on the far side of the river. At first it was easy jungle to work, chiefly scrub with the occasional large tree and patches of thorns. 'Mab and I were posted in a narrow strip of *maidan* that separated two bits of jungle,' wrote Grace. 'Mr Sanderson and Lord C were a little farther on. It was a very hot day and we just baked in the sun for about an hour while the line was coming up. There was nothing to keep the sun off one. Of course umbrellas were not allowed; and we did not have a tree to stand under.

'… when the line [of beaters] was nearly through the jungle Lord C got a shot and wounded the tiger slightly when it sprang back into a thick thorny bush from which we could not dislodge it as there was a bees' nest in it and no sane man will ever disturb a bees' nest. Following up a wounded tiger is one thing but disturbing a lot of bees is quite another story.

'While we were pottering about Stripes sneaked out and we lost sight of it for a bit and while Mr Sanderson and Lord C were beating up a bit of jungle a little way off she (it was a tigress) suddenly dashed out right in front of us with a tremendous noise and charged the elephant next to us. How frightened I was! I thought my heart was going to jump out of my body. I never knew what it was to be afraid when I was in the howdah with Mr Sanderson, not even on the day when we got the famous tiger (now in the British Museum) that charged straight at our elephant and was shot dead by Mr Sanderson only about a yard off. But having a first-rate shot in one's howdah is very different to having no one.'

Their elephant stood so firmly that the tigress changed her mind and retired into her thorn bush. Soon afterwards Lord Clandeboye arrived and, catching a glimpse of the great beast, which was preparing for another spring, finished her off with a couple of shots. 'She died pluckily, poor beast,' wrote Grace, 'and though I felt very sorry for her it was cheering to hear the old familiar cry "Allah, Allah" again. This is market day and the usually quiet little village is very noisy and in a fearful state of excitement. ... The dear old elephants looked very happy and contented having their dinner. It is pleasant to hear the 'swish, swish' of the grass as they beat it against their legs to get the earth out.'

On Saturday 6 May the journal bubbles with pleasure and excitement. 'We have had a most exciting and successful day and we are all immensely pleased with ourselves and everyone else in consequence. A villager brought in news of a kill early this morning and we started immediately after breakfast, about 9.30. We got to the jungle in about three-quarters of an hour and found all the elephants assembled awaiting orders from Mr S who had gone off to have a look around. It was a frightfully hot day. The jungle was in thick scrubby patches with a ginger swamp between two of the thickest and likeliest bits, and a small strip of *maidan* beyond, dividing two other patches.'

The first two beats resulted in nothing; in the third they were all put to flight by the wild bees – but they had heard the welcome 'it's in front' of the men and the occasional shrill scream of an elephant when it came close to the tiger, so they knew they would have what Grace called 'some sport'.

Her feelings changed later. 'After a time a tigress came through and Lord C got an easy shot at her. She staggered on a little way and he fired again when after two or three awful groans she died. Poor beast. It was dreadful to hear her. Writing of it in cold blood it seems so cruel and heartless to go out and see them shot but at the time one gets so excited that one does not think so much of it. In the meantime another tiger (her mate) had charged back and broken through the line. The beaters went back and after some time he was brought up again and went past Lord C's howdah into the thick jungle on the other side of the *maidan*. We saw him as he gained the other side and he looked magnificent as he walked quietly into the jungle and then turned round to see if he was being followed.'

Lord Clandeboye had not seen the tiger pass, so both Grace and Mabel tried to attract his attention by whistling, but neither could manage to. However the mahout succeeded and very soon had the bit of jungle the tiger was in surrounded. It was a small and rather thin patch but with very heavy jungle just beyond and if the tiger got through the line there would be very small chance of ever seeing him again.

'Mab, Bertie and I went into the line by way of a change and after we had gone a little way we heard Stripes growl and saw him spring forward just a little bit ahead of us. Lord C had a shot at him and he turned and charged the line and for the next ten minutes or so we had a very lively time indeed.

'He kept on dashing about and growling and charging the line over and over again. It was a grand sight and we saw him the whole time. The nearer we got him to the guns the more he dashed about and tried to break through. Poor beast, he fought hard for his life. The elephants and men behaved splendidly and after some time Lord C got another shot at him which brought him down, and a third shot ended his troubles. How the men shouted "Allah la la la la" again and again at the tops of their voices, each one trying to make himself heard above the rest. And how they jabbered and gesticulated and grinned as each one insisted that he had been the first to see the tiger! No one thought of listening. Everyone talked.

'The villagers, who had been posted up trees to mark the tiger's movements, crowded in to rejoice at the death of their enemy and showed their contempt of him now he could not harm them by kicking and abusing him. Just the nation's character all over. It was just 3 o'clock that the tiger was shot and after tying him to an elephant we went off to get the tigress and then started back to camp. We had a grand procession. The tigers side by side leading the way (on pad elephants of course), then ourselves on three elephants; and crowds of villagers running alongside and increasing in numbers every minute.'

Although their days and nights in the jungle brought Grace and Mabel no romantic fulfilment, they did bestow one intangible but important benefit: an impeccable seal on their social credentials. Few would now question or – more to the point – think of questioning their antecedents. Soon Grace would leave these even further behind.

William Vincent was still pursuing her. By any standards, and in particular by those of British India, he was a catch and, although he was only twenty-three, they married on 24 June 1889 in Dacca, where he was stationed. As ICS men were not supposed to marry before the age of thirty, and for the few who did special dispensation had to be obtained from the Viceroy, it says much for the high opinion in which he was held by the Service.

From that moment Grace's position in society was secure. William went on to have a distinguished career, switching from the executive side of the ICS to the judicial in 1900 and eventually becoming a judge of the Calcutta High Court in 1909. Unusually, he then switched back to the executive branch and joined the Government of India in 1911. As a member of the Government, he went up to Simla every year for six months, accompanied by Grace and, when they were not at school in England, their two daughters, Dorothy Grace (Charles Arthur's grandmother) and Isobel Wynn.

It was now the turn of Dorothy and Isobel, back from school as members of the Fishing Fleet, to enjoy dances, proposals and courtships. Enter Charles Arthur (grandfather of the present holder of the name). He had come out to India in 1905 to help out his uncle Sir Allan Arthur, whose business in Calcutta was in trouble from inattention; Allan had been President of the Bengal Chamber of Commerce several times and had served as the first Commerce Member of Curzon's Viceroy's Council. His business had suffered from his involvement in politics.

Charles, the youngest of four sons, went out from Glasgow to help his uncle pick up the pieces, and there in Calcutta met Grace's daughter Dorothy and fell in love with her – only to meet stiff opposition. Dorothy wrote to her mother in January 1914: 'What I am going to tell you now will probably surprise you a good deal, & yet I think you must have seen how things were going at Delhi. I have liked him awfully for some time but did not like to say anything until I knew my own mind better. As I am now sure that I really love him I feel I ought to let you know. I hope you will approve. I don't think you will be displeased because I know you are both very fond of him.' Obviously thinking that this might not be so she concluded with the plea: 'I do hope you will not be against it all as we should hate to do anything you would not like, and if you are pleased it will mean so much to us.'

Grace's reply was frigid. 'My dear Dorothy,' she responded coolly. 'Your letter received an hour or two ago has been a great shock to me. I am not going to write any kind of reply to it at present as I could not write as you would wish, and I do not wish to appear unsympathetic. I only ask that neither of you will give people any occasion to talk about you and I hope you will not consider yourselves engaged.'

By now so socially impregnable that she had swallowed whole all the Raj's fiercely hierarchical social protocol, Grace objected to Charles on the grounds that he came from a lower social class, declaring that 'someone in trade is not good enough for the daughter of an ICS man'. William, the ICS man concerned, was only anxious that his daughter should choose a man who would make her happy.

Grace went on to do everything she could to block the courtship: Dorothy and Charles Arthur had to exchange letters through a go-between, because Grace used to intercept any sent to the house and throw them away. But Charles was able to pursue Dorothy to Simla where, with her father a Government servant, she spent six months of every year. In Simla, with its parties and balls, it was impossible to prevent them seeing each other, dancing together and arranging meetings. It was in Simla that they married, in 1914, in Christ Church Cathedral, Grace (now Lady Vincent)* swallowing her objections sufficiently to give them a big society wedding, with

---

* William Vincent was knighted in 1913.

the marriage ceremony itself conducted by the Bishop of Lahore and the Archdeacon of Simla and the register signed by both the Viceroy and the Commander-in-Chief.

Charles and Dorothy drove off to their reception in the Lieutenant-Governor's carriage. 'Then followed one of the most memorable and remarkable processions I have ever seen,' wrote the groom's uncle. 'Most of the people were in rickshaws of which there were about 300, and, as each rickshaw requires four men, this made a rickshaw brigade. Then there were many guests on horseback, two of the clergy being mounted, and with each horseman was a syce [groom]. In addition there was a large number of camp followers and about 40 or 50 dogs, so that Charles and his bride had a marriage procession as big as an army corps.'

Charles, who spent his career in Calcutta, was to become Senior Resident Partner of Jardine, Skinner & Co., Managing Agents. Outside the business sphere he commanded the Calcutta Light Horse in the 1920s and was Sheriff of Calcutta in 1936–7, when he had the unique experience of proclaiming two new King-Emperors – Edward VIII and George VI – to the populace.

His father-in-law William went from strength to strength. In 1916 he was selected by the new Viceroy, Lord Chelmsford, for the Viceroy's Executive Council and a year later was promoted to the post of Home Member of the Government of India and President of the Viceroy's Council: a position that was second in importance, if not in status, to that of the Viceroy himself. In addition he was Speaker or Leader of the Legislative Assembly (the parliament of India created in 1919), where the Government was always a minority. He held the post of Home Member until he retired from it, aged fifty-six, when he and Grace returned to England.

Back in London his career continued. He served on the Council of India and as representative of India at the League of Nations until his final retirement in 1931. The Menai Strait farm where he had spent his boyhood through the legacy of a cousin was still in the family, but now the man who had once lived there as a poor boy travelled to it by private railway carriage hitched on to the back of the Irish Mail, stopping at the Vincents' own platform.

The story of Grace and William has a painful ending. For both, retirement could have been a life where William's many distinguished posts brought them much recognition and a wide social circle. But as soon as the Vincents returned to England Grace left her husband, to live in Cheltenham, and rarely saw or spoke to her daughter Dorothy again. It is difficult to avoid the conclusion that much of the reason for her marriage had been to escape from the curse of being Eurasian and to reclaim what she saw as her rightful place in society – and that, once at the top, she pulled up the drawbridge.

14

'Where every Jack has someone else's Jill'

The Hills

The hill stations – the small towns and stations where the altitude gave welcome coolness in the summer months – were a refuge for wives, children, soldiers and others on a week or two's leave, and Government officials, many of whom spent entire summers in one. What all of these hill stations shared was the tantalising prospect of an escape from the searing heat of the plains, where temperatures could remain at over 40°C for weeks at a stretch. Today we have air conditioning, electric fans and refrigerators; then, a dampened punkah and moistened reed mats hung over windows were the only relief.

These hill stations were essentially British in atmosphere and built within a timespan of around thirty years. Most were somewhere between 1,200 and 8,000 feet above sea level. There was more 'Englishness' in these small towns than in any other part of India, from the architecture ('the bow windows really are windows, not doors,' wrote Lady Wilson) to the climate that allowed the flowers of home – sweet peas, petunias, wisteria, wallflowers, phlox, lilac – to grow. Although the corrugated iron roofs, noisy under heavy rain and the feet of monkeys, did not look exactly homelike, at least they were pitched as at home – and effective against the monsoons.

The best known is undoubtedly Simla, the most purely British of Indian towns, with its buildings that range from Tudorbethan to neo-Gothic, some with elaborately carved and fretted eaves, others reminiscent of Swiss chalets. As the hill station for Calcutta, the seat of government until 1911, it was, from 1864, the summer capital of British India. It was also justly famous for love affairs and flirtations between married women whose husbands were working in the plains and the young officers and officials who constantly came up to Simla on leave. Immortalised by Kipling in *Plain Tales from the Hills*, it was, as Lady Reading put it, a place 'where every Jack has someone else's Jill'. It was in Simla that Frank, the son of the then Viceroy, Lord Northbrook, caused shocked gossip by forming an 'unfortunate attachment' to a married woman he had met there.

'The season blossomed and I became involved in a very gay life,' wrote Bethea Field of her first visit to Simla as a young married woman in 1928. 'I was young, attractive and had no lack of male escorts for balls, dances, cinemas and dinner parties. In the afternoons there were tennis games or picnics. I was lent horses to ride so that I could have my morning exercise and also ride down to Annandale for the races.

'To keep up with it all I had to make my own dresses and spent many hours stitching – but material in the bazaar was cheap and I was slim enough to be easily fitted. My ayah helped by pinning seams and doing up the hems. There was a big summer crowd in Simla, summer headquarters for the Viceroy, the Commander-in-Chief and the Governor of the Punjab. To add to all this, officers and civilians came on leave from the plains below. It was the Simla that Kipling had known and wrote about.

'One of the most enchanting things were the rickshaw rides at night. It was as if one were travelling through the Milky Way because all the hillside from the mall to the lower bazaar was spangled with lights. Above was the dark, velvet sky with the real stars shining so big and close.'

Bethea was often taken to Peliti's restaurant, which had a weekly dinner dance. In Rudyard Kipling's time, she noted, it was *the* place, from morning coffee and gossip to late after-theatre supper parties. 'One crossed a footbridge across a ravine with a cascading little torrent to reach it. The road just before the entrance is said to be haunted by the ghost of a woman who died in childbirth – her feet turn backwards from her ankles, though she glares at the passers-by with pale eyes. The coolies speed up and pass the dreaded spot with shouts and extra thumping of their feet, relaxing only when they are safely past.

'The rains come there in July and it can be most uncomfortable and wet. That past, there is a serene time when the sun appears again and with it the view to the plains below the hills. In the sunset they showed golden – and very welcoming.'

The amateur theatricals for which Simla was famous were considered a particular hazard to virtue, the more obvious temptations like the constant meeting with attractive members of the opposite sex and acting out scenes of passion with them heightened not only by the adrenaline rush of performance but also the holiday sense of liberation. 'For a woman who is young, comely and gifted with a taste for acting, Simla is assuredly not the most innocuous place on God's earth,' wrote Maud Diver warningly; although most Simla romances ended when both parties had left to return to normal life.

Sometimes there were more serious scandals. Just after the 1914–18 war a Mr King, who disliked dancing but was happy for his wife to attend balls, became suspicious of the way she always arrived home late from dances and in the company of his best friend, a cavalry officer. Once, when they were all staying in the same hotel for a party, he had a few drinks, picked up a poker and burst into the friend's hotel room to find the couple in bed. He flattened his friend with the poker and called in the other guests to witness what he had done and why. Knowing what the fallout would be, all three fled Simla. The cavalry officer was sent to a department called Remounts, which led Sir Harcourt Butler (shortly to become Governor of the United Provinces of Agra and Oudh) to believe that the Army had a sense of humour.

When Simla first caught the eye of Lord William Bentinck, the Governor-General of Bengal from 1828,* he wrote: 'Simla is only four days' march from Loodianah,† is easy of access, and proves a very agreeable refuge from the burning plains of Hindoostaun.' In 1864 it was officially declared the summer capital of India by the Viceroy, Sir John Lawrence, the first to move the administration the 1,000 odd miles from Calcutta to Simla and back again despite the difficulties of the journey (when the Government moved to New

---

* Later of India, when the title was created in 1833.
† Ludhiana, the largest city in the Punjab.

Delhi, the journey was cut to 250 miles). This annual spring migration of the whole of central government, files and all, took place first by train across the Ganges plain and then by bullock cart up through forests of oak, deodar and rhododendron until, finally, it arrived at this small town 7,000 feet above sea level.

What gave Simla its pre-eminent place among hill towns was, of course, the presence of the Viceroy. However far from home, however long a British subject had been away, he or she never forgot that in the person of the Viceroy was the representative of their Sovereign – and for those who served the Empire, the Sovereign was the living embodiment of the ethos that sustained them. No one, therefore, thought it odd that the Viceroy was one of only three people allowed to use first a carriage and then a car in Simla; everyone else had to use a tonga or rickshaw. The Viceroy was in residence from April until October, as were also countless officials.

Ruby Madden, who arrived in Simla on 12 March 1903, at the tail end of one of Simla's cold and snowy winters, found it freezing. 'Everything is run on English lines because of the cold,' she noted. When she went for a walk with Claude, the husband of her friend Jeanie, '[I] hitched up my skirt and with leather boots, coat, furs, muff and red cap was ready to face the elements. My goodness it was cold and fresh. Simla is very empty now but it fills up in April.' Later there would be rain – sometimes as much as six inches in two days – and thick white mists, soaking the petticoats and heavy dresses of the women who went out in this weather.

Ruby took her exercise later in the day. 'Breakfast is nominally ten o'clock but can be ordered any time. Lunch 2.15 then drift about until it's time to go out at six o'clock when we take our exercise and return glowing, to eat a huge tea at seven o'clock beside a deodar log fire, which gives out a delicious scent, and curtains drawn. Afterwards dress very much at your leisure for dinner at eight or nine, more often at nine. We don't often finish coffee until ten o'clock and any time after that we go to bed where I sleep under four blankets, an eiderdown, rezai [padded Indian quilt], hot water bottle, flannel nighty and have a big log fire as well and then just feel comfy.'

Days of serious rain were a drawback, but for the temporary inhabitants of this little hill town, newly released from the miseries of hot weather, the quest for enjoyment was paramount. A description of the determined relish with which the British of the late-Victorian Raj threw themselves into the gaieties of Simla is given by Henry Stewart Cunningham* in his 1875 novel *The Chronicles of Dustypore* (its heroine, Maud, is a Fishing Fleet girl).

'Nothing damps their ardour – not even the Himalayan rain, which effectually damps everything else. There is a ball, for instance, at the Club House; it is raining cataracts, and has been doing so for twenty hours. The mountain paths are knee-deep in mud, and swept by many a turgid torrent rattling from above. Great masses of thunder-cloud come looming up, rumbling, crashing and blazing upon a sodden, reeking world. The night is black as Tartarus, save when the frequent flashes light it up with a momentary glare.

'The road is steep, rough, and not too safe. A false step might send you several thousand feet down the precipice into the valley below. Will all this prevent Jones the Collector and Brown the Policeman and Smith of the Irregular Cavalry putting their respective ladies into palanquins, mounting their ponies like men, and finding their way, through field and flood, to the scene of dissipation? Each will ensconce himself in a panoply of indiarubber, and require a great deal of peeling before becoming presentable in a ballroom; but each will get himself peeled, and dance till four o'clock. The ladies will emerge from their palanquins as fresh and bright and ambrosial as lace and tarlatan can make them ... Is this the race which proclaims itself inadept at amusements, and which, historians gravely assure us, loves to take its very pleasures sadly?'

The town itself spread about three and a half miles from east to west and about two and a half from north to south, with all the houses on a narrow plateau which ran east to west, with some spurs projecting from it, from which descended rough slopes for about a thousand feet.

It was not a particularly beautiful town: Sir Edwin Lutyens, the architect of New Delhi, once said that if Simla had been built by monkeys, one would have said: 'What clever monkeys! They must be shot in case they do it again.' But its views were spectacular:

---

* Henry Stewart Cunningham (later Sir Henry) was a witty and charming lawyer and writer who practised in British India from 1866 and was a popular figure on the social scene. He became Advocate-General of the Madras Presidency in 1872 and in 1877 was appointed a judge of the High Court in Calcutta.

glorious sunsets and range upon range of mountains, beyond which (in the words of Lady Irwin) 'you can see the plain 120 miles away, pale cobalt blue and pinky mauve seared with silver bands, which are the rivers in flood'.

Annandale, famous first for archery contests and later for croquet, was a flat oval stadium at the foot of one of the slopes that descended from the plateau. Viceregal Lodge, huge, ostentatious and as modern as the Viceroy who built it, Lord Dufferin, could make it, stood at the west end of the plateau on Observatory Hill, with the town hall and church two miles away at the east end. Above the trees rose its towers and cupolas, made of greyish stone; inside were rooms sumptuously decorated by Maples of London. The hall was the full height of the house, its central feature a grand teak staircase that spiralled up three floors; in the hall everything was of teak, walnut or deodar, carved and moulded. The big drawing room was furnished in gold and brown silks, the ballroom decorated a lighter shade of yellow, the state dining room hung with Spanish leather in rich, dark colours.

There were large white-tiled modern basement kitchens, a huge wine cellar; there was electric light – the Vicereine, Hariot Dufferin, found this such a pleasure that she went round touching the on-off buttons from time to time – running hot and cold water in the bathrooms and an indoor tennis court. Outbuildings provided accommodation for the Viceroy's personal bodyguard and the household band. There was even a shed near the entrance where the gun for firing salutes was kept. In Curzon's day forty gardeners looked after the spacious ground with a squad of ten men whose sole duty was, to keep away the bold, thieving, chattering, monkeys that were the bane of everyone's life, Monkeys raided all the gardens in Simla, chasing each other over the red corrugated iron roofs, shrieking and clattering, stripping fruit trees and darting into houses to grab anything small or glittering, such as a silver spoon or snuff box, that caught their eye.

Viceregal Lodge was a place to impress – the tallest building on the highest spot, home to the most elevated in the country. Curzon, possibly India's greatest Viceroy and one for whom an image of magnificence was all-important ('it certainly needs no trained psychologist's eye to diagnose him at a glance as a man who would prefer to be mounted on an elephant rather than a donkey,' remarked

Lady Cynthia Asquith, daughter of one of his friends), loved Simla and entertained here freely. A typical festivity was a dinner dance at Viceregal Lodge in July 1901, with seventy to dine plus eighty in afterwards to dance (and everyone out by midnight) and around fifteen spare men so that all the women were able to dance; there were levées, a garden party, a Drawing Room, official dinners for 120 every Thursday, and innumerable smaller dinner and luncheon parties.

Lord Kitchener, Curzon's great rival and later enemy, lived almost more splendidly, with the difference that he managed to get the Government of England to pay for most of his alterations and extravagances. In Snowdon, his Simla residence, the great hall was panelled in walnut; in his new library the ceiling was a copy of the one at Hatfield. For ceilings in less visible parts of the house, he used papier mâché, composed largely of great masses of military files pounded into pulp by his two ADCs.

In the new dining room he added he entertained lavishly. 'We were forty at six tables, the centre one all gold plate and on the sideboard five gold vases,' wrote one young woman. 'We began with iced soup, just stiff enough to spoon comfortably, with little dots of truffles; next fillets of fish with mushrooms and prawns; then *filets de boeuf a la banquantine*. A *mousse de canetons*, followed by quails, constituted the fourth and fifth courses. The sixth was a dream of a fruit compote with cream ices. Then cheese and biscuits and the 8th course was a sumptuous dessert of peaches, apricots, mangoes and prunes just softened with a dash of brandy.'

The Retreat, the Viceroy's weekend cottage, at Mashobra, was to the north-east of Simla, about six miles from Viceregal Lodge and 600 feet higher. Curzon, an indefatigable worker, sent out a stream of orders, reports, diplomatic messages and proposed reforms even from Naldera, a tented camp seventeen miles from Simla where he and Mary Curzon would withdraw for a respite from official duties, where Mary could rest and Curzon could work out of doors. It was at Naldera in 1903 that Mary conceived her third child, christened Alexandra Naldera, after her godmother Queen Alexandra and the place of which Mary had such idyllic memories.

Twenty years later the Vicereine, Lady Reading, who had categorised Simla as 'a hotbed of flirtations and more,' was also seeking peace and quiet away from Simla. The Readings' retreat was Mashobra, surrounded by forests of oak, deodar, pine, maple, horse chestnut and rhododendron, the haunt of monkeys, baboons, barking deer and the occasional leopard. In 1921 Mashobra, unlike Viceregal Lodge, had no electric light, and water was still brought to the house in skins. In May 1923 Lady Reading was writing of 'irises in bloom, hundreds of coloured butterflies, and mules laden with food'. But no Viceroy was ever off duty. 'Every few hours,' she added, 'a tall bodyguard in scarlet and gold uniform on a black horse appears, carrying dispatches, letters and telegrams.'

Because it housed the whole bureaucracy of government for so many months of the year, Simla was sometimes known as 'the abode of the little tin gods'. There was plenty to keep them entertained. At nearby Annandale there were races and archery competitions; there were gymkhanas, dog shows, croquet, hunting, football, golf, the immensely popular amateur dramatics and of course club life. There were dances, concerts, polo matches, picnics and a plethora of dinner parties, all opportunities for constantly meeting the fancied member of the opposite sex in public – so much so that Maud Diver wrote that the two greatest dangers facing a woman in India were military men away from their wives, and amateur theatricals. All in all, it was a place known for its social life although at the same time protocol, especially in matters of precedence, was rigorously maintained, with the social strata as clearly delineated as ever.

Some of the most enjoyable parties were those given by The Most Hospitable Order of Knights of the Black Heart, a society founded in Simla in 1891, in abeyance in the 1914 war and revived in 1920. The motto of the Order was: 'He is no so … as he is Black' and everyone speculated on the missing word – naturally, the Knights (always bachelors or grass widowers) were forbidden to disclose it. This secret word was said to be kept in the heart-shaped lockets that Knights wore round their necks when in their Revels' 'uniform' – evening dress with knee breeches and black silk stockings, a knee-length scarlet cloak with a black heart over the left breast and a red band round the right knee. The Knights, chosen by their fellows, were an exclusive society and could not be 'living in open matrimony'.

'The dancing started with "The Lancers",' noted Bethea Williams. 'Each Black Heart chose, or was assigned, a Lady Partner. I was never in that category but it was fun to watch them. The ladies were chosen firstly by their rank – the Viceroy's wife, then the Commander-in-Chief's wife, the wife of the Governor of the Punjab and so on until it trickled down to the last few most glamorous ones. There were eight couples and the dance was very seriously performed. After that it was a "free for all" and I did not lack partners. The "Black Hearts" were so limited in number that it was a coveted honour to be invited to join them – and an expensive honour because their parties were unstinting as to wines and food and the best band Simla could produce. That year it was the dance band of the Black Watch regiment, stationed in Delhi. The supper board was loaded – smoked salmon and boar's head especially ordered from England.'

If a grass widower's wife returned to him he could attend functions in his Black Heart uniform but the red knee band was replaced by white and there was no collar badge because he had 'lost his Heart'. Any one knight could veto any item on their agenda or guest on their list. Their parties, three times in the season, were known as the best; one of them was always fancy dress. They also featured the *kalajuggah*, though with the proviso that while a couple who disappeared into one must be left alone, they also had to reappear for the next dance, thus putting paid to any serious dalliance.

The frantic gaiety of the Simla Season paused only for official mourning. Lucy Hardy, who had spent her first few months in Umballa, where her brother was stationed ('there were only two or three other girls there besides myself'), went up to Simla in May with a friend, sharing rooms in a hotel until her husband came on leave. 'Owing to the death of Queen Victoria [in January 1901], there were no big entertainments in Simla,' she wrote disappointedly, 'and Lady Curzon had gone home but Lord C gave some small dances to which we went – but as mourning had to be worn I had to appear in a black organdie gown over silk which had done much dinner duty at Umballa, instead of my best gown of white brocade with puff sleeves and trimmings of blue velvet!'

Many Bengal Europeans not in Government or official service went to Darjeeling, a favourite hill station since the days of the East India Company, then a four-day journey from Calcutta. In the twentieth century the Darjeeling Mail sped northwards as spectacular sunsets were reflected in the sheets of water that spread over green rice fields. At the end of the line, Siliguri, travellers changed to the Darjeeling Hill Railway, climbing round steep bends to the little town with its steep-roofed houses with carved and fretted woodwork and balconies. Built on hills and just under 8,000 feet above sea level, Darjeeling gave visitors plenty of involuntary exercise. Even so, 'I advise any intending visitor to the hills to take plenty of warm woollen underclothing,' wrote one traveller.

Rumer Godden, who lived for a time in a bungalow on a hill near Darjeeling, loved the landscape around it, with the pink earthen walls of the farmhouses, the orange groves, banana trees and pineapple bushes, its brilliant butterflies – black, red, yellow and blue – its streams, pools and waterfalls. Of one she wrote: 'In the crevices of the waterfall we find begonias, small ones, crisp, with heavy leaves, in colour and crispness each petal is like a delicate pink shell.'

For the Madras Presidency, the usual hill station was Ootacamund (known as 'snooty Ooty') in the Nilgiri Hills, about 8,000 feet above sea level. A popular way of reaching it was by overnight journey to the foothills, then by driving up by a road notable both for its scenery and its hairpin bends. It was perhaps the most English of them all. It was in the Ooty Club, where the game caught on, that the rules of snooker, invented by the future Colonel Sir Neville Chamberlain, then a subaltern in the 11th Foot stationed at Jubbulpore, are hung in the billiards room; it was at the Ooty Club that the Ooty Hunt met, the hunt servants and some of the field wearing pink coats but hunting jackal instead of foxes. At Naini Tal – a popular place for honeymoons – there was yachting on the lake.

Poona, a name so indelibly connected with British India that it has passed into the vocabulary of comedians to delineate certain types and experiences, was a mid-weather station for the Bombay Government, which spent four months of the year there. Only a night's journey from Bombay, its situation 2,000 feet up in the Western Ghats meant it was pleasant for most of the year, though the hot weather season was spent in the hill station of Mahabaleshwar, on the banks of Lake Venna, 4,500 feet high.

On the edge of the great Deccan plateau, Poona was the headquarters of Southern Army Command – a kind of Aldershot of the East – and also a great racing centre; in the early twentieth century Victor Sassoon kept racing stables there, and the Aga Khan owned a palace. Tan tracks, soft and sandy with a dressing of bark, ran beside most road for the benefit of horses and ponies; cork trees, with their stephanotis-like blossoms and scarlet-blooming acacias, with long pods that rattled after flowering, were planted along the sides.

Here, as well as snakes and panthers lurking in the jungle nearby, thrushes and blackbirds sang and the strawberry beds were famous. In the two large public gardens fluttered huge black and turquoise butterflies. There was also golfing, though on brown rather than green grass when the sun had dried up the links.

In the ancient city of Poona, once the capital of the Mahratta kingdom, narrow streets were flanked by the bazaar stalls – the fruit sellers, cloth merchants, jewellers, sellers of sweet, syrupy drinks and deep-fried savouries. Bullock carts jostled against the tide of walkers; the tall brick houses of the rich stood side by side with the hovels of the poor; in side lanes embroidered white pillow-cases hung from balconies – the sign that a prostitute awaited within.

The Poona Season lasted four months and began in June, with the arrival of the Governor and his officials. All who could came up from Bombay for weekends or rented bungalows there to avoid the monsoon. Newcomers were warned not to do too much and above all not to eat too many of the delicious mangoes for which the town was famous or they would get 'Poonaitis' (a euphemism for diarrhoea).

The centre of Poona life was the Gymkhana, to which the ladies drove soon after tea, the men after work. There was croquet and tennis, the women playing in white divided skirts and Aertex shirts, the men in white flannels and crisp white shirts with sleeves rolled up; others would sit, chat and sew (knitting did not come in until the war) and listen to the military band parading up and down on the lawn, playing the latest tunes from England. There was a small playground for children with a couple of swings and a seesaw. Outside the clubhouse was 'the beach' – an area covered with Alderney shingle.* On this shingle were set up small tables with chairs so that

---

* Ships carrying heavy cargo such as teak wood from India would return with Alderney shingle as ballast in their holds and places near the coast would buy this up to make carriage drives or cover for forecourts, as in front of Government House in Calcutta.

the younger set could sit around, sip their drinks, munch toasted nuts and flirt in the dim lighting of a few Japanese lanterns with candles.

On most evenings there were 'flannel dances' that lasted an hour or two, until everyone went off to dinner somewhere. The life was relentlessly unintellectual: when Iris Portal (née Butler) lived there in the late 1920, she noticed that very few of the unmarried officers called on them for the customary pre-lunch drinks on Sunday, as they did on the other married officers. Puzzled, as she knew how popular her husband was, and anxious, she asked a friendly young subaltern the reason. He looked embarrassed, then finally blurted out: 'Well – it's got about that you read poetry.'

For anyone stationed in the districts or provinces of the North-West Frontier, the usual destination was Kashmir. Robin Mallinson, whose father was in the 17th Dogra Regiment of the Indian Army, based at Jullundur in the Punjab, spent the winter in the plains and went up with his family to the hills in the summer. Some families went so often that they bought – as far as the property laws allowed – instead of rented. In Kashmir, as it was an autonomous state with a maharaja, the British were not allowed to own property. The loophole came via the water with which Kashmir is so plentifully supplied. Its capital, Srinagar, 5,000 feet high, is surrounded by lakes – and there was no law against owning a boat. Consequently, the British could buy and own houseboats – and many did (others often rented one). Usually these were on the biggest lake, the Dal Lake.

Joan Henry, after returning from her English education, was sent up to Srinagar by her widowed planter father for the hot weather in 1934. His bearer accompanied her for the three days and two nights it took to get across India. In Srinagar she stayed as a paying guest in the houseboat of an Army officer's widow, on the River Jhelum. It was one of three, one behind the other, moored to the river bank, carved inside and out – on the furniture, on the boat itself – with flowers, foliage and intricate designs (these never included animals or people as the carvers, being strict Muslims, would have considered it idolatrous). The first boat held sitting and dining rooms, the next bedrooms and bathrooms, the last the servants' quarters.

'In the summer, people would move up to Gulmarg, about 9,000 feet above sea level. From one side of it you looked across the marg, or meadow, to the chalets, known as huts; from the other side, you could look across the Vale of Kashmir towards Nanga Parbat, 26,000 feet high, almost 90 miles away,' recalled Robin Mallinson.

Gulmarg is remembered lyrically by most of those who went there. Its beauty was staggering – faintly Swiss but without the picture-postcard element: forests scented with pine and snow water, snowy peaks, icy streams beside which grew gentians and primulas, wide expanses of grass and over all a faint hint of danger. Leopards' Valley, known for its golf course, was so named because there dogs had been snatched by leopards as their owners played golf. A dog that slept on the veranda of one of the wooden huts might be taken at night by a panther that had crept into the garden; a troop of red baboons might suddenly descend the mountainside; the unwary walker could face a confrontation with a black bear, in spring just emerging from its hibernation and prepared to attack anything that looked threatening. The best defence was to stand completely still, as the bear's sight was appalling, and hope that the beast would move away. There were no cars, lorries or trucks in Gulmarg; one walked, or rode the local ponies known as *tats*, but there was a club, an hotel, a bazaar and several golf courses.

It was the great place for young families but there was also plenty of life in the club, with dancing to tunes like *Me and My Shadow, I Can't Give You Anything But Love, Baby* – or at dinner parties to which people rode on their *tats* with evening dresses hitched up. There were wonderful walks, fishing for snow trout in the Ferozpur river and – by the 1920s – skiing higher up. Best of all, perhaps, were the rides round the Outer Circular Road, with its pine woods and maidenhair fern, or up to Khilanmarg, a long slope of open, grassy ground where the snow line cuts off the forests, where you could look down on Gulmarg and the Kashmir valley with, possibly, a glimpse of K2, the second highest mountain in the world.

Mary Lloyd, whose father was in the Rajputana Rifles based in Rajasthan, went up to Kashmir every summer, her family always renting the same hut in Gulmarg. 'We would travel first by train from wherever Daddy had been posted to and then take the long, tiring and sick-inducing car or truck journey up to Kashmir. When I say "sick", I mean sick, and without exception we were sick. The smell of petrol and the whining of the engine as it struggled up the mountain roads round hairpin bend after hairpin bend is with me to this day. I clearly remember being sick on our lunchtime sandwiches and once on the cat's basket.

'Eventually, after a long, long day we would arrive in the beautiful cool fresh air of Kashmir. The lakes and the snow-capped mountains surrounding us were heaven after the searing heat we had left. We would sometimes stay a day or two in Srinagar with Aunt Emmie Walton, Grandad's sister-in-law, whose whole life had been connected with India. As a child during the Mutiny she had sheltered with her parents, who were planters, in the Calcutta Fort. She much later married Grandad's eldest brother Charles, who was also sheltering there with his mother (our great-grandmother) whilst his father was riding to relieve the garrison in the famous Relief of Lucknow. She lived in a house called Hopewell after the first boat that took the Waltons to India. It was opposite the Kashmir Nursing Home where we were all born.'

After Srinagar, the Lloyds would embark on the last lap of their journey to their beloved Gulmarg. First they would go by car up through the tall poplar trees to Tanmarg – no cars went further than this point. Here all the ponymen were gathered, each one standing by his pony, and they would each select a pony for the summer. Once chosen, they would ride their ponies up to Gulmarg, two or three miles uphill, with each pony man holding on to his pony's tail to pull himself up and encouraging the pony from behind. Up they went through steep paths winding through the pine trees, with piles of snow still lying about. 'The smell of the shrubs in flower, the pines and the fallen snow was intoxicating. We were always so excited to be back. Our luggage was carried up by coolies – masses of coolies.

'Our hut, Hut 102A, was the highest hut at one end of a valley, surrounded by forest and with a fantastic view straight down Leopards' Valley, with its streams and paths, and the towering snow-covered mountains beyond. There were flowers everywhere – primulas, pale purple irises, rhododendrons – you could grow anything. We grew poppies, forget-me-nots, a big bank of daisies. Lots of the places where the hill people lived had roofs covered in mud with irises growing on them. Always the air was scented, with pines, melting snow, viburnum.'

The Lloyds always went up earlier than most people, at the end of March or the beginning of April, which meant that there was still plenty of snow about – and quite a lot of bears. Because Gulmarg was so high it took several days to acclimatise but soon the children would be tobogganing on tin trays. 'One of our favourite tricks,' recalled Mary, 'was just as someone got started, to shout "Bear!", hoping to terrify the tobogganer – who of course was unable to stand still and hope to avoid attention.

'Mostly we would do lessons in the morning, go out for a ride or a walk in the afternoon and then have tea at a friend's house or a tea party at home. Sometimes we would have a picnic by a stream or play on the children's golf course. When we needed milk a man would come from the bazaar and milk the cow in front of my mother. She would make him roll his sleeves up because they had a trick of hiding water in their sleeves and diluting the milk with it. But even when the milking had been done in front of us we still boiled it, and all our water. We spent almost half the year in Gulmarg – we would leave in September. And how sad we were when we did.'

Jean Hilary found life in the Srinagar of May 1929 so delightful that she did not even reach Gulmarg, cancelling her planned visit there. She wrote ecstatically to her mother about the drive up to Srinagar. 'The last thirty-five miles of road here is through an avenue of silver poplars and on either side are fields of purple and white irises and every now and again a field of scarlet poppies. All the marshland is cultivated, in tiers, and it looks like a patchwork quilt. I've never seen anything to equal the colours of the birds, which fly about everywhere – green, yellow, red, blue and scarlet. Of course, we saw snow-capped mountains, with the sun on them, as soon as we left Muri, where we spent the night. It all looks quite like Switzerland, even the wooden huts of the villages. We followed the Jhelum the whole way.'

That first impression was soon superseded by an unaccustomed fit of the glooms. After being feted during the previous months in Calcutta ('I think I have realised what an awful power I have over the opposite sex'), life with her hosts, an older married couple, in their houseboat on the Dal Lake saw her dolefully bemoaning her lack of social life. 'I do rather want someone young to do things with, come to the Club with me, and get to know people. I don't know how I ever shall this way, it's all so scattered and vague. I wandered about the Club yesterday, watching the tennis tournament, and choosing books from the Library. I don't think there are many men there, as the soldiers who come up usually go off fishing and shooting.

'I am quite put off the Club and the young men here. All the decent ones only come up to shoot or fish or later on for the polo. Good regiments don't care about their young men "poodlefaking" on the river.'

Suddenly everything changed. She met a pretty young married woman with an attractive husband and some good-looking male friends. Quickly she found herself at the heart of a young and gay circle ('our men are the nicest and best-looking here') determined to enjoy themselves. There were picnics, expeditions, bathing for hours from a raft in the lake ('my new blue bathing suit is the most decent thing ever – a one-piece garment but it has kicks underneath') and daily visits to the club, now a favourite haunt. Sometimes there were ukelele bathing parties, on other days they floated across the lake in shikaras,* gramophone playing the hits of the moment; and every evening she dined out and danced. There was dinner at the Residency with twenty young people, the Resident and his wife being out for the evening, and musical chairs and sardines ('in the dark!') afterwards. 'I just go about bursting with the fun of it all,' she wrote happily to her mother.

She was, however, determined in one respect. 'I hope you won't worry,' she reassured her widowed mother, 'that I will be meeting nice regimental people and falling in love with them. It would be too awful to marry a soldier and come to some of these stations out here. Just as well my heart is quite intact – it is all too devastating.'

Jean and her companions, young, healthy and attractive, cramming every moment of the day with the pleasures of companionship, surroundings of exquisite beauty and the enjoyable frisson of sexual tension, exemplified the Raj at play. Hill stations meant holidays, with all that holidays promised in the way of carefree relaxation and romance, away from the all-seeing eyes that surrounded India's rulers in the plains.

Or, as John Masters so memorably wrote: 'Perhaps it was the mountain air that caused so many of the women to cast away their

---

* Wooden boats of different sizes, some gondola-like, that have become the architectural symbol of Srinagar.

inhibitions. Perhaps the friendly unfamiliar wood fires burning on the hearths warmed their blood and made them think with fervour of romps on tiger skin divans. Perhaps it was moonlight and bul-buls – or perhaps it was human nature ... the fact was that hill sta-tions presented an unusual picture of a race that was supposed to be frigid.'

15

'"No" would have been unthinkable'

Engagement

Getting engaged in the Raj was sometimes a bit like speed dating. Often, minds were made up and a lifelong commitment to another human being promised after only a few meetings and without the aphrodisiac bait of great wealth, a large and splendid estate, or huge personal prestige to account for such rapidity.

Violet Swinhoe, who had previously merely played a round of golf with her future husband, recalled in September 1916 of one dance: 'had two with James and he was ripping and there was a full moon and altogether everything was top hole'. After a few other meetings, at another dance on 19 March, she was writing: 'began dancing and was at the fourth when he told me he loved me. Dear thing, but I said, I was so uncertain in my mind …'. By the 30th it was fixed. 'James had final talk with Daddy and then we were engaged. Too queer for words. I lay down.'

Yet looking at the phenomenon of almost instant betrothals from the standpoint of the parties concerned, it is understandable. Most ICS men, once they reached the age when they were allowed to marry, would devote their energies to finding a wife; and if their six-month home leave brought no joy, would continue the search on the ship back to India – most returned from leave in the autumn, when the new crop of Fishing Fleet girls went out. If unsuccessful at home or on the ship but still anxious to marry, they would naturally focus on the available girls in India, who were, in the main, Fishing Fleet girls.

Once there, with a male-female ratio of about three to one, in the hothouse atmosphere of balls, parties and moonlight picnics, popular and pursued as never before, it was easy for any girl to fall headlong in love. 'Hearts are strangely inflammable under Indian skies,' wrote Maud Diver, 'and propinquity fans the faintest spark into a flame.'

Rumer Godden found herself engaged to a man she knew she did not love, simply because as an inexperienced eighteen-year-old brought up to agree with older people, this, coupled with the glamorous surroundings and the pressure of romantic expectation on all sides, was overwhelming. 'On Christmas night, after dinner, Ian took me apart on to the high foredeck of the furthest ship and, under those glittering stars, asked me to marry him ... I had no chance to say "Yes". Ian said it for me. "No" would have been unthinkable. "It is yes, isn't it?" he said, and kissed me. All his love and longing was in that kiss but I think I only blinked ... This was happening to me and it was wrong.

'Then why did I let it go on? I think I did not know how not to and I was immensely flattered, to be a chosen girl. Hostesses beamed approval on me. "Ian is such a nice man," which he was. "He deserves to be happy," which he did. Flowers came every day and Ian would take a case out of his pocket with a smile and there was a brooch, or a bracelet, once a string of pearls.' Finally, she found the courage to break it off.

More usually, courtship was a long-distance affair, with a stream of letters passing between a couple who might have met during, say, Delhi Week, thereafter to be separated by hundreds of miles as he returned to station or cantonment and she – who would never have come to Delhi Week on her own – with her hosts to where they were living.

Philip Docton Martyn (always known as PD) was an ICS man posted, when he joined in 1927, to the Presidency of Fort William in Bengal. On leave from India six years later he met his future bride, Margaret, then twenty-four; one bond was that they were both graduates of Manchester University.

They met a mere three times that summer and six months later he proposed, from India, although this meant a long engagement until he had reached the age at which marriage was permitted. It was only after four years of letters, written in the form of daily diaries and posted once a week, that he returned, married Margaret and took her back to India in 1939. (Among the advice Margaret received from a woman who lived there was to bring out a garden party dress with hat and gloves for the Christmas Garden Party at Belvedere – the Viceroy's Calcutta residence – as many evening dresses as possible, a black outfit in case of official mourning and fine lawn underwear.)

Lieutenant Leslie Lavie, stationed in Vizianagram, a town inland on the coastal plain of Bengal, halfway between Madras and Calcutta, was another for whom letters were the lifeline. He had met Florence Ross in February 1895. The youngest daughter of Dr Hamilton Ross, a former Surgeon Major to the British Army in India who lived in County Antrim, she was staying in Secunderabad with her sister Alice, married to Major Herbert Nepean.

They became engaged on 30 January 1896, and thereafter the besotted Leslie wrote daily to his beloved: long letters ('I really ought not to spend about one and a half hours a day writing to you as I have certainly let things get into arrears a little'). These told of the news of the cantonment, of the appalling and enervating heat, the illnesses from which he and his friends suffered and the general discomforts and oppression of life in the hot weather. They gave her instructions couched as wishes 'I hope you will try to get an idea of the way an Indian household should be run'), and discussed the ups and downs of their relationship ('be nice and tell me why you were so cold in your letters last week ...'); 'My own darling, you have ceased to address me like this, I suppose for some reason best known to yourself, perhaps because you no longer look on me as such ... I have tried and tried to think how I can have offended you, but don't know').

But even when there had been a spate of reproaches he was devastated when circumstances intervened to interrupt the steady stream of correspondence; when the railway broke down because of floods so that no mail got through he wrote, on 9 August, that it was 'a fearful blow to me, as my spirits and happiness depend on your letters'.

Theirs was a story that ended in tragedy. After working through financial problems, negotiating their way past the age barrier (Leslie was not quite old enough at twenty-seven) they married on 16 September in St John's Church, Secunderabad. Only seven months later he died after an illness of ten days during which, unsuspected, an abscess developed on his liver and eventually was said to have burst through his lungs. He was buried the next day in the cantonment cemetery, under a tombstone of white marble engraved with the sad little phrase, *Entered into Rest*; and on 24 July 1897 Flossie gave birth to a posthumous daughter, Leslie Mary Maud Lavie – usually called by the diminutive, Mollie.

A few years later, Flossie decided to try her luck in India again, rejoining the Fishing Fleet in the early 1900s and leaving Mollie in the care of her grandparents. Postcards arrived for Mollie at frequent intervals. One, postmarked 28 December 1905, reads 'Very many thanks for your letter. I hope you had a Happy Christmas and had plenty to eat. Mummie.' But Flossie's second Indian venture was unsuccessful, despite at least one proposal. 'It may be a waist [sic] of money your trip to India, but since you have only one life to live you might just as well enjoy it while you can,' wrote her sister Ellen from Minneapolis. 'Who did you get yourself engaged to? Unless you were quite sure you would be happy, it is as well you did not do it. It is easy to get married but not as easy to get out of it …'.

Later, Flossie said that no one she met on that second visit measured up to her beloved Leslie. Although only thirty-five, she never remarried, remaining a widow for over sixty years, until she died at the age of ninety-seven.

Not many girls become engaged on top of an elephant but one was Honor Penrose, born in 1888. One of a large family, she was brought up in Lismore Castle, the property of the Duke of Devonshire, as her father was his agent. Life in Ireland was quiet, with entertainment consisting mainly of travelling circuses and concerts, the arrival of the first bicycles ('I ran all down the drive to see one' recalled Honor) and then the motor car – a shock for this small community. 'I seen the Divil in his Hellcart coming into Athlone,' said one old man, 'and I just had time to go down on my knees and say two Aves and one Pater when "Hoot-toot!" says he and away with him.'

Honor herself was responsible for another innovation: riding astride, in those days unheard of, especially in a quiet corner of rural Ireland. Although the FANYs, the nursing yeomanry founded to ride out and give succour to the wounded in the South African War of 1899–1902, took to riding astride in 1910, they wore khaki so that their professional role was clear and therefore acceptable, despite a certain amount of tut-tutting. By contrast Lord Annaly, Master of the Pytchley 1902–14, was so outspoken in disapproval of riding astride that he would not give the Pytchley white collar to any woman who did so.* Honor, who took to riding astride because her back hurt intolerably when sitting sideways on a horse, was apprehensive on her first such outing.

'I can remember my agony of shyness arriving at the Meet and keeping my horse as close to my father's as I could to hide the terrible fact that I had two legs, even though they were covered discreetly by a divided skirt!' she wrote later. 'People were very nice to me but another girl who followed my example some time later had stones thrown at her by the cottage women and shouts of "Go home and put on the petticoat!"'

As Honor grew up there were teenage dances, conducted in the most formal way with programmes and white kid gloves. But this happy mingling of the sexes soon ceased; there were no jobs for the boys and 'one by one they departed to distant corners of the Empire to earn a living and we girls were left lamenting at home'. When in 1913 her older sister Judith was invited to India by a cousin but could not go, Honor was sent in her stead 'to find a husband,' as she later told her granddaughter. She travelled out with a married friend, Sylvia Cassels, as far as Bombay, and thence by train to Nagpur to stay with her cousin Sylvia Pollard-Lowseley, whose husband was in the Royal Engineers.

Just before Christmas she left her cousins to stay with Sylvia Cassels, whose ICS husband Seton was Commissioner for an area that contained part of the Terai, a tract of jungle at the foot of the Himalayas renowned as the haunt of tigers and other wild animals. After a duty tour with the Cassels came the highlight of the ten days' Christmas holidays, a tiger shoot, with a Colonel who served as Game Warden to the Maharaja of Kashmir, his wife and their two daughters. Also in the party was Seton Cassels's brother and his wife and another ICS man, Rupert Barkeley-Smith, always known as 'Gappy' and then aged thirty, whom Honor already knew. He was, she recalled, 'a handsome chap'.

For the tiger shoot, towards the end of the ten days luxurious

---

* From *Ladies of the Chase* by Meriel Buxton.

camping – with its sunny days, elephant rides, jungle sights and sounds, excellent meals and the romance of sitting round the blazing camp fire at night under the stars – Honor was put in the back of Gappy's howdah. It was the first tiger shoot for them both and, nervous that she would not keep quiet, he bet her that she could not remain motionless for twenty minutes.

They heard the beaters, with their drums, clashing tin cans and whacking trees. 'Suddenly in the shadows opposite I saw a flash of yellow,' wrote Honor later. 'I poked Gappy in the back and pointed. There was a bang and a great mass of yellowy brown toppled forward into the nullah [ravine] and lay there stone dead. Another shot from Gappy and a full grown cub lay dead.' As the beaters tried to steal the whiskers off the tigers for their magic properties Gappy seized his moment and asked Honor to marry him. She accepted. 'He was a rotten dancer,' his granddaughter told me, 'and thought that if he waited until they reached civilisation and he proposed to her after treading on her toes in a foxtrot she might have refused him.'

Sylvia Cassels, who felt somewhat responsible for the betrothal, since it was through her that the pair had met, sent a reassuringly enthusiastic letter to Honor's mother, its phraseology redolent of the time: 'I do hope you will be pleased. We are delighted and think it is a most satisfactory engagement in every way, and they are so happy. I am sure you will approve of him as a son-in-law, he is such a thorough "sahib" and has good brains and good looks and is healthy and sound in mind and body – and he is so very lucky to get engaged to Honor who will make a most excellent Civilian's wife! … He said to me the other day: "The dibs [rupees] are all right!" which is his way of saying he has a certain amount of money of his own.'

For a young woman with little to do except enjoy herself, all mundane necessities taken care of by a host of servants, with friendly and hospitable people delighted to see a pretty new face, the cold-weather season could seem like one long party. While she would undoubtedly notice the glamorising effect of uniform on a young, fit but otherwise perfectly ordinary young man, the fact that there was little for the life of the mind would probably pass her by. What was important was the next dance and what to wear there. As for the dance itself, even a stroll on to the veranda in those balmy nights with huge stars overhead was a potent inducement to romance.

Sometimes, with so many attractive suitors around, it seemed almost a question of luck as to which one a girl would pick, with persistence probably the strongest weapon in a young man's armoury. It certainly seemed so for nineteen-year-old Claudine Gratton. Her diary is spattered with dates with different young men. 'Ian called for me at 9.15 and took me to the New Year's Day Parade. Bad. He then took me to drinks with very queer people. Awful creature, I do detest him He more or less proposed to me last night at the flick. Grim creature.'

Soon her future husband, John Hamilton (always known as Ham), a Lieutenant-Commander in the Royal Indian Navy, then serving on the *Cornwallis,* appears in her diary. They go sailing, out to dinner, bathing and on 1 July 1939 he kisses her for the first time. Next day, however, 'Tony asked me to play polo!! I do like him.' Two days later it is dinner, in a party with Ham to see *Pygmalion*, on to the Boat Club dance, after which Ham brought her home (more kisses). 'We said goodbye for ten days as his ship has been called to Bombay.'

With Ham away, Claudine's life remained as social as before. 'Dined at home in a Scots Fusiliers lads' party, invited by Tony Johnson, we went on to the Boat Club. Had good waltzes with Watt. Home about 3.30.' Next day, 8 July, it was six people to dinner and 'on to see Merle Oberon, Laurence Olivier, Flora Robson, David Niven in *Wuthering Heights*, good but sad. Drinks Sind Club, danced at the Gym [Gymkhana Club]. Bed 3.15.' Two days later, 'Fergie took me sailing. He set the course, good one. Grand sail. Home 8.30, changed. Jim Anson called for me. We (six) saw Ginger Rogers and Fred Astaire in *Irene and Vernon Castle*.' On the 12th, 'Mike Carroll called for me and took me to a champagne party at the Noughtons. We all went on to the Boat Club for lunch.'

Only on Ham's return on 4 August did the roll-call of other young men stop. 'Went [to the Boat Club] with him and stayed there for supper. We danced to the gram. He took me to Clifton and proposed to me. "Will you be my wife?" said he. And I said: "and never see you? No! not me." I'm not really in love with him although I like him a lot. Home at 11.30-ish.'

A week later, after a cocktail party on *Cornwallis* and dancing at the Boat Club, Ham took her home. 'He proposed again, poor old thing, but I don't love him.' The following night there was a visit to the cinema to see *Mother India* and another proposal. Next morning, on 16 August, he sent her a note. 'He thinks the balloon is going up as they have been ordered to Bombay. He can't even see me to say goodbye. He seems very cut up. Wrote him a chit in bed.'

1 September. 'Germany has invaded Poland. They want Danzig. Probably war to come. Messed about. News on the wireless, lunch … I went to dinner at 1 Clifton Road with eight other men, we all went on to the Boat Club.'

Ham's pursuit of Claudine was eventually successful thanks to his tenacity. On 17 December her diary records: 'I found a letter on D[addy]'s table from H that he wants to get married!! Oh! I'm so thrilled. Don't know what to do. D arrived home from camp, want to tell him but I won't yet. Started a letter to Ham, finished it.' By the following morning she had made up her mind. 'When Daddy came to wake me up I told him that Ham and I are engaged. He was so sweet – a bit tearful too I think. I'm going to wear my marquise ring on my engagement finger till I get an engagement ring from Ham.'

When there were limited opportunities for meeting, courtship had to be an affair of speed and decision – if the loved one were not to pass irrevocably out of sight. When John Henry, manager of an indigo plantation in Bihar, went to the annual Meet in Muzaffarpur, he met a beautiful girl, Mabel Exshaw, niece of another indigo planter, staying there with her two sisters and her mother (the planter's sister). John and Mabel fell in love at first sight. But at the end of the week of socializing and gaiety, John, like every other man there, had to return to work; and Mabel, only on a short visit, would soon be leaving for England with her mother and sisters.

John was desperate – and desperate times require desperate measures. He went back to work but at the end of each afternoon he rode his horse to the nearest railway station and caught the train to Muzaffarpur, a journey of several hours. There he got a one-horse vehicle that took him out to the estate on which his beloved was staying, reaching it in time for dinner. Fortunately her uncle was a hospitable man who liked to entertain and to see his family happy.

He spent the evening courting Mabel, until the horse and cab arrived to take him to Muzaffarpur, where he caught the train to his own station. There he mounted his horse and rode back, arriving at the plantation at 6 a.m., the time when, like other managers, he rode round inspecting the fields. All his changing of clothes, washing, shaving and minimal sleeping were done in the train. He went on doing this until Mabel's mother gave her permission for the engagement.

The lovely young Violet Hanson was, as we have seen, one of the few Fishing Fleet girls who had already been married. The marriage, at seventeen, to a man who proved to be homosexual, had been annulled. Four years later, her mother had despatched her to stay with her aunt Mable, visiting her son in India.

The omens for finding a suitable husband were favourable. Mable's son was in a smart English cavalry regiment, the 4th/5th Dragoon Guards. 'There were very few unmarried girls and dozens of young unmarried men,' recalled Violet, who had gone back to her maiden name before leaving. The reason was that as well as the 4th/5th, the Secunderabad Brigade consisted of two Indian cavalry regiments – the Deccan Horse and the 3rd (Indian) Cavalry Regiment – and a battalion of the Royal Artillery and a couple of Indian infantry regiments.

Violet had plenty of admirers. One of them, Podge Gregson, in the 3rd Cavalry Regiment, had his mother staying with him for the cold weather. She was fond of entertaining, so he was in a better position to see more of people he liked than most young officers living in the mess. He was good-looking, amusing, around the same age as Violet and, as she noted thankfully, was 'the very antithesis of the men I had known in the past' – her husband had had a wide circle of intelligent, witty and almost invariably homosexual friends, to whom Podge, with his mother making a relaxed home for him, seemed quite the opposite. 'It was all so normal and conventional as to draw me like a magnet,' said Violet. 'And so I fell in love – chiefly with normality, I now think.'

They got engaged at a dance given by the Deccan Horse. 'I don't think my aunt was very pleased, as she thought I could have done much better and married into the British Cavalry – as I could have, had I wanted. There was nothing she could do and there was no real objection to the engagement except my fiancé's youth and the fact that he was not yet a captain. Men in the Indian Cavalry were not supposed to marry as subalterns. However his colonel was quite amenable, if we waited a year before we got married, so that was all settled.'

Violet's engagement meant that her mother, a woman to whom the subtle gradations of status meant much, had to balance the desired result – remarriage – against the fact that her daughter's fiancé was in a less desirable regiment. 'My mother was quite pleased though not as ecstatic as she might have been,' recorded Violet. 'She thought I might have done better than a young officer in an Indian cavalry regiment but I suppose my aunt reported favourably – and my mother was anxious that I should get married as it was embarrassing for her to have to explain why I was still Miss Hanson.'

Violet returned home as her fiancé was not due for leave that year – officers serving in the Indian Army had six months' home leave every three or four years – and spent the English summer staying with a cousin and getting her trousseau together. She returned to India in September 1924, was met by her Podge when she landed in Bombay and married the same day in Bombay Cathedral.*

Dorothy Hughes had been an unofficial member of the Fishing Fleet when she accompanied her older sister Dulcie to India. Dulcie, a young woman of difficult character, had been sent out specifically to look for a husband; Dorothy herself, at twenty, was not considered seriously in need of one at that time. She was, however, perfectly clear that marriage was her eventual goal (she later brought up her own daughters with the words: 'If you are unfortunate enough to be born clever, for heaven's sake, be clever enough to hide it.')

Soon after her return from India to the family home in Baker Street Dorothy was asked to a dinner party. 'Please come,' begged the friend who invited her. 'I've got a frightfully difficult man to cope with. You've been out to India and he lives in India – he's in the Indian Civil Service – and we're desperate to find someone to keep him amused for the evening.' Dorothy, with her beautiful figure, blonde hair, blue eyes and easy, lively manner, seemed just the girl to entertain someone clever, shy and reserved.

---

* Staying even one night in a hotel without a chaperone would have damaged her reputation severely. Many women married straight off the ship to avoid this.

This was Charles Ormerod, on record in Chapter Five as saying of his life in India, 'The people here who have a better life are the ones who are married. So when my next leave comes up I'm going to go back to England with the idea of getting a wife.' And when, in 1935, aged thirty, he had both passed the age barrier and had six months' leave, home he came with that goal in mind. Finding Dorothy placed next to him at dinner gave him immediate hope: he found this pretty young woman fascinating – but she found him rather a bore. So when at the end of the evening he asked her: 'May I have your telephone number?' she replied rudely, 'Look it up in the telephone directory if you're so keen.'

For a man accustomed to dealing with anything from a runaway horse to a crowd of angry villagers, ringing up a reluctant young woman was not difficult. He was anxious to give her an evening that she would enjoy, without the pressure of a one-to-one conversation, so arranged a party at Quaglino's, a well-known West End restaurant. It was not an unqualified success. The other guests, prepared to make the most of an evening with a generous host, had no hesitation in drinking the champagne and eating the caviar offered, but Dorothy, always conscious of people spending too much money on her, looked at the prices and was horrified, so picked the cheapest thing on the menu, an omelette. Nor did she realise he had asked the others purely for her benefit.

Shortly afterwards, a benign fate stepped in. Dorothy developed chickenpox and as she lay first ill and then convalescing at home splendid hampers began arriving from Fortnum & Mason. Her mother looked at them thoughtfully and said: 'This seems quite promising.' When she met Charles his northern roots – in those class-conscious days – told against him. All the same, their friendship developed and Charles, aware that this was his chance to realise his dream and by now deeply in love with Dorothy, pursued her until she agreed to marry him.

The wedding, in July 1936, proved to be the start of a highly successful marriage. Dorothy took to life in India at once. Charles was now a Deputy Commissioner and because his immediate superior, the Commissioner, had no wife, Dorothy became First Lady of their province at the age of twenty- two. For her this was no problem: she had all the social graces, could entertain well, was artistic, and good at bridge and tennis. Her outgoing personality and the friendliness that had originally captivated the quieter Charles was an invaluable counterbalance to his more subdued and less socially adept persona. Much of their time was spent in Delhi, whence Charles would be sent out to neighbouring areas; Dorothy would accompany him, to help the village women with hygiene and medical care.

Perhaps the strangest story was that of Rowan Mary McLeish, who knew her future husband for a mere fortnight, became engaged to him over the telephone after six years apart, and finally met him again a week before their wedding.

Mary ('I was called Mary, except at school, where there were too many Marys') was born in April 1921. Her father worked in Burma, in the trading firm started by her grandfather, and she and her brother had one of the more unhappy Raj childhoods. As she told me: 'I used not to see my father for five years at a time, after which he would come back for a year. It was really very upsetting. My parents were away most of my childhood. We were at school on Hayling Island and we lived at the school all year except for a holiday in the summer when my mother came back and I and she and my brother would meet. You can imagine how we looked forward to it. After this one lovely holiday she would go back again. For us it was devastating being left like that. My parents were almost strangers.'

One day, on one of her visits to England, Mary's mother, the prolific romantic novelist Dorothy Black,* asked her daughter if she would like to come out to India to stay with some friends. Mary jumped at the chance and they set off from Tilbury in the autumn of 1937. 'I remember we changed for dinner every night – I had to take out about six evening dresses. I was just seventeen and I'd very much had a boarding school upbringing so it was my first experience of meeting young men. There were three very nice ones on board so I had a lovely voyage, dancing every night.'

After a stop-off in Colombo, they landed in Bombay and set off for Madras by train, there to be met by a military car and taken to the cantonment where the King's Own Royal Regiment was stationed. Their host was the commanding officer. 'The following night Nigel came to dinner. I can see him now, leaping up the stairs – he

---

* She also ghosted *The Little Princesses*, by their governess 'Crawfie'.

was rather agile, with reddish hair, a good bit taller than me. He was twenty-two, and had gone out with his battalion. We clicked at once. He said: "Will you come sailing with me?"

'I'd never really done much but I said I would love to. It was a small sailing boat with one little cabin. We had a lovely time and I found I liked sailing very much. I saw him almost every day during the fortnight we spent there. At the end of the fortnight my mother and I went up to Ootacamund and I had to say goodbye to him, which made me very sad. All the time we were in Ootacamund I was wishing I could be with him in Madras.'

Nigel St George Gribbon, born in London in February 1917 during a First World War zeppelin raid, was educated at Rugby and Sandhurst and commissioned into his father's old regiment in 1937. From the point of view of Mary's mother, and everyone else in that society including Nigel himself, as a twenty-year-old Lieutenant he was far too young to marry.

Soon after Mary returned to England she was sent to Paris to improve her French. 'When war seemed a certainty the German girls at the school all went and shut themselves in their bedrooms. I was the only English girl there. I was told to go immediately to Calais and get on the first boat I could.' Back in England, Mary joined the WAAF as an aircraftwoman second class, gaining a commission after five months. 'I worked in radar, where we were constantly busy with raids, either coming in or going out.' All the time, she and Nigel were writing to each other, although there was no question of even an 'understanding'.

One day, when she was at home on leave staying with her mother, the telephone rang. 'Will you marry me?' said Nigel's voice, last heard six years earlier. He was telephoning from India. She was, she recalls, completely taken aback – but not enough to prevent her answering 'Certainly I will.' Still in the first flush of astonishment, she turned to her mother and asked: 'Shall I get engaged?' 'Yes, darling,' replied her mother. 'After all, it won't tie you down.'

'When I had said "yes", I didn't feel "Oh, what have I done?" I just felt, "How wonderful!" I knew I'd done the right thing. You see, nobody else had ever made a real dent on my heart. Partly one was so busy in the war one didn't have a real social life, and being on this very mixed radar station, although I got on with everyone very well, there was nobody tempting there.'

Nigel was not able to return to England for another four months, spending part of the voyage stuck in the Mediterranean for a while because the escorting destroyers ran out of fuel ('everyone sat there with their life jackets on wondering if the Germans would come in for the kill').

'We met in London. I was very nervous. Would I remember him properly after six years? But there he was, sitting there, looking just as he always had. I suppose I had changed quite a lot in the intervening years but somehow it hadn't affected us.

'He had one week's leave, during which we got married. I wore a white wedding dress – I'd been presented before the war and we added sleeves to my presentation dress. He was in uniform. Nigel came down to near my station for the last few days of his leave and we stayed at a grotty b and b. I had to go back on my three watches in the WAAF – eight hours on then eight hours off. So often I would have to get up in the middle of the night and leave him. When I'd thought of marriage before, this wasn't quite how I'd pictured it.'

16

Daughter of the Raj

Bethea Field

Fishing Fleet girls had to be ready to expect anything – especially in the wilder parts of India.

A girl who had come out to join her family, rather than one fresh from a London flat or house in the country, might be less taken aback by unexpected happenings since many fathers, especially in Government service, found themselves posted to remote and sometimes dangerous areas. As a child brought up in India such a little girl would become used to having a sandwich snatched out of her hands by a kite or being told 'don't go in the long grass – there may be snakes!'. In some parts, she might have seen one of her father's dogs taken by a leopard, or been tugged out of the way of a pi-dog frothing at the mouth with rabies.

When a family had been in India for generations, anything from early deaths and long journeys by bullock cart to glittering dinners in the fabulous palace of a friendly rajah became part of family history. Rather than the steady, often predictable path through the years at home, hardship, privation, adventure, luxury and exoticism were interwoven into the fabric of family life. In Bethea Field's case, there were many of these elements, plus camel-riding out to dinner in evening dress and a bullet-spattering attack by rebels.

Bethea's journal, which records them all, is notable not only for her keenly observant eye for detail but also for its unusual frankness. She makes no bones about her longing (this is not too strong a word) to meet young men and the fact that although firmly bound by the rules of convention, she has a powerful libido ('I was highly sexed'). She regarded India as home: her family, both before she was born and for subsequent generations, lived and worked there.

Her grandfather, William Field, had joined the East India Company as a cadet in 1812. His father, in the early days of the nineteenth century, had owned a furniture shop in Windsor patronised by Queen Charlotte, who became interested in the Field family. When William Field died suddenly, the Queen exercised her influence to help his widow and children, obtaining a cadetship to the East India Company for Mrs Field's son George. He left aged twelve, and his mother never saw him again.

George, who worked hard for John Company (as the East India Company was then known throughout India), also became one of the heroes of Arrah House, the 'Small House' of the Indian Mutiny, which sheltered nearby British and loyal Indian troops when the Mutiny broke out. The Indian Rebellion of 1857 began as a mutiny of sepoys of the British East India Company's army on 10 May 1857, in the town of Meerut, and soon spread, largely in the upper Gangetic plain and Central India. The sepoys were a combination of Hindu and Muslim soldiers, with over 200,000 Indians in the army, compared to about 50,000 British. The forces were divided into three presidency armies: the Bombay, the Madras and the Bengal.

Resentment had built up slowly, over a mixture of causes, from changes in terms of professional service, denial of pensions to retired sepoys, differences in pay between the three armies, to grievances over the slowness of promotions, based on seniority – many Indian officers did not reach commissioned rank until they were too old to be effective. The final spark was provided by the pre-greased cartridges supplied as ammunition for the new 1853 Enfield Rifle. To load the rifle, sepoys had to bite the cartridge open to release the powder. The grease used on these cartridges contained tallow, which if derived from pork would be offensive to Muslims, and if derived from beef would be offensive to Hindus. At least one British official pointed out, fruitlessly, the difficulties this would cause.

Unrest arose gradually throughout April and May 1857, spreading until it became a widespread revolt. On 25 July, rebellion erupted in the garrisons of Dinapur (in Bihar, north-east India). The rebels quickly moved towards Arrah and all European residents took refuge at the house of Vicars Boyle, the District Railway Engineer, together with fifty loyal sepoys. Luckily it was not only a dwelling but a mini-fort, having been an outpost in the very early days of the Company. There was a courtyard surrounded by quite thick walls, a well and stabling, stocked by one of their number with goats and grain in readiness for a siege; and a clear area of about 200 yards all round it, which proved to be their salvation.

They had small arms and some ammunition. George, a good shot, spent the daylight hours on the walls picking off any mutineers who might emerge from the woods. Apart from the fear that supplies would not last out, one of the worst moments was when the villagers, egged on by the mutineers, built a huge bonfire and threw on it at as many red chillies* as they could spare. The acrid fumes blowing across the open space and into the little stronghold blinded and choked the men inside; but the wind suddenly changed direction and it was the enemy who had to flee.

Finally, after an agonising six months, the Mutiny was stamped out and they were relieved. Bethea's grandmother Catherine (who had remained in England with her children) returned and more children arrived, including Bethea's father Charles William, born in 1863.

Charles had begun his career in the Indian Army, in the 26th Punjabis, but although he rose to the rank of Lieutenant-Colonel, after he married and had children he decided that he could no longer afford to stay in the Army, and successfully applied for a posting to the Judge Advocate-General's Department. This meant not only better pay but also relief from subscribing to all the regimental funds (upkeep of the mess, and so forth). On the debit side it meant he would no longer be called up for active duty should a war arise and no longer be in line to command the regiment or carry a field marshal's baton in his pocket. It was a move that pleased his wife Mary (always known in the family as Madre) as she disliked regimental life.

Their daughter Bethea (Betty) Helen was born in Lahore Cantonments† in the Punjab on 1 November 1899. She was a pretty

---

* These must have been *Bhut jolokia*, the world's hottest chilli, grown in north-east India and used today by the India Army as 'chilli grenades' to stun the enemy. Effects include dizziness, sweating, breathlessness, racing heart and streaming eyes.

† Then called Mian Mir, about six miles from the city of Lahore. It was where the barracks of British and Indian troops were situated.

girl, with bright blue eyes and the long curling red-gold hair inherited from her mother, a beauty for whom children tended to be an encumbrance rather than a pleasure and for whom a youthful version of herself might prove competition. When Bethea reached puberty at the age of twelve it was 'to my mother's annoyance, but *what* else could she expect?'

After education in England Bethea returned to India as a Fishing Fleet girl in 1918, to Secunderabad, where her father was now the Magistrate, responsible for law and order. Two British infantry (Territorial) regiments, one Indian cavalry and at least two Indian infantry regiments – one from Burma – were stationed there, plus various other detachments. It was a large and important station but for Bethea, newly out from England and agog for some social life, at first it seemed a desert.

'In my first weeks there I felt very lost,' she wrote later. 'The excitement of the long journey was over. Nothing seemed to happen. Father took us to the big clubhouse where mother and I read the magazines. A few people drifted past. Through my bedroom window I could see a pomegranate tree in full blossom and I enjoyed the mornings, drinking early cups of tea and eating soggy toast and bananas, but I longed for life with a big "L".'

Her first invitation was to a tennis party, where she met a young married woman, Peggy O'Cock, who 'took her up'. It was the introduction to an intoxicating new social life with a ready-made but fun-seeking chaperone thrown in. Peggy took her to her first dance, in the club. 'The only music was from a gramophone but I wore an evening dress for the first time and I was thrilled,' wrote Bethea, who found herself surrounded by would-be partners. 'That was hardly surprising, since there was only one girl or woman to every four men. My new friend Peggy introduced me to the young men of her husband's regiment and we went for rides together and picnics.'

These gaieties were temporarily interrupted by the arrival of Spanish flu, the epidemic that decimated populations worldwide. Bethea, who had had a bad attack of 'flu just before she left school in England, was unaffected but most of the servants fell ill and one died. With sudden death no rarity in India, as soon as 'the plague' was over the social round started again, with a banquet and dance, to a band provided by one of the British regiments, at the palace of the Nizam of Hyderabad.

'We were told to bring our own partners,' recorded Bethea. 'I chose a young man of whom I was enraptured at that time. He was an excellent dancer and looked very well in his mess kit. We were served in the big dining hall, hung with chandeliers. Then the ladies were taken up to meet the Nizam's wives and relations. They spoke no English and our Hindustanee must have sounded crude to them. They were dripping with jewels but we had none or little. They must have despised us and thought us immodest in our flimsy chiffon dresses.'

Another night saw a large group gather for a moonlight picnic in a ruined Moghul city called Golconda, just over twelve kilometres from Secunderabad, where it was said diamonds had been found. A few people drove there, some of the men rode and Bethea herself was driven in a buggy by her boyfriend of the moment. The night was so warm that as they ate their picnic in a courtyard all any of the women needed over their evening dress was a gauzy shawl. Little could have been more romantic than the setting of tumbled buildings – palace, mosques and tombs, some marbled and gleaming white in the soft brilliance of the moonlight.

Another moonlight picnic was to a large lake. 'Only a few of us this time,' recorded Bethea. 'A fisherman took us out in his boat and we lay on the bottom holding hands and kissing.' Bethea had been allowed by her parents to go on these jaunts by herself as the parties were organised by Peggy. But after Armistice Day on 11 November the Territorial battalions started to pack up and Peggy, her husband, and most of Bethea's beaux left.

One friend only remained: Captain Herbert McPherson of the Burma Rifles. He had joined as a wartime soldier only but no orders had been issued yet that the Rifles were to be disbanded – the British troops had priority. He was tall, good-looking, well-to-do and a man of great niceness but diffident where affairs of the heart were concerned.

'He never took any notice of the few other girls but kept his eye on me, though I was swept up here and there by the charms of Billy this or Freddie the other,' remembered Bethea. 'I think Herbert was too nice. I only know that I did not fall in love with him at all, which was a pity. It might have ripened if I had not gone up to stay with Violet, my sister, and her husband in Baluchistan. She wanted me to spend Christmas with them and my parents encouraged me to accept. The last time I saw Herbert was shortly before I left Secunderabad in the middle of December.' It was also the last of the flirtations that as a girl of just nineteen she so enjoyed.

Violet's husband, Jim (later Sir James) Acheson, was the Assistant to the Resident of Kalat state; like other states, largely independent under the Khan of Kalat but under the eye of Britain. Sibi, not far from Quetta and near the border with Afghanistan, was the winter headquarters, with a refreshing cool, dry climate. The Resident, Colonel Ramsay, and his wife were away when Bethea arrived. Jim and Violet and her little niece Janet were living in part of the residency but there was no room for Bethea, so a tent – with planked floors, veranda, bedroom and bathroom – was put up in the grounds.

At Christmas they were joined by an old friend of Jim's, Major Sydney Williams. As all of them trudged across the dry fields on Christmas Day, Jim and Sydney with shotguns in case game got up, Bethea had no idea that this older man would one day act as Cupid.

'Christmas over, I began to wish for some social life,' she wrote. 'On our side of the town there was only the Residency and the PWD officer, a Scotsman, and his guest – Mrs St John and her two small sons, seeking escape from the bitter cold of Quetta.' But across the town, three miles or so away, was stationed a regiment of Indian cavalry with British officers. Bethea began to think about them and wonder how she could meet them. Fortunately, Violet and Jim knew their commanding officer and invited him to dinner one night. He clearly realised that his young officers would enjoy meeting such a pretty single girl, since a few days later two of them rode up to the Residency, where Bethea was sitting in the garden sporadically writing, reading and sewing. She saw them 'and my heart leapt'.

But they said not a word – etiquette forbade. Instead, they dropped cards, looked at her and rode away as she sat there longingly. 'I did so hope that something would come of it. I think Jim rode over to make a return of cards but days went by before I received an invitation to dinner at the mess. I was thrilled. Violet and Jim, though included in the invitation, decided not to accept.

'The problem was, how could I get there? There was not a motor car or even a horse trap in the whole place. It would have to be one of the mares or a camel. I had become used to that form of travel when I had gone some days to the Cavalry lines to help a young mother with two sick children.' On the evening she was invited out, Bethea decided to go on camelback. 'In a long satin dress and shawl, how could I guide a pacing country horse across three miles? Camel it had to be.'

Mounting a camel was quite a procedure. The animal, brought up from the Levy lines with its rider, was ordered by the rider to squat while the 'passenger' – Bethea – stood on the near side. Laboriously the beast first doubled up its front legs, sinking down with its rump in the air, and then bending its hind legs until its body was on the ground. 'At that moment I had to climb as quick as I could into the saddle behind the rider – camels are very impatient and bad-tempered creatures. As soon as I was on the saddle I clasped my arms round the rider. The camel rose from the front legs and I was indeed grateful that I had a good grip of the rider for the angle was very steep. Then I was thrown forward as the camel raised its back legs. On the level again I could find the stirrups and some measure of confidence. The double saddle was made of wood to fit over the hump and covered with rags of old carpets. The interesting thing was that the stirrups were good British Army issue of steel but attached to the saddle by country rope – very rough. I hung on as firmly as I could to the rider – always a handsome young Baluchi, dressed in baggy white trousers and shirt and an embroidered blue padded waistcoat. He had long black curly hair which swayed in front of me – as his curls swayed I could see a thick rim of grease on the back of his waistcoat. All Indians oil or grease their hair; in the South with coconut oil but in the North with mutton fat.

'The Commanding Officer met me and the party, in the mess tent under canvas, was sedate. I was chaperoned not only by him but by a couple of other officers' wives. Strictly on time my camel was ordered up, and again successfully foiling the camel's intent to unseat me, I was ridden back.'

It proved to be merely a tempting taste of the company of young men of her own age. The regiment was sent on manoeuvres and she never saw any of them again.

The final event of the Sibi season was the horse show. This combination of market, fairground and horse show lasted for a week and attracted the population from miles around. Horses, camels, cattle and goats were bought and sold, there were stalls selling everything from food to clothes, fortune-tellers and gambling games – much the same as any English country fair. The weather was perfect and only in the middle of the day did the sun cause people to rest in the shade, after which it was time for the competitive events: horse racing, camel racing, the racing of young bullocks with small boys on their backs as jockeys. A stand had been set up for the Khan and his guests – the Ramsays, Bethea and her sister and brother-in-law and any other British there – and some of the tribal chiefs, their women, invisible, peeping through the muslin curtains of their bullock carts. Music was provided by a Baluchi band who thumped out the wailing songs of India. Bethea was quick to recognise one that recurred constantly – 'The Bleeding Heart', her father's Punjabi Regiment's march tune.

A morale-boosting frisson of excitement for Bethea was provided by a British Army vet who had come down from Quetta to look over possible remounts for the cavalry regiments. 'He was rather common,' she wrote, 'but paid me some particular attentions for which I was grateful. Violet and Jim were disapproving but then they were still caught up in the honeymoon feeling of their own early married life and had little sympathy for me and my wish for admiration.'

As 1919 began, Bethea's brother-in-law Jim moved from the Residency to the Assistant's house in Mastung (near Quetta), amid orchards of apple and apricot in bloom. But socially it was a desert. There were no other British people at all and nothing to do except play tennis on the Ramsays' court. Bethea began to fret. 'I longed to meet people – especially young men!' So she was excited to get an invitation from Sydney Williams to a fancy dress dance to be held in the Quetta Club. She planned her costume carefully.

'I remembered some friend telling me how she had gone as a powder puff so I decided that was what it should be. With some rupees in my purse I went down to Mastung bazaar, bought yards of stiff white muslin and a few yards of pale blue Indian satin – all very cheap – pleated them, frilled up the muslin and attached it to a band round my waist and made a strapped bodice and a small overskirt from the blue satin. On my head, I had white muslin covered by blue satin with a white pompom on top.' White silk stockings and satin shoes completed the costume.

Although Bethea was the only one invited to the fancy dress ball, the rest of the household decided to move to Quetta too. Going the thirty miles there presented its own problems. In 1918 cars had engines that easily overheated and to reach Quetta they had to cross a steep pass of hills – the Lak Pass. 'By the time we reached the top the engines' radiators were boiling,' remembered Bethea. 'There had to be a halt to cool down and then very cautiously the driver would open the radiator cap. Clouds of steam would gush out. As soon as that settled he would slowly trickle in water from the bucket we carried until the radiator was full again.' Once over the pass, they could coast down to Quetta.

Sydney Williams called for Bethea to fetch her for the ball and promised her mother to see her safely home again. 'He had a new Ford car. I got up beside him in my powder puff outfit and at the club we joined a party of friends of his. It was my first big dance and I was thrilled. A real band! a military one – and the ballroom full of people.'

She had the first dance with Sydney but after that crowds of eager young men – who greatly outnumbered the women there – flocked round and Sydney drifted off to join friends at the bar. Bethea was having such a good time that it was only after supper that she decided it was getting late and her mother might be worrying. She called up one of the club servants and said to him in Hindustani: 'Major Williams Sahib ke salaam do' ('please give Major Williams a request that he should attend me'). The servant bowed and went away. As she sat waiting a voice beside her said:

'You sent for me?' She looked up to see a tall man in uniform bending down. He was a complete stranger.

'No, I asked for Major Williams,' she replied. 'But I *am* Major Williams!' he said.

Bethea shook her head and told him: 'You are the wrong Major Williams! I wanted Sydney.'

The stranger bowed and went away. How attractive he was, she thought as he left. A few minutes later Sydney came up, collected Bethea and her wrap and drove her home.

Two days later cards were left for Bethea and her mother and Violet and Jim from a Major A. de C. (the initials stood for Arthur de Coetlogon) Williams, Indian Civil Service – the stranger was clearly prepared to do things properly. But Mrs Field, with no particular wish to encourage an unknown young man and in a state of irritation due to the heat and the mosquitoes, crossly pushed the cards to one side. Bethea picked them up and treasured them as a sign of the stranger's interest.

There matters might have remained but for the resourcefulness of Arthur Williams. He discovered that he and Violet had a friend in common in Quetta, Rose Patel, the daughter of a rich and influential Parsee. With her to introduce them, he could officially meet Bethea.

Soon the Fields received an invitation to tea at the home of Rose Patel. Violet accepted on behalf of them all but the unsuspecting Bethea was reluctant. 'A Parsee tea party? No thank you.' However her mother, who had been finding life in Quetta dull, was pleased. After their afternoon rest under mosquito nets she urged her daughter to get up and get dressed ready for the outing. Reluctantly, Bethea did so, putting on a blue straw hat that enhanced the colour of her eyes.

The Patel house, on the fringe of the native city, was a wide, sprawling bungalow built round a central courtyard well-shaded by trees. A fountain splashed softly in its centre. After the glare and dust outside it was cool and refreshing. Rose greeted them and they were given chairs in a shady corner.

As they drank tea and ate small delicious cakes a tall, lean young man in uniform came over to them and sat down, turning immediately to make polite conversation with Mrs Field. In a flash, Bethea remembered that he was the 'wrong' Major Williams from the fancy dress ball; and that he must have been the same Major Williams who had left cards on them. Now he was doing his best to ingratiate himself with her mother, who inexplicably became stony, so much so that to Bethea's deep disappointment he moved away to talk to others.

'Horrible man,' said her mother – and Bethea's budding romance appeared to be over before it had begun. Later, she discovered that, rather as in Victorian times when a widowed parent of either sex – including the Queen herself – felt they had the right to keep one child permanently at home as a companion, her mother hoped to keep Bethea by her side for ever. Violet, married, was out of the running and Bethea's brother had been killed in the war, so Mrs Field fought against the possibility that her last child would marry and leave her.

Back in Mastung after the Quetta visit a resentful Bethea found life duller than ever. The only amusement was when her father came up from Secunderabad on leave and they could have a tennis four. 'The interlude in Quetta had been exciting and now here I was in this isolated place, aged nineteen, growing older every day with no future – or so I thought,' she wrote despondently.

One evening, instead of playing tennis, she wandered through the garden and into an apple orchard. She climbed up into one of the trees and sat out on a branch that looked over the little valley, nursing her woes. 'I was soaked in self-pity,' she wrote. 'Nobody seemed to bother about poor little me. Then I noticed the sun was sinking and my conscience told me that the others might be worried and waiting for me, so I climbed down and went back. It was almost dusk by then. A narrow path, flanked by trees, went down to the dry stream bed – there was a little bridge across and we started up the other side. Jim and my father walked together in front, followed by my mother by herself and Violet and I side by side behind her. I think Violet sensed my depression and tried to rally me.'

Suddenly there was a succession of bangs. At first the party thought it was the villagers letting off rockets in celebration of a wedding, then Bethea saw the dust between herself and Violet being kicked up by some metallic object, and a deep nick being taken out of the side of a tree trunk. 'Almost in the same moment I saw my father ahead of us put his left hand across his right arm and hold it up in front of him. It was covered in blood.'

They were being fired upon. It was a time when there was fighting with Afghanistan and they were fairly close to the frontier. They ran back, her father to collect his revolver, Jim to alert their Gurkha guard, the others to shelter in the house. From inside, Bethea could see Jim standing on the front steps, his revolver in his hand. Round him were grouped the six Gurkhas, with their NCO beside Jim. All was quiet until they heard a tremendous tramping, which sounded nearer and nearer.

'What can two men with revolvers plus six men and their rifles do to repulse a horde?' thought Bethea desperately. 'We were in a possibly hostile region, we were at war with Afghanistan and the nearest British troops were thirty miles away with a rough ride and high hills between us. I thought it was the end.'

In the near-dark she saw that the men coming up to the drive and into the open space in front of the house carried lanterns. They were all tall, with high turbans and baggy trousers of white cotton. Most of them were bearded and they carried the strangest assortment of weapons. Some had ancient muzzle-loading guns, others large curved swords. There were men carrying lances and boys with sticks.

The Europeans stood tensely on the front steps until one man, unarmed, walked up to Jim and bowed, holding both hands beneath his face. 'Sahib, we have come to save you and your lady folk,' he said.

Jim slipped his revolver into his holster and stepped down. They shook hands – the man was the chief of the village elders – and Jim expressed his gratitude. The men left and everyone tried to settle down. Bethea's shock at the attempted massacre was such that her period not only arrived that night a fortnight early but so heavily that she thought she was suffering a haemorrhage.

A message was got to the nearest British soldiers and the family was evacuated, her father to surgery on his arm at the nearest hospital and everyone else to Quetta, apart from Jim, who remained in Mastung as the guest of the headman to sort out the reasons for the attack.

It later transpired that the night of the attack a detachment of the Mekran Levy Corps were due to march south to their headquarters in Mekran. Three of them and a new recruit, aged sixteen or seventeen, lagged behind and hid in the gully just about under the apple tree in which Bethea was sitting. They had their British-issue rifles and six rounds each, also their camels, tethered nearby. They knew that Afghanistan had declared war and they may also have thought that the British, after the long struggle in Europe, were weak and vulnerable. As they later confessed, they decided to deliver a blow themselves by killing the Resident – but mistook Bethea's tall father for the Resident, Colonel Ramsay.

At dawn a posse of village men, led by the headman, set out to track them. Since camels leave a distinctive spoor and much of the ground was sandy and impressionable, they were easily followed, caught at their next camping ground and arrested. After trial by the local court of justice, they were condemned to death and hanged – except for the youth, who was given a long prison sentence.

Back in Quetta, Bethea discovered that Arthur Williams, though a temporary Major in the Supply and Transport Unit of the Indian Army, had not been demobilised; instead, he had been re-enlisted to staff headquarters in Quetta. As her father had now been made the Cantonment Magistrate in Quetta, the family soon had their own house and a natural entrée to all the social activities of Quetta.

The delighted Bethea was quickly caught up in these, playing tennis with a girlfriend at the club in the afternoons and going to dances there or at various regimental messes in the evenings. It was the life she had dreamed of, especially now that there was romance in the offing – Arthur Williams, though not a dancing man, constantly kept his eye on her from the bar.

The more she knew him the more she liked him. As well as being tall – 6 feet 2 inches – and good-looking, with thick brown hair, warm brown eyes and a dimple in his left cheek, he was clever and had great charm. Born in September 1890, he had won scholarships to Winchester, Marlborough and then Balliol College, Oxford, where he read Classics and became a great friend of 'Cis' Asquith, son of the Prime Minister, so that he often stayed at Downing Street. Like many of the cleverest Oxbridge graduates, he joined the ICS, who would not release him to the Army when he wanted to volunteer at the outbreak of war. Instead, a month later, he sailed for India.

Soon after they had encountered each other again, Arthur took Bethea out for a picnic in his car. They returned engaged – subject to parental consent, as she was still only nineteen. The wedding had to take place quickly, because the ICS wanted him back. As Arthur's first posting, as Assistant Deputy Commissioner in Berhampore, in the Musshidalad district, was about 125 miles from Calcutta, they were married from the house of her Aunt Sybil, who had a large house there.

Before the wedding Bethea arrived to stay with Aunt Sybil, who took her off to the dressmaker to choose a wedding dress and going-away outfit. As it was only just after the war the dress, of white satin, was short and instead of a veil she wore a white satin hat under which her long red-gold hair had to be pinned up. The cake came from Firpo, Calcutta's smartest restaurant and confectioner.

Even today, brides often feel nervousness and tension as their wedding day approaches. Bethea had an added reason for apprehension. In common with most other girls of her generation, her sexual ignorance was total. 'I had shied away from the "facts of life" even though I was highly sexed,' she wrote. 'I could have learnt a lot from my school friends but I shut my ears. I preferred to look at it all with the eyes of romance and ignore the sordid details. So when my mother gave me a talk and told me "you won't like it at first" I was seized with fear and spent almost sleepless nights.'

The wedding, on 12 December 1919, in Calcutta Cathedral – 'enormous for so small a gathering' – went well. Back at the flat the food was laid out, the cake on the centre table, and the champagne was opened. Next day the couple left for Berhampore. As for those initial fears, according to family legend, Bethea quickly got over them – and, later, spent a considerable time proving this.

17

'Colonels must marry'

Marriage

Marriage in the Raj generally involved an approach quite different from the home-grown variety. As Kipling had pointed out, '[marriage] in India does not concern the individual but the Government he serves'. Even a girl's wedding day was often different from what she might have expected. Lucy Hardy – who had become engaged to her future husband Harry Grant, an officer in the Royal Artillery, when she went out to India in the 1904 Fishing Fleet on a year's visit, staying first with her brother and then with friends – could hardly have had a more disconcerting introduction to married life: with a wedding in an isolated spot threatened nightly by marauders from over the border and, on the day itself, a drive behind a runaway horse that could easily have resulted in a fatal accident.

Harry, not yet of the seniority in the Army and therefore of the financial standing to support a wife, had circumvented this obstacle by successfully applying for the post of Assistant or Second Officer with the Kashmir State Mountain Artillery, a job which carried good pay but which was not entirely wife-friendly. Meanwhile, Lucy waited at home until he could afford to send for her. When the vital cable came, she sailed for India in February 1904, and went up to Attock, close to the borders of Afghanistan and Kashmir, where her brother Willie was quartered in the old Fort. Here, with Willie, she stayed. Although Lucy had arrived in March, she and Harry could not get married until 5 April, as not until then was the nearest chaplain available – it was thirty-seven years since a wedding had taken place in the church there.

By this time it had become very hot, especially at night, as the windows of the Fort had to be kept closed on account of cross-border marauders, who lived on the opposite bank of the swift-flowing river. 'I often watched them crossing the river on inflated bullock skins,' wrote Lucy. 'They used to walk up some distance, straddle the skins and launch out into the rapid current, swimming with arms and legs till they fetched up lower down on our side.'

On her wedding day, hot as usual, she dressed with care. 'I had a very pretty white *crêpe de Chine* day dress gathered round the hips, a full skirt with a flounce at the hem, and a white tulle hat with a spray of real orange blossom from the garden.' Her brother, elegant in blue and gold full dress, was to escort her to the church, perched on a steep hill above the Fort. For this short journey he had ordered a tonga in which they planned to leave as soon as they saw her bridegroom and his best man arrive at the church door.

But the moment they stepped into the tonga the pony bolted for its stable in the bazaar and no effort of the driver could stop it hurtling along the stony track, a hair-raising ride as they narrowly missed the large boulders at each side. Finally, arriving at its stable, it stopped. There was nothing for it but to walk to the church. 'I bundled up my long skirt and then we walked back nearly a mile in the heat, both of us dripping with sweat and on my part all of a tremble! We staggered up to the church porch where they had been all amazed at our non-appearance. They got me a chair and a glass of water and I rested till I had recovered a little, and then we were married. There was only the chaplain, a sergeant who acted as verger and witness, our two selves, Willie and the best man –six people in all.' Unsurprisingly, Lucy's was the last marriage to take place at that church.

Quite apart from physical aspects such as the differences in housekeeping, climate, surroundings and so forth, there were various social and psychological factors peculiar to marriage in the Raj, many imposed by the 'rules' integral to service in the Empire.

Whereas in England a man, provided he could support a wife and family, could marry virtually whenever he chose, those who worked for the Raj – and many of those employed on plantations or in businesses – were forbidden marriage for the first years of their service. For the ICS, who usually joined a year or so after university, this in practice meant until around the age thirty. The alternative was to leave the ICS or, if permission was grudgingly granted, suffer some form of financial penalty. For soldiers, as the informal rule had it, 'subalterns cannot marry, captains may marry, majors should marry and colonels must marry'. Even so, everyone who wanted to do so had to seek his commanding officer's permission; if this was refused (almost invariably, in the case of any officer below the rank of captain) he had either to remain single or send in his papers (i.e., leave the regiment). When Henry and Margery Hall married in the 1930s Henry – who was in the Foreign and Political Department – had to get special permission from the Viceroy to marry, nor did he get the marriage allowance (only given at 'marriageable' age). The Halls lived as cheaply as they could on Henry's pay of about £15 a week, rationing themselves to one bottle of whisky a month and joining only one club – that with the best library.

Towards the end of the Raj the ban on marrying before thirty was less stringent, but as one young man wrote: 'A young married officer found it rather a struggle to furnish a house. When you were senior enough to be allocated a furnished residence most of the essentials were provided by the Public Works Department ... I remember that my wife had to use a packing case as a dressing table and a wire stretched across a corner of the room as a wardrobe. We had camp beds and small mosquito nets tied to tiny frames fixed on the ends of the beds. We could buy beautifully made furniture from the district jail, constructed to my own design by long-term prisoners. But I had to calculate my monthly budget carefully before I ordered anything and we used to estimate a large round of drinks after tennis at the club to be worth a chair that we badly needed.'

Nor was it simply a question of existing on meagre funds. In the tight-knit community of an officers' mess, a glaring discrepancy in the ability to pay your way caused embarrassment all round. 'James Hodding is coming out in May after marrying in April,' wrote Lieutenant Leslie Lavie of a brother officer of the 20th Madras Native Infantry. 'Goodness only knows how he is going to live, when I have qualms, and very strong ones, and my case is much better than his. The Major was angry about my engagement and he is very much so about his, and with even more reason; paupers in the Regiment succeed in annoying everyone and poor old Hodding! Though he is always ready to join in everything, he absolutely won't be able to afford himself a *peg* much less join the Regiment in giving anybody else one.'

For anyone who did marry early – or for many on the bottom rungs of the ladder – money was a perennial worry. There were the basic expenses such as the cost of educating children, of keeping them healthy by sending them, their mother and several servants to the hills in the hot weather and the expense of a doctor if, as almost always, one of them became ill. 'We had to weigh up how ill a child was before calling the doctor because of his heavy fees,' said Viola Bayley.

Over and above that was something that at home was less pressing: the need – to put it in modern terms – to keep up with the Joneses and, in a country where the ethos of display was a sign of elitism, to be seen to be doing so. For in British society in India there was none of the anonymity that could be preserved at home even in close-knit circles: under the glare of the Indian sun and the gaze of Indian servants everything was high-visibility, everything had to conform to certain standards of protocol and custom. If you were in a cavalry regiment, it was important to have good polo ponies; for everyone, entertaining was expected and reciprocal dinner parties could not be skimped; and a man was expected to stand his round in mess or club. Only in camp or up country was a simpler life possible.

Often, too, in Raj marriages there was an element of clinging together, like the babes in the wood. For many Raj children, childhood and adolescence were times of misery and separation. Sent home to be educated in English schools, they might see their father only once or twice during these years and their mother little more. 'When my mother went back to India my brothers went as boarders to Berkhamstead School and I to a school in Watford,' wrote Iris James. 'I was six, and I remember on the first evening sitting by the window of the common room with the laurels in the rain outside tapping against the glass, night and aloneness of a kind so desolating that all other separations take me back to it …'.

Some children were lucky enough to stay with loving aunts, cousins or grandparents and for these, if cousins and friends were also around, life was the most normal. Others less fortunate were lodged in boarding houses that catered specifically for Raj children, with unloving relations to whom children were merely a nuisance to be tolerated, or simply left at school all year. One little boy, aged six, was sent to a Dame school where the boys were not allowed to drink anything after 5.30 p.m. in case they wet their beds – suffering from thirst, they got round this by drinking their bathwater. Iris and her brothers, sent to the vicarage at Potten End (run as a home for Raj children), spent as much time as they could on the moor behind the house, eating imaginary meals 'to try and fill the gap left by the sparse vicarage fare'. When not on the moor the shy Iris 'spent a lot of time planning how not to be seen going in and out of the lavatory, which was a shed in the garden. The shame of being seen using this was not to be borne.'

Thus the idea of a home – the home they never had – was something to which these young people clung tenaciously; and a husband or wife, the one person always there for them, was the emotional equivalent. Iris James, sent home at six and brought out to India again at sixteen and a half with the express purpose of finding a husband, realised by the time she was almost eighteen that the only way to escape her difficult home life was through marriage ('at seventeen and a half I began seriously to size up my escorts'). The man she fell in love with and married, always known simply as 'Mac', was another Raj child, left at school in Scotland at the age of twelve and sent out to plant tea at nineteen. 'Now he was twenty-three and I was eighteen and we both felt needed, loved, settled.' Perhaps, too, this feeling of having at last 'come home' was the reason why so many Raj brides were undaunted by the difficulties or dangers, either physical or psychological, often faced in India.

Lack of occupation was one. Servants took care of every domestic chore. Even the ordinary excitement of making a first home together was lacking when you knew that in two or three years you might be posted somewhere completely different, with a fresh lot of furniture to rent or buy. With no libraries or radios, cultural entertainment was far down on the list; here the girl with an interest like photography or painting was lucky. Many of the more spirited would accompany their husbands on tour or camping, making the most of the sights and sounds of the jungle. For birdwatchers, India was a paradise – golden orioles that flashed through tree tops, long-beaked bee eaters, weaver birds that made loofah-like nests, pigeons, hoopoes striped in orange, black and white, the crests on their heads opening and shutting like small black fans, bright green parakeets, minah birds that mimicked everything from the songs of other birds to household noises.

One of the main hazards of married life was loneliness. Girls who married a man whose work was in the *mofussil* – anywhere up country or well away from cities, towns, stations or cantonments – were often miles from their nearest neighbour, with their social highlight a weekly visit to the club, with its leather chairs, month-old newspapers and, if enough people came, a Saturday night dance. Planters, policemen, forestry experts, missionaries, young ICS men and, often, doctors, many of whom travelled almost constantly to treat outbreaks of infectious diseases as they occurred, often led lives of great isolation – one reason why most of them were anxious to marry and gain the companionship of a wife and family – but they at least had their work.

Girls who married a man living or working in one of the big cities had a much more social time of it. In Calcutta were the Royal Calcutta Golf Club, and Tollygunge and Jodhpur Clubs. 'Tolly was the queen of clubs having almost all we needed – golf, tennis, swimming and a race course, all extra to the usual bars and dining facilities, not to mention teas. The latter were usually served on the lawns of the clubhouse until after dark when the mosquitoes drove one in,' wrote Marian Atkins in 1931.

'The clubs were expensive – I've only so far mentioned the mixed social ones – no Indians, more of that later. There were also the United Service Club and the Bengal Club, male membership only with usually an area for the ladies and a lecture room for outsiders. The Calcutta Club was rather similar to the "Slap and Tickle" but with larger grounds and mixed membership – Indians and Europeans but no dancing. Nearly all the ICS men, including judges, belonged and the richer Indians. Father wanted to belong but couldn't afford the extra – the Slap and Jodhpur did us proud but when I went out a second time we became "millionaire" members of Tolly. This meant no waiting – [normally] seven years at Tolly, four at the Jodhpur – and probably no entrance fee but a very high annual fee. For Mother's sake he had to join the Slap, and Jodhpur for the tennis and social side.

'The Saturday Club had a few dances in the hot weather, on Saturday nights, but while I was out a special jazz band was engaged for the cold weather and then we had tea dances and evening dances every day bar Sunday and sometimes special ones on certain nights. Of these I remember the Vingt-et-un, a ball given by the twenty-one richest bachelors as a thank-you to their many hostesses for much entertainment of lonely men. When a man married he resigned and was replaced as a member. It was a fancy dress ball, always given early in the season to catch the young girls out for the cold weather.'

For all but the last few years of its duration the Raj was a patriarchy, as were the indigenous cultures over which it held sway. At the beginning of its history, this merely reflected the Victorian pattern of male-dominated society in exaggerated form; Great Britain may have had a Queen but a female Viceroy to represent her would have been unthinkable. Nor were the struggles of the Suffragettes in any way meaningfully represented in the subcontinent. The Raj was run solely by men. Even as a paterfamilias a man's authority tended to be greater than in Britain since – with men of thirty securing youthful Fishing Fleet brides – he was almost always considerably older than his wife.

Thus one aspect of marriage in the Raj was that a woman tended to be subsumed into her husband's professions or interests more than was ever likely at home; her social position alone depended on his ranking and seniority in his profession. In British India there was no place for the brilliant hostess who, through advantageous friendships with the powerful, advanced her husband's career, such as Lady Londonderry and her *amitié amoureuse* with the Prime Minister Ramsay MacDonald – unless perhaps such a hostess happened to be married to the Viceroy.

While a wife who was difficult or the cause of scandal might damage her husband's prospects, one who was clever or charming did not have a similar positive weight, but would simply be appreciated for herself. The Raj was even more of a male-dominated society than Britain itself: not only was its ratio of men to women far higher, but it functioned through an all-male hierarchy, a hierarchy in which sport and energetic games, tailored largely to the male physique, played a far greater part than they did at home. And with marriage out of the question for most young men, hard, relentless exercise was the approved way to sublimate sex.

Not that they would have got very far with the girls of the Fishing

Fleet if they had preferred seduction to sport. With rare exceptions, the young unmarried girl of that era was chaste. An illegitimate baby would ruin her chances of a good marriage – often of any marriage – while scandal attached to her name would give her the reputation of 'damaged goods' and even if she had wanted to be a good-time girl she would not have known where to go for contraception. She was also sexually ignorant: sex was a subject simply not talked about, even between mother and daughter.*

When Magda McDowell, aged twenty-three, who had become engaged to her future husband Ralph Hammersley-Smith, whom she had met a few months earlier, her ignorance was total. As she sat in her bedroom on the day of her wedding waiting for her wedding dress to be brought in, her brother-in-law, to whom she was devoted, came hurrying into her room. 'He said to me: "Whatever Ralph may do tonight, remember it's all right." And that was all the preparation I had for married life. I wondered what on earth he could mean!'

With 'consorting with natives' frowned upon, the ethos from the top down was that young men should sublimate their sexual urges in hard exercise and sport. Indeed sport, it is fair to say, was almost a religion; for Army officers, this was largely because it was regarded as a physical and mental preparation for war – cavalry commanders believed that the best way to learn the skills of the cavalry charge was in the hunting field, while pigsticking taught accuracy with a lance. Jackal was hunted on the North-West Frontier, unmarried officers went on shooting and fishing leave. Any Fishing Fleet girl who married one had to realise that sport was an integral part of the marriage.

Above all there was polo, the game that originated in India and was taken up by the British in the earliest years of the Raj. In, some stations there were chukkas every day, with matches, tournaments and intense rivalry – being one of the four-man regimental polo team was every young officer's dream. 'The same qualities which bring a man to the front at polo are required by anyone who aspires to lead men,' claimed a Lancer colonel in a 1922 polo handbook.†

---

* For a previous book, the author interviewed forty-seven pre-wartime debutantes. As debs of eighteen, only two knew what were called 'the facts of life'; and none had heard them from their mothers.

† Quoted by Lawrence James in *Aristocrats*.

An ability to ride was virtually essential: for many young ICS men it was the only way to get about. The early Viceroys rode miles; Lord Northbrook once rode fifty-two miles in one day when in Simla. Women rode, played croquet – in the early days archery was popular – tennis, bicycle polo and, in the hills, golf.

As the historian Margaret Macmillan points out: 'In their copious memoirs, with a few exceptions, the men say far more about favourite horses and dogs than about their wives.' General Greaves, recounting a life of shooting, fishing, horses and dogs, mentioned his wife only once. 'Ranee [his dog] took to her at once, I am glad to say, so there were no complications.' What, one wonders, would have happened had Ranee growled?

For any Fishing Fleet bride of the early twentieth century, help was at hand in a small volume entitled *The Complete Indian Housekeeper and Cook*, which detailed everything from the best layout for a kitchen, the care and management of horses, poultry and dogs, recipes, necessities for store cupboards and medicine chest to the duties of the various servants. It was, in fact, a pocket bible for the new memsahib, even giving advice on what to wear.

'The great secret of coolness and comfort lies in wearing one well-fitting, absorbent undergarment and one only. For this purpose nothing can be better than a combination garment of silk or cellular flannel with the lower part made loose and roomy, without any knickerbockers frills and furbelows. With this, a pair of open-net stays, on to the lower edge of which a fine white petticoat buttons, and a spun-silk jersey bodice as a stay protector, and a lady will find the discomforts of clothing in a temperature over 98 reduced to the minimum compatible with European ideas ... for hot-weather nightgowns nothing is pleasanter to wear than fine nuns-veiling ... it is always advisable to buy a cheap quality of stockings as the colour goes in the strong heat ... at least four pairs of stays (if worn) should be taken, as in hot weather they get sodden and require drying and airing.' Mercifully for the well-dressed memsahib, a few years after this book was written, corsets went out for good.

Maintaining figure, complexion and hair was often difficult in India before the days of SPF50 and air conditioning. 'This is an appalling place for skins and I have suffered tortures with wind, it burns and dries up and your lips get chapped until you could scream with pain. I am brick dust colour yet always wear a veil and take all sorts of care,' wrote the appearance-conscious Ruby Madden.

There was also the dragging-down effect of constant illnesses and the general strain of a difficult climate. 'I don't think that people at home realise that the majority of people out there were often half ill, they were either sort of recovering from a burst of fever or about to have one,' said Honor Penrose, who lived for some time in Benares and later in Agra. 'They were very lethargic – when you have been out there two or three years you have to be lethargic if you're going to make a go of it.'

Sometimes boredom was a contributory factor to this apathy, if a day seems to last forever because there is so little to do, there is no point in rushing through it. At Sauga,* Violet Hanson enjoyed the early mornings and the evenings but found the days tedious. 'The climate was fairly hot during the daytime so we got up early. The Regimental Parade was about 7.00 a.m., and at that time I went for a ride. I rode side-saddle, of course (most women did at that time) – 1925. I loved riding and soon got quite good and practised jumping. After breakfast, my husband would go back to his duties and I was left to supervise the household, which was a bit strange at first, by checking the cleanliness of the cook house and compound and passing the daily accounts.

'I found the morning very long and boring, as it was too hot to go out and there weren't many women around. There was no one to talk to and very few books to read. My husband came home for lunch and after that there would be the afternoon siesta.

'Every evening we would either ride out or, if my husband was playing polo, I would go down to the polo ground and join the other ladies and non-players to watch the game. After this was the inevitable visit to the club, the social centre of all Anglo-Indian life, where everyone gathered each evening. This was where I drank the whisky that I had learned to do before in Secunderabad but I got more used to it at Sauga. Water was undrinkable unless it was boiled and even then it tasted terrible.'

Worst of all were what was known as the 'Sprees'. 'In the autumn the tea was pruned and manufacturing stopped,' wrote Iris Macfar-

* Sauga is 112 miles north-east of the state capital, Bhopal, in the United Provinces (as they were then).

lane, who married a tea planter. 'So there was a lot of free time for managers and their assistants, and this was filled with Sprees. These were day-long celebrations arranged by each club in turn, and were all exactly the same. The same teams played each other at polo, trestle tables supported the same salads, chicken and ham, souffles and trifles, our cooks sweated over similar cakes for tea and wrote over them in green icing messages like *Happy Xmas, Heep Heep Hurrah, Best Luck Sirs*. In the evening the club was converted, with palm fronds and crepe paper, into whatever the club committee had decided was to be the motif that year. It was really a waste of time, since everyone was exhaustedly drunk within the hour. A really successful Spree was one where the potted palms were used as goal posts and someone lost his trousers in a scrum-down.'

Yet at the same time India fascinated Iris and she found it difficult to shake off its spell. 'This country ... bored me and made me ill, but which also enchanted me with its moonflowers and enormous arcs of parrots flying down from the hills at dawn. With its smell of smoke and dust and frying gram and marigolds, with its beautiful people I never got to know ... '.

What India gave to Europeans in unparalleled form was its brilliant, exotic beauty, from enormous moons, fireflies, ancient buildings, temples, graceful, smooth-skinned people to – Iris again – 'the gleam and gush of the south-west monsoon, mimosa and poinsettias and butterflies the size of birds, peppermint green and primrose yellow'.

18

'No one will want to marry me now!'

Perils

In the India of the Raj sudden death was a close neighbour. You could sit next to someone apparently healthy at dinner and hear the next day that he or she had died. Illness struck like lightning, often without warning, and in any social circle; and in that time before antibiotics it was often lethal. Charlotte Canning, the wife of the first Viceroy, who had arrived in India a fit and healthy woman, died in her husband's arms soon after contracting malaria, aged only forty-four.

Desirée Hart, Personal Assistant to the Resident of Kashmir, stationed in Sialkot for the cold weather, woke up one morning to find herself so ill that she could not lift her head from the pillow to sip her early morning tea. The previous night, with a severe headache, she had acted as hostess to her boss whose wife was ill, forcing herself into the role. 'Never had I been so popular, never so good at stimulating the conversation and making the party "go".' When the doctor came he took her temperature, looked at the thermometer in disbelief, then ordered an ambulance straightaway. She was so ill that she could hardly breathe or swallow sips of cooling drinks; her thick shoulder-length golden hair was cut off for the sake of coolness and she was prayed for on church parade.

Desirée was one of the lucky ones. Suddenly the fever broke, sweat poured from her, sponged away by nurses, and she fell into a deep, lengthy sleep, waking to find herself limp but hungry. She had been struck down overnight by a combination of scarlet fever and diphtheria, on top of which she had developed jaundice. Her illness had left her with hair fallen out and turned a dull mouse colour. 'As for my face,' she later wrote, 'sunken eyes with dark shadows and hollow cheeks in a skin left yellow from jaundice and peeling from the scarlet fever. Oh how awful I look!' she wailed. 'No one will want to marry me now!'

She was wrong. During her convalescence the Resident's brother-in-law, Stuart Battye, who had broken his leg playing polo, arrived on crutches to stay at the Residency while his leg mended. Together they sat in the garden under an old banyan tree, together they read the papers, played cracked old records on Stuart's portable gramophone, together they were taken for stately drives for an hour every afternoon. In June that year Stuart turned up at the Residency in Srinagar on three weeks' fishing leave. Very early one morning he took Desiree fishing, proposing to her in the car en route to the bank of the river.

When she enquired why he had not asked her to marry him when they were convalescing together instead of at 5.30 a.m. before fishing, he told her that it had all been carefully planned. 'You were in no state to know your own mind then. It would not have been fair. As to this morning, if you'd said "yes", fine. If you'd said "no" I'd still have had a whole day's fishing to take my mind off it.' He was, she told him happily, impossible.

To the Fishing Fleet girls, merrily dancing the night away at a Government House ball or in the clubhouse of a British cantonment, the idea of life-threatening illnesses striking out of the blue or other disasters might have seemed at best unlikely, at worst far-fetched. And for most, this was perfectly true. Marriage or a visit to someone who lived up country, however, might show a different picture. There were snakes, floods, riots, houses collapsing after the foundations had been eaten away by white ants, occasional panthers in the garden, rabies, earthquakes, landslides and inexplicable fevers.

'I had not dreamed of danger and thought nothing about the journey through the jungle,' records the journal of Henry Cook, civil servant in Company days, who recounts not only the death of his own wife and child but also of an early Fishing Fleet girl. 'But about 12 days later one child was struck down with the jungle fever, then a second and a third. The nurse followed next and the infant had to be weaned suddenly; then it sickened and in a short time, died. My poor wife was the next victim, and after a few weeks she also succumbed to the disease. Everyone who had performed that night journey took fever. I lost an infant and my dear wife. A young lady, Miss Searle, had accompanied my wife and was staying with us … Her kindness and attention were beyond praise but, alas, she also was stricken down and died.'

'Vyner and a Royal Fusilier buried this evening,' wrote Violet Jacob on 2 August 1897. 'I have heard enough of the Dead March lately, for they always strike up as they pass this house, the cemetery being not far off.' A fortnight later her diary records: 'We move in on Friday. Two funerals today; thank heaven I shall not see and hear them in the new place. This season of the year is dreadful in that way.' Three weeks later, on 6 September: 'Poor Cordray died at four this morning, quite young and leaving a young wife … Things are not very cheerful in the hospital but the unhealthy season ought to be over soon now …'.

Violet put down most of the numerous but isolated deaths around her to enteric fever. Much worse, because of the speed with which it spread, was cholera; although eradicated in Britain by the twentieth century, it was endemic in India during the whole of the Raj (and after it). Almost more terrifying than its deadliness was the speed with which it struck; often it was only a few hours from the onset of the first symptoms to death. In Agra cemetery there is a monument to the memory of 146 men of the York and Lancaster Regiment who died within forty-eight hours of the appearance of cholera. During the First World War, in the state of Jodhpur cholera was so widespread that even the monkeys fell off the trees dying. Children were particularly vulnerable: all over India there are pathetic gravestones indicating a child's death – sometimes several from the same family at once. Burial had to be immediate, certainly within twelve hours, because of the climate.

Cholera had originated in India, spreading from the Ganges delta across the world. Yet unlike in England, in India cholera was a disease of the rural poor rather than the urban slum. In its home country its virulence was greatly increased when there had been a famine – rather as the Black Death in England struck hardest against those whose immunity had been weakened through hunger caused by poor harvests. It is acutely infectious, with polluted water one of the main sources, so spreads quickly through tightly packed communities such as the barracks of British soldiers in India (in the 1880s the death rate among the families of British soldiers in India was three times that in Britain).

As the theory that it was an airborne disease persisted in India until the end of the nineteenth century,* one Army technique for dealing with it was, immediately on an outbreak, to march out of barracks against the wind, to higher ground, and camp there. If there were more cases, the process was repeated (with polluted water as a main cause, coupled with the fact that water flows downhill, this was often a partial success, although not because of 'escaping the cholera miasma', as the doctors believed).

Rabies, if not caught in time, invariably meant a horrible death – for animals as well as humans. As most cantonments were haunted by pi-dogs the fear of rabies was ever-present. Without immediate treatment, a person bitten by a rabid dog invariably dies, so anyone bitten by a dog suspected of incubating this disease had to undergo a course of painful injections to ensure their survival. (In India it is estimated that one person still dies of rabies every thirty minutes.) Before the Pasteur Institute was established at Kasauli in 1900, victims sometimes had to be rushed to Paris where the Pasteur Institute had been administering the vaccine since its discovery in 1885. Thus in military cantonments, the sight of a soldier on a motorbike, rifle slung over his back, in pursuit of a rabid pi-dog, was a familiar sight.

Fortunately, it was fairly easy to tell from a dog's behaviour if it might be a risk.† If the animal appeared mad, aggressive or frothing at the mouth it almost certainly had rabies; when rabid, even a timid dog often bites rather than running away. Even before these symptoms appeared it was usually clear if a dog was ill. Sam Raschen, sharing a bungalow with three other subalterns in Rawalpindi, made great friends with their dogs, two of which were a couple of three-month-old Airedale puppies. 'One of them, Titus, loved to play by worrying fiercely anything he could get his pin-sharp

---

* The cholera microbe was isolated and identified in 1883 but medical advances took a certain time to reach the Raj.

† There was no ban on bringing dogs into India. The first legislation imposing quarantine on animals being brought back from India was the Importation of Dogs Order 1897, which came into force on 15 September and made provision for animals to be quarantined for six months.

Driving in a tonga along the road to the Khyber Pass, through a rocky, desolate landscape. In 1912, the year this photograph was taken by the twenty-one-year-old Lilah Wingfield, armed sentries guarded the heights in this dangerous territory between India and Afghanistan.

Leila Blackwell mounted on a yak on an excursion from Gilgit.

Mary Lloyd in a doolie – the Gulmarg version of both pram and carrycot.

(*left*) Rosemary Cotesworth and William Redpath leaving the church after their wedding in 1936.

(*bottom left*) At seventeen, Iris Butler was presented at Court and almost immediately left for India, in the autumn of 1922. It was the start of an intensely social two years.

(*bottom right*) Gervase Portal in his 'lungee', or parade dress turban, brilliantly coloured in emerald, gold, deep blue and scarlet which was worn with a matching cummerbund on formal occasions, including at his wedding to Iris.

Iris Butler on her wedding day in 1927. She refused to carry the bouquet her father pressed into her hands at the last minute, describing it as 'a tightly packed bunch of vegetation packed into a ham frill' and snatched up an ostrich feather fan instead.

Billy Fremlin on her wedding day, aged twenty-two.

Ralph Fremlin on safari, with two porters.

'The Smoking Concert', held in the Durbar Hall, Mercara, in 1910. Pam and Billy's father Ralph is in the centre of the top row, their mother Maud is the third woman from the right in the centre row.

Pam Fremlin, Billy's younger sister, arriving at the Bangalore Hunt Breakfast in 1935. The Fremlin plantation was seventy miles from Bangalore.

A meet of the Bangalore Hunt at 4-Mile Old Madras Road, in August 1935. Pam Fremlin, aged twenty-one, is second from left at the back.

(*top left*) Sheila Hingston, just before she came out to India in September 1929. She was just eighteen.

(*top right*) George Blackwood Reade, always known as Jerry, who became Sheila's husband.

(*centre right*) Lieutenant Colonel C.A.F. Hingston, Sheila's father. 'Hinkie' was the most popular doctor in Madras.

(*below*) Greenwood, the house in Ootacamund that belonged to Sheila's mother Gladys. In front are the family car and driver and beside them Gladys and the eight-year-old Sheila, on her pony, held by a syce. In the background the ayah holds Sheila's one-year-old brother Clayton.

Gladys Hingston entertaining in Madras: (*from left to right*) Rosita Forbes, the glamorous and well-known traveller, Gladys Hingston, Princess Nilufer – who was married to the second Prince of Hyderabad – and Sir George Stanley, Governor of Madras.

The Opening Meet of the Ooty Hunt. Since 1894, this had been taking place at the Maharaja of Mysore's summer palace, Fernhill, presided over by the Maharaja as official host.

The ultimate goal for any Fishing Fleet girl was of course a wedding to the man of her choice. These could be lavish social occasions, such as this one in Poona in 1905 *(above)*; for the Elgin wedding even the cake was larger than life. It stood 5 feet 7 inches high, weighed 650lbs and took two months to make.

little teeth into – often my hands! One day Titus was visibly out of sorts, the next his owner announced that rabies was suspected, so the poor little chap had to be destroyed (an examination of his brain confirmed the diagnosis).'

None of those in the bungalow could be sure that they had not been scratched and then licked in romping with Titus, so they were sent off immediately for treatment. As well as remaining teetotal, they had to have two injections, deep into the stomach, every day for a fortnight. 'Towards the end,' wrote Raschen, 'one felt like a walking pincushion. All the male patients stood in a queue, holding up the front of their shirts, rather undignified but little time was wasted.' There was still time, however, to play a joke on the other poor sufferers. 'The trick lay in arriving early to be at the front of the line, giving a dreadful grimace after receiving one's jabs and muttering audibly about the shocking bluntness of the needles today.'

'It is awful the way dogs go mad in India,' wrote Lilah Wingfield in December 1911. 'Captain Mitford has lost three lately, through rabies. It is thought they get bitten by a mad jackal originally, then one dog bites another and so it goes on. Mr Palmer's delicious smooth-coated black retriever which he had in camp at Delhi with him, started rabies a day or two before we left Pindi. He tied it up and had it carefully watched and at length the poor beast had to be shot.'

Between the mid-1880s and the early 1920s India was struck by a series of major epidemics. As well as malaria and cholera, both endemic, there was Spanish flu and bubonic plague.

For well over twenty years, plague was a major killer and caused an estimated ten million deaths. It spread from Bombay, where the death toll rose to 183,984 between 1896 and 1914. When the outbreak first began, it was not known in India that plague was spread by rat fleas – only in the twentieth century was one woman able to write grimly: 'When a dead rat falls from the rafters of the roof, you know that bubonic plague has come to town.' Instead, the city was scoured with sea water and carbolic. Drains were flushed out, disinfectant sprinkled in tenements and alleyways.

In 1897, to halt the spread of plague, the Government forbade fairs and pilgrimages, segregating suspected plague cases, examining and where necessary detaining travellers by road and rail to examine them, dividing queues at railway stations into male and female. But this fell foul of India's caste system, whereby even a touch by a white person could pollute, while for women, accustomed to purdah and strict modesty, a public examination for swollen lymph glands was deeply offensive. The result was that many potential cases were smuggled out of the city, taking the plague with them.

In 1898, so bad was the plague in the city and district of Poona that 1,200 British troops were employed for months searching out 'plague' houses, so that these could be disinfected or destroyed. 'When a case was detected, the family was removed to a special camp, after being thoroughly washed in a strong solution of perchloride of mercury,' wrote General Sir Henry Beauvoir De Lisle.* After this, the house was disinfected and whitewashed; later still, when it was considered safe, the survivors could return. What made the job difficult was that, to avoid being sent to the camp, the inhabitants of a house where someone had died of the plague that night often buried the body under the house's floor; unless detected, the infection remained through plague fleas.

Unlike most of the other diseases, plague was transmitted in the cold weather, when people huddled together for warmth, with outbreaks peaking in the spring and summer. Doctors who treated it were known as plague sahibs. 'Driving through the district it is easy to tell the villages where the plague is really bad,' wrote Margaret Munson, who had come out in the Fishing Fleet to marry a man in the Indian Medical Service. 'The houses are empty and along the roads nearby are huts of grass and wood built by those afraid to remain in infected villages.' IMS doctors had a mobile dispensary camp, travelling ten to twelve miles a day by bullock cart, doing small operations such as cataracts, with local anaesthetic and careful sterilisation of their instruments between operations.

During the British Raj, India experienced some of the worst famines ever recorded, including the Great Famine of 1876–8, in which 6.1 million to 10.3 million people died, and the Indian famine of 1899–1900, in which 1.25 to 10 million people perished. The main reason was the British insistence on Indian farmers growing jute or cotton – to facilitate trade – rather than food crops such as rice and

---

* In *Reminiscences of Sport and War* (Eyre and Spottiswoode, 1939).

wheat. In times of shortage, this policy was catastrophic.

Smallpox was another killer: between 1868 and 1907, there were approximately 4.7 million deaths. And after the First World War came Spanish flu, the pandemic that lasted from March 1918 to June 1920 and killed up to fifty million people worldwide. In India it accounted for between ten and seventeen million deaths.

By the 1930s children could be inoculated against smallpox, cholera and plague, but dysentery and diphtheria (which accounted for over two thousand deaths a year in Britain) still carried off many.

When in 1898 Sir Ronald Ross, working in the Presidency General Hospital in Calutta, finally proved that malaria was transmitted by mosquitoes, as many precautions as possible were taken against their bites, from mosquito nets to the wearing (by women) of light boots under their evening dresses in 'mosquito-ey' areas. Even so, malaria was so common that most people treated it as almost unavoidable. 'We took five grains of quinine and five grains of aspirin every six hours until the fever broke,' wrote Monica Campbell-Martin. 'The rapid drop from a high temperature to one that was well below normal brought the body out in such a heavy sweat that the bed sheets were wringing wet. Once the fever had broken people were supposed to remain in bed for twenty-four hours and take things easy.'

Sometimes malaria arrived in epidemic form. Joan Henry, newly married to sugar plantation manager Geoffrey Allen, was one of the few who never caught malaria, although 500 died around them in Pandaul village, and Geoffrey suffered for a week each month with repeated attacks, with the typical very high temperature, shivering, vomiting, headaches and pains. During the times he was on his feet he brought in squads of low-caste Hindus to burn the corpses – the villagers themselves were so weak from malaria that they were throwing these into the nearby water supply. It was only this swift action that prevented a cholera outbreak from contaminated water.

Along with malaria, dengue fever, still endemic in more than one hundred countries, was another disease transmitted by mosquitoes. Although most people survived, it was a truly painful experience, involving anything from bleeding gums, pain behind the eyes, red palms and feet to a high temperature, as described by this sufferer:

'One morning in July I woke up barely able to move. Every bone in my body felt as though it were being crushed in a vice, with hot knives stabbing into my brain. Wrenching myself out of bed, I went to the bathroom and vomited what felt like everything in my system.

'Over the next couple of days my body temperature became extremely erratic; one minute I would be drenched in sweat, burning up; the next I would be screaming for blankets, desperate to stop chills so extreme and rapid in onset that it felt as if I had plunged into icy water.

'The pain hammering my bones and joints was the hardest to bear; the disease lives up to its nickname of breakbone fever. Nausea and vomiting left me unable to contemplate the tiniest morsel of food while the bone pain robbed me of sleep so that I became extremely weak … there is little doctors can do except control symptoms, so I was put on a saline drip …'.

In the damp heat of the hot weather, skin infections could be a problem. One particularly nasty one, supposedly transmitted by the bite of tiny, almost invisible sand flies, was known as 'Delhi boils', a self-explanatory term. These began as itching red spots on exposed skin such as the face, hands, feet, elbows, ankles; for men, left in the plains while women and children sought the coolness of the hills, a common place was the back of the neck.

Disease was not the only peril faced by the Fishing Fleet girl. Throughout the duration of the Raj there were outbreaks of fighting and sporadic rioting, with almost constant battling of one kind or another along the North-West frontier, then as now such engagements almost a hobby among those warlike people. 'There is fighting at Malakund, which saw a number of the soldiers depart,' wrote Lady Elisabeth Bruce in 1897. 'One man, a major, had a Pathan servant who asked him very earnestly if he was not going to the front to fight. "Why?" said the officer. "Because I long to go too, that I may get a shot at my father-in-law," said his servant.' Later she heard news of another outbreak on the frontier, near Peshawar, and as the month progressed half her father's soldier ADCs left for the front.

Women, of course, did not fight – but natural disasters were no respecters of gender.

On tour in Gilgit, Rosemary Redpath and her Political Officer husband Alexander sometimes heard 'the familiar crackle which heralded the arrival of boulders and rubble from high up on the mountainside'. On those occasions there was little time for the Redpaths, travelling along a narrow track with a sheer precipice on one side, to decide whether to gallop ahead, stay put, or turn on the proverbial sixpence and retreat.

Once, halted for a midday meal, they heard a loud crack and on looking up saw 'enormous rocks the size of houses virtually standing out in mid-air thousands of feet above us. We all took to our heels leaving, I regret to say, horses and baggage ponies tethered where they were.' Luckily the avalanche was diverted by a couloir, leaving the Redpaths – and their horses – in the clear as it thundered to the bottom of the valley.

In Bihar, on 15 January 1934, Monica Campbell-Martin heard a noise like the rushing of an express train, then the walls of her bungalow started to ripple as if made of cloth and she rushed into the garden. 'The hills, the mountains, the trees, all were dipping and swerving. A hill disappeared like a scenic backdrop as I looked at it. Hundreds of birds flew by, screeching their terror.'

Joan Henry had a similar experience, in the same Bihar earthquake. At 2.13 in the afternoon as she was resting on her bed she heard a rumbling that at first sounded like the wind that heralded the monsoon. As the noise grew louder, the first shock waves hit. 'My bed rocked and I leapt off and tore out of my room, but it was difficult to run as the floor behaved like a roller coaster, up one moment and down the next.'

Outside 'the lawn was like a billowing sea, great waves instead of flat grass. Two cars, parked outside the garage, were rolling backwards and forwards in unison, partners in a formal dance – brakes were often forgotten in such a flat area. As I gazed at them, the ground under my feet cracked open, splits appeared around me, and out of these spouted high gushes of hot liquid, a muddy mixture.' The garden was left under a mixture of mud, sand and water but the Henry household was safe. They, and those nearby, were lucky: the quake, which measured 8.5 on the Richter scale, killed something like 30,000 people and caused immense structural damage, with collapsed buildings, railway lines twisted like writhing snakes, bridges broken and flooding.

Much later the same year there was a meeting in Patna, attended by the Governor and involving the most senior men in the province to discuss what was to be done in the aftermath of the earthquake. Here one of the ADCs decided to tell a funny story he had heard about a lady who had been caught in her bath when the quake struck. She had rushed out of the bathroom dripping wet, clutching only a small towel, and shouting in her poor Hindi a sentence which translated as 'Five rupees a look!' None of the laughs the young man had hoped for materialised; instead there was a frozen silence, broken by the District Commissioner (the top ICS man in the district) saying in a frigid voice: 'That was my wife.'

There was not such a happy ending for Edward Wakefield of the Indian Civil Service. He survived the Quetta earthquake of 1 May 1935, in which between 30,000 and 60,000 people died, but it killed one of his two small daughters. Two days later, camping in the Residency gardens, he wrote to his mother-in-law; first telling her that his wife Lalage had survived, he described the events of that terrible night, when they had gone to bed about 12.35 (the earthquake occurred at 3.02 a.m.).

'I was woken up, in pitch blackness, by an indescribable roar of noise. I had time, so Lal tells me, to say "My God, what's that?" before the crash came; but to me it seemed that I had hardly woken from a deep sleep and, alarmed, had half turned towards Lal, when the whole world collapsed on me. Everything tumbled on me – beams, rafters, bricks, mortar – from above and from both sides. I was surprised, when all this falling of the house had stopped, to find myself alive. I called to Lal, but she could only groan in reply ... there was a big beam across her back, that hurt her frightfully, and she could not move. I then struggled desperately to move but could not manage to. My head was wedged between two rafters and the beam that was across Lal's back was also across my thighs. My legs and body were covered deep with bricks and plaster.'

The only part of his body that Edward Wakefield could move was his right hand With it, he tried to remove what bits of bricks and plaster he could touch. But soon he realised that to do this would be dangerous, as when some plaster was dislodged it almost filled the small breathing space that was left to him. Somehow he managed to breathe, though not freely, and working away very gently and cautiously with his one hand, he managed to release most of his arm. Now, better able to use his hand, he could clear a space by his wife's head so that she could breathe more easily.

'Meanwhile, I heard Nurse, from a great distance it seemed, shout for help, and I also heard Bold One crying; but no sound from Imogen. After I had found it quite impossible to free myself or help Lal, I simply lay still, as did Lal, and we waited. Eventually (after about ten minutes) I heard sounds of people moving; I shouted but got no reply. Nurse also shouted and it seemed that people answered her shouts.

'After that, things are confused in my mind. I remember feeling relief at the thought that Bold One had got away with Nurse, though how I knew they had been pulled out I cannot say; perhaps the fact that Nurse's shouts for help had stopped and men's voices were heard made me deduce that they had escaped.'

He shouted again for Ghulam Mohammad, their bearer, and eventually a voice replied from what seemed to the barely conscious Edward an infinite distance. Then, as he later recalled, the worst period of all followed: he could not move at all, he was in pitch darkness and Lalage was silent, in great pain and possibly dying. The rescuers were making no headway, as they had no light and no tools to dig with and could only guess where the Wakefields were lying. After what seemed hours, they managed to clear away the bricks and plaster above the couple, and at last got to the beam lying across them. They tried to move it – and failed. They tried again, and again failed. And, to Edward's despair, they said it could not be moved. All this was still in the threatening dark. Time passed, and he began to feel that the rescuers had begun to give up hope of getting them out. 'I had that last horror of feeling that Lal and I could not even kill ourselves.'

Eventually the rescuers (a sweeper, a driver and another man from their compound, and a prisoner from the lock-up behind the house) tried approaching the trapped couple from a different direction. At last they got Edward and Lalage's heads free and after that he was able to show them how to get Lalage out. First they cleared all rubble away from the upper part of her body and legs, then took some of the strain of the beam off her and drew her out by the shoulders. It was another ten minutes before Edward was pulled out in his turn and just as he found himself on the drive in front of their house, up came the Superintendent of Police with reinforcements to help – a party of the West Yorkshire Regiment who had come from their cantonment. The end was a tragedy.

'It was still too dark to see much but the parties kept at work with the help of hurricane lanterns and, from the servants' quarters, bodies, dead or alive, were continually being extracted. The party looking for Imogen worked for two and a half hours before they came on one of her feet, and then I did not look any more but waited near by.'

Although among Europeans death by snakebite was comparatively rare, to the Western mind one of the greatest terrors of India was snakes. As a consequence, some British would sleep with a revolver by their side in case of a snake's sudden appearance in bedroom or bathroom. Again, snakes were largely a peril of the hot weather (in the cold, they hibernate). In March, as the heat began, frogs would seek the cool, damp quietness of bathrooms, with their convenient drainage hole entrance, and snakes, scenting prey, would follow them. As snakes love long grass, bungalow compounds in regimental cantonments were inspected to see that grass was cut short.

The most deadly snake was the krait, common in northern India. Small – seldom more than two feet in length – and an inconspicuous grey-brown colour, it is probably responsible for more deaths than any other snake in India. It is mostly nocturnal, said to kill in twenty minutes and is generally lethargic. As it lies in the dust unnoticed, anyone who goes barefoot is at risk, especially because as it is deaf it does not, like most other snakes, slither quickly out of the way if it gets a chance.

Because it can only raise its head about a quarter of an inch, Europeans, who wear shoes and boots, are generally safe, unless it drops off the top of a door or curtain rod where it sometimes lies. A krait fell on the head of Betsy Macdonald's (née Anderson) husband Tommy as he was opening the garage door of their bungalow in Bihar. 'Luckily,' wrote Betsy afterwards, 'he was wearing his topi.'

Perhaps because, instinctively, most people feel an atavistic fear of snakes that somehow connects with the depth of the subconscious, there was also a curious fascination with snake charmers. 'The Sanp-wallah, or Snake People, are short, dark-skinned people with broad faces that suggest Dravidian ancestry, long hair in ringlets or pinned on top of the head and thick beards. Their snakes live in baskets, carried in yokes. Traditionally, they wear orange robes,' wrote Evelyn Barrett, who witnessed their mysterious ability seemingly to call wild snakes to them.

'In our compound, one patch of grass, fifteen feet by twelve feet, remained uncut. Before this, the men took up position, the elder retiring a few paces and dropping his load. Pacing up and down before the grass and scrutinising it carefully, the boy then raised his pipe and started to play.

'He sauntered back and forth, never taking his eyes off the grass, as the beckoning notes rose and fell. A rustle was answered by a stirring in the music. Leaning forward, the charmer now played with urgency, a summons that seemed to strike and follow the rippling grass until, almost unnoticed, a small, dark snake lay writhing at his feet. When the music stopped it started whipping and hissing, but at the first notes of the pipe it flattened and calmed, coiling ever more closely until, at a sign from the boy, the older man stepped forward and seized it behind the head, flicking it, hissing, into a sack. A second snake was similarly dealt with.

'Next came a cobra. It was writhing on the ground before anyone saw it leave the grass. As before, when the music stopped, the snake seemed to lose purpose, and started to writhe and hiss. As before, at the first notes it flattened and undulated towards the player. Then it 'danced'. Facing the pipe, hood spread, it reared and swayed from side to side, while its forked tongue ceaselessly flickered. Holding the pipe to within an inch of its head, the charmer played the snake, drawing it to and fro as certainly as though it were attached to his pipe. Before disappearing into a sack, it was made to bite a leaf and we were shown the two viscous fang prints. Cobras are always found in pairs, so not until the second was disposed of was the performance concluded.

'"Now," said my husband, "get us a wild snake! These were doped."

'A ten-rupee note silenced expostulations. This time, both were taken aside, stripped and searched by my husband and another officer, before being allowed to continue the performance. Everyone was then ordered by the sanp-wallah to stand back and neither speak nor move.

'As before, the boy paced before the grass, staring at it closely. The older man now stood up. After a deep salaam, with eyes closed and palms joined against his breast, he started rapidly intoning. I caught the words 'Hazur' (Presence) and 'Mehtar' (Prince) at each mention of which he salaamed. Gathering momentum his voice rose, to fall to desperate mutterings, the while his hands were lowered in supplication. Now the pipe was speaking, softly, calling, calling.

'Suddenly the boy ceased his pacing and, half-crouching, played with frenzy at a point in the grass. Hissings followed. As these grew louder, the boy retreated in dancing, circling steps, always facing the grass and never for an instance ceasing to play. The older man now stepped aside. Next instant three feet of skewbald snake shot from the grass, and as quickly withdrew. The hissings now became frantic and the boy leapt as a snake flung itself, hissing and writhing, at his feet. It was about five feet long, coloured pink and sand, and in the wildest rage. Fresh hissings now broke out as a second and even longer snake broke from the grass. Anyone unfamiliar with snakes can have no idea of the lightning speed of a roused six-footer.

'To us horrified onlookers it was hardly possible to follow the movements of the snakes. Although we realised that both reptiles were frantic from fear, and were only trying to regain the shelter of the grass, the odds against the naked, prancing boy and his pipe seemed overwhelming. Again and again, the snakes were turned by a dancing toe. Gradually the hissings subsided, the thrashing bodies closed in ever-tightening coils until, for a second, one snake lay motionless at the foot of the charmer. On the instant it was snatched behind the head by the older man and flung, hissing, into a sack. Five minutes later the second snake was similarly dealt with. For no baksheesh on earth will a sanp-wallah kill a snake.

'Streaming with sweat, chest heaving, the boy stood up. Physically and nervously he was exhausted. Throughout the performance not a word had been uttered. Now a babel of voices broke forth – flat, English voices, falling strangely on that Indian garden of scent and sun and secret, thrilling power. Only the sanp-wallah were apart, silently and methodically adjusting their garments and fastening the sacks.

'Baksheesh to the extent of twenty rupees (about thirty shillings), to these people a fortune, seemed little enough for what we had witnessed.'

Disease, avalanche, snakebite – Fishing Fleet girls who stayed in India were threatened by them all. But few could have had the experience of Olive Crofton, married to a District Officer and setting off by train from Central India in 1920. 'There had been trouble on the railways lately with train thieves, including several murders,' she wrote laconically; and at her husband's instigation packed her revolver in her dressing case.

Her carriage had a detachable chair, more comfortable than the ordinary seats, and while she sat reading in this, her back to the window, a reflection of something flickered on the glass of her spectacles. She turned round to see a large man, who had been crouching out of sight on the footboard, clambering through the window, a leaded stick in his right hand and a large knife in his belt.

Luckily her dressing case was open on the bunk beside her. She reached in, picked up her revolver, released the safety catch and pointed it at him in one swift motion while saying in Urdu: 'Do you want to be shot?'

'An expression of utter horror came into his face as he threw himself backwards out of the window,' she wrote later. 'And the last I saw of him was rolling over and over like a shot rabbit down the high railway embankment.' A woman who could coolly tackle an armed robber, one feels, could tackle anything.

'As I inspected ours I sighed a bit'

The First Home

In 1889 Anne Wilson, newly married to a Deputy Commissioner, wrote to a friend of her first impression of her new home in the Punjab: 'Picture to yourself, then, a square one-storied flat-roofed house, with a pillared veranda at each side, nine rooms, three in a row, without an entrance hall or any passage, each room opening into the other as rooms do in an *étage* abroad, each room having one or two door-windows into the bargain, and then count how many doors or windows there must be – a blessing no doubt in the hot weather but not ornamental in the cold …

'Every room looks as high as a country church, the roofs are of upholstered rafters, the doors are folding doors, bolted in the middle. If you wish to keep them shut, you must bolt them. If you wish to keep them open, you have to fix a wooden block in, behind the hinges. At present a white cotton, sheet-like curtain hangs from a wooden rod before each …'

She went on to speak of the extraordinarily primitive kitchen arrangements – which, in the majority of bungalows, persisted into the twentieth century. There was no pantry, dresser, shelves, cupboards or even hot or cold running water – not even a proper kitchen, with a scullery or larder, let alone a plate rack for drying dishes. 'The kitchen is a little dark room, with a board on the floor to hold the meat, two tumble-down brick "ranges" in one corner, a stone receptacle in another into which the water is thrown, which runs out through its hole in the wall into a sunk tub.

'There are two shelves, on which are an array of pots, a hatchet, drainer, one or two tin spoons and some pudding and pate shapes.' After the first shock, she was cheered to learn that a brick floor could be laid and a sink built while they were in camp, and anything in the way of tables or kitchen equipment could be ordered.

Furniture was sparse, usually left or sold by the previous resident. Single beds, pushed into the centre of the room to avoid any creature that might crawl down the walls, were the rule because the nights were so hot. Bungalows were always whitewashed; wallpaper would have been eaten by white ants. To soften the appearance of these high bare walls the authors of *The Complete Indian Housekeeper and Cook* recommended a painted band around the base of the wall, with patterns around the top. Floors were often of beaten mud – termites loved wood – covered with grass or bamboo matting. Until electricity arrived during the twentieth century, light came from paraffin or coconut oil lamps and candles.

'As I inspected ours I sighed a bit,' wrote newly wed Fishing Fleet girl Cecile Stanley Clarke, on arrival at their first home – her husband Henry's regiment was stationed in the Fort at Calcutta. 'The furniture consisted of two single beds covered in mosquito nets, two rather battered little tables, a couple of chairs and a kind of cupboard. The drawing-room had a table, a sofa – very hard Victorian horse-hair type – two armchairs of the same vintage, and six brown flowerpot stands on long legs.' These latter, she continued mournfully, were beloved of the Indian contractors, 'and as no one saw eye to eye with them the junior subalterns were generally landed with the lot ... our dining room had a table, with a blotchy kind of surface (only colonels' and majors' wives had ones with a high polish), six chairs, and a kind of sideboard affair.'

Violet Hanson found the same dilapidated bareness awaiting her when she and her husband returned from honeymoon to the Indian Cavalry School at Sauga, where her husband was to take the Cavalry course – obligatory for all Indian cavalry officers.

'Sauga was a very old military station and the bungalows were of the most primitive kind. They were furnished by the Public Works Department with a minimum of functional furniture: the usual wooden and cane chairs, iron beds with mosquito netting, dining table and chairs, and a chest of drawers for dressing tables. The floors were bare with rush matting covering them and we got some material from the bazaar for curtains.

'The ceilings were nothing but ceiling cloths, which were much-patched cotton material stretched beneath the rafters of the roof. These cloths hung fairly slackly and a colony of various little creatures lived under the roof. Looking up, you could see the imprint of their little feet running from side to side over the ceiling cloth and hear squeaks and rustling. A colony of bats lived in one corner of my bedroom, with a separate entrance hole, so that they would emerge at night to fly about the room. When my husband was dining in the Mess (as he had to do at least once a week) I would have my dinner in bed, under the relative safety of the mosquito netting.'

As Violet sat in bed eating she would see muskrats, harmless little creatures but with a strong smell that gave them their name, scuttling round the sides of the room by the skirting boards. Less pleasant were other, bolder rats which ran across the room 'sometimes over my feet while I was dressing. There were insects of all kinds, of course, and lizards on the wall, that ate the spiders and flies.'

Occasionally a bungalow would have a justified reputation as 'queer'. Before she married, Cecile Stanley Clarke and her mother stayed in one, rented for them by Cecile's brother-in-law Hubert Gough. It had been the old Madras Regiment's mess in Indian Mutiny times and, thought Cecile, there was a 'something' that still lingered. Later, at 12.30 one night, it manifested itself. Here is Cecile's account:

'"Mamma, I can hear something!"

'"Go to sleep," she replied, lighting our bedside light; but not before I had seen the most horrible yellow face pressed against the window.

... '"I saw something." I continued, with chattering teeth.

'"Rubbish," she replied, though with not much conviction.

'I got up and ran to the window – nothing to be seen.

'"You must have dreamt it," said Mama, but I hadn't and I can see the face now, grinning hideously at me.

'"Golly! I don't like this at all", I said.

'There was a veranda running round just outside our bedroom. I opened the doors and went out to have a look round. The moonlight was making great shadows and the stars seemed so near that I felt I could stretch out a hand and pluck one from the sky.

'"Chowkidar," I called. "Have you seen anyone?"

'"Banshee," replied the man, with no hesitation at all.

'"I don't like this," I said. "Let's go back to Dorset tomorrow."

'I went to the great cupboard and hunted round for the little bottle of holy water I had been given for just such an emergency, then went round the room flipping it about. "That will keep them out of here, anyway," I said, climbing back into bed and pulling the sheets over my head. Mama kept the light on and read a book.

'When I told Hubert about it the next morning he just laughed. Not so my sister Mary. "You are right," she said. "There is something funny about this bungalow; it has been empty for years, because of course no one would take it as it is haunted." She and I made such a fuss that in the end Hubert had a police guard put on the two staircases that led up to our veranda.

'Night after night, just as we were having dinner, we would hear footsteps pattering about above our heads. "Banshees," we would yell, and all rush up and have a ghost hunt, but we never saw anything. Our police guards put sand on the floors and strands of cotton across the veranda, the footsteps continued but the feet left no marks, nor was the cotton broken.'

The sound of clanking was what woke Fishing Fleet girl Violet Field on her first night of married life on her husband's station in the Punjab. She asked her new husband, Jim Acheson, what the noise was, to be told that it was made by the chains worn by the gardeners working in their garden. They were all prisoners from the local prison, he explained. Violet would have none of this. 'No one will wear chains in *my* garden!' she said. After that, every day the prisoners would come, have their chains struck off, work in the garden and then undergo a rigorous head count before being chained up again to go back to gaol.

For Ruth Barton and her husband Pete their garden brought glamour. After arriving in Bombay they went straight to Secunderabad in the Deccan where her husband's battalion of the Rajputana Rifles was stationed. Here they dined outside, their table under a gold mohur tree in the garden, shaped like an open umbrella. In mid-March it was brilliant with scarlet blossoms against its bare branches. They hung a light in the tree so that all the insects hovered round it, and little owls swooped down and feasted on the insects.

Then came feathery leaves and then more scarlet flowers. On clear nights they slept in the garden, well away from the heat-soaked walls of the bungalow, where a 'blessed coolness rose with the dew and the fragrance of tobacco flowers and night-scented stock filled the air'.

Some things were permitted that would be frowned on at home – in India, for example, it was quite permissible for young ladies to have a chota peg as a sundowner (indeed, it was medically advised), whereas in England a young woman downing whisky would have been very *mal vu*.

But the importance of keeping up standards was felt strongly. 'You seem to think, dearie, that it's only people who come from out of the way places who get untidy or careless in their appearance,' wrote Leslie Lavie to his fiancée Flossie in March 1896. 'I can name numbers of people in Secunderabad who seem to have no scruples about white petticoats ... I'm sure you would never get like that, degenerating as the climate of Vizianagram is. I like, or should I think like, ladies of my household to wear sort of light tea gowns during the day in India, than which nothing is more becoming; instead of which you generally see, if you surprise anybody suddenly, some very old and untidy costume.'

Fifteen years later, in a paper she read to young women planning marriage, Florence Evans, wife of Joseph Evans in the Royal Corps of Armourers, made the same thing clear: 'It has been particularly impressed upon me that this paper would not be complete if I did not mention *curl pins*,' she wrote. 'These I am led to understand are particularly disliked by the male sex, therefore they should be carefully laid aside before the return of the men; not only this but we should be neatly dressed in our house to please our *husbands* as well as others.'

Even in small stations like the little railway outpost of Arkonam, where Hilda Bourne lived with her husband Jim, formality reigned. Jim, who first went to India as a civil engineer for a railway company, did so well that he was soon responsible for the Nilgiri Railway (one of India's famous Hill Railways) that linked the fashionable hill station of Ootacamund to the main system. Hilda and Jim had been childhood sweethearts, and she joined the Fishing Fleet of autumn 1903 with her wedding cake in her luggage. They married in Bombay a week after her arrival, settling down in a company bungalow in Arkonam, almost 660 miles distant, soon after their honeymoon.

Here in this town, supposedly one of the hottest in India (sometimes the temperature was 43°C for several days running), at a time when flannel was worn next to the skin and no lady was considered dressed without corsets and petticoats, the small British community gave constant dinner parties, almost all of which had to have eight courses, with the correct wine for every course. As the only meat available locally was goat or chicken – supplemented occasionally by what was shot for the pot – one of the chief ingredients of these meals was the cook's imagination, although for special occasions European food was sent up from Madras.

None of this entertaining, of course, could have happened without the servants who were an integral part of life in India. Buffer and link between the stranger and the vast land of his responsibility, their loyalty was a miracle of the Raj. 'I sometimes wonder they do not cut off all our heads and say nothing about it,' wrote Emily Eden, sister of Lord Auckland, the Governor-General 1836–42.

The size of a bungalow was irrelevant to the number of servants employed. This conformed to a basic quota and consisted of: bearer (personal servant, also valet to the master of the household), khitmagar (butler), khansamah (cook), messalgie (pantry boy), bheestie (water carrier) and sweeper. For a 'married' bungalow, with children, nanny (ayah) and nursery boy would be added. A dhobi (laundry man) usually came from outside.

Outside were mali (gardener) and as many boys (chokras) as he could wangle. For anyone with horses there would be a jemadar-syce (head groom) and a syce per horse or (polo) pony. Finally there was the chowkidar (night watchman), 'a stalwart who spent most of the night snoring in a corner of the veranda'. The bearer was the head servant, responsible for overseeing running the household, engaging other servants, paying wages and overseeing expenses and doing the bidding of his master. A good one was invaluable; a bad one could make life irritating, difficult and distracting.

Anne Wilson found herself with thirteen servants – including a groom, water carrier and milkman – but soon realised that supervision was needed. 'One must look after the filter [on the water supply], see to the milk, the feeding of cow, sheep and poultry, the making of butter, bread and cakes, the careful trimming of the lamps, to the dusting of books, pictures, furniture, to the tinning of pots and pans, to the way the cook uses his dishes or his dusters.'

For Indians, domestic service carried no stigma but rather conferred status. Servants, like soldiers, were drawn from the highest strata of village society, their regular wage a wealth normally undreamt of. Like English servants in great houses, they reflected the standing of their employers; thus the bearer of a British cavalry colonel claimed higher wages and status than that of a British infantry colonel; to be in the Viceroy's household was to be at the pinnacle. Entertaining also added prestige; Anne Wilson found that her servants invariably laid places for four even when she and her husband were alone 'as if they were in a state of constant hospitable expectation'.

Memoir after memoir has described how one could come home after a drink or a swim at the club at 8.30, tell the cook that there would be six guests for dinner that night – and know that an excellent dinner would somehow be conjured up out of the kitchen's hole-in-the-ground oven and handle-less saucepans.

Nor did it matter how basic the newlyweds' silver or china cupboard was; what was needed would be borrowed from a nearby bungalow to maintain the honour of the household. Many a bride was surprised to see her newly acquired salt cellars or candlesticks appearing, without a word said, on the dinner table of her hosts. 'The Brigadier's pearl-handled fruit knives figured at our parties as regularly as our green coffee cups graced the Colonel's table,' wrote Evelyn Barrett. 'Of course no one said anything.'

In the same way the gardener, whose first duty was to produce flowers, always managed this even when there were none growing in the garden. One story, perhaps apocryphal, tells of a man leaving for England who gave his gardener a reference that read: 'This gardener has been with me fifteen years. I have no garden, I have never lacked flowers and he has never had a conviction.'

In England, just as children of the upper and middle classes often lived a life completely separate from their parents, going down brushed, combed and smartened up, to see them for an hour after tea, with their nurseries quite likely on a different floor, so servants, too, had their own quarters away from the rest of the family.

But in India, living in a bungalow, where rooms often opened out of one another, there was far less separation; and the servants, who did not knock and walked noiselessly on bare feet, could often be in a room before anyone was aware of their presence. The bearers would be in attendance all day long; others would wait at table, another might be waiting on the veranda for orders. Although their dwellings were completely separate, nevertheless they managed to know everything that was going on in the bungalow, from a surreptitious love affair to ill-health and the beginning of a pregnancy; next to her husband, the sweeper, who emptied the thunderboxes, had the most intimate knowledge of a woman's bodily functions.

Hygiene meant full-time vigilance, from boiling water and milk, washing all fruit and vegetables in water sterilized with permanganate of potash, lining meat safes with mosquito netting to deter flies and pouring paraffin and boiling water down the cracks in the floors to keep away white ants, to filtering water. This was done by setting three large jars one above the other in a frame, with holes in the bases of the top two. In the top jar was put a mixture of gravel and charcoal, through which the water ran into the second jar, in which there was clean sand, which also took away the flavour of the charcoal. A further refinement was putting some minute pieces of sponge in the holes in the base of the second jar. The result was water so purified that if it came from a natural source it was fit to drink, though any from a well or stream near a village still had to be boiled.

Betsy Macdonald, who had married the owner of an up-country sugar factory in Bihar, had to rely on her husband to give the orders until she had learnt sufficient of the language. She managed to get a decent kitchen built; her next struggle was with the dhobi. Although the clothes and tea towels he brought back each evening were spotlessly white and impeccably washed and ironed, she suspected he had been using a lot of bleach and laying them out in the sun, which would soon rot them.

'I followed him one day and to my horror my worst fears were confirmed as I was led to the buffalo pool. Everything and everybody washed there – dogs, buffaloes, children and villagers. It intrigued me how they changed their clothes in the water and came out of the murky pond looking cleaner … [but] I did not relish the idea of our washing being done there and then slapped to shreds on the rocks.' She put an end to it, telling the man he could use as much hot water as he liked at the bungalow, and giving him a packet of Lux. He took to this arrangement, soon extolling the merits of 'Lukkus sahopu'.

20

———•———

'But what about horses?
And polo? And parties?'

Iris Butler

Iris Butler was a quintessential daughter of the Raj. Her father's career was in India, much of her childhood was spent as an 'Empire orphan' and it was as a Fishing Fleet girl that she returned to India – and marriage to an Indian Army cavalry officer. Like so many governors' daughters, her choice fell on a man serving as ADC to her father.

Her family on either side was profoundly linked to India. She herself was born in Simla on 15 June 1905, the daughter of Montagu Butler, who had passed into the Indian Civil Service in 1896, and, after being knighted, was Governor of the Central Provinces 1925–33. Her mother, Ann Smith, was the daughter of a Scottish Presbyterian family with Indian connections stretching back over three generations. Her mother's elder brother, James Dunlop-Smith, was Secretary to the Viceroy; her grandfather had gone to India at the age of twenty-one to teach at Doveton College, Calcutta, a school for Eurasian boys, but soon gave this up to become editor of *The Friend of India*, the forerunner of India's leading English-language newspaper *The Statesman*. The husband of another aunt, on her father's side this time, was the Legal Member of the Viceroy's Council; her father's elder brother, Harcourt Butler,* was Foreign

---

* Sir Spencer Harcourt Butler, who joined the ICS in 1890, was the first Governor of the United Provinces of Agra and Oudh, from January 1921 to December 1922.

and Political Secretary to the Government of India.

In 1911, aged six, Iris, her sister Dorothy and her brothers Austen and Jock were brought back to England by their mother in order to undergo an English education, staying first with an aunt in Cambridge. That July, in a letter to her husband, their mother Ann summed up the terrible dilemma that faced most Raj wives (and, incidentally, the priority given to boys in those days): 'I can't stand a year again [of separation]. And yet I can't stand being away from the boys ... still it is far and desperately worse for you, who are without either half.'

For Iris, England was a profound shock, both culturally and emotionally. 'I stood in the window of the dining room of that tall, dark house and looked out at rain falling.' Everyday living brought her face to face with other unwelcome facts. 'One had to get used to sharing a bathroom; indeed, I have never got used to it. Naturally in 1911 there were very few houses with more than one bathroom. My grandfather Smith when he returned from India at the end of the nineteenth century found this so intolerable that he made himself an extra one for his exclusive use in his house in Edinburgh.'

Worse was to come. When Iris was eleven she suffered the fate common to almost all Raj children – years of separation from her parents. Her mother, wretched at being away from her husband for so long and her children now safely in boarding schools, left for India. First, in October 1916, she came to say goodbye to Iris. For this special occasion, at evening service in the school hall, Iris was allowed to sit beside her mother, in the place reserved for visitors. When they turned to kneel against their chairs for prayers the little girl was overcome by weeping. 'I heard my tears plop on to the hymn sheet and thought in a detached way: "I have read about the sound of tears falling – so it really happens."'

After this, parental contact was limited to letters. Many of the other girls at her school were also 'orphans of the Empire', so there was always great excitement on the day when the mail from India arrived. 'We would come together, asking: "Have you had your Mail?" I remember rather despising a girl whose father was a Madras civilian, for I had been inoculated with the snobbery of the Punjab.'

At seventeen, Iris left school and was presented at Court. Rules had been relaxed a trifle since the 1914–18 war: although veils and feathers had made a return, trains were modified in length, bouquets could be dispensed with and the colour of the presentation dress was now optional – though most debutantes still stuck to white (if only because this expensive garment could later be converted into a wedding dress).

'Coming out' – that is, doing the London Season as an adult – was an ordeal. In 1922 girls still 'put up' their long hair* and were expected to leap from the persona of shy boarding-school miss into full grown-up mode overnight, to have mastered what Edith Sitwell called 'the heavy art of light conversation' and to have smartened up their appearance. Here Iris found herself at a disadvantage. 'My mother bought my clothes with an eye to cost rather than fashion; I had no idea what to do with my hair or nails and certainly not my face. In any case there was little time between leaving school in July and embarking on SS *Olympia* of the Anchor Line at Glasgow in October.

'Life on that ancient coal-burning hulk seemed to me the height of sophistication. As soon as we were past Port Said we slept on deck and were woken at 5.00 a.m. by lascars swabbing the decks. Sleeping under tropical stars became very much part of my life as time went on and I have never forgotten the wonder and beauty of it. We ate at long tables with "fiddles" put on in rough weather … and at Aden we were all ordered ashore for coaling to take place. Every door and port hole was sealed and an unending procession of little black emaciated figures toiled up the gang planks bowed down each under his sack of coal. It was a scene from Conrad and I never made a voyage like it again.'

'When we went ashore at Bombay there was Gokal, my father's bearer, impassive on the docks amid the yelling coolies and the rattle of anchors and cranes. He had originally been sent to my father by Uncle Harcourt, the elder brother, when father first landed in India as a "griffin" in the Indian Civil Service. He could never wait at table or go anywhere near our food as he was so high caste. One of my mother's first injunctions to me when I rejoined the household was never to disturb Gokal or ask him for anything between the hours of two and five pm as he needed that time to go through the ritual of his main meal and its attendant purification.'

* The bob, the shingle and short skirts came in a year or two later.

Iris and her mother travelled north from the coast on the Bombay, Baroda and Central Indian Railway, watching from the window as the panorama of India rolled out against a red and gold sunset. Slow trains of bullock carts wandered towards tiny villages where evening cooking fires twinkled and smoked, and mist rose to the height of a man's shoulder. Their destination was Delhi, where her father was now working, as Secretary in the Department of Education, Health and Lands in the Government of India. This meant living in Delhi during the cold weather and departing for Simla with the rest of the Government of India when the hot weather began. The Government offices were then housed largely in what might later have been described as Nissen huts – everything had been moved up from Calcutta just before the 1914–18 war and this had delayed the building of the new city. But the Delhi of those days had many fine old trees and bungalows, the Butlers' bungalow stood among them, back to back with the Commander-in-Chief's.

Fortunately for Iris, she had grown up beautiful, and quickly began to have a good time. She went out hawking with one of her father's Indian friends, Sir Oomer Hyat Khan, head of the Tiwana clan from the northern Punjab. 'Father had spent his earliest days in India among them. Sir Oomer came to Delhi to attend Meetings of the Council of State and he brought with him his horses, hounds and hawks and a collection of wild feudatory retainers. We met at dawn; across the Jumna on the Meerut road and set off just as the sun rose, riding in medieval cavalcade, Sir Oomer with favourite hawk on wrist, others carried by followers who held the Afghan hounds on leashes. These hounds put up hares and goshawks were flown at the same time, turning the hares into the jaws of the hounds. Smaller falcons and merlins were flown at black partridge and quails. It was exhilarating and romantic in the diamond air of a winter morning. The retainers all looked like hawks themselves. As the sun became hotter we paused in some shady grove and chatted amicably over coffee and curry puffs.'

As an unmarried daughter of a father based at Government headquarters Iris was automatically included in invitations to official functions and meals. 'It never occurred to me to refuse. I would not have been allowed to – nor would I have been allowed to find such functions dull.' The dinners and lunches were formal, with a printed plan; every woman was told in advance the name of the man who would 'take her in' to dinner. The niceties of conversation – right up to the fish course, then to the left – were observed, as were the curtseys at Viceregal Lodge.

In Simla, where Iris spent two summers, life was one long party. 'I never thought of anything but amusing myself It was excessively gay.' Night after night she went to dances, usually riding with her skirt hitched up above her waist as a rickshaw (one with a mackintosh cover) was deemed too extravagant unless there was one of the regular Simla downpours. Her record was twenty-six nights running of dancing, 'after which I fell asleep at one of my mother's official dinners when sitting next to a very woolly old judge, for which I was afterwards severely reprimanded.'

She was taken up by a vivid and eccentric character called Edward Buck, known to everyone as Bucky, Reuter's agent with the Government of India and an old friend of her parents. As children Rab and Iris had played with his daughter Lorna. Now that Iris was grown up, Bucky asked her to his weekend parties at his large and lovely house some way out in the mountains, in wild, secluded surroundings with a view straight on to the snows. His weekend house parties conformed to the social ruling that a young girl must never be entertained alone with a man but only in a party with a married woman as chaperone – but his chaperones were the giddiest and most lively of the young Simla matrons.

'I have no doubt that there were distinctly Edwardian antics after lights were out,' wrote Iris later. 'But to seduce young girls simply was not done. In that enclosed society it would have provoked extreme embarrassment, even disaster, for all concerned. So I rode out to Bucky's house with some bright youth and wandered among the deodars with him. We gossiped and played bridge by huge log fires in the evening and early in the morning before dawn the whole house party would assemble on a massive divan in a bay window looking on the snows to watch the sunrise. We came in dressing gowns, with much giggling and chatter. Bucky would supervise benignly, saying: "Now you know the rule of the house, a blanket between each of you." I had no idea what he meant!'

When Bucky took Iris to a dinner party with a famous lawyer called Eardley Wilmot he told her not to tell her father; the man was Eurasian, and the social barrier between Europeans and those with Indian blood was such that Bucky knew Iris would have got into trouble at home. Only a few years later she was to feel horrified at this ('It is shaming to admit that I would not have been allowed to mix socially with Eurasians at that period'), but at the time she took it for granted. She sat between two Indian guests and drank liberally of the champagne that she was not allowed at home.

'I accepted it as part of a splendid adventure, and did not analyse the social aspects for I was intent on my own life, this glorious freedom from cold, grey school and cold, grey England. The next dance, the next gymkhana, whether Captain So-and-so would ask me to dance at the Viceregal Lodge, were in the forefront of my thinking; also the extraordinary beauty around me in Delhi – the tombs, the gardens where we went for moonlight picnics, the gallop past of a Horse Battery in the New Year Parade – and in Simla the snow line of the Himalayas, the dark deodars marching up the mountain side.'

At the end of the summer of 1924 her mother decided to return to England to see the two boys and her sister Dorothy. Iris had to go too. Her father, worried because of the number of landslides owing to that year's exceptionally heavy monsoon, suddenly broke down and wept at the last dinner with his wife and daughter. 'It was when I saw tears on his face that I realised, with shock, what this parting meant – and that it was parting from mother and not from me that mattered. It was the first acute parting of my adult life, to be repeated with different individuals and in different places again and again, the penalty of empire.'

She and her mother set off in a rail motor, an open coach with wheels that ran on the railway track. Iris found it less sick-making than the Hill Railway, called by Rab the 'Little Ill Train' because of its effects. With them in a basket went Phra, Iris's Siamese cat, destined for a new home with friends in Bombay, as her father did not care for it. Only a few miles out of Simla they turned a corner to find the track obliterated by a landslide. There was no room in the tiny waiting room as the passengers of two earlier trains, brought to a halt by landslides, were jamming it. Fortunately the Butlers' bearer, Gokal, who had gone ahead with the luggage, was safe and told them of a missionary who had tea equipment. The missionary proved a real good Samaritan, offering warm stockings and blankets and insisting they shared her carriage.

'Then came the problem of Phra, the Siamese. Anguished cries came from her basket. "I must let her out. Where can I get some earth for her?" I asked. I took her to what had once been a flower bed by the platform.' In two minutes Phra and Iris were soaked and the frightened cat bolted down the platform and leapt into the window of a carriage further down. Out of it burst an agitated Hindu gentleman crying: 'Take that unclean animal away – she is prowling round the ashes of my mother!' Iris plunged through the huddled crowd, managed to catch Phra and returned her to their carriage, where the missionary took charge, firmly telling Iris to shut the distraught animal in the bathroom (even in the tiny Simla trains first-class carriages had bathrooms). 'She can make the best of the bare floor and we can wash it down through the hole!'

Once the cat was shut in, Iris and her mother went to apologise to the Hindu family – who were very nice about Phra, and explained that the ashes were being taken down to be scattered on the Ganges. The delay caused by the landslides was such that the ship on which they were to travel to England, which had already waited a few hours, was now steaming out in the huge bay where they just managed to catch it, thanks to a special motor launch, chartered by Iris's father by telegraph.

While her mother went back to Hove to be near her sons, Iris stayed in a hostel in London, spending a lot of time on voluntary work for children. Then came the news that her father had been made Governor of the Central Provinces and Berar. What were the Central Provinces? wondered Iris, and went down to Hove to find out from her mother what this new life would be like. These provinces were full of jungles and tigers, said her mother.

'But what about horses? And polo? And parties?' asked Iris. 'Oh, that will be a bit different,' replied her mother. 'More formal. You can be a great help as an extra ADC – we will only have two on the staff and of course a Private Secretary and Military Secretary. Tom Paterson and friend are coming as the former and he has suggested someone called Portal as an ADC.'

Portal, always known as 'Squire', had, she later discovered, put in for the job because he wanted to shoot tiger in the Seeonee jungle made famous by Kipling. He was a cavalryman in the British Indian regiment the 2nd Royal Lancers, better known by its original name of Gardner's Horse, as also was Tom Paterson; so perhaps, thought Iris, between them they might have a horse or two, although it seemed odd to her that anyone could leave the joys of cavalry soldiering to shoot tigers. She did not want to leave London for somewhere she did not like the sound of, so set out for India again in October 1925 in a deep sulk and on comparatively bad terms with her mother.

Her father met them at Nagpur* station, complete with Military Secretary and ADC, Captain Portal. Although thirty-five to Iris's twenty, his impact on her was immediate. 'I was aware of a presage about the latter. Not love at first sight, just a presage that here was someone important.'

Gervas Portal was one of a family of brilliant brothers by whom, because of his wit and sense of humour, he was called Buzz ('there he goes again, buzzing about with his jokes'). He was tall, thin and good-looking, with great charm and ease of manner, and very attractive to women. Delicate as a child, he had been educated at Malvern because of its supposed health benefits while his brothers went to Eton. He was commissioned into the Berkshire Regiment and fought at Gallipoli, where his friends were all killed around him and he himself had been recommended for the Victoria Cross – but with no officer present the recommendation did not go through.

Later, in the search for adventure and because he was a brilliant horseman who loved riding, he joined Gardner's Horse and almost on arrival was asked if he would like to go and be an ADC to the Governor of the Central Provinces. As he also had a somewhat shamefaced desire to shoot tiger, he accepted at once.

In contrast to the bubbling excitement and joy of the first return to India two years earlier, Iris felt flat and unexcited when she arrived this second time. From the start, everything felt dreary and disappointing. The journey from Bombay along a new and different route had been depressing, over endless miles of flat cotton and sugar cane country and, to Iris, even the air seemed dead and stale in contrast to that of the north. After the crisp efficiency of Delhi and Simla, the ragged salute given by the escort of police welcoming His Excellency and family was deeply unimpressive.

What she did not then realise was that her father had been

---

* The capital of Central Provinces and always considered the exact centre of India.

appointed to this seeming backwater by the Viceroy, Lord Reading, for the express purpose of implementing the Montagu-Chelmsford reforms, which were to introduce self-governing institutions to India as part of the gradual evolution towards independence.

Government House in Nagpur, from its buildings, which she thought insignificant and uninspired, to its environs and appurtenances, was a shock after the panoply and efficiency of the viceregal and other gubernatorial palaces Iris had seen. The furniture was in a sorry state, with sinister-looking stains on the backs of the chairs, probably caused by sweat; the kitchen was a place of horror and the official cars could only be persuaded to start when two hefty men whacked them with spanners – any broken parts were tied up with sock suspenders. In the garden the flowers were drooping ('rows of dusty zinnias'), but there were some fine trees and, in the middle of the lawn, a handsome eighteenth-century gun on a plinth.

Gradually Iris's spirits improved. At Christmas the family went camping – pleasurably and luxuriously. The tents were pitched in a grove of teak trees on a small hill beside a river, beyond which thick forest clothed a low range of hills. Each spacious tent had its own bathroom; the family met for meals under an awning and after dinner, wrapped in rugs against the cold, sat round a huge bonfire.

The servants' encampment was in a nearby grove, where the huge shapes of the elephants swayed at their pickets and the police ponies were hobbled well away from them (horses do not like elephants). Every evening after the day's shooting the elephants came up to the Butlers' camp to salaam and be given chapattis rolled round a big lump of unrefined sugar by Iris and her parents. 'Then the mahouts, sitting on the elephants' heads, called for a salute and up would go the trunks with a loud "Hurrumph!", and so to bed.'

What Iris noticed was how carefully shooting was regulated.* The decimation of the jungles came later and was due to a combination of factors: poaching, appropriation of land for grazing by domestic cattle, and the destruction of large tracts of jungle through the spread of industrialisation. 'Anyone then wanting to shoot rented a block from the Forest Department,' wrote Iris, 'and the game in it was strictly rationed: a tiger or two was allowed, one good Chital stag, one sambhur perhaps as well. Even if they were

---

* Except in the princely states, where the maharajas did more or less as they pleased.

shot in the first few days, no more were allowed. The Forest Officers kept a close watch and in those days the forest guards, all Indian, were not corruptible by Europeans or fellow Indians. Poaching was almost unknown, although in the most remote and dense jungles the aboriginal tribes had regular battues when all game was driven into nets and killed with bows and arrows. They did this to feed themselves but their inroads made no more difference to the tiger population than a farmer's rabbit shoot made to rabbits in the days before myxomatosis.'

Iris was twenty, and finding life difficult. She had asked her father to give her some sort of work connected with child welfare and he had put her on one of her mother's voluntary committees. 'I dare say I spoke too loud. My parents told me to keep quiet as I was the most junior person on the committee and I left in a huff.' By this time Squire had fallen in love with her, but he was sixteen years older than her and a committed regimental soldier who at thirty-six had been a bachelor for a long time. Then, with the question of marriage still hanging in the air, he returned to his regiment in Poona. With the man she was finding increasingly attractive gone and no work, a tedious vista of days seemed to stretch before Iris. 'There seemed no purpose in anything I was doing,' she thought drearily.

Then came an invitation to the Poona 'Week' from a friend of her mother's, a dashing widow who had remarried. As her new husband had got a divorce in order to marry her, Montagu Butler did not wish his young daughter to go and stay with her and the tempting invitation seemed out of reach. Fortunately the new Viceroy, Lord Irwin, came to stay at Nagpur, before going on to Poona. And when the Viceroy suggested that Iris could travel with the viceregal party even her father could not refuse him.

At Poona Iris's hostess met her with a flow of words that clearly indicated that she thought her duty was to fix Iris up with a suitable – i.e. rich or with good prospects – husband. 'That man Portal has been round but I discouraged him,' she said. 'He is not an ambitious soldier and he has no money. I have a dinner party tonight for you and have asked a brilliant young ICS man who will certainly be a Governor one day and also a very rich gunner. His father owns Monkey Brand soap.' The ICS man, noted Iris dryly, turned out to be married and the Monkey Brand Gunner looked like the monkey on his soap packets.

Next day Squire Portal came round and asked them all to a dinner dance at the Club of Western India that night – the club allowed women in once a month only. He was not on her hostess's dinner list, and Iris was of course chaperoned, so courtship chances would be few. Squire did not intend to waste them. That evening, during the last dance, he proposed to Iris and she accepted. The following morning she wired the news of her engagement to her parents and her father wired back sweetly: 'Much too good for you.'

They were married in Nagpur in early 1927. As befitted the Governor's daughter, it was a grand wedding, with a large tented encampment for guests; one of her father's old friends from the north, Bahadur Khan, travelled for four days to be present. A minor but important hiccup was caused by the Bishop of Nagpur, who married them. The Bishop, who had spent most of his life in the jungle as a missionary to the Gonds (the ancient tribal peoples of Central India), was not used to soldiers and refused to allow Squire to wear a 'lungee' (the regulation parade dress turban worn by all Indian cavalry) in church. Both Iris and Squire found it impossible to get him to understand that the Indian officers from the regiment, some of whom had come from as far away as Poona, would be horrified and shocked at what they would regard as an indecency – a bare head in uniform.

All appeals left the Bishop unmoved. Finally Monty Butler said to Iris: 'I shouldn't argue with the Bishop if I were you – he's an amateur boxing champion.' The only solution was to have Squire's orderly lurking in the porch: as the bridal couple emerged he sprang forward and planted the lungee – askew – on the bridegroom's head so that at least he did not appear in public improperly dressed. As a lungi constructed off the head hardly ever holds together, this made the reception, cake-cutting and speech an anxious business.

Iris had had her own problem. As she left Government House in her bridal finery with her father, he pressed into her hands what she later described as 'a tightly packed bunch of vegetation packed into a ham frill', telling her that it was her bridal bouquet. 'I can't walk up the aisle with this,' said Iris, nearly in tears. 'You must,' answered her father. 'It has been prepared and presented by the Agricultural Department of the Central Province.' Such a provenance weighed not at all with Iris; recalling that there was a large white ostrich feather fan in the display of wedding presents, she dashed off and snatched it up, with a defiant glare at her father. As any further argument would have made them late, she got her way.

The honeymoon too had its bumps – ups and downs that could only have happened to a Raj bride. They went to the Seeonee district jungles, taking with them as provisions only a cured ham and the remains of their wedding cake – Squire was a very good shot and assumed he could provide for the pot. It was not at all as described in *The Jungle Book*, and there was no sign of the Council Rock – although the villagers' cattle, driven out to graze on the edge of the settlements, were guarded by small boys like Mowgli. Squire had no luck with game, as beating to one gun did not work and he felt he could not shoot either doves or peahens on the ground. He did not like women shots but eventually shortages meant that Iris was pressed into service with a 20-bore she had been lent.

She was installed in a hide near a waterhole where peafowl came to drink. No peahen came and after a while darkness fell. Hyenas began to call, one to the right and one to the left. 'I knew they were hyenas but their cry is so eerie and baleful it froze the blood,' wrote Iris, 'then I heard monkeys chattering – not whooping. That meant they were seriously alarmed and warning each other of something.'

She listened but heard nothing. Soon came lights and trampling through the trees and Squire appeared with the forest ranger, some villagers and his big-game rifle. 'You'll have a long walk back,' he whispered. 'A tiger has killed a young village buffalo about three hundred yards behind you so we must make a detour.'

Soon afterwards she developed a high temperature and a large swelling on the back of her neck, later diagnosed as Indian tick fever, picked up during her time in the hide. The doctor whom Squire managed to summon from fifty miles away arrived drunk and could think of nothing bar prescribing quinine – to which she was allergic. When the fever finally wore itself out, she had to spend the rest of the honeymoon travelling in a small bullock cart instead of on foot.

In their subsequent life, Iris and Gervas both followed the familiar Raj pattern, with their two daughters both sent home as children, just as Iris had been. When Gervas was appointed Commanding Officer of the Governor's Bodyguard in Bombay, Iris was able to immerse herself in the welfare work she had always wanted to do, among the young soldiers' wives and their families. Gervas was a keen and popular regimental soldier and his subsequent postings took them, as with most Raj families, around the subcontinent – to Poona, Bombay, Hyderabad and Bihar.

During the Second World War, while Gervas was first in Basra, then Cairo and subsequently Burma, Iris helped as an auxiliary nurse at the Salvation Army hospital in Ahmednagar and in the military hospital in Ranchi, before finally leaving India in 1943, her ship dodging U-boats on the way back. Gervas was demobbed in 1946; when he returned to England the couple settled in Norfolk, where they often had Indian friends to stay in their freezing house. Gervas died in 1961 and Iris, who became a biographer,* in 2002. Of her time in India she wrote: 'When I returned to England for the last time in 1943, I was in a state of mind similar to bereavement.'

---

* After being widowed, Iris wrote three biographies: *The Rule of Three: Sarah Duchess of Marlborough and her Companions in Power* (1967), *The Viceroy's Wife: Letters of Alice, Countess of Reading, from India 1921–5* (1969) and *The Eldest Brother: the Marquess Wellesley, the Duke of Wellington's eldest brother* (1973). All were published by Hodder and Stoughton.

—•◦•—

21

'Just lift up your skirts and you'll be all right'

Up Country

The destination of some Fishing Fleet girls was the *mofussil*, often in a remote area where there was no other British family.

For the Fishing Fleet girl plunged into such a life when she married, the experience could be harsh, even traumatic. Gone were the warm, jasmine-scented nights under which she had strolled with an admirer on the smooth lawns of the club, huge stars lighting up a velvet sky to the sound of dance music from a regimental band – the India of glamour and romance about which she had heard and was experiencing.

Instead, there were habits, difficulties, attitudes and even perils unheard of in the London street or quiet English country village in which she had been brought up. She could be a hundred miles from the nearest doctor, in which case she had to keep a well-stocked medicine chest and know how to deal with everything from malaria to snake bite (cut the puncture marks, suck and spit out the poison, rub in permanganate of potash crystals, tie a tourniquet and then pray).

For girls like 'Billy' Fremlin, who had been brought up on a plantation, the isolation of a 'jungly' life was no deterrent.

Billy had been educated in England, arriving back in India in 1924 at the age of seventeen to stay with her father, having survived the last ravages of the Spanish flu pandemic. 'I very nearly didn't go out. At school we all had the most appalling flu, it was killing everybody off like flies, several members of our staff died, people were dropping dead in the streets with it. Kay and I had it together, we were really very ill, and Mummy came to see us. She thought we were being starved so she got special food for us. I got thinner than ever, I was always just exactly like a beanpole but then I went absolutely down to nothing. Then I had rheumatic fever and that put me back. I was off a whole two terms with it so I was never allowed to learn Latin which I wanted to do.'

She finally left for India – unusually, travelling quite alone. 'I'd always looked forward more than anything else to going out to India, to my father. I adored him. I was so excited I could hardly believe it.' Her father met her in Madras, where they stayed with friends of his, then journeyed by train to his coffee estate, seventy miles from Bangalore in upstate Mysore. It was a trip that led past plantations of sugar cane, banyan and fig trees, women in brilliant saris carrying brass pots on their heads and carts drawn by the creamy coloured bullocks of Mysore, with their backward-curving horns.

Billy, slim, blonde and pretty, was always treated exactly like a boy by her father Ralph – her parents' four eldest children, all boys, had died soon after birth. Her father had longed for a son, especially as he was a noted shot and wanted a son to carry on this tradition, so gave his favourite daughter her boy's name. Soon after her arrival she was even given a small coffee estate, approximately an acre of bushes, of her own, 'where I kept the proceeds. It was so happy and so exciting.'

Ralph's brilliance as a shot – he was so unfailingly successful that he would often go shooting with a professional skinner, in effect a taxidermist – was such that film-makers Robert and Frances Flaherty used him as the white hunter in their story *Elephant Dance*. There was plenty of jungle round about the estate; the sign of elephant jungle was when the milestones on the roads were painted black instead of white. 'Elephants hate white ones and root them up,' wrote Frances Flaherty later, describing how, if elephants made inroads on paddy fields, sometimes they were shot by the game preserve officer – who would aim at the earhole or the top of the trunk in front. Often, a deep trench would do the trick: 'A four-foot wide trench is an insuperable obstacle to an elephant, which cannot step across it and cannot jump,' she noted.

With such a father, determined that in all respects his daughter would become the son he never had, Billy's life was eventful – finally, too eventful. 'We used to do the most amazing things. We used to go out on shikar [hunting] after tiger or wild pig or occasionally after bison. He was a good shot himself and he wanted me to be a good shot, so I thought I'd try. I hated killing things but I'd do anything for him and I became quite a good shot, with a shotgun or a rifle. We used to go right up into the jungles, and we used to beat, and if I did shoot anything Daddy was so proud of me that I felt I would do *anything* to please him.'

The final test was to go after bison, known for their formidable size and power, into very deep jungle. 'We were after a very special huge bison that was famous and the beaters spotted it, but I could not see it. Daddy could because he had wonderful knowledge of the jungles but I looked and looked and couldn't see it – he wanted me and nobody else to kill it, you see. But I couldn't see it and in the end we went on and it went. But there was a younger bison so I killed that instead and that was quite close to. He said to me afterwards "Weren't you frightened?" And I said: "I'm never frightened with you." He had no fear. There was great rejoicing among the beaters because they all had food for weeks.'

For light entertainment, Billy would drive the seventy miles to Bangalore to dance in the club – her father taught her to drive in an old Ford car – usually staying with friends afterwards. 'I loved dancing in Bangalore, the Highland Light Infantry were there and the Wiltshires, and I had some very pretty dresses I'd brought out with me so altogether it was a contrast to tiger drives in the jungle.'

Inevitably, she got malaria. Sitting in a *machan*, motionless for hours as the slightest movement might alert the quarry, she could not even raise a finger to brush away a mosquito. The attacks got worse and worse, with only quinine for remedy, until eventually the doctor who treated her said she must go home or die. Her father came back with her on the ship and, before returning to India, bought her a little Austin Seven.

It was through this car that she found romance. Driving herself to a dance in it when she was twenty-one, she arrived a little late and slipped quietly into her hosts' house, where she stood by the huge fire in the hall. Suddenly in came the man she later married, who said: 'Oh you're late too.' And from then on they danced the whole evening together. For Billy, as she said: 'It really was love at first sight.'

Some Fishing Fleet girls became 'junglies' through marriage – that is, they married one of the police, forestry or political officers or mining engineers, surveyors, railway engineers and geologists who lived in the remotest regions. For them it was a tough, outdoor life, with only the occasional sighting of a fellow European and the constant threat of accident or illness. Such things as hairdressers, books and radios were luxuries of distant civilisation. They travelled with their husbands through jungles and across mountains, through forests, tribal territories or deserts, by elephant, bullock cart, camel, horse or boat, living in camps for which all supplies, from medicine and stationery to unbreakable enamel plates, had to be brought by animal, usually the sure-footed mule.

One of these girls, Olivia Hamilton, whose husband Arthur was an Assistant Divisional Forestry Officer, wore 'up-country' clothes for such trips: breeches, lace-up canvas gaiters and deer-skin boots,* a tweed jacket and a topi – if a topi did not come off, its thickness made it a good head protector. They lived in these camps for weeks while Arthur, whose headquarters were in Lahore, surveyed vast tracts of forest. Olivia took to it as to the manner born.

On arrival, Olivia's first duty was to 'turn over every stone all round the tent to see how many scorpions from underneath I could kill, before they got into our slippers or our beds'. Meanwhile the cook would be making his fire and sending a messenger to buy charcoal from the nearest settlement, before producing a meal (which could be pigeon or pheasant that one of the Hamiltons had shot).

After supper, Arthur settled in his 'office' tent to write up reports on what he had seen that day while the enterprising Olivia would make flies for fishing from the feathers of the game birds they had shot (higher up, she would shoot and skin birds for their collector friends in Simla). 'I sent them as far away as Kashmir sometimes and I once bought myself an evening dress on the proceeds.'

---

* They were usually made from the skin of a sambhur, India's largest deer; their quality of noiselessness made them a favourite choice for anyone shooting or stalking.

In the late evenings they would sit round the camp fire watching the flying squirrels scampering up one tree then floating across to another.

Occasionally they shot the panthers and black bears that lived in the higher forests, especially if they had been harrying the villagers. The hill women reassured Olivia that bears would never attack a woman. 'Just lift up your skirts and you'll be all right,' they told her. But she was not prepared to put this to the test.

When, after months in the solitude of the Himalayan uplands, the Hamiltons finally returned to Simla, with its social life and its beautifully dressed women with well-coiffed heads and the latest gossip at their fingertips, they felt, as Olivia put it, 'like hoboes'. Arthur had grown a shaggy beard in the jungle, which had to be shaved off, leaving his chin an anaemic white against his sunburnt face while Olivia's hair, cropped short, was uneven and jagged and her clothes' sense, after months in breeches, in need of revival.

Camping could range from sophisticated and enjoyable, with home comforts prepared by efficient servants, to an endurance test with attendant horrors. Beatrix Scott, who went with her husband to Assam soon after their marriage in 1910, found that leeches were her worst nightmare – although sandflies, against which no mosquito net was proof, and a giant bluebottle-type insect that could sting through leather boots ran them pretty close.

'They [the leeches] did not worry us much till we met them in the jungle in the rains. Then it seemed that every blade of grass, every leaf-tip, had its looping thread-like organism waiting to hurl itself at the passer-by. We always marched in single file. The first man gets few leeches; his passing just puts them on the *qui vive*. As far as possible, each man picked leeches off his own front and off the back of the man ahead of him; at intervals the front man went to the back.

'In spite of all this, towards the end of the march we were all dripping gore from the leeches that had escaped our vigilance and having gorged themselves had dropped off. They leave a tiny triangular hole from which the blood flows freely because of some substance injected by the animal that prevents coagulation. At the end of a march when we could remove our clothes we often picked a score of leeches off one another. To this day, my pet particular nightmare is that I am in a pit with leeches …'.

The girl who married into this kind of life had to be tough, resourceful – and in good health. Up country there were few, or no, doctors or dentists. When in the 1920s Monica Campbell-Martin, living at Tisri where her husband worked in a mica mine, suffered from toothache it meant getting to the nearest railway station, thirteen miles from the house, then a twelve-hour train journey over the 500 miles to Calcutta, and staying there anything from a week to ten days because dental treatment often took that length of time; so that rail fare, hotel bill and incidental expenses added up almost to a month's salary. Because of these costs, many junior officials or workers delayed treatment.

Housekeeping meant borrowing a car once a fortnight to drive the eight miles to the local bazaar, returning with live chickens, kid meat, vegetables and eggs. Dry goods came from Calcutta every two or three months. There was little to do and boredom was often acute – there was no tennis, no golf, they had no radio, and there was no library near. Besides themselves, there was only one other European, her husband's assistant.

They kept in touch with the outside world by mail – the office was also a post office, where stamps were available; the mail was sent off by a mail runner, the mailbag slung over his shoulder on a stick, to the next village thirty miles away; it was a condition of his employment that he did not walk but trotted. When they moved house it was by bullock cart, which went at about two miles an hour – the carts were a series of flat boards between two enormous wheels.

Viola Bayley had no previous connection with India and went to join her husband Vernon, in the Frontier Constabulary, which had the job of keeping order between British India and the Tribal Territories. For a girl who had been 'brought up in the security of a small Sussex town, it was a fairly traumatic experience to start married life in Hangu, a tiny link on the road that led from Peshawar to Kohat and Bannu and finally to the Khyber Pass'.

In Hangu, two armed constables accompanied her and her new husband when they first walked out together, 'which was not conducive to the pleasure of a honeymoon stroll'. But their garden, its irrigation channels made by prisoners from the local gaol (always full) brought in by armed guard, was a delight. 'Our violet bed stretched the length of our garden and scented the whole air.' The backdrop was equally beautiful. 'All along the valley there were orchards pink with peach blossom and carpeted with small iris. There were lady's finger tulips and blue ixiolerion. There were oleanders flowering in the dry waterbeds ... Hoopoes pecked at grubs on our lawn and bulbuls sang. It was so idyllic I could hardly believe that the menace of the hot weather would soon be upon us.'

When Betsy Anderson married Tommy Macdonald, their first home was on a sugar plantation in Bihar. Tommy was the third generation of Macdonalds to live and work there on what had originally been an indigo plantation; when indigo cropping came to an end his father had the machinery for a sugar factory shipped out from Glasgow to Calcutta, then to the plantation by barge, rail and bullock cart. Betsy was kept busy learning the language, to be able to ask the cook such questions as: 'How did you manage to use six dozen eggs yesterday when we had chicken and rice pudding?'

Although several miles from their nearest neighbours, she was never frightened, even when Tommy had to be away for a night. 'The only creepy sound was the beating of the tom-toms from the villages [that supplied the native labour for the factory]. When alone, I would lie awake, imagining that they were sending strange messages to each other, like stories of Red Indians. The noise of the jackals was scary and always gave me the shivers, their yells were horrible and unearthly, rising to a crescendo and ending in ghastly screams.'

Their bungalow – or rather the trees in their garden, including a huge and ancient banyan – was home to a number of langurs, big grey monkeys with long arms and prehensile tails, who from time to time featured in an extraordinary and inexplicable episode.

Fun though the langurs were to watch, especially when teaching their babies to jump, hang and swing from the rope-like branches of the banyan tree, they were very destructive, uprooting plants, ripping branches of favourite shrubs, running along the marble veranda and stealing what they could from the house if they found an open window. As the hot weather approached their behaviour got worse and eventually the 'monkey man' had to be called.

On payment of his fee he would stand beneath the banyan, the chosen centre of monkey life, calling to them. Soon afterwards the Macdonalds would see them, jumping one by one from tree to tree and then disappearing into the sugar cane fields. After every visit of the monkey man, the garden was empty of langurs for some time.

Some Fishing Fleet girls were lucky enough to enjoy what is best described as 'grand camping', as the guest of someone reasonably senior. Honor Penrose, who went out to India in 1913, toured with her friends the Cassels in the Terai, at the foot of the Himalayas. En route Seton Cassel, Commissioner for that area, visited villages, if any, talked to the headman, heard complaints, inspected crops, roads, bridges and much else beside. Their retinue went ahead, taking baggage, food, cooking utensils, tents, and finding a site near – but not too near – the next village on the Commissioner's itinerary.

'Some days there were no villages and mounting the elephants we dived into the jungle alert for wild animals, or shooting for the pot an occasional jungle mirghi [wild hen],' recorded Honor. 'This being the dry season, the grass and fallen leaves were dry as tinder and would crackle at a touch, yet these elephants with their enormous feet wove their way in and out of the trees, soundlessly, like phantoms in a dream. Another wonder was how the mahouts kept their sense of direction. We might turn and twist north, south east or west looking for game yet, always in time, we arrived at the next camp.' Whenever they arrived, their tents had been put up by the servants, there was water for a bath and a delicious dinner was ready.

Somewhat on the same lines was the self-sufficiency needed in a remote station like Gilgit, virtually cut off from the outside world by heavy snows from late September until the following spring. After spending the summer in Gulmarg, Lucy Hardy and her husband Harry Grant set off one September in the early 1900s for this distant outpost of the Empire, where Harry was stationed with his Mountain Artillery Battery. To survive in Gilgit, in a valley in the Karakoram range, meant not only organising almost a year's supplies of essential stores but also provisions for themselves and their servants on the long and arduous journey.

'We had to collect servants willing to go – cook, ayah, sweeper, dhobi, syces etc, and supply them with a warm outfit each and blankets. Then H bought me a pony and sidesaddle. Then we got a dandy for ayah and baby son, and a well-made dhoolie for Charles [her older son, aged two], it was carried by two men on a long bamboo pole which ran through iron rings on top. It had reed curtains and being on four short legs made a very cosy bed at night.

'All our permanent supplies – tea, coffee, tinned milk, biscuits, baby food and so forth – had to be sent off during the summer as the passes are only open for pony transport from May to September.' Harry had already acquired a flock of twenty-four sheep, looked after by the Indian officers of the Battery along with their own goats but, as Lucy later said disgustedly, they were so small and skinny that 'the leg only gave the two of us one roast and one made-up dinner'.

The road to Gilgit with a caravanserai of babies, coolies, equipment and food for the journey was long and arduous. 'Fifteen miles a day doesn't sound a long ride but when one has to walk it up, up, up and down, down, down on very rough paths – and day after day – it is very tiring. The road is supposed to be nine foot [wide] and no parapet of course, not much width when meeting strings of pack animals coming down to the valley.' They crossed over the 14,100-feet Komri Pass, and broke the twenty-six-mile journey on to where they halted for the summer in two tents so freezing that Lucy, who kept her baby son warm by clasping him to her all night, could not sleep for a cold-headache.

Ruttu was a rough plateau 10,000 feet up surrounded by hills, one of which provided summer grazing from May to September for the Battery mules, looked after there by sepoys who built their own lines. For their British officer, they had also added two new rooms to an existing hut, into which Lucy subsided with thankfulness for a month and cheerfully made the best of, mud floors and all. 'Our sitting room, when decked with cretonne covers and cushions, muslin curtains, jars of wildflowers etc, looked quite civilised.' The dining room in the old hut had a table and chairs, some numdahs on the floor and an improvised sideboard made of boxes with a cloth over it.

Her husband was busy with the Battery all day; during the evenings he would take his gun and they would wander after game or explore. Sometimes they ate snow trout from the nearby river; occasionally the sepoys managed to get them a few eggs and fowls from villages in the neighbouring nullahs. 'After a month, the mules having eaten all available grass, the battery prepared to march for Bunji for winter quarters but a bungalow in Gilgit thirty-seven miles further on had been allotted to us as the doctor had his quarters there and we thought it wiser for the sake of the two babies to be near him.'

Little had changed twenty-five years later when Fishing Fleet girl Leila Phillips set off for Gilgit in the autumn of 1929 with her friends Captain and Mrs Lloyd – he was being sent to Gilgit on duty. There were just a few more British officers stationed there, about half a dozen by now, with their families. Stores still had to be ordered in April so that they would arrive before the passes were snowed-up but now they came on mules, which could carry packs of up to 80lbs hung on each side.

If you did not want to wait weeks for photographs to be returned from Srinagar, noted Leila, you took your own printing and development kit. Gilgit was 200 miles from Bandipur, where the motor road from Srinagar ended.

On the journey, the snow glare and wind burned their faces so badly that they blistered. Leila's was in such a state that she had to tie on cotton wool and handkerchiefs to cover it when she went out for a walk the next day.

Once in Gilgit, the Lloyds had to be almost entirely self-sufficient. They were 400 miles from the nearest railway station, there were no European shops and anything ordered might take several months to arrive. They kept a cow, made their own butter and cream, and also had hens and sheep, in addition to ducks and geese, all of which had been brought on the long journey to Gilgit. Local fruit, mainly cherries, strawberries and apricots, was delicious and plentiful and they made jam and crystallized or tinned other fruits, taking the tins to the blacksmith to be soldered. Along with the rest of the livestock, they had luckily brought two cats as there were countless rats, appallingly bold – they even ate the fruit in the dining room and chewed up a string of Lucy's beads, which had been put out of the way on the top of a high cupboard.

Remote as it was, there were a number of amusements: riding amid wonderful scenery, tennis that went on all winter and polo matches for Cassels's soldiers. This was not polo as played in cavalry stations all over India, but more a form of non-lethal inter-tribal warfare. The field was a strip of not very even turf approximately twenty-five yards wide and one hundred and twenty-five yards long (village fields were usually much smaller). There were eight instead of four men a side, riding very small but fast and handy ponies and wielding locally made polo sticks that were always breaking. Each chukka lasted half an hour rather than the usual seven minutes and the sides played all out, encouraged by the crowd, who sat round the field on a low mud wall shouting advice.

Also squatting on the wall was the band, keeping up its noisy performance all the time, increasing in volume whenever a goal was scored. The player who had scored it, holding the ball in the same hand as his polo stick, would fling it high in the air, hitting it before it reached the ground – often scoring another goal. Another strange aspect of this polo was the rule that allowed a player to catch the ball at any time and try to ride through the goal. If he did this he was immediately set upon by all the other side who tried to snatch the ball from him.

Tournaments carried even more risk. 'There were no chukkas,' recorded Leila. 'A game went on for one hour or until one side had scored nine goals. In the final, two of the teams (Hunza and Nagar) were hereditary enemies, and a free fight broke out, while the rival bands tried to drown each other out.'

When Rosemary and Alexander Redpath were sent to Gilgit in 1939 they travelled from the Gurez valley over the Burzil Pass (13,780 feet). At the highest point of the pass stood a wooden hut perched on stilts forty feet high – an indication of the depth of snow in winter – used by mail runners, who could only negotiate the pass on a clear night when the surface snow was frozen hard enough to support their weight.

Self-sufficiency was still the order of the day and all cooking was still done on wood from the nearby forests; regulating the heat was an art in itself. Their cook baked by placing a tin on top of the embers to produce wonderful cakes and pastry. Preserving tins for the abundant summer fruit were made in the bazaar from kerosene oil tins, filled with fruit and syrup and a lid with a small hole in it was soldered on; the tins were then placed in a fish kettle of boiling water and kept at the correct temperature for a specified time and finally a small disc was clapped over the hole in the lid and soldered on.

Bread was of course home-made, the cook using yeast from packets of dried hops. In this Hindu state beef was not available but, wrote Rosemary: 'The butcher came round our houses with a freshly killed carcase and we bought what we wanted from him – eating the offal first and letting the bigger joints hang for a day or two. We also ate chickens and, in the winter, game like duck which we shot ourselves. In the season we had trout from the Kurgah. We also had well-stocked vegetable gardens on which we relied. We entertained each other frequently, usually sitting and talking till all hours after dinner.'

Gilgit polo had scarcely changed by the time the Redpaths arrived, although a three-foot stone wall had replaced the original mud one. 'When I first watched this violent game, in which I knew I would soon have to participate,' wrote Alexander later, 'I experienced a twinge of apprehension. There were no recognisable rules. You could reach across the front of your opponent's pony to play the ball – if by doing so you brought the pony and its rider down, they were just unlucky. You could knock your opponent's stick out of his hand in any way practicable and if his head got in the way it was just too bad.

'Your opponent could grab your pony's reins and wrestle with you while the rest of his team could seize your team's bridles and so prevent any attempt at passing the ball. You could cross immediately in front of your opponent if you thought it worth bringing him and probably yourself down in order to prevent a goal being scored against you.

'When a player scored a goal he was given the ball; he then tied his reins in a knot and, holding them and the ball in his left hand, set off at a gallop down the middle of the field with his team in echelon behind him – spectators roaring, bands playing furiously – and when about to reach the halfway mark, threw the ball forward and hit it full-toss towards his opponents' goal.'

For his debut in this free-for-all Alexander wore a topi with a strong chinstrap, thick breeches and, to protect his shins, puttees over five-week-old folded copies of *The Times*. 'Thus protected I escaped many bruises and was only brought down twice and only once sustained a painful injury – a wild swipe by an opponent missed the ball but hit my left hand, smashing two bones. It was noticeable that the local players avoided involving "the sahibs" in anything really dangerous; and I only saw one man killed during a game.'

The Redpaths, who lived in Gilgit for three years, found the disadvantages – isolation, long delays in getting home news, no electricity, restriction of supplies – more than offset by the advantages. 'We looked across over the Gilgit valley to a continuous wall of rock some three miles away which changed colour with every hour of the day and variation of light,' recorded Rosemary. 'I never tired of looking at it. I do remember however longing to see the sun rise or set, for the valley must have been roughly east-west, with high mountains to the south blocking out the sun in winter – on the shortest days we only had an hour or two of sunshine.'

For Alexander Redpath the joys were: 'no cars, lorries or trains, the exhilaration of being among mountains, trekking and riding everywhere, dealing with people one could not help liking and an equable climate. Winters were cold with occasional snowfalls in Gilgit itself, spring was a delight and so were summers except for a couple of months when the temperatures reached 100°F. During that period our families moved to two log cabins in a Swiss-like valley called Naltar at a height of about 10,000 feet. For both of us Gilgit was a unique experience.'

In the jungle, too, there were entertainments, notably the Kadir Cup,* desired by every regiment and all the more sporting members of the ICS. It was, basically, an annual hog-hunting competition held in the Kadir jungle near Meerut. Cavalry officers trained for it whenever they could. 'Lucknow was a paradise for cavalry officers,' wrote Douglas Gray, who won the Cup as a subaltern in 1932. 'It had four polo grounds, a racecourse and some good shooting nearby.

'But best of all, the surrounding country provided the finest horse activity in India which was hoghunting, or pigsticking, as it was more commonly called. This involved the finding, hunting and killing of wild boars with a lance called a hog-spear. Falls were frequent, and accidents, though inevitable, were accepted as part of the thrill which comes with pursuits involving some danger.'

The Kadir Cup was held over three days and involved heats of three or four riders, each attempting to be the first to show the blood of a boar, driven towards them by beaters, on their spear. As these wild pigs were extremely fast – as well as fierce – jinking and turning often under the horse's belly, it was not a sport for the faint-hearted. 'There were about 50 elephants and 500 beaters

---

* Held every year since 1873; it was discontinued after 1939. It is now displayed at the Cavalry and Guards Clubs, London.

driving across the riverine country which was the haunt of wild pigs, occasional panthers and even a tiger (once seen during a pig-sticking heat).'

When Gray competed there was a record entry of 120 horses, almost all ridden by cavalry officers from British and Indian regiments. Riders drew for places in heats of four, taking their turns on the line – left, central and right, each with an umpire carrying a red flag. There were about 300 beaters on foot and, behind them, some twenty elephants used as moving grandstands for spectators; women who watched sat in howdahs on these elephants.

In March 1937 one of these spectators was Lord Baden-Powell, who had himself won the Cup in 1883 and wrote to a friend to describe the final day. 'We spent from 9 a.m. to sunset out on a vast yellow grass plain – the whole day under blazing hot sun, wobbling along on elephants with the excitement of watching the competitors racing after pig and, in one case, hunting and killing a panther.'

The rules were simple. As a rideable boar got up, the nearest umpire followed with his heat and, shouting 'Do you all see him? NOW RIDE', dropped his flag and away they galloped, competing for first spear; this would advance the winner to the next round. Heat followed heat over the next three days until the final was reached.

'That night,' wrote Gray of the day he won, 'in the large tented camp under the mango trees, and with all the elephants lined up as a background in the light of the bonfires, a last-day party was held and as the lucky rider, I was obliged to attempt the traditional Hog-hunter's song:

'Over the valley, and over the level
Through the rough jungle now go like the devil
Here's a nullah in front, but a boar as well.
So sit down in your saddle and ride like hell!'

22

'Cheerio, old girl'

Sheila Hingston

Families that lived and worked in the Raj for generations – rather than spending a greater or lesser amount of time there – almost unconsciously developed certain patterns of behaviour. Although they clung to the attitudes and customs of home, sometimes more tenaciously than those who actually lived in England, the blazing suns and torrential rains, perils and sudden deaths, the beauty, stoicism and sheer vastness of their adopted land seeped into their psyches. To stay English, in a land so alien to English culture, required the cultivation of some of the most English of virtues.

In the women, this bred a particular kind of fortitude. Not making a fuss was high on the list, as was 'getting on with it', whether this be packing up a home for the umpteenth time to move to somewhere a thousand miles hence, dealing with unexpected illness when floods had swept away the only road along which the distant doctor could drive or ride or coping with the monotony of life in a remote outpost. It was not usually the sudden crisis that sapped the spirit – most women rose admirably to the challenge – but the prospect of days spent doing virtually nothing that stretched endlessly ahead.

Most crucial of all, though, was something that Raj daughters had themselves suffered from and that they accepted would continue: the sending home of their children somewhere between the ages of five and ten for an English education, in the knowledge that it might be years before they saw them again. It posed an agonising dilemma that few could solve: whether to abandon the husband who needed them, to live in England, probably on very little money, so that they could be with the children in the school holidays, or to stay with the husband they loved and leave their children with others. In some families, boys and their Fishing Fleet sisters had spent childhoods that ranged from happy – usually with aunts and cousins – to wretchedly lonely with strangers. Yet such was the pull of India, especially with a family out there, that it seemed only natural to return to the land of their birth and, in their turn, take up this inheritance.

Sheila Hingston was one of these. She came from a family that had spent three generations in India. Her grandfather, Clayton William James Hingston, was born in Antigua in 1849; his mother's family owned a sugar plantation and his grandfather, Lieutenant-Colonel James Hingston, briefly the Governor of the Gold Coast, died in 1857.

He was brought up in Antigua by an aunt and her husband, a judge, and sent to England to be educated. His career was always going to be the Army, so he was sent to Wellington College and then to Sandhurst. He went out to India with the 62nd Regiment of Foot, Wiltshire, arriving in February 1870, and was based in Lucknow. He transferred to the 10th Bengal Native Infantry and in 1874, aged twenty-five, he married a Fishing Fleet girl, twenty-two-year-old Mary Clementina Gray, who was visiting her eldest brother, the Chaplain of Jabalpur. The couple were stationed at Barrackpur for six years, during which time Clayton Alexander Francis Hingston was born, in May 1877.

Clayton Hingston was, in the usual fashion, sent home to be educated, staying in England another five years after he had left school to take a degree and be trained as a doctor and surgeon at the Medical School of the Middlesex Hospital, where he passed the College of Surgeons and College of Physicians joint examination. After this he returned to India, joining the 16th Madras Native Infantry when he was twenty-five. For some time he served as a regimental soldier, then decided he wanted to work on the civil side of the Indian Medical Service, which paid better, and successfully applied for the job of Assistant Superintendent of the Government Maternity Hospital in Madras – the largest gynaecological and maternity unit in the British Empire outside the British Isles.

At thirty-one he likewise married a Fishing Fleet girl, twenty-year-old Gladys Scroggie, the sister of a brother officer in the 16th

Madras Native Infantry. Gladys had spent most of her life in India, only being sent home to be educated. It was while Gladys, always known as Glad or – owing to her flirtatious nature – Glad-eyes, was staying with her brother Willie that she met Clayton Hingston, always known as Hinkie.

Hinkie was an extraordinarily popular and able man, ready to deal with all eventualities, from removing an appendix on a hastily scrubbed-up kitchen table, operating on the fetlock of a friend's horse in the absence of a vet, to repairing the face, disfigured in a car crash, of a friend's beautiful wife – so well did he do this that her friends said she looked better than before. His speciality, though, was gynaecology and obstetrics, for which his reputation spread throughout South India; young married women, some former members of the Fishing Fleet, often came out to Madras simply to be cared for by him – to be 'pupped by Pops'* as one of them put it.

Hinkie and Glad's daughter, Sheila Violet Lena Hingston, was born in Madras in July 1911. The family lived at Pantheon House, an imposing, marble-floored Palladian mansion built in East India Company days, that went with Hinkie's job and was next door to the Women and Children's Hospital. Hinkie and Glad had thirty servants, including gardeners and syces, with even a small boy to groom and de-tick the dogs and run messages. As a little girl Sheila was taken for a daily outing in a governess cart drawn by a pony called Flying Fox, her sola topi held on by a white *broderie anglaise* scarf. Like other English children during the Raj, she was forbidden to play with Eurasian children when she went to the beach, a prohibition approved of even by her beloved ayah, who once smacked her with a hairbrush for doing so.

Sheila and her mother Glad were staying in an hotel in Kanoor, Kerala, when the 1914 war broke out. Although almost forty, Hinkie wanted to volunteer for service at once and was only dissuaded by a petition signed by all the women in Madras. He was not only a brilliant gynaecologist but also a first-rate paediatrician, surgeon and all-round general doctor and in 1917 he was appointed Superintendent of the Hospital.

For Sheila, life went on much as usual. Three years after the war

---

* Pops was his children's name for him, often used by his wife and thence picked up by younger patients.

had ended and now ten years old, Sheila was brought home to England to be educated at Southlands School in Exmouth. One reason for choosing it was that nearby was an excellent children's home for 'Raj orphans'* run by a former Norland Nurse called Alice but always known as Adgie. The kindly Adgie took care that the six or so children staying there felt that they were in a family and enjoyed themselves. For Sheila this was lucky, as she did not see her mother again for four years.

When she was sixteen, her mother returned to England and Sheila was gradually introduced to grown-up entertainment: a month in Le Zoute in Belgium where there were lots of parties with other English people, a visit to the Dublin Horse Show, with races and a Hunt Ball thrown in, a party at the Savoy and more racing at Goodwood.

After seven years at Southlands, Sheila left school when she was seventeen, in July 1928. Her parents offered her the choice between 'coming out' as a debutante and doing the Season in London, or going to a finishing school in France. The idea of being a debutante did not really interest Sheila, so she chose the finishing school, with its promise of art, museums and music. The one selected was Madame Mombrey's in Paris, where a fellow pupil was the squash and tennis player Susan Noel. However, Madame Mombrey's turned out to cost twice as much as the Hingstons had originally been told, and with one son at Malvern and another still to be educated, Hinkie decided to whisk Sheila away after only one term. She was delighted. 'I was only too pleased to be out in the world and not to have to go to school again,' she said.

So what next? She thought vaguely of taking up nursing in England, but 'First come out to India and have a really nice holiday,' urged her parents, adding 'Then you can go back and find a job, if you want to.' She accepted with alacrity.

With her father now back in India and the boys settled in school, Sheila and her mother embarked on a shopping spree for the gaieties ahead in Madras. The first priority was evening dresses for balls

---

* As their parents could only visit at intervals, unless children were lucky enough to have aunts, grandparents or cousins with whom to live, they had to stay either at their school or in children's homes for their holidays. Some of the latter were very good, some appalling.

and parties; Sheila's two favourites were a dress in red taffeta and a wonderful confection of white velvet and chiffon, which Glad said would be perfect for balls at Government House. Arriving in India in September 1929, with six stylish dresses apiece, they were soon known as the most fashionably dressed women in South India.

Sheila, young, beautiful and, as one of that season's intake of Fishing Fleet girls, a novelty, soon had a wonderful time. She was plunged straight into the heart of Madras society: Glad and Hinkie were enormously popular and famous for their parties, often giving dinners for thirty people. They were also close friends of the previous Governor of Madras, Lord Willingdon,* and Lady Willingdon, a closeness that continued with the advent of the new Governor, so Sheila, along with her parents, was invited to all the events at Government House. Such was the protocol, with its immediate downgrading of everyone in 'trade', that those in Government service, like Hinkie, went in through a private entrance for banquets and parties; those in 'commerce' had a different door.

The Hingstons' closeness to the Government House circle meant that Sheila quickly got to know all the ADCs, one of whom taught her to ride on the enormous Madras Guards troop horses – there was a riding school at Government House. She took to it – a skill that would later stand her in good stead.

Her social diary was packed. She dined and danced at the Adyar Club and strolled on its lawns sloping down to the river, played golf and tennis, was taken rowing on the river, went to the races and spent evenings at friends' dinner parties. Another boyfriend taught her how to drive and there was also one of British India's favourite recreations, amateur theatricals.

Her family owned a house in Ootacamund, the hill station for Madras – her mother had bought it with the proceeds of the sale of a tea plantation – so when the hot weather began in July Sheila and her mother moved there, with her father arriving for the occasional week when he could manage to get away. It was here, in Ooty, that Sheila's fate was decided.

Ooty was extremely social. Sheila hunted, played golf and went to parties in the Maharaja of Mysore's house (where musical chairs was a popular game), at the club, with its parquet floors, rosewood

---

* Viceroy, 1931–6.

furniture and ballroom bedecked with tiger, leopard and bear skins and the heads of bison, deer and sambur, and at Government House, where the uniformed Government House band would play. There, one evening, at a hunt ball, she spotted a tall and handsome man leaning against the bar chatting to friends. His appearance attracted her at once. 'He's bound to be married,' she thought to herself pessimistically. 'All the nice ones are.'

Later that week she saw the good-looking stranger, again, once more with a crowd of friends, at the Golf Club, on the outskirts of Ooty. Here, because everyone knew everyone, she was introduced to him and discovered that his name was George Reade but that he was universally known as Jerry – and that he was a bachelor. She wondered if she would see him again; with luck, yes, as Ooty was a social place and their paths had already crossed twice.

Shortly afterwards a high-ranking friend in the ICS gave a party at the Ooty Club where seating at dinner was arranged by the simple method of putting papers with all the men's names in a hat, each woman drawing one out. Luck was now definitely on Sheila's side: out of all the scraps of paper in the hat, her mother had drawn the one with Jerry's name on it, and did not need much persuasion to swap it for the one her daughter was holding.

Sheila, at the age where first love strikes hard and fast, found Jerry just as fascinating as a partner for the evening as she had thought him at first glance. He was a tea planter on the Stanmore Estate in the Annamallais (the Elephant Hills) and older than her by eleven years. Although women found him attractive he was very much a man's man, with interests that were mainly sporting – hunting, shooting and fishing. The outdoor life in the Annamallais suited him down to the ground.

These hills were still a wild, untamed area, a paradise for both naturalists and keen shots. As their name denotes, there were elephants. Bison herds often roamed the swamps in the tea fields – frequently scaring the tea coolies on their way to morning muster at 6.30 – and there were periodic visits by herds of wild pigs. There were no jackals as these were kept away by the packs of wild red dogs. Of the smaller animals, porcupines were a pest, but good to eat. In the teak forests below lived the Indian sloth bear, tigers, panthers, huge herds of spotted deer, monkeys, mongooses and squirrels, civet cats, tiger cats and panther cats. Birds abounded, from the grey Junglefowl (ancestor of our domestic poultry) to bulbuls, giant black serpent eagles, kites, kestrels, harriers and their chief prey, pigeons of different sorts.

The isolation did not worry Jerry. The odd bursts of gaiety at Ooty were enough for him. The previous year his sister Joan had been a member of the Fishing Fleet, coming out to stay with him, and they had had a week in Ooty to the delight of their mother, who must have wondered if Joan would find a mate on Ooty's lively social circuit. 'I can't tell you how glad we are that you may get a chance of seeing such a lovely hill station and *enjoying* the parties of a Hunt week & Government House Ball,' she wrote to Joan. 'It is all thrilling. I quite know what you feel about clothes for such an auspicious occasion and we will do the best we can. The sales will be on the 1st week in July and I shall go up for a browse round. What do you think of a gold colour? It always suited you, or a flowered chiffon? You could not go in a black frock to the G.H. Ball, I think.'

At home in Sussex the two daughters of a family friend who lived nearby were both keen on Jerry and, although he rather liked the younger one, serious thoughts of marriage had not yet entered his head. Now he had met Sheila he wanted to see more of her but, as the Annamallais were a hundred miles away from Ooty across the plain, his visits were necessarily few.

After Glad returned to England to be with the boys, Sheila moved into an hotel in Ooty. Jerry came over from Stanmore as often as he could to see her and they used to hunt together. One of his friends said he could never remember seeing Jerry off a horse and in horse-mad Jerry's eyes it was a huge mark in Sheila's favour that she went so well to hounds.

In other ways he was not always the romantic lover of a young woman's dreams. In true Raj male style,* he would visit his beloved hounds before going on to see Sheila; when she remonstrated at the order of his priorities, he would simply remark gently that he loved them both very much but in different ways. And when he first wrote to her when she returned to Madras, he would dictate his letters to his clerk, who would type them up for signature. 'Dear Sheila,' these cheerful little notes would begin, ending 'Yours ever'.

---

* For many lonely, sports-oriented men it seems to have been theoretically women and children first but dogs and favourite polo ponies before either.

By March 1931 hints of his feelings began to trickle out. 'You were just in time with that letter! I was beginning to think that you didn't like me any more. Probably quite true, too …'. And on 29 March: 'Morning Sheila dear, Thank you so much for your letter. I wasn't ticking you off in the least, I only wanted to know if I still had your "luv". I can well believe Madras is sweltering, even up here at 4,000 feet the heat is too – – for words and everyone is getting very short-tempered as a result. The sooner we get some rain the better it will be for all concerned. We have had to stop polo as the ground is like steel.'

Throughout April and early May Jerry's focus was entirely on hunting, but the letters continued. 'I hear you have just started hunting,' on 27 April. And on 2 May: 'Do you know Ireland well? I'm fixing up to put in 10 days in November at a place called Kilcreene Lodge, Kilkenny, where one can hunt 6 days a week with the Kilkenny, Waterford, Carlow, Tipperary or Kildare. I've never hunted in Ireland before, and have always wanted to have a "go" at their banks and stone walls, but this is the first time that opportunity has offered. I imagine that it must be quite different from hunting in England, and I have no doubt but that I shall be up-ended in some of their ditches before the finish. Cheerio, old girl, don't go and overtire yourself with these rehearsals. Thine …'.

After his next visit to Ooty, feelings for Sheila rather than horses or hounds crept in. 'It was lovely seeing you again, Sheila, and still lovelier to think that I shall see you again so shortly,' he wrote on 15 May. This next visit was the pivotal one; and his letter showed that they had reached an understanding (Sheila said later that he had never actually proposed but simply assumed they would get married). 'My Darling,' he wrote after leaving her. 'This is hell! I came down the ghat yesterday in such a temper that I could hardly speak and woke up this morning in a worse one if anything. Thank God, it is only for a fairly short time, otherwise I don't think I could stand it.'

The moment marriage was agreed between them, Jerry wrote to Hinkie. 'I wrote to your father this morning (I send a copy for what it's worth).' I didn't say much as it seemed to me there was nothing much to be said beyond a straightforward statement of facts, and am quite sure that he didn't want to be burdened with the vapourings of someone who is violently in love. … The social life up here is nearly as bad as at Ooty. I appear to be dining out five nights this week. But it keeps me from brooding which is something.'

However, passion did not prevent him giving news of the pack. 'Hounds are all fit and they killed the hunt before last. All love, sweetheart.'

On 12 June he was able to write joyously: 'My darling – we're off. I had the most awfully nice letter from your fond father. No one could have asked for a nicer letter or a fairer one … Sheila darling, I could dance for joy. I must admit that whilst waiting for his reply I felt rather as if waiting for the starter's flag to drop in a steeplechase at home on a bitterly cold March afternoon when the clouds are about 100 ft up, it's raining, one's saddle is damp, the reins are slippery, one's teeth are chattering, one's clad to all intents and purposes in a bathing dress and the first fence looks ten feet high and as black as Erebus. However the flag has dropped, and we've landed over the first fence, galloping, and with six inches to spare. Forrard on, and the devil take the hindmost.'

Deeply in love as he was, Jerry was aware that the life on his isolated tea plantation that suited him so well might not be to the taste of a nineteen-year-old girl who had only left England a year earlier and who was accustomed to the rich social life in the best circles of Madras and Ooty. 'God knows what you will think of this Club on a Saturday night,' he wrote. 'Still, one has one's own friends and doesn't bother about the rest. All love, sweetheart mine, your very loving, Jerry.'

Sheila had better see for herself, he thought, and preferably when things were at their worst, so that she would know what she would be in for. So he invited her up to the Annamallais, in the height of the monsoon, when four inches of rain a day* fell out of the sky. She stayed, of course, with married friends of his, as anything else would have been unthinkable, even for an engaged couple, in those days of chaperonage.

It was a brave move: not only the beauty of the landscape but the inevitability of a solitary life would be laid before her. Sheila grasped this at once, thinking to herself: 'How on earth am I going to stick this? What am I going to do all day?' She nearly broke off

---

* The average rainfall from 1899 to 1941 was 137.2 inches. The year with the greatest rainfall, 204.3 inches, was 1933 – the year after Sheila's marriage.

the engagement but her passionate love for Jerry swayed the balance. With the optimism of youth and the stoicism of a daughter of the Raj she thought that if she 'gritted her teeth' it would be all right.

The next step was for Jerry to meet her father – her mother was still in England. Hinkie gave the young couple a big engagement party in Madras, partly as a test for Sheila's hitherto unknown fiancé; Hinkie believed that you could always tell a man's true colours when he was drunk. In pursuance of this theory he plied Jerry with drink all evening but at about two in the morning he took Sheila to one side to say: 'I'm giving up. He simply gets politer and more charming the more I give him to drink.'

Sheila and Jerry had cabled Glad in England when they got engaged. Glad smartly cabled back, with the warning: 'Do be careful.' From the perspective of many years of marriage, she knew how lonely her daughter would be in the Annamallais, miles from anywhere, when the first intoxication of passion had worn off. Sheila, now twenty, was a very young bride, used to a social life with people of her own age and tastes – and Jerry's life was bound up in hunting, shooting, fishing and his work as a tea planter, with its long hours out of doors and away from his house. But Sheila's mind was made up.

Both Sheila and Jerry were anxious to marry in England so that both families could be present. It was only on the ship, found Sheila, that she and Jerry really got to know each other. As in many Raj courtships, especially where distance was involved, they had only met comparatively few times, a dozen at most; and, difficult as it is, perhaps, for us to realise now, when they were courting they were always surrounded by others – at parties, at the club, in the hunting field. Among strangers on the ship, they could be together undisturbed.

Their wedding took place on 14 January 1932 at the beautiful Nash church of All Souls, Langham Place, with a reception at the nearby Langham Hotel, London's first grand hotel, made famous by – among others – Somerset Maugham, Noël Coward, Anna Neagle and (a few years later) Wallis Simpson. Sheila was an all-white bride, from her satin dress with train and bouquet of white carnations and lilies of the valley to the orange blossom that held her white lace veil in place. Even here, with the bride an ethereal vision, hunting had its place, in the two little figures in hunting clothes mounted on bay horses, representing bride and groom, on top of the wedding cake.

The newlyweds went back to India by ship and Sheila settled down to her new life on the tea plantation; home leave, which they always tried to coincide with the hunting season, was only every four years. For the first few years there was no electricity or running water; sanitation was by thunderbox or outside privies ('long drops'), water was brought by the water carrier and heated in two-gallon drums over wood fires for the evening bath and lighting was by oil lamps and candles. Most basic supplies came from the estate bazaar; tinned food could be ordered from Madras city but was so expensive that it was only an occasional luxury. There were plenty of small chickens and the butcher killed a sheep every week; fish, though, was unobtainable and no one ever ate pig or cow. Yet even though alone, they still changed for dinner every night – Jerry in a dinner jacket and Sheila in evening dress – because, as she later told her daughter: 'It was felt that one must keep up standards and not let oneself go native.'

At first Sheila would ride round the tea gardens with Jerry, but as he settled back into the demands of his work and former life the lack of occupation that had worried her during her engagement made itself felt. 'There was absolutely nothing to do,' she later told her daughter. '*Nothing.*' The Annamallais were breathtakingly beautiful, the climate excellent – rather that of a ski resort when the sun is out – but for a young bride one vital essential was missing: other people.

She longed for a friend but the nearest white woman lived five miles away. Often, desperate for companionship, Sheila would walk the five miles through the tea plantations to see her and then walk back. She took up tapestry work but it occupied only so much of the day; she asked Jerry 'Can I have a piano?' but gave up the idea when he replied, astonished, 'Whatever for?' There was an awful moment when he forgot her twenty-first birthday – 'he was very thoughtful but it just slipped his mind on the day and I didn't like to remind him,' she said later. Instead, she got unhappily on a horse and rode the fifteen miles to the house of great friends, the Ireland-Joneses. 'You poor thing,' said Mrs Ireland-Jones. 'We must celebrate.' All she had to hand was a tin of pears, a luxury from Madras, which they opened and ate.

But Sheila was a true daughter of the Raj, brave and uncomplaining – grumbling, she thought, was boring and tedious. Instead, she simply got on with things. As the years passed, life became a bit more social. When the Anamallais Club was founded the Reades would go there and play tennis, and Sheila would sometimes play golf (Jerry did not play); and on Saturday nights they would visit it regularly, as did everyone within reach. On short leaves they would go hunting together in Ooty, Sheila riding side-saddle (she normally rode astride), which gave a firmer seat. 'She went like the wind,' said Jerry proudly.

Sheila's eldest daughter, Diana, was born in the spring of 1933. India did not really suit her. As a small child she had boils under her arms and her legs were always swathed in bandages because every time she was bitten by an insect the bite would turn septic. Hinkie, by now one of the most senior and respected physicians in the subcontinent, told Sheila that that his granddaughter would never be really well in India and would be much better off in England, with its temperate climate and almost total freedom from biting insects. This brought the familiar Raj dilemma sharply into focus several years earlier than expected: to go to England with her child – or to stay in India with Jerry.

Staying with Jerry won; and the bandaging continued until their next home leave, in 1939, when Diana was to go to school, as a boarder at St George's, Ascot – a Raj child, like her mother and grandmother before her. Sheila's wretchedness at leaving her six-year-old daughter was tempered by the fact that Jerry's sister Joan, who had been teaching at Heathfield, was now at St George's and so would be able to keep an eye on Diana, and that Diana would be able to spend her holidays staying with Joan and her grandfather in Sussex.

But while all of them were in England war was declared. Sheila and Jerry had to return when their leave was over and, as Sheila wrote later: 'It was the worst day of my life leaving Diana behind and not knowing when I would see her again.' As they left during the first months of war – known as the 'phoney war' – when leaflets rather than bombs were being dropped over Germany, there was no way of knowing that the war would last six long years.

They wrote to Diana every week, letters that were censored. They sent her sweets and tea – rare commodities in wartime England – but with the sinking of so many ships were never sure if their letters got through, or if this was the reason that Diana's were sometimes irregular. One arrival that did generally make it through the difficulties of a wartime postal service was the magazine *Country Life* which both read eagerly, sometimes spotting people or places they knew. For Sheila in particular, with nothing to do except worry about her daughter, the war years were a time of acute strain.

As all the younger men were called up the older ones like Jerry (now forty) were left to run the five Stanmore estates, 5,000-odd acres in all. During the six war years Jerry, as General Manager, would get up at 5 a.m. every day, have breakfast, set out for the estates, return for lunch and then work in a bedroom now turned into an office until about midnight, with Sheila bringing him sandwiches and cups of tea or coffee at intervals. But there was still little for Sheila to do.

The men who were left formed a 'Dad's Army' in case the Japanese invaded, practising by marching about in the pouring rain with umbrellas because there were no guns then. They also had a hut built in the Grass Hills higher up, at about 8,000 feet, the idea being that if the Japanese did invade the Annamailais the women and children could escape up to this hut, where they would spend the night, then make their way on to the High Range and down to the west coast of India and, with luck, a boat back to England.

In practice, the hut was used for fishing weekends. Sometimes Sheila and Jerry would have a walking weekend in the Grass Hills, driving part of the way then walking up through the jungle from about 4,000 feet to 7,000 feet.

Like other daughters of the Raj, Sheila suffered some serious illnesses. The worst was smallpox, probably contracted from the bite of an insect that had bitten someone in the Annamallais bazaar, where there was an outbreak of the disease. Jerry wired down to his father-in-law in Madras – the recently acquired telephone system did not reach that far – and he and Glad arrived the following day to find their daughter covered in spots from head to foot.

Before he came up Hinkie had asked the advice of an Indian doctor on the latest treatment; he was told to paint each spot with a 2 per cent solution of manganese permanganate and, of course, never to scratch or dislodge them. A disinfected sheet was hung over the door of Sheila's bedroom, Jerry, Glad, Hinkie and the nurse he had brought with him and all the servants were vaccinated and Sheila's meals were all brought to her on a tray by the nurse. The only other person allowed to enter her room was Hinkie, who when there chain-smoked the whole time, as he thought inhaling the smoke would help prevent him catching the disease.

'It was like being social pariah,' said Sheila later. 'It was weeks before people would come near me, although I stayed in quarantine three weeks longer than medically necessary.' When the scabs eventually came off, leaving purple marks behind them, there were so many that Sheila had to surround herself with newspaper, later burnt, to catch them. She had been very careful never to scratch, and the purple marks eventually faded until, finally, she was left with an unblemished skin.

A few years later there was an outbreak of bubonic plague,* but when Sheila learned that several friends who had been immunised against it had had problems with side effects from the drugs they were given – one man had phlebitis for the rest of his life – she said she would not be immunised unless a rat actually fell dead within the house. Fortunately, the nearest dead rodent was in the office, one hundred yards away. Strangely, malaria, one of the commonest illnesses in the Raj and one that in many frequently recurred, only affected her once.

Just before VJ day, Sheila had another daughter, Helène. This time Hinkie, the famous gynaecologist, missed the date and could not attend to his daughter; instead Helène was delivered by a vet.

After partition, Jerry joined the South Indian Parliament – known as the Legislative Assembly – as the Planting Member of the United Planters' Association of Southern India. Sheila and Jerry finally returned to England in 1950.

Sheila was delighted to be back. She had, as Glad had predicted, been bored and lonely during the eighteen years she had spent in the Annamallais; but she had managed to survive everything without complaint, and with her love for her husband intact. When they

---

* She may have been referring to an outbreak of Relapsing Fever, caused by the bite of a louse or tick, of which rodents are sometimes the carrier. Without antibiotics, mortality could be high. Shortly before her arrival twenty coolies had died of Relapsing Fever on a neighbouring estate.

were engaged, Jerry had written to her: 'Looking back on things now, it strikes me more and more forcibly that events could never have gone any other way from the time last September when I sat out a dance with you and said that if you came home this year I'd give you a job on condition you promised to take it on.' She had indeed taken it on – and triumphantly succeeded.

EPILOGUE

'The cruel wrench'

Did the Fishing Fleet girls have any real influence on the conduct of affairs in this vast country that was home to so many of them during the time of the Raj?

The short answer is no. The Raj was entirely run by men, in the kind of hierarchical fashion that precluded a sudden leap to the top by a man of outstanding brilliance who might normally have been considered an outsider. Ramsay MacDonald, for instance, the illegitimate son of a farm labourer who was virtually self-educated, became Prime Minister of England whereas he would never have been considered as Viceroy. It is true that for the first sixty years of the Raj there was no woman in the British Government either – the first to take her seat, Nancy Astor,* was only elected in 1919 when her husband was elevated to the peerage, and after that women only gradually began to filter into Parliament – but it is inconceivable to think of a woman becoming an ICS District Officer or the Magistrate of a cantonment. In the Raj, the role of the British female was as wife, helpmeet and mother.

Here came one hideous caveat peculiar to the Raj, causing a wretchedness impossible to over-estimate. 'Separation is the dark cloud which hangs over an Indian existence; husbands and wives, mothers and children, forced asunder, perhaps at the very time when union is most delightful, and living (how maimed and sad a life!) in the absence of all that is best-beloved,' wrote H.S. Cunningham in *The Chronicles of Dustypore.*

---

* The first woman to be elected was the Countess Markievicz, a member of Sinn Fein, who stood for a Dublin seat while in Holloway Prison in London in 1918. She won – but never took her seat in the House of Commons.

To be a Fishing Fleet girl who married into the Raj was to face this appalling, inescapable burden: separation from either husband or children, sent home at a tender age to England for their education. 'Early or late the cruel wrench must come – the crueller, the longer deferred,' wrote Maud Diver. 'One after one the babies grow into companionable children; one after one England claims them, till the mother's heart and house are left unto her desolate.' Quite apart from separation, in many cases, from the land where she was born.

Only the rich – and there were few of those in the service of the Raj – could afford the cost of constant sea passages back and forth to spend holidays with the children and ameliorate this anguish (until the last few years of the Raj, flying was almost unknown).*

Sending children home meant that they would not be classed as 'domiciled'. This was an important distinction, especially in the early days of the Raj, stemming from Lord Cornwallis's edict in the late eighteenth century that reduced those British born in India – even if of pure English blood – to a status below that of native-born Englishmen.

Even in the twentieth century there were echoes of this: when Jim Acheson said at a dinner party in 1914 that he liked a certain commissariat colonel from Army headquarters in Simla, adding that with a name like Moriarty he must be Irish, he evoked the response from a fellow diner: 'You mean a *Mussoorie* Irishman, don't you, Mr Acheson?' At first Jim did not understand but later realised that the poor man was regarded as being not 'quite quite' because he belonged to the domiciled community.

Snobbishness is one of the justified criticisms that has always been hurled at the Anglo-Indian wife, a snobbishness based on petty distinctions of manner, birth or behaviour. Along with the dedication that left India, after independence, with an enviable infrastructure, a democratic Government and a common language came a concern with social matters that reflected – indeed, outdid – that at home.

'If I were asked what struck me as the chief concern of English

---

* The first direct Air Mail service from London to Karachi was in 1933. Early passenger flights involved not only many stops but also changing to rail and seaplanes between flights. In 1935 Imperial Airways took a total of 983 people to and from India, on 104 flights. By 1937 a direct flight to India by flying boat from Southampton to Karachi took five days.

social life in India, I should answer: "to seek Precedence and ensure it." ... Precedence is the focal point of India's social nonsense, convulses the home and has even, it is said, convulsed the government,' said Yvonne Fitzroy who, as Private Secretary to the Vicereine, saw India from the top of the heap. The effect of this preoccupation was more stifling than that of the home-grown variety, in part because of the lack of alternative concerns but chiefly because, in England, talent, intelligence and beauty were powerful social coinage that added mobility and leaven to the status quo. But in the hierarchy of the Raj position was fixed, according to service, rank and seniority in an unalterable grading, like so many butterflies on pins, within which there was room for petty nuances that could be painful and damaging. Was a man in a 'good' regiment? In 'trade' as opposed to a 'profession'? If in the ICS had he caught the approving eye of Government? The young Fishing Fleet bride, moulded by the attitudes and customs of the 'mems' higher up in the pecking order, might adopt this unattractive way of thinking.

Yet these were the same girls prepared to have a baby alone in a bungalow fifty miles from the nearest doctor, to suffer the cruel deaths of sometimes several in succession of their children, to up sticks and move house for the thirtieth time in succession without a murmur, to offer hospitality cheerfully and unstintingly to friends of friends of friends.

For other Fishing Fleet girls, India meant loneliness, living perhaps on an isolated plantation, the only excitement a weekly dance at the club fifteen miles away. They coped with it, as they coped with almost everything the country threw at them – the vagaries of the climate, illnesses or a perpetual feeling of being 'below par', the feeling of desperation if the longed-for mail did not bring a letter.

For still others, the stultifying boredom of small-town society was the chief memory brought back to England after a husband's retirement. 'If there is a hell for me it'll be an endless day in a club in the North Indian state of Assam; a day of staring through dazzling white dust at men galloping about on polo grounds; of sitting in sterile circles drinking gin with their wives; of bouncing stickily round an unsprung dance floor, clutched to their soggy shirts, of finally being driven home at night by one of them peering woozily over the wheel, tipping old villagers in bullock carts into the ditch. I spent thirty years on a tea plantation enduring such days and nights.' So wrote Iris Macfarlane after she left India in 1936.

'Seldom in history have women been subjected at one and the same time to so many discomforts, so much monotony, and so many temptations,' summed up John Masters. Yet plenty of them managed to extract the maximum advantage from their situation. 'Many things were unforgettable about our life at Ramkolah [close to the borders of Nepal], particularly our rides home through the sunsets, dew replacing the dust, the sky aflame with vivid colours until it turned suddenly to deep blue,' recalled Betsey Macdonald. 'We would smell the pungent smoke rising from the village fires as we trotted by, the exotic scents from the shrubs and flowers as we returned to our garden.'

Rumer Godden, at her happiest in India, characterised its appeal as 'the honey smell of the fuzz-buzz flowers, of thorn trees in the sun, and the smell of open drains and urine, of coconut oil on shining black human hair, of mustard cooking oil and the blue smoke from cow dung used as fuel; it was a smell redolent of the sun, more alive and vivid than anything in the West ...'.

Some felt its magic all their lives, enthralled by the beauty and grace of the people, the landscape that ranged from steamy jungle to the glittering, ethereal purity of the high Himalayas and the wild creatures, the elephants, grey langurs, and above all the birds – friendly little bulbuls with red and yellow rumps, green parrots, golden orioles that flashed from tree to tree, hoopoes in their Art Deco plumage of orange, black and white, Paradise flycatchers with tails like long white streamers. As Veronica Bamfield put it: 'I was one of the lucky few on whom India lays a dark, jewelled hand, the warmth of whose touch never grows cold to those who have felt it.'

Many did what they could to take part in the life of the country or to help those around them. Their scope was limited as Government policy was to interfere as little as possible with the habits and customs of 'the natives'. Plenty helped with simple medication, Army wives concerned themselves with the welfare of the wives and children of their husbands' soldiers, still others taught. Flora Annie Steele,* appointed Inspectress of Girls' Schools in the Punjab, campaigned successfully against the selling of degrees at the Punjab University; Anne Wilson made a serious study of Indian music;

---

* Co-author of *The Complete Indian Housekeeper and Cook*.

Violet Acheson was awarded the Kaisar-i-Hind Gold Medal for Public Service in India.

Most prescient, perhaps, was Anne Wilson, writing (at the end of her camping tour) in 1895, in sentiments that expressed not only her realisation of the possible impermanence of British rule but also the idealism that inspired the best of the Raj: 'When a century or two have gone, will all traces of those tents and their occupants have disappeared? ... Or will our rule in India be permanent, if not in its present form, at least in its effects? Will it gradually confer on this immense population, numbering a quarter of the inhabitants of the globe, not only greater material prosperity and greater knowledge but a higher intellectual, moral and religious standard, and so permanently raise a mighty people in the scale of humanity?

'Should this be the result of all our labours spent in India – as assuredly it will, if only we fulfil our trust – they will not have been spent in vain, and history will acknowledge the truth of the saying that India is the brightest jewel in England's crown.'

ACKNOWLEDGEMENTS

My special thanks are due to the following: the Rev. Malcolm Acheson for permission to use *An Indian Chequerboard* by his grandfather James Acheson; Charles Arthur for the diary of his great-grandmother Grace Trotter; Keith Atkinson for the well-documented story of his great-great-grandfather Michael Edward Smith; Susan Batten and Lady Williams for the memoir by their mother Iris Butler; Malcolm Chase for the memoir of his mother Marian Atkins; James Collett-White for letters sent to his mother Patience Home and those sent by her to his father; Thomas Courtenay Clack for the memoir by his mother Marjorie Fremlin; Jessica Douglas-Home for letting me see the diary of her great-aunt the Hon. Lilah Wingfield; Simon Durnford for permission to use the memoir of his grandmother Bethea Field; Eric Evans for the letter and transcript of talk from his grandmother; Nick Phillips for *A Year in the Gilgit Agency* by his mother Leila Blackwell; Harriet and Toby Garfitt for permission to use their mother Annette Bowen's memoir; Julia Gregson for her kindness and help, and Richard Gregson for the memoir by his mother Violet Hanson; Mary Gribbon for our long conversation together about her days in India as Mary McLeish; Sukie Hemming for the diaries of her grandmother Lady Elisabeth Bruce; Lyn Homan for the diary of her mother Hermione Claudine Gratton; Ann Jameson for the memoir by her great- grandfather Alfred Stowell Jones V.C.; Clare Jones for the memoir by her grandmother Honor Penrose; Charles Joynson for the memoir by his grandmother Cecile Stanley Clarke; Mary Lloyd for her reminiscences of Gulmarg; Jean Lovatt-Smith and Peter Whitestone for their kind permission to use extracts from the journal of their grandmother Florence Badgley; Katherine Prentice for talking to me at lengh and for lending me her memoir (written

as Katherine Welford); Colonel Dan Raschen for *Sam's India*, a
memoir by his father Sam Raschen; Helène Reade for permission
to use her parents' letters and her unpublished story of her family's connection with India; Andrew Redpath and his daughter Leila
Redpath for the memoir of Andrew's mother Rosemary Cotesworth
and the journal of Alexander William Redpath; Caroline Saville for
the letters of Lieutenant Leslie John Germain Lavie to his fiancée
Florence Ross; Jonathan Scott for letting me see the diary of his
grandmother Maude Bingham; Anne Storey for permision to use
her aunt Kathleen Griffith's memoir; Nicholas Thompson for letting
me see the letters of his mother Jean Hilary; Stan Turner for his private book about his great-great-grandmother Mary, Mrs Templeman;
Valerie Welchman for talking to me and for permission to use
her memoir (written as Valerie Pridmore Riley); and Ralfe Whistler
for the story of his mother Margaret Joan Ashton.

Among others I would like to thank are Keith and Nancy Atkin-
son, Joy Bailey, Barbara Durnford, Lord and Lady Elgin, Major
John Girling, Richard Goodwin, Charles Greig, Mary-Clare Grib-
bon, Jill, Duchess of Hamilton, Dr Rosie Llewellyn Jones, David
Lovatt-Smith, Professor Margaret Macmillan, Charlotte Martin,
Penelope Mayfield, Nick Rander, Mike Waring, John Welchman,
Ralfe Whistler, David Swain (then Secretary of the Oriental Club),
the staffs of the London Library and the Centre of South Asian
Studies, Cambridge, and last but not least, my wonderful editor Bea
Hemming.

BIBLIOGRAPHY

Allen, Charles (ed), *Plain Tales from the Raj* (André Deutsch, 1976)

Allen, Charles, *Raj: A Scrapbook of British India 1877–1947* (André Deutsch, 1977)

Allen, Joan, '*Missy Baba' to 'Burra Mem'* (BACSA, 1998)

Anon., *The Englishwoman in India* (Smith, Elder and Co., 1864)

Aspinall, A., *Cornwallis in Bengal* (Manchester University Press, 1931)

Ballhatchet, Kenneth, *Race, Sex and Class under the Raj* (Weidenfeld & Nicolson, 1980)

Bamfield, Veronica, *On the Strength: The Story of the British Army Wife* (Charles Knight & Co., 1974)

Barr, Pat, *The Dust in the Balance: British Women in India* (Hamish Hamilton, 1989)

Barr, Pat, *The Memsahibs* (Secker & Warburg, 1976)

Battye, Evelyn Desirée, *The Kashmir Residency* (BACSA, 1997)

Beames, John *Memoirs of a Bengal Civilian* (Chatto & Windus, 1961)

Beauman, Francesca, *Shapely Ankle Preferr'd: A History of the Lonely Hearts Ad 1695–2010* (Chatto & Windus, 2011)

Beaumont, Penny and Roger, *Imperial Divas: the Vicereines of India* (Haus Publishing, 2010)

Bhatt, Vikram, *Resorts of the Raj* (Mapin Publishing Pvt, 1998)

Brendon, Vyvyen, *Children of the Raj* (Weidenfeld & Nicolson, 2005)

Brown, A. Claude, *The Ordinary Man's India* (Cecil Palmer, 1927)

Buettner, Elizabeth, *Empire Families: Britons and Late Imperial India* (OUP, 2004)

Butler, Iris, *The Viceroy's Wife* (Hodder & Stoughton, 1969)

Buxton, Meriel, *The High-Flying Duchess* (Woodperry Books, 2008)

Campbell-Martin, Monica, *Out in the Midday Sun* (Cassel & Co., 1951)

Collingham, E.M., *Imperial Bodies* (Polity Press, 2001)

Cunningham, H.S., *The Chronicles of Dustypore* (Smith, Elder & Co., 1875)

Dalrymple, William, *White Mughals* (HarperCollins, 2002)

Diver, Maud, *The Englishwoman in India* (William Blackwood & Sons, 1909)

Douglas-Home, Jessica, *A Glimpse of Empire* (Michael Russell, 2011)

Du Boulay, F.R.H., *Servants of Empire* (I.B. Tauris, 2011)

Fitzroy, Yvonne, *Courts and Camps in India* (Methuen, 1926)

Flaherty, Frances, *Elephant Dance* (Charles Scribner's Sons, 1937

Forster, E.M., *A Passage to India* (Edward Arnold, 1924)

Gill, Anton, *Ruling Passions* (BBC Books, 1995)

Gilmour, David, *The Ruling Caste* (John Murray, 2005)

Godden, Rumer, *A Time to Dance, No Time to Weep* (Macmillan, 1987)

Hammerton, A. James, *Emigrant Gentlewomen* (Croom Helm, 1979)

Hilton Brown(ed.), *The Sahibs* (William Hodge and Co. 1968)

Howarth, David and Stephen, *The Story of P&O* (Weidenfeld & Nicolson, 1986)

Hunt, R. and Harrison J., *The District Officer in India 1930–1947* (Scolar Press, 1980)

Hyam, Ronald, *Empire and Sexuality* (Manchester University Press, 1990)

Jacob, Violet, *Diaries and Letters from India 1895–1900* (Canongate, 1990)

Jalland, Pat, *Women, Marriage and Politics 1860–1914* (Clarendon Press, 1986)

James, Lawrence, *Raj* (Little, Brown, 1997)

Jenkins, Sir Owain, *Merchant Prince* (BACSA, 1987)

Kaye, M.M., *Golden Afternoon* (Viking, 1997)

Kincaid, Dennis, compiled by Laurence Fleming, *British Social Life in India, 1608–1937* (Radcliffe Press, 2004)

Kipling, Rudyard, *Plain Tales from the Hills* (Thacker, Spink & Co. 1888)

Kranidis, Rita S., *The Victorian Spinster and Colonial Emigration* (St Martin's Press, 1994)

Macdonald, Betsy, *India … Sunshine and Shadows* (BACSA, 1938)

Macfarlane, Iris, *Daughters of the Empire* (OUP, 2006)

MacMillan, Margaret, *Women of the Raj* (2006)

Martyn, Margaret, *Married to the Raj* (BACSA, 1992)

Masters, John, *Bugles and a Tiger* (Michael Joseph, 1956)

Morris, P.A., Van Ingen and Van Ingen, *Artists in Taxidermy* (MPM Publishing, 2006)

Nevile, Pran, *Sahibs' India* (Penguin Books India, 2010)

Nicolson, Nigel, *Mary Curzon* (Weidenfeld & Nicolson, 1977)

Padfield, Peter, *Beneath the House Flag of the P&O* (Hutchinson, 1981)

Royal United Services Institute journals, April 1895, October–March 1896, October 1899–1900

Rutledge, Helen (ed.), *A Season in India: The Letters of Ruby Madden* (Fontana/Collins, 1976)

Saumarez Smith, William, *A Young Man's Country: Letters of a Subdivisional Officer of the Indian Civil Service, 1936–7* (Michael Russell, 1977)

Steel, F.A. and Gardiner G., *The Complete Indian Housekeeper and Cook* (Heinemann, 1921)

Stocqueler, J.H., *Handbook of India* (W.H. Allen, 1844)

Taylor, Stephen, *The Caliban Shore* (Faber & Faber, 2004)

Toovey, Jacqueline (ed.), *Tigers of the Raj: The Shakar Diaries of Colonel Burton, 1894–1939* (Alan Sutton, 1987)

Trevelyan, Humphrey, *The India We Left* (Macmillan, 1972)

Trevelyan, Raleigh, *The Golden Oriole: Childhood, Family and Friends in India* (Secker, 1987)

Trollope, Joanna, *Britannia's Daughters: Women of the British Empire* (Hutchinson, 1983)

Trudgill, Eric, *Madonnas and Magdalens* (Heinemann, 1976)

Venning, Annabel, *Following the Drum* (Headline, 2005)

Wakefield, Sir Edward, *Past Imperative: My Life in India* (Chatto & Windus, 1966)

Wilkinson, Theon, *Two Monsoons* (Duckworth, 1976)

Wilson, Anne, *After Five Years in India* (Blackie & Son, 1895)

Wood, Maria L., ed. Jane Vansittart, *From Minnie with Love* (Peter Davies, 1974)

Wright, Maisie, *Under Malabar Hill* (BACSA, 1988)

Yeats-Brown, Francis, *Bengal Lancer* (Victor Gollancz, 1930)

Younger, Coralie, *Wicked Women of the Raj* (HarperCollins, 2001)

UNPUBLISHED SOURCES

The diary of Sir William Adamson
The diary of Maude Bingham
The diary of Lady Elisabeth Bruce
The diary of Marjorie Fremlin
The diary of Claudine Gratton
The diary of Violet Hanson
The diary of the Hon. Lilah Wingfield
The journal of Florence Badgley
Journal extracts, Evelyn Barrett
The journal of Alexander William Redpath

BIBLIOGRAPHY

Memoir: 'An Indian Chequerboard', by James Acheson
Memoir: Marian Atkins
Memoir: Frances Annette Bowen
Memoir: Iris Butler
Memoir: Bethea Field
Memoir: Kathleen Griffiths
Memoir: Alfred Stowell Jones, V.C.
Memoir: Honor Penrose
Memoir: 'A Year in the Gilgit Agency', by Leila Phillips
Memoir: Valerie Welchman (née Pridmore Riley)
Memoir: 'Sam's India', by Sam Raschen
Memoir: Rosemary Redpath
Memoir: Katherine Prentice (née Welford)
'In Search of Henry', by Cecile Stanley Clarke
'Mary, Mrs Templeman', by Stanley Richard Turner
Letter and talk, Eric Evans
The letters of Harold Edwin Collett-White
The letters of Jean Hilary
The letters of Patience Home
The letters of Lieutenant Leslie John Germain Lavie (Caroline Seville)
Letters and unpublished transcript, Helene Reade

INDEX

Abdur Rahman, Amir of
    Afghanistan, 118
Acheson, Janet, 221
Acheson, Jim (later Sir James),
    47–50, 50n, 62, 221, 223, 224,
    226, 227, 253, 302
Acheson (*née* Field), Violet *see* Field
    (later Acheson), Violet
Acton, Dr, 14
Adamson, William, 18, 20, 21, 22
ADCs (aides–de–camp), 62–3, 64,
    99, 109, 110, 111, 113, 135,
    137, 138, 250, 265, 271, 272,
    296
Aden, 18n, 28, 267
Adyar Club, Madras, 104, 162, 296
Adyar River, 102–3, 104
Afghanistan, 118–19, 226, 227
affairs, 151
Africa, 18
Aga Khan, 194
Agra, 48, 49, 50, 100–1, 147, 168,
    243
Ahmednagar, 277
Ainley, Mrs, 144
Ajmer, 59
Alderney shingle, 195 and n
Aldous, Aline, 143
Aldous, Hugh ('Bodie'), 143
Aldous, Louise, 143
Alexandra, Queen, 125, 191
Alexandria, 21, 22
Ali Khan (son of Nawab of Jaora),
    155
Allahabad, 10, 118, 129
Allen, Geoffrey, 149, 247

Allen (*née* Henry), Joan *see* Henry
    (later Allen), Joan
All-India Muslim League, 170
All Saints College, 34
All Souls, Langham Place, 301
Alwar, 77
    Maharaja of, 77
America *see* United States
Amritsar, massacre of (1919), 170
Anchor Line, 267
Anderson (later Macdonald), Betsy,
    90, 100–1, 142–3, 154, 250,
    263–4, 284, 310
Anglo-Indians, 34, 35, 56, 166, 168,
    308
Annaly, Lord, 206
Annamallais (Elephant Hills), 297–8,
    300, 301
    married life in, 302–8
Annamallais Club, 303
Annandale, 186, 190, 192
Anson, Jim, 208
Antigua, 293
Antrim, Lady, 133
Arabia, 39 and n, 49
Arabic, 49
Arcadia, 45, 47
Arkonam, 260, 261
Army *see* British Army; Indian
    Army
Army Cup Week, 146
Arnold, Dr, 57
Arrah House, 217–18
Arras, 78
arrivals, 72–84
Arthur, Sir Allan, 181

319

Simla: courtship and wedding of
Dorothy and Charles Arthur in,
182–3; Elisabeth Bruce in, 110–
11, 111–12, 113, 115, 116–18,
121, 122–3, 129; life in,
185–93, 263; Queen's Diamond
Jubilee celebrated in, 117–18,
129–30; as summer capital
of the government, 91,185–6,
187–8; brief references, 17, 41,
50, 63, 74, 85, 93, 150, 152,
173, 181, 265, 268, 270, 282,
308
Simon Artz store, 27–8, 85
Simpson, Wallis, 295
Sindh (Sind), 58, 69
Singh, Rajendar, Maharaja of
Patiala, 164–5
Sitwell, Edith, 267
skin infections, 248
Skinner's Horse, 62
Slater, Richard, 74
smallpox, 241, 298–9; vaccine, 30
Smith (later Butler), Ann see Butler
(née Smith), Ann (Iris Butler's
mother)
Smith, Lieutenant Michael Edward,
9–10
snake charmers, 252–3
snakes, 81, 252–4
snobbishness, 302–3 see also
precedence; status
Snowdon (Kitchener's Simla
residence), 191
social life, 94–107
Socotra, 45
Sonmarg, 91
South African War, 123, 128, 205
Southampton, 22
Southampton, 19–20
Southampton Water, 18, 20
Southern Army Command, 194
South Indian Parliament (known as
Legislative Assembly), 305
Southlands School, Exmouth,
295
Spanish flu, 219, 245, 247, 278–9
spinsters, difficulties faced by, 11–13

sport, 66–7, 159, 237–8 see also
names of sports
Sprees, the, 233–4
Srinagar, 91, 196, 198, 199–200,
242, 287
stabilisers, 31 and n
Stanley, Lady Beatrix, 104 and n
Stanley, Sir George, 104, 138
Stanley Clarke, Cecile, 53, 161–2,
169–70, 257, 258–9
Stanmore Estates, 297, 298, 304
Star of the South, 157
Statesman, The, 265
status, 97 see also precedence
Steele, Flora Annie, 304
Steele, Captain Gordon, 45–6
Steele, Lady, 17, 18
stinkbugs, 90
Stock, Thomas, 53
Stopes, Marie: Married Love, 15
storms at sea, 24–5, 30–1
Strefford, Lady, 44
Stuart, Major-General Charles
'Hindoo', 167
Subdivisional Officer/Assistant
Magistrate, 59–60
Sudan, 18n
Suez, 21, 22
Suez Canal, 10, 18n, 22, 29
Sutherland Highlanders, 9
Swinhoe, Violet, 202

Taj Mahal, 100–1, 147
Tanmarg, 198
Taylor, Robert, 107
teaching, 11
tennis courts, 93
Tennyson, Lord: 'Flowr in the
Crannied Wall', 121
tent-pegging, 102 and n
Terai, 206, 285
Thomas Cook, 51
tigers, 160, 270; shooting, 66, 160–1
and n, 177–81, 206–7
Tilbury, 17, 18, 38, 47, 149, 213
Times, The, 5, 120
Tisri, 277
Tiwana clan, 268

blog and newsletter

For exclusive short stories, poems, extracts, essays, articles, interviews, trailers, competitions and much more visit the Weidenfeld & Nicolson blog and sign up for the newsletter at:

www.wnblog.co.uk

Follow us on

 and **twitter**

Or scan the code to access the website*